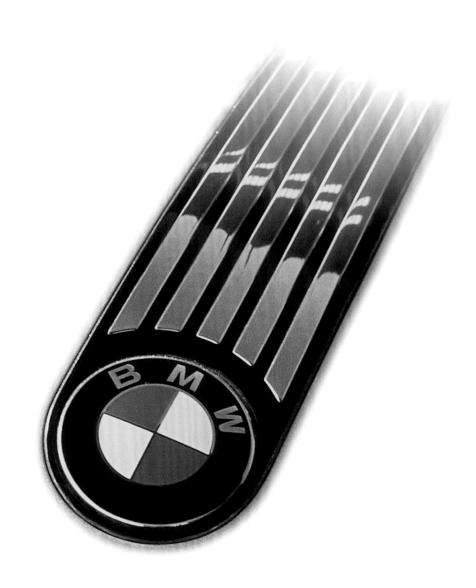

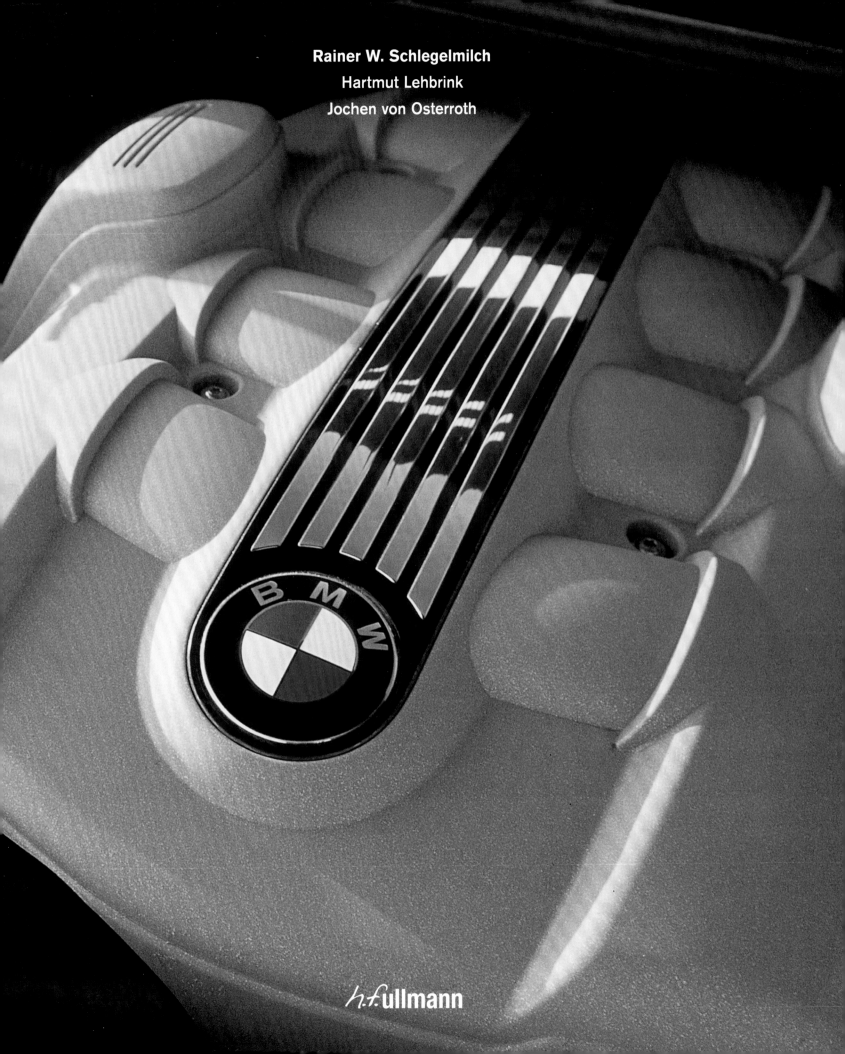

Rainer W. Schlegelmilch

Hartmut Lehbrink

Jochen von Osterroth

h.f.ullmann

BMW—The Ascent of the World Brand
6   **BMW – Aufstieg zur Weltmarke**
BMW devient une marque internationale

Contents
Inhalt
Sommaire

BMW—The Ascent of the World Brand
BMW – Aufstieg zur Weltmarke
BMW devient une marque internationale

Good things come in threes: the Bayerische Flugzeugwerke AG (BFW) aviation company, registered in Munich's Commercial Register on 7 March 1916; the conversion of the Rapp Motorenwerke GmbH on 21 July 1917 into the Bayerische Motoren Werke GmbH; and a man called Franz-Joseph Popp. Popp, a qualified engineer, imperial and royal lieutenant in the reserves of the Austro-Hungarian navy, and an expert in aero engines, was in search of suitable engines for the Austro-Hungarian Dual Monarchy. After all, there was a war on, and Austro-Daimler had a contract for the construction under license of 224 aircraft engines to allocate. Rapp was chosen—on the condition, however, that Popp would supervise the work. Max Friz, an excellent mechanical engineer, joined the company at this time, having quit Paul Daimler of Stuttgart because of the latter's refusal to increase Friz's salary by 50 reichsmarks. Popp's support and encouragement for Friz was so strong that Karl Rapp started to fear that he would be usurped by the duo. So he made a snap decision to withdraw to his retirement cottage. Popp took over the company, and in October 1917 had the BMW trademark registered with the Imperial Patent Office in Munich; the logo remains largely unchanged to this day. It symbolizes the rotation of a propeller, dividing the Bavarian state colors into four. A propeller, because the plans for the company's vast range of products included not only agricultural machines, land and water craft, and all kinds of engines, but also the construction of aircraft.

Friz soon developed a 220 bhp, six-cylinder aero engine that, thanks to an ingenious high-altitude compressor, lost only half of its performance at the oxygen-poor height of 20,000 feet (6000 meters). Because it was ideal for use in war, this innovation resulted in an order for 600 engines. Now the Bayerische Motoren Werke had to allocate licenses for production, since their premises on the Schleißheimer Straße were bursting at the seams. In order to secure financing, the company was made a stock corporation, with Popp as its General Director. Friz then produced an even better engine that still provided 250 bhp at 10,000 feet (3000 meters). After the war, 3500 employees at BMW lost their employment, since the Treaty of Versailles forbade the construction of aero engines and airplanes. BMW managed to stay afloat with a contract from Knorr-Bremse AG, Berlin, to provide brakes for the Bavarian railway. Far from being discouraged, Popp and Friz quietly carried on with their developments. So there was really no need to ask which engine set a new record height of 32,021 feet (9760 meters) on 19 July 1919 from Munich's Oberwiesenfeld.

In 1922, Camillo Castiglioni, a financier and banker from Vienna who had introduced Popp to Rapp, acquired the Bayerische Flugzeugwerke (Bavarian Aircraft Works) for BMW. The so-called Bayern-Motor was created here—a sturdy four-

Aller guten Dinge sind drei: die Bayerische Flugzeugwerke AG (BFW), am 7. März 1916 im Münchener Handelsregister registriert, die Umwidmung der Rapp Motorenwerke GmbH am 21. Juli 1917 in Bayerische Motoren Werke GmbH und ein Mann namens Franz-Joseph Popp. Diplomingenieur Popp, K.u.K-Oberleutnant der Reserve der österreichisch-ungarischen Marine und Experte für Flugapparate, ist auf der Suche nach geeigneten Triebwerken für die Donau-Doppelmonarchie. Schließlich befindet man sich im Krieg, und Austro-Daimler hat einen Lizenzbau-Auftrag über 224 Flugzeugmotoren zu vergeben. Rapp wird auserkoren, freilich unter der Bedingung, dass Popp die Arbeiten überwacht. Mit Max Friz – bei Paul Daimler in Stuttgart wegen einer abgewiesenen Gehaltserhöhungs-Forderung von 50 Reichsmark gegangen – tritt ein hervorragender Motoren-Ingenieur in die Firma ein. Popp fördert ihn derart, dass Karl Rapp seine Entmachtung durch das Duo befürchtet. Er zieht sich kurzerhand auf sein Altenteil zurück. Popp übernimmt die

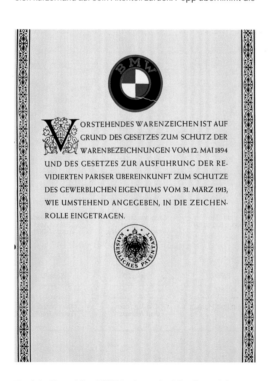

Registration of the BMW trademark at the Imperial Patent Office in Munich. The year is 1917.

Eintrag des BMW-Firmenzeichens beim Kaiserlichen Patentamt München. Man schreibt das Jahr 1917.

Inscription de l'emblème de la marque BMW à l'Office impérial des brevets de Munich en 1917.

Jamais deux sans trois, dit-on, et la naissance de BMW semble confirmer le dicton: immatriculation de la Bayerische Flugzeugwerke AG (BFW) le 7 mars 1916 au registre du commerce de Munich, transformation de Rapp Motorenwerke GmbH en Bayerische Motoren Werke GmbH le 21 juillet 1917 et apparition d'un certain Franz-Joseph Popp. Cet ingénieur diplômé, lieutenant-colonel de réserve dans la marine austro-hongroise et expert en engins volants, recherche des moteurs adaptés pour la double monarchie danubienne. Mais le pays est en guerre et Austro-Daimler doit passer une commande sous licence pour 224 moteurs d'avion. Rapp est choisi mais à la condition expresse que les travaux soient supervisés par Popp. L'entreprise recrute alors un ingénieur extrêmement compétent spécialisé dans les moteurs: Max Friz, qui a quitté Paul Daimler à Stuttgart, ce dernier ayant refusé d'accéder à une demande d'augmentation de salaire de 50 reichsmarks. Popp le soutient tellement que Karl Rapp craint d'être dépossédé de son pouvoir par le duo et prend rapidement sa retraite. Popp reprend la direction de l'entreprise et, en octobre 1917, fait breveter par l'Office impérial des brevets de Munich l'emblème de la marque BMW dont seule la police a été, depuis, légèrement modernisée. Il représente la rotation d'une hélice découpant en quatre les couleurs de la Bavière. L'hélice est choisie car la large gamme de produits prévus ne comprend pas uniquement des véhicules terrestres, agricoles et amphibies mais également aéronautiques.

Friz développe en peu de temps un moteur d'avion de 220 ch qui grâce un carburateur à haute altitude ingénieux ne perd que la moitié de sa puissance à 6000 mètres, altitude où l'oxygène se fait rare. Cette innovation arrivant à point nommé en temps de guerre se voit récompensée par une commande de 600 moteurs. Les Bayerische Motoren Werke doivent maintenant céder des licences de fabrication car les locaux de la Schleißheimer Straße manquent de capacité. Pour s'assurer le financement nécessaire, la firme doit se transformer en société anonyme et Franz-Joseph Popp est nommé directeur général. Friz développe un nouveau moteur amélioré qui a encore une puissance de 250 ch à 3000 mètres d'altitude. La fin de la guerre prive les désormais 3500 collaborateurs de BMW de leur base de travail, le traité de Versailles interdisant la fabrication de moteurs d'avion et d'appareils aéronautiques. Une commande passée par la firme berlinoise Knorr-Bremse AG pour des circuits de freinage destinés à l'administration des chemins de fer bavarois, maintient l'entreprise hors de l'eau. Popp et Friz ne se laissent pas décourager et poursuivent leurs recherches dans le plus grand secret. Inutile, dans ces circonstances, de demander quel moteur parvient à établir un nouveau record en atteignant une altitude de 9760 mètres en 87 minutes, le 19 juin 1919, au départ de l'Oberwiesenfeld de Munich.

Dixi-land: 3/15 Dixis, lined up in front of the administration building of the BMW works in Eisenach.

Dixi-Land: Dixi-Wagen vom Typ 3/15, aufgereiht vor dem Direktionsgebäude der BMW-Werke Eisenach.

Au pays de Dixi : des Dixi 3/15 alignées devant le bâtiment des usines BMW à Eisenach.

13 cylinders: a Junkers 52 with nine combustion chambers flies nimbly over the BMW four-cylinder in 1983.

13 Zylinder: Eine Junkers 52 mit neun Verbrennungseinheiten überfliegt 1983 behäbig den BMW-Vierzylinder.

13 cylindres: un Junkers 52 doté d'un moteur à 9 cylindres survolant le bâtiment de BMW «à quatre cylindres» en 1983.

cylinder engine with eight liters of cubic capacity and ideal for lorries, tractors, other agricultural machines, and motorboats. This "bull" in BMW's stables was soon joined by a "calf": the Bayern-Kleinmotor (Bavarian mini-engine). This air-cooled, two-cylinder 494 cc boxer engine was ideal for motorbikes, a developing industry in this postwar period.

In 1923, BMW unveiled its first motorbike, the R32. This was the beginning of a success story on two wheels that continues to this day. As the strictures of the Treaty of Versailles were relaxed, and following the inflation, the construction of aero engines expanded at BMW. In 1927, the share capital was increased to ten million reichsmarks. At the same time, Dr. Emil Georg von Stauss, the Chairman of the Supervisory Board, tried to restrict the influence of Castiglioni, who was also on the Board. As BMW had now also set its sights on automobile construction, Castiglioni entered into negotiations with Gothaer Wagon-Fabrik with the aim of acquiring its subsidiary, the Eisenacher Fahrzeug-Fabrik. This factory, overlooked by the Wartburg castle, came with a price tag of one million—200,000 reichsmarks to be paid in cash, the rest in BMW shares.

Founded by Heinrich Erhardt in 1896, the Eisenach factory commenced vehicle construction in 1898. Its most legendary product was the Dixi; by 1929, 15,822 had been built, the most recent being the Dixi 3/15 PS, a construction under license of the British Austin Seven! BMW's somewhat "Germanized" version was released with the designation 3/15PS DA2. Whether the sedan or the two-seater DA3 sports coupé, the cut-price little car burst cheerfully onto the terrain previously dominated by Opel's "Laubfrosch" (tree frog). The company kept the car at an affordable level during the difficult years following the Wall Street Crash of 1929—helped considerably by its running costs of just 5.11 pfennigs per kilometer. The "shrimp's" success in the Alpenfahrt rally with an average speed of 26 mph (42 kph) emphasized its all-round capability.

Geschäfte und lässt im Oktober 1917 das bis heute nur im Schrifttyp leicht modernisierte BMW-Markenzeichen beim kaiserlichen Patentamt zu München eintragen. Es symbolisiert die Rotation eines Propellers, der die bayerischen Landesfarben viertelt. Propeller deswegen, weil zur geplanten großen Produktpalette nicht nur Land-, Landwirtschafts- und Wasserfahrzeuge sowie Motoren aller Art gehören sollen, sondern auch der Flugzeugbau ins Auge gefasst wird.

Friz entwickelt in kürzester Zeit einen 220-PS-Sechszylinder-Flugmotor, der dank eines genialen Höhen-Vergasers auch in dem sauerstoffarmen Environ von 6000 Metern nur die Hälfte seiner Leistung einbüßt. Diese kriegstaugliche Innovation wird mit einer Order von 600 Triebwerken belohnt. Nun müssen die Bayerischen Motoren Werke ihrerseits Lizenzen zur Fertigung vergeben, da ihre Hallen in der Schleißheimer Straße aus den Nähten zu platzen drohen. Um die Finanzierung zu sichern, erfolgt die Umwandlung in eine Aktiengesellschaft, mit Popp als Generaldirektor. Friz wartet sogar mit einem verbesserten Triebwerk auf, das in 3000 Metern Höhe noch 250 PS abgibt. Nach Kriegsende wird den mittlerweile 3500 BMW-Mitarbeitern die eigentliche Arbeitsbasis entzogen, denn der Versailler Vertrag verbietet den Bau von Flugmotoren- und geräten. Mit einem Auftrag der Knorr-Bremse AG, Berlin, zur Bremsherstellung für bayerische Eisenbahnen hält sich BMW über Wasser. Popp und Friz lassen sich nicht entmutigen, und so wird in aller Stille weiterentwickelt. Ergo erübrigt sich die Frage, mit welchem Motor am 19. Juni 1919 vom Münchener Oberwiesenfeld aus in 87 Minuten eine neue Rekordhöhe von 9760 Metern erreicht wird.

1922 vereinnahmt der Wiener Bankier Kommerzialrat Camillo Castiglioni, der Popp bei Rapp eingeschleust hatte, für BMW die Bayerischen Flugzeugwerke. Hier entsteht der so genannte Bayern-Motor, ein uriger Vierzylinder mit acht Litern Hubraum, ideal für Lastwagen, Traktoren und sonstige Landwirtschaftsmaschinen, aber auch für Motorboote. Neben diesem „Bullen" bereichert auch ein „Kälbchen" den BMW-Stall, apostrophiert als „Bayern-Kleinmotor". Dieser luftgekühlte Zweizylinder-Boxer mit 494 cm³ eignet sich besonders für Motorräder, einer aufstrebenden Nachkriegs-Fahrzeugsparte. 1923 präsentiert BMW mit der R32 das erste Motorrad aus eigener Produktion, Beginn einer Zweirad-Erfolgsstory bis zum heutigen Tage. Mit der Lockerung der Versailler Bandagen und nach der Inflation gewinnt der Flugmotoren-Bau bei BMW zunehmend an Fahrt. 1927 erfolgt eine Erhöhung

En 1922, Camillo Castiglioni, banquier et conseiller commercial viennois, que Popp avait fait rentrer chez Rapp, rachète les Bayerische Flugzeugwerke au nom de BMW. On y crée le «moteur de Bavière», un quatre-cylindres rugueux de 8 litres de cylindrée, idéal pour les camions, les tracteurs et toutes les machines agricoles, mais aussi pour les bateaux à moteur. En plus de ce «taureau», l'étable BMW s'enrichit d'un «petit veau», surnommé le «petit moteur bavarois». Ce bicylindre à plat de 494 cm³ refroidi par air est surtout employé pour les motos, de plus en plus utilisées après la guerre. En 1923, BMW présente sa première motocyclette, la R32, qui marque le début du succès jamais démenti de la marque dans le secteur des deux-roues. Avec l'assouplissement des conditions draconiennes du traité de Versailles et après l'inflation, la construction de moteurs d'avions est relancée chez BMW. On entreprend d'augmenter le capital, qui passe à dix millions de reichsmarks, en 1927 tandis qu'Emil Georg von Stauss, président du conseil de surveillance, cherche à limiter l'influence de Castiglione qui siège lui aussi au conseil. BMW s'intéressant désormais aussi à la construction automobile, Castiglione entre en négociations avec la Gothaer Wagon-Fabrik pour racheter sa filiale, la Eisenacher Fahrzeug-Fabrik. L'usine à l'ombre de la Wartburg coûtera un million de reichsmarks dont 200000 en espèces et le reste en actions de BMW.

Fondée en 1896 par Heinrich Erhardt, la firme construit des automobiles depuis 1898 à Eisenach. Modèle légendaire, la Dixi, construite en 15822 exemplaires jusqu'en 1929, sous le nom de Dixi 3/15 PS pour les dernières, est en réalité une Austin Seven sous licence. La version de BMW un peu adaptée au goût allemand est présentée sous le nom de 3/15 PS DA2. Berline ou cabriolet sportif deux places DA3, la petite voiture progresse effrontément sur le terrain de la «grenouille» d'Opel dans une véritable guerre des prix. Au cours des années difficiles suivant le krach de 1929, cette voiture reste accessible, d'autant que ses coûts d'exploitation ne s'élèvent qu'à 5,11 pfennigs au kilomètre. La victoire de cette naine à la Coupe internationale des Alpes avec une vitesse moyenne de 42 km/h souligne sa polyvalence.

La motocyclette BMW R2 (à partir de 1931) et la réplique du neuf-cylindres en étoile de Pratt & Whitney pour l'industrie aéronautique aident la marque à surmonter la crise économique mondiale. Les bonnes relations de l'entreprise avec Daimler-Benz se manifestent par des postes réciproques

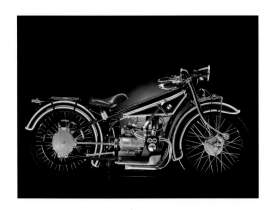

A legend in its own lifetime: the R32, the first motorcycle of the Bayerische Motoren Werke.

Schon zu Lebzeiten eine Legende: die R32, das erste Motorrad der Bayerischen Motoren Werke.

Une légende dès sa création : la R32, la première moto de Bayerische Motoren Werke.

BMW's R2 motorbike (from 1931) and reproduction of Pratt & Whitney's nine-cylinder radial engine for the aviation industry helped the brand through the world economic crisis. The excellent relationship with Daimler-Benz was confirmed when each company appointed an individual from its own Supervisory Board as a director on the other's board. So BMW boss Popp was well placed, both in Munich and in Stuttgart. The tremendous demand from Germany's aviation industry in the 1930s prompted a reorganization, with the creation of BMW Flugzeugmotorenbaugesellschaft mbH for the construction of aero engines, while work in Eisenach focused more on orders for developments required by the Luftwaffe. On a good day, the "Tante Ju" (the Junkers 52) with its three BMW radial engines can still be seen flying over her old home today.

Following the ending of the Austin license agreement, BMW introduced the 3/20 PS in 1932 with attractive bodywork that had been fitted out at the Mercedes-Benz body plant at Sindelfingen. The debut of the 303, whose six cylinders provided just 1173cc, also marked the birth of the unmistakable BMW kidney-shaped radiator grille. This "3" is widely regarded as the forerunner of the 326 of 1936, which wrote its own chapter in the success story of the blue-and-white marque. It was also followed by motor sports successes on two and four wheels: three wins at the German Motorcycle Grand Prix in 1933, and Ernst Henne's victory in its class with a BMW 328 at the Eifelrennen in 1936; he also set a new motorbike speed record the following year of 173.675mph (279.503kph). Simply sensational were the three triumphs in the 2-liter class at Le Mans in 1939. And in 1940, Baron Fritz Huschke von Hanstein and his co-driver Walter Bäumer even achieved the overall victory at the Mille Miglia. This was just the boost BMW needed, but then the Second World War brought down the curtain on the company's production for the civilian market.

Now there was a demand for all types of vehicle, and BMW shone with its turbojet engine for the Heinkel 162 "Volksjäger" ("People's fighter") which, despite its superior speed of 522mph (840kph), could not steal a march on the enemy's machines of the time. Instead, British and American bombs destroyed the major BMW manufacturing plant sites. The Eisenach plant was the only one to remain relatively unscathed, and the Americans handed it over to Soviet

des Aktien-Stammkapitals auf zehn Millionen Reichsmark, zugleich versucht der Aufsichtsratsvorsitzende, Dr. Emil Georg von Stauss, den Einfluss von Castiglione – ebenfalls in seinem Gremium – in Schranken zu halten. Da von BMW nun auch der Automobilbau ins Visier genommen worden ist, führt Castiglione Verhandlungen mit der Gothaer Wagon-Fabrik, um ihre Dependance, die Eisenacher Fahrzeug-Fabrik, abzukaufen. Eine Million, davon 200 000 Reichsmark bar und der Rest in BMW-Aktien, kostet das Werk am Fuße der Wartburg.

1896 gegründet durch Heinrich Erhardt, werden in Eisenach seit 1898 Fahrzeuge gebaut. Legendär der Dixi, der es bis 1929 auf 15822 Einheiten schafft, zuletzt als Dixi 3/15 PS, ein Lizenzbau des Seven von Austin! Die von BMW etwas germanisierte Ausführung wird unter der Typenbezeichnung 3/15 PS DA2 vorgestellt. Ob als Limousine oder zweisitziges DA3-Sportcabriolet, das kleine Auto prescht frech in das von Opels „Laubfrosch" beherrschte Terrain mit einem echten Kampfpreis. Er hält das Fahrzeug gerade in den schweren Jahren nach dem Wallstreet-Crash von 1929 auf einem erschwinglichen Niveau, zumal die Betriebskosten mit lediglich 5,11 Pfennigen pro Kilometer angegeben werden. Der Gewinn des Winzlings bei der Alpenfahrt mit einem Schnitt von 42 Stundenkilometern unterstreicht seine universelle Tauglichkeit.

Das BMW-Motorrad R2 (ab 1931) und der Nachbau des Neunzylinder-Sternmotors von Pratt & Whitney für die Flugzeugindustrie helfen der Marke bei der erfolgreichen Bewältigung der Weltwirtschaftskrise. Die guten Beziehungen zu Daimler-Benz manifestieren sich in der gegenseitigen Besetzung eines Aufsichtsratspostens. So steht BMW-Chef Popp in zweierlei Hinsicht unter einem guten Stern – in München und in Stuttgart. Die große Nachfrage der deutschen Flugzeugindustrie in den dreißiger Jahren resultiert in der Ausgliederung dieses Firmenzweiges in eine BMW Flugmotorenbaugesellschaft mbH, während in Eisenach vermehrt Luftwaffen-Entwicklungsaufträge eingehen. Noch heute fliegt die legendäre „Tante Ju" (Junkers 52) mit ihren drei BMW-Sternmotoren an schönen Tagen über ihrer alten Heimat.

Nach dem Auslaufen der Austin-Lizenz präsentiert BMW 1932 den 3/20 PS, eingekleidet im Mercedes-Benz-Karosseriewerk Sindelfingen. Das Debüt des 303, der auf seine sechs Zylinder lediglich 1173 cm³ verteilt, gilt gleichzeitig als Geburtsstunde der unverwechselbaren „BMW-Niere". Dieser Dreier gilt als Vorläufer des 326 von 1936, der ein eigenes Erfolgskapitel in der Geschichte der weiß-blauen Marke schreibt. Diesem schließen sich motorsportliche Meriten auf zwei und vier

dans les deux conseils de surveillance. Le directeur de BMW, Franz-Joseph Popp, se trouve ainsi à double titre sous une bonne étoile, à Munich comme à Stuttgart. La demande importante de l'industrie aéronautique allemande dans les années 1930 aboutit au détachement de cette branche de l'entreprise qui devient la BMW Flugmotorenbau GmbH tandis qu'Eisenach reçoit de plus en plus de commandes pour le développement des forces aériennes. Le légendaire «Tante Ju» (Junkers 52) avec ses trois moteurs en étoile BMW vole aujourd'hui encore lorsqu'il fait beau dans le ciel de sa patrie.

Après l'expiration du contrat de licence signé avec Austin, BMW présente en 1932 la 3/20 PS «habillée» dans l'usine de carrosserie de Mercedes-Benz à Sindelfingen. Le lancement de la 303, qui répartit ses six cylindres sur seulement 1173 cm³, annonce la naissance des «naseaux» BMW, visage singulier de la marque. Cette «Série 3» est considérée comme précurseur de la 326 de 1936 qui pose elle aussi un jalon dans l'histoire de la marque bleue et blanche. À ce succès viennent s'ajouter des exploits sportifs sur deux et quatre roues : trois victoires au Grand Prix d'Allemagne pour motocyclettes en 1933, une victoire d'Ernst Henne dans sa catégorie au volant d'une BMW 328 lors de la course d'Eifel en 1936, qui récidive l'année suivante avec un nouveau record du monde de vitesse à moto avec 279,503 km/h. Le triomphal triplé dans la catégorie deux-litres en 1939 au Mans fait sensation. Le baron Fritz Huschke von Hanstein et son copilote Walter Bäumer remportent la victoire au classement général des Mille Miglia en 1940. La réputation sportive de la marque n'est plus à faire mais l'ombre de la Deuxième Guerre mondiale plane déjà sur la production civile BMW.

On réclame désormais des véhicules tout-terrain et BMW s'illustre dans le segment des moteurs d'avion avec le turboréacteur du «chasseur du peuple» He162 qui, malgré sa vitesse de 840 km/h, ne jouera plus aucun rôle contre l'ennemi de l'époque. Les bombardements anglo-américains anéantissent en effet les plus grands ateliers de production BMW. Seule la filiale d'Eisenach a été en grande partie épargnée et est remise par les Américains aux soldats soviétiques. Une main-d'œuvre autochtone efficace s'occupe immédiatement de la poursuite de la fabrication et se trouve placée en 1946 sous la tutelle de la société anonyme étatique soviétique Avtovelo. En 1951, BMW est rebaptisée pour la voiture provenant de la zone est. La modification est des plus simples : seule la première lettre change et BMW devient EMW (pour Eisenacher Motoren Werke) tandis que le bleu de l'emblème est remplacé par du rouge. En 1952, l'usine est transmise au groupe IFA de RDA.

BMW motorcycles were used not just for peaceful purposes: parade on Hitler's birthday on 20 April 1936.

Nicht nur friedlichen Zwecken wurden BMW-Motorräder zugeführt: Parade zu Hitlers Geburtstag am 20. April 1936.

Les motos BMW n'étaient pas utilisées qu'à des fins pacifiques: ici, la parade pour l'anniversaire d'Adolf Hitler, le 20 avril 1936.

soldiers. The local workforce took the initiative and continued production, and in 1946 Soviet state company Awtowelo took over the plant. In 1951 BMW changed the name of the car produced in the Soviet zone. Nothing was easier: the first letter was simply changed to "E" and became "EMW" (Eisenach Motor Works), and the blue in the badge was replaced by red. In 1952 the factory was handed over to the GDR concern IFA.

While BMWs were once more being rolled out from the premises in Thuringia—albeit it only for state officials—the BMW range in Munich was limited to an unusual product combination of baking sheets and whisks, bicycles and small agricultural machines for sowing and harrowing. This situation particularly incensed Georg "Schorsch" Meier, who in 1939 had won the Isle of Man's famous "Tourist Trophy" motorcycle race. He was appointed—or demoted, depending on how you view the position—as head of the BMW factory police force, and he urged that the company should find its feet amidst all the chaos and confusion by returning to the manufacture of motorcycles. The R24 with 250 cc—the Allies would not allow more at the time—was launched at the Geneva Motor Show in 1948, and was an instant hit. By 1950 it had already delighted more than 10,000 two-wheel enthusiasts, and BMW produced an even better version in the form of the R51 once the quarter-liter cubic capacity limit had been lifted.

It was in 1951 that the 501, known as the "Baroque angel," first floated out of the Munich BMW plant. The nickname given to the car, solid and with extragavant curves, was actually not fair: even the design genius Pinin Farina, whose own body design for the 501 was rejected by BMW, was fulsome in his praise of the four-door vehicle in fashionable black. However, this underpowered, relatively expensive car proved to be a false dawn. The eight-cylinder 502 and the two beautiful creations by Count Goertz failed to match up to the competition from Stuttgart. Instead, all that was available was a place in the small car sector. BMW designed a mini car called the Isetta, lovingly nicknamed the "Knutschkugel" ("cuddle box") by young people. From this two-seater and the later, larger BMW 600 it was just a small step to a true small car that would be able to conquer the racing tracks. The 700, the first BMW to have a self-supporting chassis, proved to be a real success—and just in time, since despite a cash injection from the Bremen wood entrepreneur Hermann Krages, the days of the Munich company had seemed seriously numbered. There were tumultuous scenes at the annual meeting of shareholders on 9 December 1959, when the workforce, dealers and minor stockholders joined forces to battle for the company's survival. This so impressed the major stockholder Dr. Herbert Quandt that he invested even more capital and thereby saved it. The 700 Coupé—a total of 188,212 of the 2+2 version were built—was joined by a convertible and a sedan.

Following its economic recovery, BMW entered the mid-size car market in 1962. The 1500, a well-designed modern automobile, was the basis for a range of models that was continually extended, culminating in 1969 in the 2000 tii touring version. Sales of the 1600-2 totaled 252,786 between 1966 and 1975: BMW was finally established in the mid-size range. Thus encouraged, the company initiated a return to the popular six-cylinder engines, beginning with the 2500 and 2800 sedans, and the 2800CS. There was also an increase in racing activities. Hubert Hahne's daring exploits on an 1800ti have never been forgotten—especially at the Nürburgring, where, on 1 August 1965, he covered the Nordschleife circuit in 10 minutes 12.02 seconds. BMW Motorsport GmbH was founded in 1972, while the "Vierzylinder" ("four-cylinder"), the new administrative building, soared

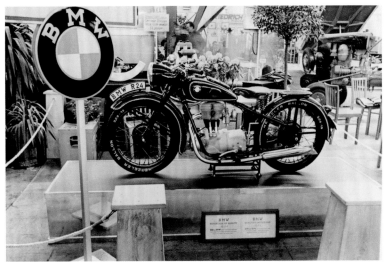

Prototype of the R24 at the Hanover Export Fair in May 1948. The machine turned into a big seller.

Prototyp der R24 bei der Exportmesse in Hannover im Mai 1948. Die Maschine wird ein Renner.

Le prototype de la R24 à la Foire des Exportations de Hanovre en mai 1948. Cette moto sera un best-seller.

Rädern an: Drei Siege beim Großen Preis von Deutschland für Motorräder 1933, Klassensieg mit einem BMW 328 beim Eifelrennen 1936 durch Ernst Henne, der im Folgejahr auch einen neuen Motorrad-Geschwindigkeits-Weltrekord mit 279,503 km/h aufstellt. Einfach sensationell: Dreifach-Sieg in der 2-Liter-Klasse 1939 in Le Mans. Baron Fritz Huschke von Hanstein und sein Copilot Walter Bäumer holen sich 1940 sogar den Gesamtsieg der Mille Miglia. Für sportliches Image ist reichlich gesorgt, doch dann schließt sich der Vorhang des Zweiten Weltkriegs über der zivilen BMW-Produktion.

Geländegängiges ist nunmehr gefragt, und bei den Flugzeugmotoren brilliert BMW mit der Strahlturbine für den „Volksjäger" He162, der dem damaligen Feind freilich nichts mehr abjagen kann, trotz seiner überlegenen Geschwindigkeit von 840 km/h. Stattdessen zermalmt der anglo-amerikanische Bombenhagel die größeren BMW-Fertigungsstätten. Nur Eisenach bleibt weitgehend verschont und wird von den Amerikanern den Sowjetsoldaten übergeben. Flinke einheimische Hände bauen sofort weiter und werden 1946 dem sowjetischen Staatsbetrieb Awtowelo unterstellt. 1951 erwirkt BMW eine Namensänderung für das Auto aus der Ostzone. Nichts einfacher als das: Es wird lediglich der erste Buchstabe geändert in EMW (Eisenacher Motoren Werke) und das Blau im Signet gegen Rot ausgetauscht. 1952 geht das Werk an die DDR-Gruppe IFA über.

Während in Thüringen wieder BMW-Mobile – wenngleich nur für Funktionäre – aus den Hallen rollen, beschränkt

Alors qu'en Thuringe des véhicules BMW recommencent à sortir des usines, même s'ils ne sont destinés qu'à des fonctionnaires, l'offre munichoise de la marque se limite à un curieux assortiment de produits allant de plaques de cuisson et fouets de cuisine à des bicyclettes et petites machines agricoles en passant par des scies et des herses. Cette situation irrite au plus haut point Georg Meier, vainqueur en 1939 du «Tourist Trophy», célèbre course de motos organisée sur l'Île de Man. Plus connu sous le surnom de «Schorsch», celui qui a été élevé – ou ravalé, selon l'estime que l'on porte au poste – au rang de chef des vigiles de l'usine BMW, insiste pour que l'entreprise recommence immédiatement à construire des motocyclettes. La R24 de 250 cm³, cylindrée maximum autorisée à l'époque par les Alliés, est présentée à Genève en 1948 et connaît un succès fulgurant. Dès 1950, elle fait le bonheur de plus de 10 000 adeptes de deux-roues. Avec la R51, BMW lance ensuite une moto de 500 cm³ au ronronnement mélodieux, le plafonnement de cylindrée ayant été supprimé entre-temps.

À partir de 1951, ce n'est pas l'«ange Aloisius» mais un «ange baroque» qui plane au-dessus des usines BMW à Munich. La 501, imposante avec ses courbes plantureuses, ne mérite pas vraiment son surnom car le génie du design Pinin Farina lui-même, dont le propre prototype n'avait pas reçu un accueil favorable, reconnaît une certaine élégance à cette quatre portes commercialisée exclusivement dans un noir très distingué. Cette voiture sous-motorisée et

Single cylinder and V8— this combination proved unpalatable in the 1950s.

Einzylinder und V8 – dieser Spagat erweist sich in den fünfziger Jahren als wenig bekömmlich.

Monocylindre et V8 – dans les années 1950, ce grand écart s'avérera peu favorable au constructeur.

Admired and scolded: "Nischen-Paul" Hahnemann.

Viel bewundert und viel gescholten:
„Nischen-Paul" Hahnemann.

Très admiré mais souvent en proie aux critiques :
Paul Hahnemann, surnommé « Paul la niche ».

heavenwards on Munich's Petuelring. The new flagship, the BMW 3.0 CSL, made motor sports history as one of the most successful coupés of all time: it won the European Touring Car Championships no fewer than six times between 1973 and 1979. As an engine partner to March Engineering in Formula 2, BMW won five titles with Jean-Pierre Jarier, Patrick Depailler, Jacques Laffite, Bruno Giacomelli, and Marc Surer. This was added to by Hans Stuck making runner-up in 1975; his father was one of the icons in German motor sports, and he even showed his mettle as a 60-year-old in winning one of the most famous European Alpine races in a BMW.

By increasing its production facilities at the Dingolfing factory, BMW's 28,989 employees there achieved a turnover of 3.2 billion deutschmarks in 1975. BMW of North America formed a Bavarian bridgehead over the Atlantic, and BMW assembly lines were operating at full tilt in South Africa. The Munich team relished its role as a global player from the outset. The company's 50th anniversary as an automobile manufacturer was another record year for the blue-and-white marque, producing 290,236 cars and 31,515 motorcycles, which were now being manufactured in Berlin. In 1978 BMW presented the M1, a thoroughbred sports car that had its own racing series ahead of the major racing events—at least at most of the European Grands Prix. This Procar series, in which the five fastest F1 pilots were "obliged" to participate at the end of their training, offered extremely exciting motor sport. There were world-class performances by Niki Lauda (Procar Champion 1979) and Nelson Piquet I, who proved his world-class skills in 1980.

BMW conquered the pinnacle of international motor sports in 1983: Paul Rosche's perfected four-cylinder turbo engine, which produced 1280 bhp at full throttle, secured Formula 1 victory for Nelson Piquet's Brabham BT52—the first F1

sich das Münchener BMW-Angebot auf eine seltsame Produktmischung von Backblechen und Schneebesen über Fahrräder bis zu kleinen Landmaschinen zum Säen und Eggen. Diese Situation bringt besonders Georg Meier, der 1939 das berühmte Motorradrennen auf der Isle of Man, die Tourist Trophy, gewonnen hat, in Rage. „Schorsch", zum Leiter der BMW-Werkspolizei ernannt oder degradiert – je nach Einstufung dieser Position – regt die unverzügliche Wiederaufnahme der Motorrad-Produktion an. Die R24 mit 250 cm³ – mehr erlauben damals die Alliierten noch nicht – reüssiert 1948 in Genf und ist auf Anhieb ein Renner. Bereits 1950 erfreut sie mehr als 10 000 Zweirad-Enthusiasten, und mit der R51 setzt BMW ein Halbliter-Sahnehäubchen oben drauf, denn inzwischen ist die Hubraum-Restriktion gefallen.

Nicht der Engel Aloisius, sondern ein „Barockengel" schwebt ab 1951 aus dem Münchener BMW-Werk. Dass der Typ 501, gewichtig und mit üppigen Rundungen versehen, diesen Spitznamen erhält, ist eigentlich ungerecht, denn selbst das Design-Genie Pinin Farina, dessen eigener Entwurf für BMW nicht auf Gegenliebe gestoßen war, attestiert dem in vornehmen Schwarz gehaltenen Viertürer eine gewisse Eleganz. Diesem untermotorisierten, relativ teuren Wagen bleibt jegliche Fortune versagt. Auch der 502 mit acht Zylindern und die beiden bildhübschen sportlichen Kreationen des Grafen Goertz sind der Konkurrenz aus Stuttgart nicht gewachsen. Stattdessen bietet sich eine Belegung des Kleinwagensegments förmlich an. BMW stellt einen Kabinenroller namens Isetta auf die Räder, von jungen Leuten liebevoll „Knutschkugel" genannt. Von diesem Zweisitzer und dem größeren Nachfolger, dem BMW 600, ist es dann nur noch ein kleiner Schritt zu einem echten Kleinwagen, der auch wieder die Rennpisten erobern kann. Der Typ 700, erster BMW mit einer selbsttragenden Karosserie, erweist sich als Senkrechtstarter, gerade rechtzeitig, denn den Münchnern droht trotz einer Finanzspritze des Holz-Großhändlers Hermann Krages das wirtschaftliche Aus. Tumultartige Szenen in der Hauptversammlung am 9. Dezember 1959: Verbissen kämpfen Kleinaktionäre und Belegschaft ums Überleben! Das imponiert dem Großaktionär Dr. Herbert Quandt derart, dass er noch mehr Kapital einbringt und das Unternehmen damit rettet. Dem 700er Coupé, insgesamt werden 188 212 Exemplare des 2+2-Sitzers gebaut, gesellen sich noch ein Cabrio und eine Limousine hinzu.

Wirtschaftlich wieder erholt, steigt BMW 1962 in die Mittelklasse ein. Der 1500, ein gediegenes, modernes Automobil, bildet den Grundstock für eine Modellpalette, die ständig erweitert wird und 1969 im 2000 tii – einem Renn-Tourenwagen – gipfelt. 252 786 verkaufte 1600-2 zwischen 1966 und 1975: Damit hat sich BMW endgültig in der Mittelklasse etabliert. Solchermaßen ermutigt beginnt mit den Limousinen 2500 und 2800 sowie dem 2800 CS die Rückkehr zu den bewährten Sechszylinder-Reihentriebwerken. Gleichzeitig werden die motorsportlichen Aktivitäten verstärkt. Unvergessen bleiben die Husarenritte von Hubert Hahne auf einem 1800 ti, besonders auf dem Nürburgring, wo er am 1. August 1965 in 10:12,2 Minuten die Nordschleife umrundet. 1972 wird die BMW Motorsport GmbH gegründet, während am Münchener Petuelring der "Vierzylinder", das neue Verwaltungsgebäude, in den Himmel schießt. Das neue Flaggschiff, der BMW 3.0 CSL, geht in die Motorsport-Historie als eines der erfolgreichsten Coupés ein: Zwischen 1973 und 1979 gewinnt es sechs Mal die Tourenwagen-Europameisterschaft. Als Motorenpartner von March in der Formel 2 heimst BMW mit Jean-Pierre Jarier, Patrick Depailler, Jacques Laffite, Bruno Giacomelli und Marc Surer fünf Titel ein. Dazu gesellt sich die Vizemeisterschaft 1975 von Hans-Joachim

relativement chère ne rencontre pas le succès attendu. La 502 huit-cylindres et les deux magnifiques créations sportives du compte Goertz ne feront pas non plus le poids face à la concurrence de Stuttgart. En revanche, le segment des voiturettes se renforce radicalement. BMW propose un « motocoupé », l'Isetta, surnommée affectueusement « l'œuf à roulettes » ou le « pot de yaourt ». Le pas à franchir n'est plus très grand pour passer de cette deux places et de celle qui lui a succédé, la BMW 600, à une véritable petite voiture capable de s'illustrer sur les circuits. La 700, première BMW à carrosserie autoportante, connaît un vif succès, pile à temps, car, malgré une injection de capitaux du négociant en bois Hermann Krages, les Munichois sont au bord de la faillite. En témoignent les scènes tumultueuses lors de l'assemblée générale du 9 décembre 1959 : les petits actionnaires et le personnel de l'entreprise se battent âprement pour la survie de la marque ! Le gros actionnaire Herbert Quandt est tellement impressionné qu'il injecte encore plus de fonds et sauve l'entreprise. Un cabriolet et une berline viennent s'ajouter au coupé 700 dont 188 212 exemplaires en tout seront produits.

Remise sur le plan économique, BMW fait son entrée sur le segment intermédiaire en 1962. La 1500, une voiture moderne et sobre, constitue la base de la nouvelle gamme de modèles qui sera sans cesse élargie pour culminer en 1969 avec la 2000 tii, une voiture de tourisme sportive. Avec 252 786 exemplaires de la 1600-2 vendus entre 1966 et 1975, BMW s'est définitivement établie dans le segment intermédiaire. Ainsi encouragée, la marque renoue avec les moteurs six-cylindres en ligne bien rôdés avec les modèles 2500, 2800 et 2800 CS. Les activités dans le domaine du sport automobile se renforcent également à ce moment-là. Les exploits d'Hubert Hahne au volant d'une 1800 ti, en particulier le 1er août 1965 sur le Nürburgring, dont il parcourt la boucle nord en 10.12,2 minutes, restent inoubliables. La BMW Motorsport GmbH est fondée en 1972 tandis que le nouveau siège social de la marque, un bâtiment en forme de « quatre-cylindres », s'élève dans le ciel le long du Petuelring à Munich. Le nouveau produit phare de la marque, la BMW 3.0 CSL, devient l'un des coupés les plus récompensés de l'histoire du sport automobile : entre 1973 et 1979, il est sacré six fois champion d'Europe des voitures de tourisme. Partenaire de March en Formule 2, les moteurs BMW raflent cinq titres avec Jean-Pierre Jarier, Patrick Depailler, Jacques Laffite, Bruno Giacomelli et Marc Surer. En 1975, Hans-Joachim Stuck remporte le titre de vice-champion ; son père, figure emblématique du sport automobile allemand, triomphe lui-même à 60 ans, au volant d'une BMW, dans la plus célèbre course en montagne d'Europe.

En augmentant ses capacités de production avec l'usine de Dingolfing, BMW réalise en 1975 un chiffre d'affaires de 3,2 milliards de marks et emploie 28 989 personnes. Avec BMW of North America, la marque possède désormais une tête de pont décisive outre-Atlantique, tandis que les chaînes de montage BMW tournent à plein régime en Afrique du Sud. Dès le début, les Munichois jouent leur rôle de « global player » avec le plus grand investissement. Le cinquantenaire de la marque bleue et blanche en tant que constructeur automobile est célébré par de nombreux records : 290 236 voitures construites et 31 515 motocyclettes, qui sont désormais fabriquées à Berlin. En 1978, BMW présente la M1, une voiture de sport racée pour laquelle est créée une série de courses en lever de rideau des grandes compétitions, en particulier des Grands Prix européens. Ces courses de Procar à laquelle les cinq pilotes de F1 les mieux classés aux essais sont « obligés de participer », sont la promesse d'un spectacle extrêmement intense de sport mécanique. Niki Lauda (champion de Procar

title for a turbocharged car. Austrian Dieter Quester became the touring car champion in the same year—like his father-in-law, Alex von Falkenhausen, another of BMW's founding fathers. Another high point was the Touring Car World Championship for a BMW M3 driven by Roberto Ravaglia in 1987. Over the following years, the M3 touring car garnered awards as if they were coming off a conveyer belt.

A welcome return to familiar territory came in 1990 when BMW and Rolls-Royce joined forces for the manufacture of aircraft engines—with excellent prospects for the future.

A new production record was achieved in 1993: BMW entered a new stage of expansion with 598,000 automobiles and 35,000 motorcycles a year. An impressive facility was built at Greensville, near Spartanburg in South Carolina, and the production lines began operating in September 1994. Various subsidiaries—including an automobile assembly facility in Vietnam—sprang up like mushrooms around the globe, although the takeover of the ailing Rover Group proved to be a flop. BMW later shed this costly load, but held on to the Mini, which went on to enjoy a renaissance. Overall, BMW's results for 1995 were nominally remarkable: the addition of Rover meant that the group broke the one-million barrier, producing 1,098,582 automobiles. The German capital also announced another record of 52,655 motorcycles. In 1998 BMW ascended to the highest sector of luxury car production with the take-over of Rolls-Royce's automobile division. The blue-blooded British company was given a new home near Goodwood. "Royal carriages" are produced there under German management—as with the Mini—using high-tech components from Bavaria. In 2003, Mini boss Anton Heiss had two reasons to celebrate: the bubbly first flowed for the annual production of 174,366 Minis, and then again when his paint shop began running at full capacity.

Another Bavarian-British liaison, this time with Williams in Formula 1, celebrated its third position in the Constructors' World Championship of 2000 and 2001, and in the following two years BMW-Williams even achieved runner-up position—behind Ferrari, but ahead of McLaren-Mercedes. BMW's Sauber team has competed in this prestigious

Collected works: the first BMW 1500s being delivered to the dealers in 1963. Bright colors were preferred.

Gesammelte Werke: Die ersten BMW 1500 werden 1963 an die Händler ausgeliefert. Man bevorzugt helle Farben.

Œuvres réunies: les premières BMW 1500 sont remises aux concessionnaires en 1963. Les couleures claires ont la cote.

Stuck, dessen Vater schon zu den Ikonen des deutschen Motorsports gehört und selbst als 60-jähriger Draufgänger noch bei den berühmtesten Bergrennen Europas auf einem BMW siegt.

Durch Erweiterung der Produktionskapazitäten auf das Werk Dingolfing verzeichnet BMW 1975 einen Umsatz von 3.2 Milliarden Mark, erwirtschaftet von 28989 Mitarbeitern. Mit BMW of North America hat man einen wichtigen Brückenkopf über den Atlantik geschlagen, und in Südafrika laufen BMW-Montagebänder auf vollen Touren. Die Münchener spielen ihre Rolle als „global player" von Anfang an mit viel Engagement. Zum fünfzigjährigen Jubiläum als Autohersteller gibt es ein weiteres Rekordjahr für die weiß-blaue Marke: 290236 produzierte Pkw und 31515 Motorräder, die fortan in Berlin gefertigt werden. 1978 präsentiert BMW mit dem M1 einen reinrassigen Sportwagen, der eine eigene Rennserie im Vorfeld großer Rennveranstaltungen – zumeist bei den europäischen Grands Prix – erhält. Diese Procar-Serie, zu der die fünf schnellsten F1-Piloten des Abschlusstrainings teilnahmeverpflichtet werden, bietet extrem spannenden Motorsport. Weltmeisterliche Darbietungen liefern Niki Lauda (Procar-Champion 1979) und Nelson Piquet, der 1980 seine Extra-Klasse unter Beweis stellt.

Den Olymp des internationalen Motorsports erklimmt BMW 1983: Der von Paul Rosche zur Perfektion getriebene Vierzylinder-Turbomotor, der bei vollem Boost 1280 PS entfaltet, treibt Nelson Piquets Brabham BT52 zum Titel des ersten Formel-1-Weltmeisters mit einem Turbo im Rücken. Tourenwagen-Champion wird im gleichen Jahr der Österreicher Dieter Quester, wie sein Schwiegervater Alex von Falkenhausen ein BMW-Urgestein. Weiterer Höhepunkt: die Tourenwagen-Weltmeisterschaft für einen BMW M3 durch Roberto Ravaglia 1987. In den Jahren danach sammelt der M3 Tourenwagen-Siege im Fließbandverfahren.

Seliger Rückfall in vertrautes Terrain: 1990 gründen BMW und Rolls-Royce eine Gesellschaft zur Fertigung von Flugzeug-Triebwerken – mit hervorragenden Zukunftsperspektiven.

Neuer Produktionsrekord 1993: Mit 598000 Automobilen und 35000 Motorrädern per anno tritt BMW in eine neue Expansionsphase ein. In Greensville bei Spartanburg, South Carolina, entsteht ein stattliches Werk, in dem bereits im September 1994 die Bänder anrollen. Tochtergesellschaften rund um den Globus – sogar ein Montagebetrieb in Vietnam – wachsen wie Pilze aus dem Boden, doch die Übernahme des angeschlagenen Rover-Konzerns erweist sich als Flop. Später entledigt sich BMW dieses teuren Ballastes, behält aber Mini, der eine strahlende Renaissance erlebt. Immerhin beschert das Jahr 1995 BMW ein nominell bemerkenswertes Resultat, denn mit dem Anhängsel Rover überschreitet der Konzern die Millionengrenze: 1098582 produzierte Automobile. Rekordmeldung auch aus der deutschen Hauptstadt mit 52655 Motorrädern! 1998 steigt BMW in das höchste Luxussegment auf Rädern ein und übernimmt die Automobilsparte von Rolls-Royce. Dem noblen Briten wird ein neues Zuhause in der Nähe von Goodwood spendiert. Unter deutscher Leitung – wie bei Mini – entstehen dort „königliche" Gefährte mit High-Tech-Komponenten aus Bayern. 2003 stößt Mini-Chef Anton Heiss gleich zweimal an: einmal mit Schampus auf die Jahresproduktion von 174366 Minis und zweitens an die Kapazitätsgrenze seiner Lackierwerkstätten.

Eine weitere bayerisch-britische Liaison, nämlich mit Williams in der Formel 1, feiert 2000 und 2001 den dritten Rang in der Konstrukteurs-Weltmeisterschaft, und in den zwei Folgejahren gelingt BMW-Williams sogar hinter Ferrari, aber vor McLaren-Mercedes, die Runner-Up-Platzierung. Basierend auf dem Sauber-Team tritt BMW seit 2006 unter

They called him "Camshaft Paul": racing car engineer Rosche.

**Sie nannten ihn „Nocken-Paul":
Rennmotoreningenieur Rosche.**

**Il était surnommé «Paul la came»:
l'ingénieur et motoriste Paul Rosche.**

1979) et Nelson Piquet senior en 1980 y font pour leur part des démonstrations magistrales.

En 1983, BMW accède à l'Olympe du sport automobile international: le moteur turbo quatre-cylindres de 1280 ch à plein régime conçu à la perfection par Paul Rosche emporte la Brabham BT52 de Nelson Piquet vers le titre de premier champion du monde de Formule 1 sacré avec un moteur turbo. La même année, l'Autrichien Dieter Quester devient champion des voitures de tourisme, comme son beau-père, Alex von Falkenhausen, vieux routier BMW. Autre grand événement: le titre de champion du monde des voitures de tourisme est remporté en 1987 par Roberto Ravaglia au volant d'une BMW M3. Au cours des années suivantes, la M3 remportera des victoires «à la chaîne» dans ce type de compétition.

Retour bienheureux en terrain connu: en 1990, BMW et Rolls-Royce fondent une société de construction de moteurs d'avions aux perspectives d'avenir mirobolantes. Nouveau record de production en 1993: avec 598000 automobiles et 35000 motocyclettes par an, BMW entre dans une nouvelle phase d'expansion. À Greensville, près de Spartanburg en Caroline du Sud, BMW ouvre une imposante usine dont les chaînes commencent à tourner dès septembre 1994. Les filiales poussent comme des champignons tout autour du globe, dont une usine de montage au Vietnam, mais la reprise du groupe Rover en pleine difficulté s'avère un échec. BMW se débarrassera par la suite de ce poids coûteux mais conservera la Mini qui connaît alors une flamboyante renaissance. Quoi qu'il en soit, l'année 1995 réserve un résultat nominal remarquable car avec Rover, le groupe dépasse la barre du million: 1098582 automobiles produites. Record également dans la capitale allemande avec 52655 motocyclettes construites! En 1998, BMW fait son entrée dans le plus haut segment du luxe sur roues en reprenant la branche automobile de Rolls-Royce. La prestigieuse marque britannique se voit offrir un nouveau foyer à proximité de Goodwood. Sous direction allemande, comme chez Mini, on y fabrique des véhicules «royaux» aux composants haute technologie d'origine bavaroise. En 2003, le chef de Mini, Anton Heiss, fait coup double: en sabrant le champagne une première fois pour fêter la production annuelle de 174366 Minis et une seconde fois parce qu'il a atteint la limite des capacités de sa ligne de peinture.

Une autre alliance anglo-bavaroise, avec Williams en Formule 1, décroche en 2000 et en 2001 la troisième place

motor sports league under its own management since 2006, and after a year's preparation once more established itself in the top trio of constructors. On 29 July 2009, BMW announced that it would be adopting new, more environmentally friendly technology.

BMW took part in the Touring Car World Championship when it reappeared in 2005, the previous one having been in 1987, and its driver, Britain's Andy Priaulx, achieved the title of world champion. BMW also secured the manufacturers' prize with the 320i. Priaulx won the title again in 2007 with a dramatic finale on the urban circuit of Macau. It has long been a tradition for BMW to play a key role with Super Production cars in national and international touring car championships, and it is one that continues to this day.

The BMW product range became broader than ever in 2008, and now has something for everyone. There are 5 and 3-door versions of the 1 series, which has been in the portfolio since 2004, plus a coupé and a convertible. The 3 series range is even greater. The 5 series is similar, although the coupé and convertible are classed as 6 series. The fifth generation of the flagship 7 series was produced in 2008. Since 1996, those with sporty aspirations have been able to satisfy them with the Z3 from Spartanburg and, since 2002, with its successor, the Z4. And between 1999 and 2003, people who fancied some James Bond-style excitement could find it in the exclusiveness of a Z8. The X5 and X3 enjoyed such sales success in the Sports Activity Vehicle

eigener Regie in der Königsklasse des Motorsports an und hat sich nach einem Lehrjahr wieder in dem Top-Trio der Konstrukteure angesiedelt. Am 29. Juli 2009 verkündete BMW den Ausstieg zugunsten neuer, umweltfreundlicher Technologien.

In der seit 2005 ausgeschriebenen Weltmeisterschaft der Tourenwagen knüpft BMW dort an, wo man 1987 aufgehört hat: mit dem Weltmeistertitel – diesmal für den Briten Andy Priaulx. Außerdem sichert sich BMW mit dem 320i auch die Herstellerwertung. 2007 kann Priaulx in einem dramatischen Finale auf dem Stadtkurs von Macau erneut den Titel holen. Dass bei nationalen und internationalen Tourenwagen-Meisterschaften für seriennahe Fahrzeuge BMW eine Schlüsselrolle spielt, hat Tradition – bis heute.

Breitgefächerter denn je stellt sich die BMW-Produktpalette ab 2008 dar und deckt alle Segmente ab. Der 1er, seit 2004 im Programm, wartet mit 5- und 3-Türern auf, flankiert von einem Coupé und einem Cabrio. Noch größer ist das Spektrum der 3er-Reihe. Der 5er bietet ähnliches, wobei Coupé und Cabrio als 6er eingeordnet sind. In der fünften Generation bewegt sich 2008 das Flaggschiff, der 7er. Sportlich Ambitionierten kommen seit 1996 der Z3 aus Spartanburg und als Nachfolger ab 2002 der Z4 entgegen. Wer das Besondere à la James Bond wünscht, konnte sich zwischen 1999 und 2003 die Exklusivität eines Z8 gönnen. X5 und X3 feiern im SAV-Segment derartige Verkaufserfolge, dass BMW im Herbst 2008 auch eine Studie des künftigen X1 präsentiert. Eher einem Zwitter gleicht dagegen der X6, dessen

This 'cabin scooter' proved to be the ideal vehicle for driving in cities, but did not win the acceptance that BMW had hoped for.

Dieser „Kabinen-Motorroller" erwies sich als ideales Stadtgefährt, fand aber nicht die erhoffte Akzeptanz.

Ce «scooter à habitacle» était un véhicule idéal en ville mais n'a pas reçu l'accueil espéré.

The BMW World introduces itself in the Munich handover center, complete in every aspect—even with a museum.

Die BMW-Welt präsentiert sich in dem Münchener Auslieferungszentrum mit allen Facetten – sogar mit einem Museum.

L'univers BMW se présente sous toutes ses facettes dans le centre de livraison des voitures neuves à Munich – on y trouve même un musée.

au championnat du monde des constructeurs et les deux années suivantes, BMW-Williams se place deuxième après Ferrari mais devant McLaren-Mercedes. Fort de sa Sauber-Team, BMW entre, à partir de 2006, de manière indépendante dans la cour royale du sport automobile et après une année d'apprentissage se place de nouveau dans le trio de tête des constructeurs. Le 29 juillet 2009, BMW annonce pourtant que son écurie se retire au profit de technologies nouvelles, plus respectueuses de l'environnement.

Dans le championnat du monde des voitures de tourisme annoncé depuis 2005, BMW reprend là où elle s'était arrêtée en 1987: avec un titre de champion du monde – cette fois pour le Britannique Andy Priaulx. BMW s'assure par ailleurs la coupe des constructeurs avec la 320i. En 2007, Priaulx remporte de nouveau le titre lors d'une finale palpitante sur le parcours de la ville de Macao. Il est désormais de coutume que BMW joue un rôle primordial lors des championnats nationaux et internationaux des voitures de tourisme pour des véhicules proches d'une fabrication en série.

À partir de 2008, l'offre BMW se présente plus diversifiée que jamais et couvre tous les segments. La Série 1, commercialisée depuis 2004, existe en versions 5 et 3 portes, agrémentées d'un coupé et d'un cabriolet. La palette de la Série 3 est encore plus vaste. La Série 5 propose une offre similaire, mais le coupé et le cabriolet sont classés sous la désignation «Série 6». Le modèle phare, la Série 7, en est en 2008 à la 5e génération. La Z3 de Spartanburg depuis 1996 et la Z4, qui lui a succédé en 2002, viennent quant à elles répondre aux attentes des amateurs de voitures sportives. De 1999 à 2003, ceux qui s'imaginent dans la peau de James Bond peuvent s'offrir l'exclusivité avec une Z8. La X5 et la X3, dans le segment des SAV, se vendent tellement bien que BMW présente aussi à l'automne 2008 une étude pour la future X1. La X6 enfin ressemble plus à un hybride avec son châssis à quatre roues motrices surélevé sur lequel repose un coupé. Ce premier «Sports Activity

sector that BMW revealed its plans for the future X1 in the fall of 2008. The X6 is more like a hybrid: a coupé with a high 4WD chassis. This first "Sports Activity Coupé with Dynamic Performance Control" was another godsend for the BMW "M" Motorsport company, and was to be fitted with a 460 bhp twin turbo. Even the X5 was targeted by the "M-men" in 2008, who apparently only showed restraint with the elegant 7 series.

"Better dynamics, lower consumption, and even more driving pleasure"—this philosophy is integral to the BMW Group's innovative concepts for progress. The "High Precision Injection" fuel injection technology and regenerative braking were introduced in 2007, and the "Active Hybrid" drive concept was promoted for high-performance models from 2008 onwards. The expansion of the global production network also continues apace. In addition to the eight German factories, the Spartanburg site in South Carolina, USA, has also grown so much that its current production capacity of 450,000 vehicles far exceeds that of currently the largest BMW plant at Dingolfing. The BMW network includes 30 production and assembly sites all over the world. In addition to its tremendous commitment in Shenyang (China), Chennai (India), Kuala Lumpur (Malaysia), Jakarta (Indonesia), and since 2014 in Araquari (Brazil), BMW had also gained a foothold in Kaliningrad (Russia). However, production there remained far below expectations.

Following the record-breaking years of 2012 (1,845,188 vehicles) and 2013 (1,963,798), BMW Group crossed the two-million threshold in 2014 with 2,117,965 units, with 1,811,719 for BMW, 302,183 for Mini and 4063 for Rolls-Royce. Never before in the 111 years of its history has the Anglo-German marque sold so many cars in a single year. However, the motorcycle branch of BMW also enjoyed a 7.2-percent growth to 123,495 units. So there are plenty of good reasons for BMW to celebrate their centenary in style in 2016.

hochgelegter Allrad-Unterbau ein Coupé befördert. Dieses erste „Sports Activity Coupé mit Dynamic Performance Control" ist für die BMW M GmbH ein weiteres gefundenes Fressen und soll mit einem 460-PS-Biturbo ausgestattet werden. Selbst der X5 rückt Ende 2008 ins Visier der M-Mannen, die sich offenbar nur beim vornehmen 7er scheuen, die Muskeln spielen zu lassen.

„Mehr Dynamik, weniger Verbrauch und noch mehr Freude am Fahren", diese Devise begleitet die innovativen Antriebskonzepte der BMW Group. Haben die Benzin-Einspritztechnologie „High Precision Injection" und die Regeneration der Bremsenergie bereits 2007 Einzug gehalten, wird ab 2008 vermehrt das Antriebskonzept „Active Hybrid" für leistungsstarke Modelle forciert. Vorangetrieben wird auch der Ausbau des weltweiten Produktionsnetzwerks. Neben den acht Werken in Deutschland ist auch Spartanburg in South Carolina, USA, derart gewachsen, dass die Produktionskapazität von 450 000 Fahrzeugen das bisher größte BMW-Werk Dingolfing bei weitem übertrifft. Zum BMW-Netzwerk gehören 30 Produktions- und Montagestätten weltweit. Neben dem großen Engagement in Shenyang (China), Chennai (Indien), Kuala Lumpur (Malaysia), Jakarta (Indonesien) und seit 2014 Araquari (Brasilien) hatte BMW auch in Kaliningrad (Russland) Fuß gefasst. Dort freilich blieb die Produktion weit hinter den Erwartungen zurück.

Nach den Rekordjahren 2012 (1845188 Fahrzeuge) und 2013 (1963798) knackte die BMW Group 2014 die Zwei-Millionen-Marke mit 2117965 Einheiten, davon 1811719 BMW, 302183 Mini und 4063 Rolls-Royce. So viele Wagen der deutsch-britischen Edelmarke wurden in ihrer 111-jährigen Geschichte noch nie in einem Jahr verkauft. Aber auch die Motorradsparte von BMW konnte sich über einen Zuwachs von 7,2 Prozent auf 123495 Maschinen freuen. Viele gute Gründe also für die Münchner, ihr 100. Jubiläum 2016 ausgelassen zu feiern.

Coupé» à «Dynamic Performance Control» représente une nouvelle aubaine pour BMW M GmbH et doit être équipé d'un moteur biturbo de 460 ch. À la fin 2008, la X5 réapparaît elle aussi dans la ligne de mire des hommes de BMW qui ne redoutent visiblement de miser sur les muscles que pour la distinguée Série 7.

«Plus de dynamisme, une consommation réduite et un plaisir de conduire accru», cette devise illustre le concept de moteur innovant du groupe BMW. La technologie d'injection «High Precision Injection» et la récupération de l'énergie au freinage ont déjà fait leur apparition en 2007, mais à partir de 2008, BMW mise de plus en plus sur le concept moteur «Active Hybrid» pour les modèles les plus puissants. Le groupe s'attelle aussi à l'expansion du réseau mondial de production. Parallèlement aux huit ateliers de production allemands, le site américain de Spartanburg, en Caroline du Sud, a connu une telle croissance que sa capacité de production de 450000 véhicules a largement dépassé celle de l'atelier BMW de Dingolfing, qui était jusque-là le plus grand. Le réseau BMW comprend 30 sites de production dans le monde entier. Outre des investissements d'avenir à Shenyang (Chine), Chennai (Inde), Kuala Lumpur (Malaisie), Jakarta (Indonésie) et depuis 2014 à Araquari (Brésil), BMW a également mis le pied à Kaliningrad (Russie). La production y reste cependant bien inférieure aux attentes.

Après les records de 2012 (1845188 véhicules) et 2013 (1963798) le groupe BMW a dépassé la barre des deux millions en 2014 avec 2117965 unités, dont 1811719 BMW, 302183 Mini et 4063 Rolls-Royce. La marque de prestige germano-britannique n'avait encore jamais vendu autant de véhicules en une année au cours de ses 111 ans d'histoire. Mais la division moto de BMW a également pu se réjouir d'une croissance de 7,2 pour cent, avec 123495 machines. Autant de bonnes raisons pour les Munichois de fêter leur centenaire en grande pompe en 2016.

"May I get an upgrade to first class, please?" "For sure!" The sixth Seven, introduced in the summer of 2015, caresses passengers in both seat rows with a cornucopia of gadgets to turn ride time into favorite pastime. And it's got built-in valet parking.

„Kann ich bitte ein Upgrade in die Erste Klasse haben?" „Aber sicher!" Die sechste Generation 7er, vorgestellt im Sommer 2015, öffnet über beide Sitzreihen ein Füllhorn an Gimmicks für Komfortsteigerung und Fahrzeitvertreib. Und sie parkt sich selbst ein.

«Pouvez-vous me surclasser en première?» «Mais bien sûr!» La sixième génération de la Série 7, présentée en été 2015, régale ses passagers avant et arrière d'une profusion de gadgets pour un confort incomparable. Et elle se gare toute seule.

Wartburg Motorwagen 1898

On 3 December 1896, a bank consortium led by Privy Councilor and Group Chairman Dr Heinrich Ehrhardt founded the Fahrzeugfabrik Eisenach AG vehicle factory with the intention of building military vehicles and bicycles. Dr Ehrhardt with his Rheinmetall Group was a growing competitor of Krupp and was to pump 1.25 million goldmarks into the new company at Eisenach. The resourceful businessman had realized the potential of the Imperial Army as a profitable source of major orders. Ambulances and ammunition trucks, in addition to mobile kitchens, were all items appearing in large quantities on the commander's list of provisions.

There was another product intended for use outside the battlefield being sold in large quantities. This product was a bicycle with ratios designed for uphill cycling via a shaft drive, tailor-made for cycling up to the Wartburg castle. So the first mountain bike was named after the Landgrave of Thuringia's former seat and Martin Luther's refuge during the Reformation.

A new reformation was occuring, but this time Luther did not need to spill any ink to make Ehrhardt understand its consequences: he clearly saw the success that Daimler and Benz enjoyed with their volume-produced motorcars. To save both the time and money involved in an original development, Ehrhardt obtained the manufacturing license for the French Decauville-Voiturettes.

Like the bicycle, this car was also christened "Wartburg." Presented in Düsseldorf at the first German motor show in September 1898, it appeared alongside names such as Benz, Daimler, Opel and Dürkopp. Despite such stiff competition, it acquitted itself well.

This vehicle was also known as the "Wartburg motorized carriage" because of its carriage shape. Depending on how many people were sitting on the coach box and the opposite bench, it could reach road speeds of up to 28 mph (45 kph). There were alternative two-cylinder engines available: an aircooled design (479 cc, 3.5 bhp) and a water-cooled motor delivering 5 bhp. Initially, the transmission only had two speeds, a third being introduced later.

The front suspension technology offered leaf-sprung comfort, recognizable today, but a lack of rear axle suspension meant that passengers' backs suffered. A single steering bar was employed, a conventional steering wheel was only introduced for the new generation of motorcars in 1902/03. This did not seem to affect the car's sporty characteristics. "Wartburg" cars gained excellent double victories in the major Dresden-Berlin and Aachen-Bonn car races of 1899. The carriage car won a total of 22 gold medals, including an award for elegance.

Of the six original cars remaining today, one is still capable of performing at competition level. This Wartburg, chassis number 88, had slumbered like Sleeping Beauty from 1903 to 1959 in Landsberg/Lech before being woken up by the Munich vintage car enthusiast Georg Schlautkötter.

Wiesloch 1964: Schlautkötter's Wartburg caused a sensation at the Bertha Benz memorial rally, demanding that the fire brigade leap into action. At the turn of the century, the local constabulary in Wiesloch stipulated that the fire brigade spray the streets with water whenever a motorcar was filled with petrol from a pharmacy. This is exactly what happened at the veteran event in which this car took part.

Den Bau von Militärfahrzeugen und Fahrrädern im Visier, gründet am 3. Dezember 1896 ein Bankenkonsortium unter Leitung des Geheimen Baurats Generaldirektor Dr.-Ing. e.h. Heinrich Ehrhardt die Fahrzeugfabrik Eisenach AG. 1,25 Millionen Goldmark pumpt der findige Unternehmer, der mit seinem Rheinmetall-Konzern bereits Krupp Konkurrenz macht, in das Eisenacher Werk, denn dicke Rüstungsaufträge winken. Sanitäts- und Munitionswagen sowie Feldküchen – allesamt in größerer Stückzahl – stehen auf der Beschaffungsliste des Berliner Kriegsministeriums.

Aber auch ein ziviles Nebenprodukt findet reißenden Absatz. Ein Fahrrad mit Bergübersetzung und Kardanantrieb – ideal für Fahrten hinauf zur Wartburg. Und so wird dieses erste „Mountain-Bike" nach dem ehemaligen Sitz der Landgrafen von Thüringen und Zufluchtsort Martin Luthers benannt.

Um Ehrhardt auf die bevorstehenden Umwälzungen des 20. Jahrhunderts vorzubereiten, bedarf es keines Reformators. Schwarz auf weiß gedruckt sieht Ehrhardt die Erfolge der Firmen Daimler und Benz im Bau serienmäßiger Motorwagen. Um die Kosten einer eigenen Entwicklung zu sparen und Zeit zu gewinnen, erwirbt er die Lizenz zum Nachbau der französischen Decauville-Voiturettes.

Wie das Fahrrad auf den Namen „Wartburg" getauft, stellt sich das Lizenz-Produkt im September 1898 auf der ersten deutschen Automobil-Ausstellung in Düsseldorf dem Vergleich mit Benz, Daimler, Opel und Dürkopp, und der fällt gut aus!

Wegen seiner Kutschenform auch „Wartburg-Kutschier-wagen" genannt, läuft dieses Gefährt je nach Anzahl der Passagiere auf dem Kutschbock und dem gegenüber lie-genden Kinderbänkchen bis zu 45 Stundenkilometer. Zwei Zweizylindermotoren stehen zur Auswahl: Ein luftgekühltes Triebwerk (479 cm³, 3,5 PS) und ein wassergekühlter Motor, der 5 PS leistet. Das Getriebe beschränkt sich erst auf zwei, dann drei Gänge.

Während die Vorderradaufhängung geradezu modern anmutet, malträtiert die ungefederte Hinterachse die Band-scheiben der Passagiere. Gelenkt wird mit einer Kurbel. Erst die junge Motorwagen-Generation 1902/03 bekommt ein Lenkrad. Der Sportlichkeit tut es keinen Abbruch, denn in den großen Rennen Dresden–Berlin und Aachen–Bonn anno 1899 erringen die Wartburg Doppelsiege. Insgesamt 22 Goldmedaillen – darunter auch Edelmetall für seine Eleganz – heimst der Kutschwagen ein.

Von den sechs erhaltenen Exemplaren des Ur-Wartburg ist eines noch wettbewerbsfähig. Dieser Wagen mit der Chassis-Nummer 88 hatte von 1903 bis 1959 in Landsberg/Lech einen Dornröschen-Schlaf gehalten, ehe ihn der Münch-ner Oldtimer-Enthusiast Georg Schlautkötter weckte.

Wiesloch 1964: Der Wartburg Schlautkötters erregt bei der Bertha-Benz-Gedächtnis-Rallye Aufsehen und sorgt für einen Einsatz der Feuerwehr. Beim Betanken eines Motor-wagens mit Benzin – aus der Apotheke (so eine Anordnung der Wieslocher Gendarmerie der Jahrhundertwende) – muss die Feuerwehr die Straße spritzen. So geschieht es auch bei dieser Veteranenveranstaltung.

Le 3 décembre 1896, un consortium bancaire dirigé par Heinrich Ehrhardt, ingénieur diplômé *honoris causa,* fonde la Fahrzeugfabrik Eisenach AG dans l'intention de construire des véhicules militaires et des bicyclettes. L'offensif industriel, qui se pose déjà en concurrent de Krupp avec son groupe Rheinmetall, injecte 1,25 million de marks or dans l'usine d'Eisenach, car il a en vue d'importantes com-mandes d'armes. Des ambulances, des transporteurs de munitions et des cuisines de campagne – le tout en quantité très importante – figurent dans les carnets de commandes des stratèges à Berlin.

On s'arrache aussi un produit qui s'utilise en dehors des champs de bataille. Il s'agit d'une bicyclette avec dérailleur pour la montagne et transmission à cardan – idéale pour monter sur la Wartburg. C'est ainsi que ce premier « vélo tout-terrain » est baptisé du nom de l'ancien siège des Landgraves de Thuringe où Luther trouva refuge lors de la Réforme.

Mais une nouvelle Réforme se prépare et cette fois Luther n'a pas à intervenir pour que Ehrhardt en mesure les conséquences. Il observe les succès de Daimler et de Benz qui construisent en série des automobiles. Pour s'épargner les coûts de son propre développement et gagner du temps, il acquiert la licence de la voiturette française Decauville.

Baptisée, comme la bicyclette, du nom de « Wartburg », la voiture construite sous licence est exposée en septembre 1898 au premier Salon de l'automobile d'Allemagne, à Düssel-dorf, où on la compare aux Benz, Daimler, Opel et Dürkopp. La comparaison est flatteuse !

Surnommé « la calèche motorisée de Wartburg » en rai-son de sa forme rappelant celle d'une calèche, ce véhicule peut atteindre 45 km/h selon le nombre de personnes qu'il transporte sur le banc et sur la banquette opposée. Pour les moteurs, on a le choix entre deux deux-cylindres : l'un refroidi par air (479 cm³, 3,5 ch), et l'autre refroidi par eau, qui déve-loppe 5 ch. La boîte a d'abord deux, puis trois vitesses.

Alors que la suspension avant présente un confort moderne, l'essieu arrière non suspendu maltraite la colonne vertébrale des passagers. La direction est à manivelle. Il faudra attendre la nouvelle génération de voitures à moteur de 1902–1903 pour voir apparaître un volant. Cela ne porte aucunement préjudice à la sportivité puisque, lors des grandes courses Dresde–Berlin et Aix-la-Chapelle–Bonn en 1899, les Wartburg signent un magnifique doublé. La voitu-rette rafle au total 22 médailles d'or, dont un prix d'élégance.

Des six exemplaires qui existent encore, un seul est encore en mesure de courir. Cette Wartburg, numéro de châssis 88, avait sommeillé dans une grange de 1903 à 1959 à Landsberg/Lech avant d'être réveillée par Georg Schlaut-kötter, un Munichois fanatique de voitures de collection.

Wiesloch 1964 : lors du rallye commémoratif Bertha Benz, la Wartburg de Schlautkötter fait sensation, mais grâce à l'intervention des pompiers. Lors du ravitaillement d'une voi-ture à moteur en benzène de pharmacie – selon les instruc-tions de la gendarmerie de Wiesloch à la fin du XIXᵉ et du début du XXᵉ siècle – les pompiers doivent inonder la route. Et c'est donc ce qu'ils ont fait lors de ce rassemblement de voitures anciennes.

A technically interesting vehicle: this delicate-looking motor vehicle, just over 4 feet (1.25 meters) wide, is steered by a hand crank via a rack-and-pinion and started with a hand wheel located alongside the driver's seat. During travel, the magneto ignition can be adjusted using two levers.

Ein technisch interessantes Fahrzeug: Der filigran wirkende, nur 1,25 Meter breite Motorwagen wird per Handkurbel über Zahnstangen gelenkt und mit einem Handrad, das sich neben dem Fahrersitz befindet, angeworfen. Während der Fahrt lässt sich die Magnetzündung an zwei Hebeln verstellen.

Une voiture intéressante sur le plan technique : cette automobile à l'aspect fragile, de seulement 1,25 m de large, possède une direction à manivelle via une crémaillère. Son moteur démarre à l'aide d'un volant placé à côté du siège du conducteur. Deux manettes permettent de régler l'allumage magnétique durant le voyage.

The engine sits unprotected beneath the "coach-box," generating 3.5 bhp in the air-cooled version and 5 bhp in the water-cooled version. A feature that stands out is the linkage of the cam-adjusted rear wheel brakes. The front wheel suspension, with its encased helical springs and overhead transverse springs, is also ahead of its time.

Ungeschützt unter dem „Kutscherbock" arbeitet der Motor, der luftgekühlt 3,5 PS und wassergekühlt 5 PS leistet. Auffällig ist das Gestänge der mit Nocken verstellbaren Hinterradbremse. Die Vorderradaufhängung mit gekapselten Schraubenfedern und hochliegender Querfeder ist ebenfalls ihrer Zeit voraus.

Le moteur, d'une puissance de 3,5 ch dans la version à refroidissement par air et de 5 ch dans la version à refroidissement liquide, est exposé aux intempéries sous la banquette de cocher. Bien visible, la timonerie du frein arrière est réglable par cames. La suspension du train avant, avec ressorts hélicoïdaux protégés de la poussière et un ressort transversal surélevé, est également en avance sur son temps.

Dixi 3/15 PS 1929

Strange but true: BMW cars are of British ancestry. Financially troubled, the Eisenach Dixi factory could not make use of the bank loan available for mass production of a small car as BMW did not have its own automotive design. The stock exchange speculator Jakob Schapiro, who had interests in several wagon and car companies, also controlled the Dixi factory. Without hesitation, Schapiro decided to buy the license to build the Austin Seven. This uncomplicated car with its 750 cc four-cylinder engine had sold strongly in Britain since 1922.

As well as the manufacturing license, Schapiro immediately obtained 100 Austin Sevens for the first Dixi 3/15 PS customers. These preliminary cars were sold with few alterations: even UK right-hand drive was retained.

In December 1927, the factory began producing its own Dixi 3/15 PS, type DA1. DA stood for Dixi Austin or "Deutsche Ausführung" meaning "German construction." A touring version of this diminutive car, just 970 lbs (440 kg), was created using the original plans and production documents from England. The 15 bhp were achieved at 3000 rpm, giving the vehicle a top speed of 47 mph (75 kph). Fuel consumption was correspondingly modest: 39.5 miles to the gallon (6 liters per 100 km). Just 42 tourers were built in December 1927, sales scheduled to begin in January 1928.

When BMW took over the busy but broke Dixi factory on 16 November 1928 for ten million reichsmarks, production of the 3/15 initially continued unchanged. In 1928/29, 9308 Dixi DA1s left the factory in the shadow of Wartburg castle. The majority (4831 units) were tourers. The BMW-badged DA2, a considerable development of the basic Austin design, was mass-produced from summer 1929 onward. The DA2 was the first of the Eisenach cars to carry the BMW name.

In the final months of production, the Dixi was available through special finance deals (discounts and 24 monthly installments). The DA1 was provided with a battery since the original magneto ignition was unreliable. No longer did customers gamble with the brakes ("they work more … or less"), but BMW would improve this aspect.

As well as the tourer and sedan (for three large or four smaller passengers), the open-top two-seater was very popular. Dixi prices were between 2750 and 3200 reichsmarks, a real market niche!

"It accords with the wishes of the sporting lady and the gentleman driver, who wish to drive a light two-seater vehicle with modern lines and elegant exterior," claimed BMW as it took over the Dixi legacy. What would "Grandfather" Austin say in the 1990s, now that BMW has again adopted British "grandchildren" at Rover and Rolls-Royce?

Eigentlich ist der Urahn aller BMW ein Brite. Die Eisenacher Dixi-Werke sind in finanziellen Schwierigkeiten, und dem Bankkredit für eine Serienfabrikation eines Kleinwagens steht keine brauchbare Entwicklung gegenüber. Börsenspekulant Jakob Schapiro, der an mehreren Waggon- und Fahrzeugfirmen beteiligt ist und auch die Dixi-Werke kontrolliert, besorgt kurzerhand eine Nachbau-Lizenz des Austin Seven. Dieser unkomplizierte Wagen mit einem 750-cm³-Vierzylindermotor verkauft sich auf der Insel seit 1922 prächtig.

Schapiro erwirbt nicht nur die Lizenz, sondern lässt auch gleich 100 Austin Seven kommen, um sie als erste Dixi 3/15 PS zu verkaufen. Diese „Vorabserie" geht fast unverändert – sogar noch mit Rechtslenkung – an die Kunden.

Im Dezember 1927 beginnt die Eigenproduktion des Dixi 3/15 PS, Typ DA1. Dabei steht „DA" als Kürzel für „Dixi Austin" oder für „Deutsche Ausführung". Nach Originalplänen und Fertigungsunterlagen aus England entsteht das 440 Kilo leichte Wägelchen in der Tourer-Version. Die 15 PS werden bei 3000 Umdrehungen pro Minute erreicht und beschleunigen das Gefährt auf bis zu 75 Stundenkilometer. Ähnlich bescheiden ist der Verbrauch: sechs Liter auf 100 Kilometer. 42 Tourer werden im Dezember 1927 gebaut, der Verkaufsbeginn wird auf Januar 1928 festgelegt.

Als BMW am 16. November 1928 für 10 Millionen Reichsmark die hochverschuldeten, aber emsig produzierenden Dixi-Werke übernimmt, wird der 3/15 erst einmal unverändert weitergebaut. 1928/29 verlassen 9308 Dixi DA1 das Werk in Sichtweite der Wartburg. Den Hauptanteil trägt die Produktion des Tourers mit 4831 Einheiten. Der DA2, eine erheblich weiterentwickelte Konstruktion, geht im Sommer 1929 parallel vom Band und trägt erstmals den Namen BMW.

Zurück zum Dixi, der in den letzten Monaten seiner Fertigung zu Sonderpreisen erhältlich ist – Rabatte und Ratenzahlung in 24 Monaten. Dem DA1 wird eine Batterie eingebaut, da die Magnetzündung des Austin-Originals unzuverlässig arbeitet. Auch der Unsicherheitsfaktor Bremsen („they work more … or less") wird behoben.

Neben Tourer und Limousine (für drei große oder vier kleinere Passagiere) erfreut sich der offene Zweisitzer großer Beliebtheit. Die Dixi-Preise liegen zwischen 2750 und 3200 Reichsmark – eine echte Marktnische!

„Er entspricht dem Wunsche der sporttreibenden Dame und des Herrenfahrers, die ein leichtes zweisitziges Fahrzeug mit moderner Linienführung und elegantem Äußeren zu steuern wünschen." Mit dieser Werksaussage übernimmt der BMW das Erbe des Dixi. Was hätte „Großvater" Austin wohl gesagt, hätte er gewusst, dass BMW mit Rover und Rolls-Royce Jahrzehnte später wieder englische „Enkel" adoptieren würde?

L'ancêtre des BMW est en réalité une anglaise. Retour en arrière : les usines Dixi d'Eisenach rencontrent des difficultés financières et les crédits accordés par les banques pour la fabrication en série d'une petite voiture ne permettent pas de construire une automobile digne de ce nom. Un spéculateur, Jakob Schapiro, qui tire les ficelles de plusieurs entreprises de wagons et d'automobiles et qui contrôle aussi les usines Dixi, achète sans hésiter une licence pour produire une réplique de l'Austin Seven. Cette première voiture avec un petit moteur à quatre cylindres de 750 cm³ se vend comme des petits pains en Angleterre depuis 1922.

En plus de l'achat de la licence, Schapiro fait venir dans la foulée 100 Austin Seven pour pouvoir vendre à ses clients les premières Dixi 3/15 PS. Cette première série est vendue pratiquement sans modification – elles ont même conservé le volant à droite.

En décembre 1927 commence la production à Eisenach de la Dixi 3/15 PS, type DA1 (pour Dixi Austin et, à partir de 1928, pour «Deutsche Ausführung», fabrication allemande). Selon les plans originaux et les dossiers de fabrication en provenance d'Angleterre, cette voiturette de 440 kg est fabriquée en version tourer. Les 15 ch sont délivrés à 3000 tr/min et confèrent à l'engin une vitesse de 75 km/h. La consommation est modeste : 6 litres aux 100 km. Quarante-deux voitures de tourisme sont construites en décembre 1927 et la commercialisation est fixée à janvier 1928.

Quand BMW reprend pour 10 millions de reichsmarks les usines Dixi criblées de dettes, mais qui tournent à plein régime, le 16 novembre 1928, la 3/15 est, dans premier temps, usinée sans modification. En 1928–1929, 9308 Dixi DA1 quittent l'usine à un jet de pierre du château de la Wartburg. Avec 4831 exemplaires, la tourer se taille la part du lion de la production. La DA2, un modèle beaucoup plus perfectionné, est produite parallèlement à partir de l'été 1929. Et seule la DA2 porte le nom BMW.

Mais revenons à la Dixi qui, durant ses derniers mois de production, est vendue à un prix spécial (avec une ristourne et même payable en 24 mensualités). La DA1 est pourvue d'une batterie, car l'allumage magnétique de l'Austin d'origine n'est pas fiable. Le comportement des freins («ils fonctionnent plus … ou moins») est, lui aussi, revu et corrigé. Avec la tourer et la berline (pour trois grands ou quatre petits passagers), la biplace découverte jouit aussi d'une grande popularité. Les Dixi coûtent entre 2750 et 3200 reichsmarks. Une véritable niche!

«Elle répond aux besoins de la femme sportive et du gentleman qui veulent conduire une voiture biplace légère aux lignes modernes et à l'allure élégante», vante le slogan publicitaire de BMW lors de la reprise de l'exploitation de la Dixi. Qu'aurait dit le «grand-père» Austin dans les années 1990, s'il avait su que BMW, après Rover, tente encore, avec Rolls-Royce, d'adopter une autre «petite-fille» britannique?

The galloping centaur—the symbol of the Dixi works at Eisenach—captured the hearts of motorists. It stands at the prow of the DA1, of which 9308 were produced during 1928 and 1929, under license to Austin. The tourer model depicted here accounted for the bulk of production.

Der galoppierende Zentaur – Symbol der Dixi-Werke Eisenach – stürmt mit dem DA1 in die Herzen der Automobilisten. 1928/29 werden 9308 Exemplare davon nach Austin-Lizenz gebaut. Der Hauptanteil der Produktion entfällt auf das hier abgebildete Tourer-Modell.

Le centaure au galop – emblème des usines Dixi d'Eisenach – a su conquérir le cœur des automobilistes avec la DA1. En 1928–1929, 9308 voitures de ce type sont construites sous licence Austin. Le modèle tourer représenté ici s'est taillé la part du lion de la production.

In the cockpit of the Dixi, instruments, switches and levers are reduced to a bare minimum. The fuel supply when idling is regulated by a lever fitted on the rim of the steering wheel. For the sake of simplicity, this also serves to bring the car to a standstill. The footbrake operates on the rear wheels and the handbrake on the front wheels.

Im Cockpit des Dixi sind Armaturen, Schalter und Hebel auf das Notwendigste reduziert. Das Standgas wird über einen Hebel auf dem Lenkradkranz reguliert. Er dient der Einfachheit halber auch gern zum Abstellen des Motors. Die Fußbremse wirkt auf die Hinterräder, während die Handbremse vorne greift.

Dans le cockpit de la Dixi, les cadrans, leviers et manettes se limitent au strict minimum. Un levier placé sur le volant permet de régler le ralenti. Astuce géniale : il sert aussi à couper le moteur. La pédale de frein agit sur les roues arrière alors que le frein à main agit sur le train avant.

Taking a look under the hood, the Dixi's engineering comes across as simple but functional: the klaxon fitted above the 15 bhp engine with its laterally-mounted sidedraft carburetor may be a few decibels less loud than modern horns, but it is certainly more original.

Einfach, doch funktionell präsentiert sich die Dixi-Technik auch bei einem Blick unter die Haube: Die „Tröte" über dem 15-PS-Motor mit seitlich stehendem Flachstromvergaser ist heutigen Hupen zwar um einige Dezibel unterlegen, dafür aber umso origineller.

Simple et fonctionnelle: telle est la mécanique de la Dixi même sous le capot. La corne qui trône sur le moteur de 15 ch à carburateur horizontal placé sur le côté est, certes, beaucoup moins puissante que les klaxons d'aujourd'hui, mais nettement plus originale.

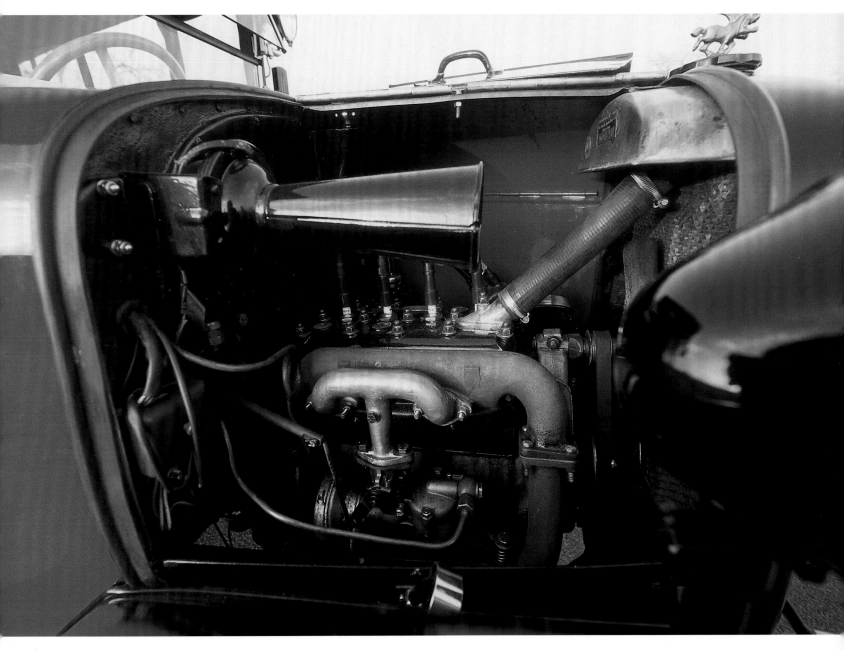

BMW Wartburg DA3 1930

Mr W. from Munich is entitled to call himself the Croesus of veteran cars, for his stock of BMWs of the 3/15 PS category has been likened to a Dixi band with 20 soloists. The tone is set by a particularly beautiful Wartburg DA3. Machines such as the DA3 appear just six times in the archive lists of Jürgen Pollack, membership officer of the BMW Veteran Club.

On the subject of the DA3, Pollack defers to another expert: "I'm sure that Kasimirowicz in Düsseldorf will know more about that." Helmut Kasimirowicz, who has already assisted several BMWs to return to their old glory, including a rare express pick-up truck, does know more: "I know another three DA3 owners, I'm one of them."

The DA3 of Jürgen and Brigitte Klöckner possesses an original chassis with number and associated documentation which was only produced 150 times. Conversation about the refinements of the engine with copper suction pipe and double exhaust immediately turns to a special carburetor. Tested by the motor magazine *Motor und Sport* in 1930, the "Atmos carburetor" produced a performance increase of 1.4 bhp.

In the DA3, weighing no more than 904 lbs (410 kg) with its aluminum chassis, 18 to 19 bhp were sufficient to produce a car with "a full personality and spirit and all the signs of a thoroughbred sports car," wrote *Motor und Sport*.

On 17 April 1931, *ADAC-Motorwelt* added: "The low air resistance of the light and racy sports chassis contributes to the achievement of a good speed." When the windscreen—made of shatter-proof glass back then—was folded, the agile little DA3 neared 62 mph (100 kph).

Steering and handling of the small car surprised its contemporaries. A lowered front axle with transverse leaf-sprung suspension enabled a ride height reduction of almost 4 inches (10 cm) compared to the DA2, benefitting roadholding.

The sporting attributes also included the spare wheel fixed to the side of the bonnet, an absence of doors and the instruments. The latter were restricted to a roller speedo and an oil pressure gauge flanking the ignition switch.

In his *Motor und Sport* report of 1930, the author noted: "The Wartburg is a car for good drivers. Bad drivers do not deserve to own this automobile." Probably the best Wartburg driver was Robert "Bobby" Kohlrausch, born in Eisenach in 1904. Professionally, Bobby advanced from apprentice fitter in the Dixi works to engineer. The motorcycle which his father gave him as a reward for his hard work—modified as a racing machine by Bobby—earned him many cups, but also almost cost him his life. On the promise of never racing motorcycles again, his Dad gave him a BMW. So began an incredible career with 62 wins and four world records. Nobody had said anything about four-wheeler motor sports. Each year in May, when the "DA pilgrims" are engaged in their pilgrimage to Eisenach, one of the most beautiful Kohlrausch cups is reverently passed around.

Herr W. aus München darf sich Oldtimer-Krösus nennen, denn sein Bestand an BMW der 3/15-PS-Kategorie gleicht einer „Dixi-Band" mit 20 Solisten. Den Ton gibt freilich ein besonders schönes Exemplar des Typs DA3 Wartburg an. Solche DA3-Raritäten finden sich lediglich sechsmal in den Archiv-Listen von Jürgen Pollack, dem Mitglieder-Betreuer des BMW-Veteranen-Clubs.

Beim Thema DA3 verweist Pollack gern an einen Kenner: „Sicherlich weiß da der Kasimirowicz aus Düsseldorf noch mehr." Helmut Kasimirowicz, der schon einigen BMW, so auch einem seltenen Eil-Lieferwagen, zu altem Glanz verholfen hat, weiß tatsächlich mehr: „Ich kenne drei weitere DA3-Eigner, einer davon bin ich."

Der DA3 von Dr. Jürgen und Brigitte Klöckner verfügt über ein Originalfahrgestell mit Nummer und dazugehörigem Brief, wie er nur 150 mal ausgestellt wurde. Angesichts des Motors – mit kupfernem Ansaugrohr und doppeltem Auspuff – kommt die Sprache sofort auf eine spezielle Vergaserbestückung. Solchermaßen exerziert von den Testern der Fachzeitschrift *Motor und Sport* im Jahre 1930, bringt ein so genannter „Atmos-Vergaser" einen Leistungszuwachs von 1,4 PS.

Bei dem nur 410 Kilo leichten DA3 mit Aluminium-Karosserie sorgen 18 bis 19 PS für „eine vollwertige Autopersönlichkeit mit Temperament und allen Anzeichen eines gutrassigen Sportwagens" (so *Motor und Sport*).

Und die *ADAC-Motorwelt* vom 17. April 1931 fügt hinzu: „Der geringe Luftwiderstand der leichten und schnittigen Sportkarosserie trägt zu einer guten Fahrgeschwindigkeit

bei." Bei heruntergeklappter Windschutzscheibe, die bereits aus splitterfreiem Glas besteht, kommt das behände Wägelchen an die 100-km/h-Marke heran.

Lenkung und Handling des schmalen Wagens erstaunen die Zeitgenossen. Eine durchgekröpfte Vorderachse mit Querfeder macht es nicht nur möglich, das Auto gegenüber dem DA2 um fast 10 Zentimeter tieferzulegen, sondern verbessert auch die Straßenlage.

Sportliche Attribute sind auch das seitlich neben der Motorhaube montierte Reserverad, der türlose Einstieg und die Instrumentierung, die sich auf einen Walzentacho, das Öldruckmanometer und das dazwischenliegende Schalt-Zündschloss beschränkt.

In einem *Motor und Sport*-Bericht von 1930 vermerkt der Autor: „Der Wartburg ist ein Wagen für gute Fahrer. Schlechte Fahrer verdienen nicht den Besitz dieses Automobils." Der wohl beste Wartburg-Lenker ist Robert „Bobby" Kohlrausch, 1904 in Eisenach geboren. Beruflich bringt es Bobby vom Schlosserlehrling in den Dixi-Werken bis zum Ingenieur. Das vom Vater als Lohn des Fleißes geschenkte Motorrad – von Bobby zur Rennmaschine umgebaut – fährt viele Pokale ein, kostet ihn aber auch fast das Leben. Gegen das Versprechen, nie mehr Motorradrennen zu fahren, spendiert der Papa einen BMW. Es ist der Beginn einer unglaublichen Karriere mit 62 Siegen und vier Weltrekorden. Von vier Rädern war ja nicht die Rede! Jedes Jahr im Mai, wenn die „DA-Pilger" gen Eisenach ziehen, wird einer der schönsten Kohlrausch-Pokale andächtig herumgereicht.

Monsieur W., de Munich, peut légitimement se considérer comme le Crésus des collectionneurs de voitures anciennes, car sa collection de BMW de la catégorie 3/15 PS ressemble à un «orchestre de Dixi» qui comprendrait 20 «solistes». C'est toutefois un superbe exemplaire du type Wartburg DA3 qui donne le ton. Posséder une DA3 est exceptionnel puisqu'on en dénombre seulement six sur l'inventaire de Jürgen Pollack, qui gère le club des propriétaires de vieilles BMW.

Concernant la DA3, Pollack vous dirigera cependant volontiers vers un connaisseur: «Je pense que Kasimirowicz, de Düsseldorf, en sait encore plus.» Helmut Kasimirowicz, qui a déjà restauré de nombreuses BMW, dont une fourgonnette de livraison expresse assez rare, en sait plus en effet: «Je connais trois autres propriétaires de DA3, et je suis l'un d'eux.»

La DA3 du Dr Jürgen Klöckner et de son épouse Brigitte possède un châssis avec le numéro et la carte grise d'origine, qui n'a été délivrée qu'à 150 exemplaires. Quand on évoque les raffinements du moteur avec tubulure d'aspiration en cuivre et double pot d'échappement, on ne peut pas manquer de parler aussi des particularités de son carburateur. Lors d'un essai réalisé par la revue spécialisée *Motor und Sport* en 1930, le carburateur «Atmos» permet d'obtenir un gain de puissance de 1,4 ch.

Avec un poids de seulement 410 kg pour la DA3 à carrosserie aluminium, 18 ou 19 ch garantissent que «cet engin possède une identité et du tempérament, bref tous les ingrédients d'une voiture de sport racée», rapporte *Motor und Sport*.

L'*ADAC-Motorwelt* du 17 avril 1931 ajoute: «La faible résistance aérodynamique de la carrosserie sport, légère et racée, contribue à atteindre une bonne vitesse.» Avec son pare-brise rabattu, déjà en verre de sécurité, cette petite voiture rapide peut franchir les 100 km/h.

Le volant et le maniement de cet étroit engin étonnent ses contemporains. Un essieu avant galbé avec ressort transversal permet de la surbaisser de près de 10 cm par rapport à la DA2 ce qui entraîne une meilleure tenue de route.

D'autres caractéristiques permettent de la qualifier de voiture de sport: la roue de secours montée sur le côté du capot moteur, l'absence de portières et le tableau de bord constitué d'un tachymètre à tambour, d'un manomètre d'huile et d'une clé de contact entre les deux.

Dans un reportage de *Motor und Sport* de 1930, l'auteur souligne: «La Wartburg est réservée aux bons conducteurs. Un mauvais conducteur ne mérite pas de posséder une telle automobile.» Le meilleur conducteur de Wartburg est sans aucun doute Robert «Bobby» Kohlrausch, né en 1904 à Eisenach. Il commence sa carrière comme apprenti-ajusteur aux usines Dixi et finit ingénieur. Une fois transformée par Bobby en engin de compétition, la motocyclette que lui a offerte son père pour le récompenser de son travail gagne de nombreuses coupes, mais a failli lui coûter la vie. Contre la promesse de ne plus jamais courir en moto, son père lui offre une BMW: ce sera le début d'une incroyable carrière avec 62 victoires et quatre records du monde. Il n'avait, en effet, jamais promis de ne pas courir sur quatre roues! Chaque année en mai, lorsque le «pèlerinage des DA» prend la direction d'Eisenach, on se transmet respectueusement de main en main l'une des plus belles coupes de Kohlrausch.

A motor magazine observed in 1930 that "the Wartburg is a car for good drivers." And apparently they were happy to crank up the 18 bhp engine in all weathers in order to get behind the wooden steering wheel and go for a spin. The folding windscreen was already made of shatter-proof glass and stays up "as an exception."

1930 heißt es in einer Fachzeitschrift: „Der Wartburg ist ein Wagen für gute Fahrer." Und die werfen den 18-PS-Motor offenbar bei jedem Wetter an, um sich hinter das dicke Holzlenkrad zu klemmen. Die umlegbare Windschutzscheibe besteht bereits aus splitterfreiem Glas und bleibt „ausnahmsweise" oben.

En 1930, une revue spécialisée proclame: «La Wartburg est réservée aux bons conducteurs» qui n'hésitent pas à mettre en marche le moteur de 18 ch par tous les temps pour se glisser derrière l'épais volant en bois. Le pare-brise rabattable est déjà en verre de sécurité et reste rarement à la verticale.

Max Friz, an engine designer who had left Daimler-Motoren-Gesellschaft due to unfulfilled salary expectations and a lack of interest in his project for high altitude flight-engines, was one of BMW's first pioneers. He was a genius in his field, capable of finding the engine to suit any purpose, especially to power planes, but also trucks, boats and motorbikes.

The BMW license agreement with Austin came to an end on 1 March 1932. As it had, in any case, been a thorn in his flesh, Friz, who had since become a company director, began to work on his own design for a two-stroke car engine with front-wheel drive transmission. Immersing himself in engine practice and suspension theory, Friz was forced to concede that the proposal of Eisenach staffers to adapt designs which were already in existence was a quicker means of achieving his objectives.

Transforming these designs to create the first proper BMW began with an engine whose stroke was lengthened by 80 mm while the original bore was retained. This extended stroke could deliver 20 bhp as opposed to the previous rating of 15 bhp, a fact mirrored by the new creation's name: 3/20 PS (PS is a German alternative measure of realistically rating horsepower). The modifications made to the crankshaft drive, cylinder head and side-mounted camshaft (now driven by a duplex chain instead of cast iron spur gears) meant that the design was effectively brand new.

One of the biggest departures from the British original could be seen in the chassis. The main features constituted a central frame (instead of U-section rails) and a propshaft extended right back to the swing axle. The front axle, one of the components most in need of updating, remained unaltered. Therefore, the driving characteristics continued to be somewhat less than driver-friendly, particularly since the new car's sturdy, but heavy body (from Daimler-Benz at Sindelfingen) meant that it weighed 396 lbs (180 kg) more than the earlier 3/15 DA2.

Daimler-Benz built all four designs: sedan, tourer, convertible and roadster. What was even more confusing was the type designation AM1 for "1. Auto München" (1st Munich car). One of the special car bodies did, however, come from Munich: a cute roadster by Ludwig Weinberger. Some 7215 chassis (AM1–4) were manufactured from April 1932 to the end of 1934, all destined to cater for a wide variety of designs. 53 were destined for pick-up trucks.

Four of the 59 BMW 3/20s listed in the BMW Veteran Club Germany have the same owner: the lucky man is a Dutchman from Gouda. A Warsaw owner is even more fortunate: in addition to an AM4, he owns a truly rare model, the 1932 AM1 Roadster.

Die Daimler-Motoren-Gesellschaft hat er wegen unerfüllter Gehaltswünsche und allgemeinem Desinteresse an seinem Höhenflugmotoren-Projekt verlassen. Bei BMW ist der Motorenkonstrukteur Max Friz einer der Männer der ersten Stunde, ein genialer Kopf, der allem, was „kreucht und fleucht" – besonders Flugzeugen, aber auch Lastwagen, Booten und Motorrädern – die richtigen Triebwerke verpasst.

Der Lizenzvertrag mit Austin, der Friz ohnehin ein Dorn im Auge ist, wird zum 1. März 1932 gekündigt, und sofort macht sich Friz – inzwischen zum Direktor avanciert – an eine eigene Konstruktion. Das Ziel ist ein Zweitakter mit Frontantrieb. In Motorenpraxis und Fahrwerkstheorie tiefschürfend, muss Friz bald erkennen, dass der Vorschlag der Eisenacher, Vorhandenes umzukonstruieren, schneller zum Ziel führt.

Die Mutation zum richtigen BMW beginnt beim Motor, dessen Hub unter Beibehaltung der Bohrung auf 80 Millimeter verlängert wird. 20 statt 15 PS bringt die so erzielte Hubraumvergrößerung, und damit steht auch der Name des Debütanten fest: 3/20 PS. Änderungen an Kurbeltrieb und Zylinderkopf sowie der Antrieb der seitlichen Nockenwelle über eine Duplexkette anstelle der gusseisernen Stirnräder sprechen für eine „Fast-Neukonstruktion".

BMW 3/20 PS 1932

Noch mehr vom Insel-Original entfernt man sich beim Chassis. Wichtigste Merkmale sind der Zentralrahmen anstelle des U-Profils und eine bis nach hinten zur Pendelachse durchlaufende Kardanwelle. Ausgerechnet die Vorderachse, die eigentlich nach einer besseren Lösung verlangt, bleibt unverändert. Und so bleiben auch die Fahreigenschaften äußerst gewöhnungsbedürftig, zumal der Wagen mit seiner soliden, aber schweren Karosserie, gebaut im Daimler-Benz-Werk Sindelfingen, 180 Kilo mehr wiegt als der 3/15 DA2.

Daimler-Benz baut alle vier Aufbauten: Limousine, Tourer, Cabriolet und Roadster. Umso mehr verwirrt die Typenbezeichnung AM1 für „1. Auto München". Immerhin stammt eine der Sonderkarosserien aus der Isar-Metropole: ein schnuckeliger Roadster von Ludwig Weinberger. Von April 1932 bis Ende 1934 werden 7215 Fahrgestelle (AM 1–4) für die verschiedensten Aufbauten gefertigt. Davon erhalten 53 einen Lieferwagenaufbau.

Von den 59 im BMW-Veteranen-Club Deutschland e.V. registrierten 3/20 befinden sich vier in einer Hand: Ein Holländer aus Gouda ist der Glückliche. Es gibt aber auch einen Überglücklichen, und der kommt aus Warschau: Ihm gehört neben einem AM4 eine echte Rarität, der AM1 Roadster von 1932.

Après avoir quitté la Daimler-Motoren-Gesellschaft qui avait refusé sa demande d'augmentation de salaire et ne s'intéressait pas à son projet de moteur d'avion, le motoriste Max Friz est, chez BMW, l'un des hommes de la première heure. C'est un génie qui dessine des moteurs qui s'adaptent à tous les engins – en particulier les avions, mais aussi les camions, les bateaux et les motos.

La licence d'exploitation accordée par Austin, la bête noire de Friz, est résiliée le 1er mars 1932 et, immédiatement, Friz – entre-temps promu directeur – s'attaque à son propre projet : un moteur à deux temps destiné à une traction avant. Parfait connaisseur de l'utilisation des moteurs et de la théorie des châssis, Friz doit admettre que la proposition des ingénieurs d'Eisenach consistant à adapter des plans déjà existants était un moyen plus rapide d'atteindre ses objectifs.

La transformation de ces plans pour créer la véritable première BMW commence avec le moteur, allongé à 80 mm pour un alésage inchangé. L'augmentation de cylindrée permet ainsi d'obtenir 20 ch au lieu de 15 et, par la même opération, donne son nom à la voiture : 3/20 PS. Des modifications sur l'embrayage et sur la culasse ainsi que sur la prise de force pour l'arbre à cames latéral à l'aide d'une chaîne duplex – et non plus d'engrenages en fonte – justifient le qualificatif de modèle quasiment nouveau.

Pour le châssis, on est encore plus éloigné de l'original. Les caractéristiques les plus importantes sont le cadre central (à la place de profilés en U) ainsi que la transmission par cardan allant jusqu'à l'essieu arrière oscillant. Quant à l'essieu avant, qui mériterait pourtant d'être amélioré, il reste en l'état. Sa conduite demande donc, pour le moins, une certaine accoutumance, d'autant que la voiture à la lourde mais solide carrosserie (fabriquée par l'usine Daimler-Benz de Sindelfingen) pèse 180 kg de plus que la 3/15 DA2.

Daimler-Benz assemble chacun des quatre modèles : berline, tourer, cabriolet et roadster. La dénomination de AM1 pour «1re Auto Munich» est d'autant plus troublante. Toujours est-il que l'une des carrosseries spéciales provient de Munich : il s'agit d'un joli petit roadster signé Ludwig Weinberger. D'avril 1932 à la fin de 1934 sont construits 7215 châssis (AM1–4) pour les carrosseries les plus diverses (dont 53 en version camionnette).

Sur les 59 BMW 3/20 enregistrées auprès du BMW-Veteranen-Club Deutschland e.V. (le club des collectionneurs de vieilles BMW), quatre se trouvent aux mains d'un seul homme : l'heureux propriétaire est un Hollandais de Gouda. Mais un propriétaire de Varsovie est encore plus chanceux : non seulement il possède une AM4 mais aussi un authentique roadster AM1 de 1932, ce qui est exceptionnel.

The BMW 3/20 PS is a rock-solid vehicle, but at 1430 lbs (650 kg)
a relatively heavy one. Despite this, 7215 chassis were produced
for a variety of different bodies, even including 53 panel vans. The
bodies were mounted in Sindelfingen—by Daimler-Benz.

Der BMW 3/20 PS ist zwar ein grundsolides, aber mit 650 Kilo Gewicht
doch ein relativ schweres Vehikel. Immerhin werden 7215 Fahrgestelle
gefertigt. Die verschiedenen Aufbauten, darunter auch 53 Lieferwagen,
werden in Sindelfingen montiert – von Daimler-Benz!

La BMW 3/20 PS est, certes, une voiture inusable, mais, avec ses 650 kg,
tout de même relativement lourde. 7215 châssis seront néanmoins
construits pour différents modèles, dont 53 camionnettes. Les
carrosseries sont montées à Sindelfingen – par Daimler-Benz!

The dashboard is compact and well-designed. Underneath the hood, plenty of spare room is left by the small straight-cylinder engine with its laterally-mounted camshaft driven by a duplex chain.

Gebündelte Ordnung herrscht auf dem Amaturenbrett. Viel Platz unter der Haube lässt der kleine Reihenmotor, dessen seitliche Nockenwelle über eine Duplexkette angetrieben wird.

Tout est bien ordonné sur le tableau de bord. Le petit moteur en ligne dont l'arbre à cames latéral est actionné par une chaîne duplex est loin d'occuper la totalité du compartiment moteur.

BMW 303 1933

The 3/20 formula delivered 5 bhp per cylinder. How do you get 30 bhp? Correct, install six cylinders. So a miniscule BMW engine was born; 1173 cc, meaning it was the smallest automotive six cylinder of all time. Like the whole BMW 303 car, it was an interim solution, but provided a basis for follow-up designs of the 1930s.

The six cylinders featured long stroke dimensions, measuring 56 × 80 mm, utilizing overhead valves. The pressurized lubrication now took a liter and a half (three pints) more oil than a 3/20 and the carburation system had also been uprated with two Solex sidedraft carburetors.

The engineers from Eisenach developed a modern frame design with tubular steel longitudinal beams and four box-section cross beams. The 309, 315, 315/1, 319 and 329 models also followed this construction. New conscientious solutions had also been researched and developed for the suspension, which had previously been the car's Achilles' heel: control arms and transverse springs at the front, semi-elliptic springs at the live axle rear. This was an enormous technological advance on BMW's DA and AM predecessors.

Thanks to fine-tuning of shock absorbers and springs alongside direct rack and pinion steering, the 303 provided

a completely new driving sensation. Pleasure in driving was disseminated and marketed by an advertising campaign involving a 1250 mile (2000 km) publicity trip through the German Reich.

Every fourth car of the 2300 BMW 303s built was a four-window convertible. The models on offer—only in production for a year—were completed by special designs, such as the Gläser sports convertible. Only two examples were manufactured of the tourer and the convertible sedan bodies.

The Wartburg area was still covered by the snow which fell in the winter of 1933/34: by then it was already clear that the 303 was old hat. In February, the exterior of the subsequent BMW 315 model was trimmed to give a final body style, one made unmistakable by six parallel cooling slots on each side of the hood. A 1.5 liter engine (to which the "fifteen" numeral after the "three" prefix refers in 315) was completed and installed from April onwards.

Theoretically, the increase in cubic capacity should, in percentage terms, produce 8 bhp more. That prediction was inaccurate, for an increase of only 4 bhp was achieved. This was, however, enough to enable the European 100 kph (62 mph) barrier to be breached.

Fünf PS pro Zylinder lautet die Gleichung beim 3/20. Wie kommt man also auf 30 PS? Richtig, indem man mit sechs Zylindern rechnet! So entsteht bei BMW mit 1173 cm³ der hubraumschwächste automobile Sechszylinder aller Zeiten – eine Interimslösung wie das ganze Auto, aber eine Grundlage für die Folgekonstruktionen der dreißiger Jahre.

Über den sechs langhubigen Zylinderröhrchen mit je 56 × 80 mm liegen im Zylinderkopf hängende Ventile. Gegenüber dem 3/20 passen anderthalb Liter Öl mehr in den Druckumlauf, und auch das Vergasersystem wird der neuen Situation gerecht.

Die Ingenieure aus Eisenach entwickeln eine moderne Rahmenkonstruktion mit Stahlrohrlängsträgern und vier Kastenquerträgern. Auf dieser Basis entstehen auch die Modelle 309, 315, 315/1, 319 und 329. Für die Radaufhängungen, den bisherigen Schwachpunkt, gibt es ebenfalls durchdachte Lösungen: vorn mit Querlenkern und -feder, hinten mit halb-elliptischen Blattfedern – ein enormer technischer Fortschritt gegenüber den DA- und AM-Vorgängern.

Dank der gefühlvollen Abstimmung von Stoßdämpfern und Federn und einer direkten Zahnstangenlenkung

vermittelt der 303 ein völlig neues Fahrgefühl. Fahrfreude kommt auf, und die wird bei einer 2000 Kilometer langen Tour durch das Deutsche Reich werbewirksam vermittelt und vermarktet.

Jeder vierte der 2300 gebauten 303 ist ein Cabriolet mit vier Fenstern. Seltene Sonderaufbauten wie das Sport-Cabriolet von Gläser runden das Angebot dieser Baureihe, die nur ein Jahr lang in Produktion bleibt, ab. Vom Tourer und der Cabrio-Limousine werden jeweils nur zwei Fahrzeuge gefertigt.

Die Wartburg hüllt noch der Schnee des Winters 1933/34 ein, da ist schon klar, dass der 303 bereits Schnee von gestern ist. Im Februar wird das Outfit auf das Nachfolgemodell BMW 315 getrimmt, leicht erkennbar an den sechs unterteilten Kühlschlitzfeldern auf jeder Seite der Motorhaube. Auch der 1,5-Liter-Motor, für den die 15 hinter der 3 steht, ist fertig und wird ab April eingebaut.

Die Rechnung, dass das neue Modell nun proportional zur Hubraumvergrößerung 8 PS mehr an die Räder bringen könnte, geht freilich nicht auf: Es sind lediglich vier Pferdestärken mehr, aber genug, um die „Schallgrenze" von 100 Stundenkilometern zu erreichen.

La BMW 3/20 développe 5 ch par cylindre. Comment obtenir 30 ch? Avec six cylindres bien sûr! C'est ainsi que naît chez BMW un minuscule moteur qui est, avec ses 1173 cm³, l'automobile six-cylindres la plus petite de tous les temps. Comme pour la BMW 303, cette voiture est une version intermédiaire mais qui jettera les bases des réalisations qui auront lieu dans le courant des années 1930.

Les six minuscules cylindres à longue course aux cotes respectives de 56 × 80 mm ont des soupapes en tête. Le circuit d'huile renferme un litre et demi de plus que celui de la 3/20 et le carburateur aussi est adapté à ce nouvel environnement.

Les ingénieurs d'Eisenach mettent au point un châssis-cadre moderne avec longerons longitudinaux en tube d'acier et quatre poutres transversales en caisson – un châssis en échelle que reprennent également les modèles 309, 315, 315/1, 319 et 329. Pour les suspensions, le talon d'Achille de ces voitures, on trouve également des solutions: des bras et ressorts transversaux à l'avant et des ressorts semi-elliptiques à l'arrière. C'est un énorme progrès qui est accompli sur le plan mécanique par rapport aux DA et AM de la génération précédente.

Grâce à la précision du réglage des amortisseurs et des ressorts ainsi qu'à une direction à crémaillère directe, la 303

donne des sensations absolument inédites à son conducteur. On ressent un réel plaisir de conduite – une campagne publicitaire effectuée sur 2000 km à travers le IIIe Reich en assure la promotion.

Près d'un quart des 2300 BMW 303 construites sont des cabriolets à quatre fenêtres. Les modèles proposés – qui ne seront fabriqués que pendant un an – dans cette gamme seront complétés de séries spéciales comme le Sport-Cabriolet de Gläser. Seulement deux exemplaires de la tourer et de la berline cabriolet seront fabriqués.

La Wartburg frissonne encore sous le manteau de neige de l'hiver 1933–1934, et il est clair que la 303 n'en est plus à son premier printemps. En février, son esthétique est alignée sur celle de la BMW 315, aisément reconnaissable par les six fentes de refroidissement disposées de chaque côté du capot moteur. Le moteur de 1,5 litre, symbolisé par le «quinze» derrière le «trois», est prêt techniquement et est lancé en avril 1934.

L'équation selon laquelle l'augmentation de cylindrée pourrait se traduire proportionnellement par 8 ch supplémentaires est fausse puisqu'ils ne sont qu'au nombre de quatre – mais cela suffit pour atteindre le «mur du son» de l'époque, les 100 km/h.

The new engine, with twin vertical carburetors and developing 30 bhp, was the smallest six-cylinder automobile of all time with its cubic capacity of 1.2 liters. The hinged windscreen ensures plenty of ventilation for the roomy interior.

Der neue Motor, der mit seinen zwei Vertikalvergasern 30 PS leistet, ist mit 1,2 Litern Hubraum der kleinste automobile Sechszylinder aller Zeiten. Für Frischluft im geräumigen Innenraum sorgt die ausstellbare Windschutzscheibe.

Le nouveau moteur de 1,2 litre, qui développe 30 ch avec ses deux carburateurs verticaux, est le plus petit six-cylindres de toute l'histoire de l'automobile. Le pare-brise relevable permet d'aérer l'habitacle spacieux.

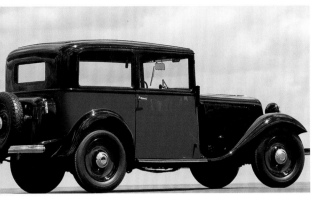

For the 303 the engineers from Eisenach developed a modern frame incorporating tubular steel longitudinal beams and box-section cross members. The bodywork styling found great favor with motorists, as a promotional tour through the German Reich revealed, but the car's performance left something to be desired.

Für den 303 haben die Ingenieure aus Eisenach eine moderne Rahmenkonstruktion mit Stahlrohr-längsträgern und Kastenquerträgern entwickelt. Die Form der Karosserie findet bei den Automobilisten – wie sich bei einer Werbetour durch das Deutsche Reich herausstellt – großen Anklang. Die Leistung lässt indes noch Wünsche offen.

Pour la 303, les ingénieurs d'Eisenach ont conçu un châssis moderne à caissons avec des longerons longitudinaux creux en acier et des poutres transversales. Comme le clame une campagne publicitaire qui a traversé tout le IIIe Reich, sa carrosserie est tout à fait au goût des automobilistes, bien que sa puissance laisse encore à désirer.

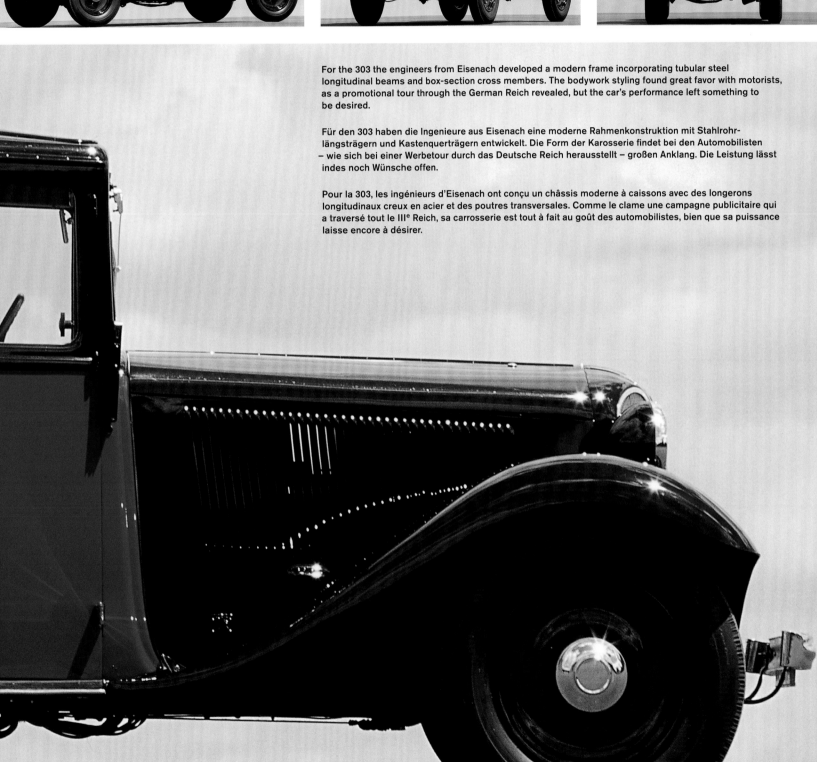

BMW 315/1 1934

In 1933 a dramatic change took place. BMW abandoned its small-volume, four-cylinder baby engine and redesigned it as a six-cylinder. The result was an 1173cc engine, which was the smallest in the world. It only took a few weeks before engineers at Eisenach recognized the engine's potential and increased the volume to 1490cc. This motor move provided the basis for the BMW 315, which sold a total 9765 units to be highly successful. The bigger engine also laid the foundations for an attractive small sports car providing 40bhp. It proved to be so successful in motor sport that the English company Frazer-Nash acquired the license to build it.

BMW engine size was increased again to achieve sporting success in the 2-liter class. That 1911cc development produced 55bhp at 4000rpm and an 81mph (130kph) top speed, 10kph more than the smaller six-cylinder engine delivered.

Both sport two-seaters, the 315/1 and the 319/1, look almost identical. The "bigger brother" boasts three decorative strips on the grills on the side of the hood and features a small ventilator window, slightly reducing drafts around the necks of passengers. This sport two-seater should only be driven open-topped, for the raised fabric folding top gives a rather ugly appearance. A coupé top, designed by the Vereinigte Werkstätten in Munich (workshop for car bodies and coach building) remained a short-lived oddity and was not a styling triumph.

In contrast to the 315 sport convertible and the 319/1 edition from the Munich BMW dealer and specialist bodywork producer, Ludwig Weinberger, the 315/1 Sport-Zweisitzer was notable for the delicate and refined style of its covered rear wheels.

All in all, the 315/1 was an uncomplicated vehicle with a simple chassis (at the front: lower control arm suspension, transverse spring on top, plus rigid rear axle suspension via semi-elliptic spring). Interestingly, it already used an electric fuel pump for the 11-gallon (42-liter) tank. Maneuverability and a good power-weight ratio destined the 315/1 for motor sport, its only occasional drawback being the erratic drum brakes.

Both sport two-seaters correspond to the classic idea of a roadster, starting with the spartan cockpit. Two large round instruments dominate: the clock on the left and the speedometer with odometer on the right. Two smaller round instruments for water temperature and oil pressure, as well as many little levers and push-buttons (located above the glove compartment) are the only dashboard decorations. The small front windscreen with its parallel wipers is adjustable.

Even the doors, with their recessed armrests, are pure roadster: there are no handles to open them; a small lever inside works the mechanism. Of course there are no bumpers or external mirrors. One thing which is important, however, is the spare wheel, situated where you would expect the trunk to be.

Ein Umsturz vollzieht sich 1933: BMW wendet sich von seinem hubraumschwachen Vierzylindermotörchen ab und steigt auf sechs Zylinder um. Heraus kommt der mit 1173 cm³ kleinste Sechszylinder der Welt. Welche Möglichkeiten in diesem Triebwerk stecken, erkennt man in Eisenach schon nach wenigen Wochen und vergrößert das Volumen auf 1490 cm³. Das ist die Basis des mit insgesamt 9765 Einheiten recht erfolgreich verkauften BMW 315, eine Baureihe, zu der auch ein attraktiv aussehender kleiner Sportwagen mit 40 PS gehört. Dieser ist im Motorsport so erfolgreich, dass die englische Firma Frazer-Nash das Recht zum Lizenzbau erwirbt.

Um auch in der 2-Liter-Klasse sportlich reüssieren zu können, wird der Motor nochmals vergrößert. Aus 1911 cm³ werden bei 4000 Touren 55 PS geholt. Das bedeutet 130 Stundenkilometer Spitze – zehn mehr als mit dem kleineren Sechszylinder möglich sind.

Beide Sport-Zweisitzer, der 315/1 und der 319/1, unterscheiden sich optisch kaum. Der „große Bruder" protzt mit drei Zierleisten auf den seitlichen Motorhauben-Gittern und verfügt über ein kleines Ausstellfenster, das die Luftverwirbelung im Nackenbereich der Passagiere etwas reduziert. Diese Sport-Zweisitzer sollte man nur offen fahren, denn das geschlossene Stoffverdeck wirkt ziemlich ungehobelt. Ein Coupé-Aufsatz, entworfen von den Vereinigten Werkstätten in München, der stilistisch wenig gelungen ist, bleibt kurzlebiges Kuriosum.

Im Gegensatz zum 315 Sport-Cabriolet und der 319/1-Ausgabe des Münchner BMW-Vertreters und

Sonderkarosserie-Herstellers Ludwig Weinberger wirkt der 315/1 Sport-Zweisitzer zierlich und mit seinen abgedeckten Hinterrädern elegant.

Insgesamt gesehen ist der 315/1 ein unkompliziertes, sportliches Fahrzeug mit simplem Fahrwerk – vorn verfügt er über einen Querlenker unten, eine Querfeder oben und hinten über eine starre Aufhängung mit Halbfedern. Interessant ist, dass er bereits eine elektrische Benzinpumpe für den 42-Liter-Tank aufweist. Wendigkeit und gutes Leistungsgewicht prädestinieren diesen Wagen zum motorsportlichen Einsatz, wo Freude und Erfolg nur ab und zu durch Schwächen der Trommelbremsen getrübt werden.

Beide Sport-Zweisitzer entsprechen den klassischen Roadster-Idealen, beginnend mit dem spartanischen Cockpit. Ins Blickfeld fallen zwei große Rundinstrumente: links die Uhr und rechts der Tachometer mit Kilometerzähler. Zwei kleinere Rundinstrumente für Wassertemperatur und Öldruck sowie einige Hebelchen und Zugknöpfe (selbst über dem Handschuhfach) sind die einzige Zierde des Armaturenbretts. Die knapp bemessene Frontscheibe mit den Parallelwischern ist verstellbar.

Aber auch die mit Armausschnitten versehenen Türen erinnern an einen Roadster: Griffe zum Öffnen fehlen, die Schlösser betätigt ein Hebelchen von innen. Natürlich sind auch keine Stoßstangen und Außenspiegel vorhanden. Wichtig ist allerdings das Reserverad, das sich dort befindet, wo man den Kofferraum vermutet.

En 1933, année révolutionnaire, BMW met au placard ses asthmatiques quatre-cylindres de petite cylindrée pour se tourner vers les six-cylindres. Avec 1173 cm³, c'est le plus petit six-cylindres du monde. Il n'a fallu que quelques semaines aux ingénieurs d'Eisenach pour s'en apercevoir et augmenter sa cylindrée à 1490 cm³. Il est l'âme de la BMW 315 qui connaîtra un succès enviable puisqu'elle sera vendue à 9765 exemplaires, une BMW 315 qui sera aussi épaulée par une séduisante petite voiture de sport de 40 ch. Celle-ci remporte tant de succès en compétition que la firme britannique Frazer-Nash achète une licence pour sa construction.

Pour lui assurer le succès sportif dans la catégorie deux litres également, la cylindrée de son moteur est encore majorée. Les 1911 cm³ délivrent 55 ch à 4000 tr/min: la vitesse de pointe est de 130 km/h, dix de plus qu'avec le petit six-cylindres.

Sur le plan esthétique, il est bien difficile de distinguer les deux biplaces de sport, la 315/1 et la 319/1. La «grande sœur» affiche trois joncs décoratifs sur les grilles d'aération latérales du capot moteur et possède un petit déflecteur qui réduit légèrement les courants d'air à hauteur de la nuque des passagers. On ne peut, en effet, conduire cette biplace de sport pratiquement qu'en décapotable, car la capote en toile fermée amoindrit la beauté des lignes. Un hard-top dessiné par les Vereinigte Werkstätten München (atelier de carrosserie et d'automobiles de Munich), qui n'est pas non plus une grande réussite esthétique, disparaîtra rapidement.

Contrairement à la 315 Cabriolet Sport et à la 319/1 carrossée par Ludwig Weinberger, un concessionnaire munichois

de BMW qui fabrique aussi des carrosseries spéciales, la 315/1 Sport biplace affiche un style délicat et raffiné avec ses roues arrière carénées.

Globalement, la 315/1 est une voiture sportive et peu compliquée avec un châssis simple (bras transversaux inférieurs et ressort transversal supérieur à l'avant et, à l'arrière, suspension rigide à ressorts semi-elliptiques). Un détail intéressant est qu'elle possède déjà une pompe à essence électrique pour son réservoir d'une capacité de 42 litres. Maniabilité et un bon rapport poids/puissance prédestinent cette voiture à la compétition dont la seule faiblesse chronique provient des freins à tambour.

Les deux biplaces de sport correspondent au schéma classique du roadster, à commencer par leur cockpit spartiate. Deux gros cadrans circulaires sautent aux yeux: à gauche, l'horloge et, à droite, le tachymètre avec compteur journalier. Deux cadrans ronds de plus petit diamètre pour la température de l'eau et la pression d'huile ainsi que quelques petites manettes et boutons (même au-dessus de la boîte à gants) sont la seule décoration du tableau de bord. De petite dimension, le pare-brise à essuie-glaces parallèles est réglable.

Quant aux portières servant d'accoudoirs, elles sont dans le plus pur style des roadsters: il n'existe pas de poignées pour les ouvrir, un petit levier actionne le mécanisme de l'intérieur. Naturellement, il n'y a pas non plus de pare-chocs ni de rétroviseurs extérieurs. La roue de secours, en revanche, est indispensable et se trouve dans le coffre.

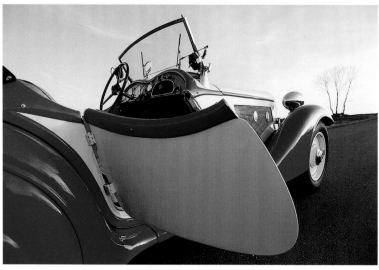

Sporty elegance and performance to match are the main features of the 315/1, which also had considerable success on the racetrack. The clock and speedometer, reading up to 93 mph (150 kph), are the dominant features of this roadster dashboard.

Sportliche Eleganz und ein ansprechendes Leistungspotential kennzeichnen den 315/1, der sich auch mit vielen rennsportlichen Meriten schmücken darf. Die Uhr und ein Tacho, der bis zu 150 Stundenkilometer anzeigt, sind die beherrschenden Rundinstrumente auf dem Roadster-Armaturenbrett.

Une élégance sportive ainsi qu'un potentiel intéressant caractérisent la 315/1 qui remportera de nombreuses victoires en compétition. Deux cadrans circulaires, la montre et le tachymètre gradué jusqu'à 150 km/h, trônent sur le tableau de bord du roadster.

Harmony of form and function from all angles. The front windscreen of the stylish automobile is adjustable, the soft top is easy to operate, and the tapered "trunk" at the rear only has room for the spare wheel.

Harmonie von Form und Funktion aus jeder Perspektive. Die Frontscheibe des schnittigen Fahrzeugs ist verstellbar, das Verdeck leicht zu bedienen, und in dem auch nach hinten abgerundeten „Kofferraum" findet lediglich das Reserverad Platz.

Harmonie des formes et de la fonction quelle que soit la perspective: le pare-brise de cette élégante voiture s'ouvre et la capote s'escamote aisément, mais le «coffre» arrondi n'héberge que la roue de secours.

BMW 326 1936

The 326 proved to be the most successful prewar BMW, despite the fact that it was thought to be somewhat conservative when it was presented in February 1936. This model had a 50 bhp six-cylinder engine, which fired the imagination of bodywork designers. Some 5500 convertibles were built in addition to more than 10,000 sedans, whose bodies were manufactured in Berlin-Johannisthal.

Coach builders Autenrieth in Darmstadt were a major player in the automotive sector and offered two-door as well as four-door body designs. A 1938 prototype caused a sensation with its safety-conscious sliding doors. This was a beautiful car, one which is still in the best of health lovingly preserved to this day.

The convertible offered by the Vereinigte Werkstätten in Munich for car bodies and coach building listed two doors, four seats, four windows. The two-seater convertibles by Drauz, Weinberger and Gläser were far sportier. Erdmann & Rossi's roadster appealed to the purists and could provide drivers with a wonderful slipstream sensation, one broken only by the windscreen.

The bumpers turned out to be a means by which the passage of each succeeding year could be determined: they

appeared in pairs until 1938 and in a single blade from 1939. In the year of the car's "birth," the 326 had disk wheels, followed by perforated rims from 1937.

As already indicated, the "crowning glory" was the new six-cylinder engine, which had 1971 cc instead of 1911 cc and therefore took the 2-liter class to the limit. This extremely long-stroke engine (66 × 96 mm equals a bore-to-stroke ratio of 1.45) made a compact cylinder block possible due to the small gaps between cylinders.

The crankshaft and the four-bearing camshaft with a duplex chain drive were correspondingly small. A pair of downdraft Solex 26 BFLV carburetors were part of the basic 326 equipment range. For reasons of cost, BMW decided to install just one carburetor in the 320 and 321 models, although this was at the expense of 5 bhp.

Depending on the version and equipment range, a 326 convertible cost between 5800 and 8000 reichsmarks. The chassis and engine alone cost 4450 reichsmarks. All in all, this mid-range convertible was relatively expensive, which made the strong sales figures even more surprising.

Als erfolgreichster BMW der Vorkriegsgeschichte entpuppt sich der 326, der bei seiner Vorstellung im Februar 1936 einen eher biederen Eindruck macht. Doch der 50-PS-Sechszylindermotor dieses Typs beflügelt offenbar die Phantasie der Karosserieschneider. Denn neben mehr als 10 000 Limousinen, deren Karosserien in Berlin-Johannisthal entstehen, werden auch 5500 Cabriolets gebaut.

Autenrieth in Darmstadt ist groß im Geschäft und bietet vier- und zweitürige Ausführungen an. 1938 wird ein vielbestaunter Prototyp mit Sicherheits-Schiebetüren vorgestellt, ein bildhübscher Wagen, der sich noch heute „bester Gesundheit" erfreut.

Zwei Türen, vier Sitze, vier Fenster, so lautet die Cabriolet-Offerte der Vereinigten Werkstätten für Karosserie- und Wagenbau in München. Weitaus sportlicher wirken die zweisitzigen Cabriolets von Drauz, Weinberger und Gläser. Erdmann & Rossis Roadster wendet sich an die Puristen und bietet ein nur von der Windschutzscheibe getrübtes Fahrtwind-Erlebnis.

Die Jahrgänge lassen sich an den Stoßstangen ablesen: Bis 1938 sind sie doppelt, ab 1939 nur noch einfach ausgeführt. Im „Geburtsjahrgang" sind die 326 mit Scheibenrädern ausgestattet, die ab 1937 durch Lochfelgen ersetzt werden.

Des „Pudels Kern" ist aber der neue Sechszylinder, der mit 1971 cm³ (zuvor 1911 cm³) die 2-Liter-Klasse voll ausschöpft. Dieser extreme Langhuber (66 × 96 mm entsprechen einem Bohrung-Hub-Verhältnis von 1,45) ermöglicht wegen seiner kurzen Zylinderabstände einen kompakten Block.

Entsprechend kurz sind die Kurbelwelle und die vierfach gelagerte Nockenwelle mit Duplex-Kettenantrieb. Zwei Vertikalvergaser Solex 26 BFLV gehören zur Grundbestückung, während sich BMW aus Kostengründen bei den Modellen 320 und 321 auf einen Vergaser beschränkt und somit fünf PS „verschenkt".

Je nach Ausführung und Ausstattung müssen zwischen 5800 und 8000 Reichsmark für ein 326 Cabriolet bezahlt werden. Allein 4450 Reichsmark kostet das Fahrgestell mit Motor. Damit ist dieses Mittelklassecabriolet vergleichsweise teuer. Umso mehr überraschen die Verkaufszahlen.

La 326 sera la BMW produite en plus grand nombre durant l'avant-guerre bien que, lors de sa présentation en février 1936, elle fut perçue comme quelque peu conservatrice, mais le six-cylindres de 50 ch de cette version donne apparemment des ailes à l'imagination des constructeurs, car, en plus des plus de 10 000 berlines dont les carrosseries sont montées à Berlin-Johannisthal, BMW fabrique également 5500 cabriolets.

Autenrieth, à Darmstadt, fait également de bonnes affaires avec ses versions en deux et en quatre portes. En 1938, il présente un prototype à portières de sécurité coulissantes qui fait sensation, une magnifique voiture qui est aujourd'hui encore merveilleusement conservée.

Deux portes, quatre places, quatre fenêtres, telle est la formule choisie pour les cabriolets proposés par les Vereinigte Werkstätten München. Mais les cabriolets biplaces de Drauz, Weinberger et Gläser sont autrement plus sportifs. Le roadster d'Erdmann & Rossi est destiné aux puristes et offre les mêmes sensations qu'une décapotable que ne tempère qu'un petit pare-brise.

Les millésimes respectifs se distinguent par leurs parechocs : jusqu'en 1938, ils sont doubles, puis simples à partir de 1939. En 1936, l'année de leur mise sur le marché, les 326 possèdent des jantes à voile plein, puis des jantes perforées à partir de 1937.

Mais le chef-d'œuvre mécanique est le nouveau six-cylindres en ligne qui, avec une cylindrée de 1971 cm³ (contre 1911 cm³), exploite à fond la classe deux litres. Ce moteur à course extrêmement longue (66 × 96 mm donnent un rapport alésage/course de 1,45) autorise un bloc compact grâce aux faibles intervalles entre les cylindres. D'autant plus courts sont donc le vilebrequin et l'arbre à cames à quatre paliers avec entraînement par chaîne duplex. Deux carburateurs verticaux Solex 26 BFLV font partie de la dotation de série alors que, par souci d'économie, BMW se contente d'un seul carburateur, et renonce ainsi à 5 ch, pour les versions 320 et 321.

Selon la version et la finition choisies, une 326 Cabriolet coûte entre 5800 et 8000 reichsmarks. À lui seul, le châssis avec moteur coûte 4450 reichsmarks. Ce cabriolet du segment intermédiaire est finalement assez cher et son succès est donc d'autant plus surprenant.

The four seats, four side windows and two large doors of this BMW 326 Cabriolet make for a well-heeled mid-range car with a generously equipped interior offering plenty of passenger comfort.

Vier Sitze, vier Seitenfenster und zwei große Türen offeriert dieses BMW 326 Cabriolet: die gehobene Mittelklasse mit einem reich ausgestatteten Interieur und viel Fahrkomfort.

Cette BMW 326 Cabriolet offre quatre places, quatre vitres latérales et deux grandes portières : un certain luxe déjà, avec un habitacle richement équipé et un grand confort.

The driver's gaze is drawn over the large three-spoke steering wheel through the windscreen (no longer adjustable) to the free-standing headlamps. By the time the BMW 327 came along, these had been integrated into the wings.

Über das große Dreispeichenlenkrad fällt der Blick durch die nicht mehr ausstellbare Windschutzscheibe auf die freistehenden Lampen. Beim BMW 327 werden diese bereits in die Kotflügel integriert sein.

Derrière le grand volant à trois branches, le regard se dirige, à travers un pare-brise désormais fixe, vers les phares proéminents. Sur la BMW 327, ceux-ci seront déjà intégrés aux ailes.

The six-cylinder engine developed 50 bhp. The striking double fenders of the 326 disappeared from the BMW range in 1939.

Der Sechszylindermotor mobilisiert 50 PS. Die geteilten, besonders markanten Doppelstoßstangen des 326 verschwinden 1939 aus dem BMW-Programm.

Le six-cylindres délivre 50 ch. Les doubles pare-chocs divisés de la 326, particulièrement marquants, disparaîtront du programme BMW en 1939.

A successful model: more than 5500 of this attractive Cabriolet were sold, despite the price tag of almost 8000 reichsmarks. Apart from a few exceptions, Autenrieth of Darmstadt built the Cabriolet bodies.

Erfolgsmodell: Mehr als 5500 dieser attraktiven, nahezu 8000 Reichsmark teuren Cabriolets werden verkauft. Bis auf wenige Ausnahmen führt Autenrieth in Darmstadt den Cabriolet-Aufbau durch.

Un grand succès commercial : plus de 5500 exemplaires de ce joli cabriolet qui coûtait près de 8000 reichsmarks seront vendus. À quelques rares exceptions, les carrosseries seront l'œuvre d'Autenrieth, de Darmstadt.

BMW 328 1937

A feast for the eyes: slim fenders which extend full length, with elegantly integrated headlights. In sports tradition, no bumpers cover the small BMW kidneys at the front of the radiator of this roadster. The BMW 328 is not only a benchmark symbol of automotive esthetics but it also promises endless soft top fun.

Two leather belts secure the hood, which covers an engine capable of producing 80 bhp at 4500 rpm, a motor fed by three downdraft carburetors. To avoid developing a completely new engine, the existing six-cylinder unit was provided with a cylinder head whose brilliant design was worth a patent certificate in itself. Its tuning potential enabled power increases up to 120 bhp without difficulty, or 136 bhp for the final factory racing versions.

A consistently lightweight construction of only 1782 lbs (810 kg) and a balanced chassis ensured the best behavior even on the worst roads. This was a full-blooded sports car without any moodiness to spoil the fun. There is just one small fault: changing gear is like entering a labyrinth.

With the agility of a weasel, the 328 could outmaneuver many more powerful cars in the sports category, and on the racetrack it became a sporting legend in just three years with 405 wins and 154 second places. Indeed, races often

featured internal BMW warfare, for there were starting grids made up exclusively of 328s.

The achievements of the racing version with the avant-garde aerodynamics of Carrozzeria Touring in Milan is worth a chapter in its own right. The series 328 also provided the basis for two streamlined versions built by the Wendler coachworks in Reutlingen, which reduced the drag coefficient and allowed very high maximum speeds.

Just 464 cars were built up to 1940. Frazer-Nash, British BMW importer since 1932, also built the 328 under license, converting it to right-hand drive.

The engine of the 328 experienced a comeback in postwar Britain and was used for several vehicles in the UK. Fritz Fiedler, one of the leading BMW designers, developed versions for Bristol and AFN. Last but not least, the Swiss automobile conversion company, Sbarro, contributed to the paeans of praise for the 328 with a replica in more recent times.

What was the 328? A classic or a vintage car? Perhaps a prestige badge for the company, a trendsetter of the 1930s for the sports cars of the postwar period? Maybe it was even a myth? Cult objects are a matter of taste. In the case of the 328, it is a fact that this timelessly elegant roadster has survived the era of automotive tin boxes and has remained forever youthful.

Eine Augenweide sind die schlanken, ganz nach hinten gezogenen Kotflügel mit den elegant integrierten Lampen. Keine Stoßstange verdeckt die sportlich schmalen BMW-Nieren vor dem Kühler dieses Roadsters. Der BMW 328 ist nicht nur ein Symbol automobiler Ästhetik, sondern verheißt auch schier endloses Cabriolet-Vergnügen.

Zwei Ledergurte sichern die Haube um das 80 PS bei 4500/min leistende Triebwerk, das von drei Fallstromvergasern beatmet wird. Um eine Neuentwicklung zu sparen, hat man den herkömmlichen Sechszylinder mit einem Zylinderkopf bestückt, dessen geniale Konstruktion eine Patenturkunde wert ist. Dieses Tuning erlaubt klaglos weitere Kraftschübe bis 120 PS und für die Rennversionen noch mehr.

Die konsequente Leichtbauweise (nur 810 Kilo) und ein ausgewogenes Fahrwerk sorgen für bestes Fahrverhalten selbst auf schlechtesten Straßen – ein Vollblutsportler ohne Launen. Kleines Manko: Die Schaltwege ähneln einem Labyrinth.

Mit der Wendigkeit eines Wiesels umkreist der 328 so manchen PS-Protz in der sportlichen Kategorie, und auf dem Rennparkett wird er mit 405 Siegen und 154 zweiten Plätzen in gerade mal drei Jahren zum Sportwagenmythos, wobei der Sieger oft als *primus inter pares* auftritt, denn

letztlich gibt es Startfelder, die sich ausschließlich aus BMW 328 rekrutieren.

Das Ruhmesblatt der Rennversionen mit avantgardistischer Aerodynamik von Carrozzeria Touring in Mailand ist ein eigenes Kapitel wert. Aber auch auf Basis des serienmäßigen 328 werden von dem Karrosseriewerk Wendler in Reutlingen zwei Stromlinien-Exemplare mit niedrigem Luftwiderstand gebaut.

Bis 1940 werden 464 Exemplare gebaut. Frazer-Nash, seit 1932 britischer BMW-Importeur, führt die BMW 328 ein und baut sie auf Rechtslenkung um. Der Motor des 328 erlebt im Nachkriegs-England ein Comeback und beflügelt so manches Fahrzeug der Insel. Fritz Fiedler, einer der maßgeblichen BMW-Konstrukteure, entwickelt Derivate für Bristol und AFN. Last but not least stimmt der Schweizer Autoveredler Sbarro mit einer Replika in das Hohelied auf den 328 ein.

Was ist er nun eigentlich: ein Klassiker, ein Oldtimer, ein Firmenaushängeschild, ein Trendsetter der dreißiger Jahre für die Sportwagen der Nachkriegszeit oder gar ein Mythos? Kultobjekte sind Ansichtssache, aber beim 328 ist Tatsache: Dieser zeitlos elegante Roadster hat jede „Blechkultur" überlebt und wirkt noch immer jung.

Ces fines ailes élancées vers l'arrière et ses phares élégamment intégrés sont un véritable plaisir pour les yeux. Aucun pare-chocs ne couvre le radiateur de ce roadster aux naseaux d'une délicatesse et d'une sportivité sans conteste. La BMW 328 n'est pas seulement un symbole d'esthétique automobile, elle incarne aussi le plaisir infini de la conduite en cabriolet.

Deux courroies de cuir fixent le capot sous lequel ronronne un moteur qui délivre 80 ch à 4500 tr/min grâce à trois carburateurs inversés. Pour éviter de développer un moteur totalement nouveau, BMW a coiffé le six-cylindres conventionnel d'une culasse dont l'ingéniosité a mérité le dépôt d'un brevet. Son potentiel permet sans difficulté de faire monter la puissance jusqu'à 120 ch voire plus pour les versions course.

Une construction allégée de série (seulement 810 kg) et un châssis équilibré lui permettent d'offrir un comportement sans défaut même sur les plus mauvaises routes. Un pur-sang sans allure ! Elle n'a qu'un petit défaut : changer de vitesse est un véritable casse-tête.

Très maniable, la 328 rivalise avec des voitures de sport beaucoup plus puissantes. Elle s'impose sur les pistes du monde entier : avec 405 victoires et 154 deuxièmes places en trois ans, elle devient un mythe parmi les voitures de sport, une sorte de *primus inter pares* (le premier entre ses égaux).

Dans certaines courses, les grilles de départ sont composées exclusivement de 328.

Le tableau de chasse des versions course à l'aérodynamique d'avant-garde signée par la Carrozzeria Touring à Milan mérite que l'on y consacre un chapitre spécifique. En s'inspirant de la 328 de série, le carrossier Wendler, à Reutlingen, construit deux exemplaires aérodynamiques qui en diminuent le C_x et qui permettent d'atteindre des vitesses maximales très élevées.

Jusqu'en 1940, 464 exemplaires seront produits. Frazer-Nash, importateur de BMW en Grande-Bretagne depuis 1932, importe des 328 et les transforme pour la conduite à gauche. Dans l'Angleterre de l'après-guerre, le moteur de la 328 fait un come-back et est utilisé sur plusieurs véhicules en Grande-Bretagne. Fritz Fiedler, l'un des grands ingénieurs de BMW, en développe les dérivés pour Bristol et AFN. *Last but not least,* le préparateur suisse Sbarro lui a rendu hommage récemment avec une admirable réplique.

Mais qu'est-ce qu'une 328 ? Une voiture classique ou un millésime ? Peut-être une carte de visite pour l'entreprise, un modèle des années 1930 à imiter par les voitures de sport de l'après-guerre, ou même un mythe ? Les avis sont partagés. Mais, pour la 328 une chose est acquise : ce roadster d'une élégance intemporelle a survécu à toutes les modes et reste indémodable.

A long slender kidney grill and sporting lines with no frills or flourishes and also no fender: the 328 is without doubt one of the most beautiful roadsters ever built. With its patented hood catch involving two leather straps to hold the engine hoods together, it has achieved cult status among BMW enthusiasts.

Eine schmale lange Niere und eine sportliche Linienführung ohne Schnörkel oder Stoßstangen: Der 328 ist zweifelsohne einer der schönsten Roadster, die je gebaut wurden. Mit den zwei Lederriemen, deren Patentverschlüsse die Motorhauben zusammenhalten, ist er ein automobilistisches Kultobjekt.

Des naseaux minces et étroits ainsi que des lignes sportives sans fioritures ni pare-chocs: la 328 est incontestablement l'un des plus jolis roadsters qui aient jamais été construits. Avec les deux courroies en cuir dont les fermetures brevetées maintiennent fermées les ailes du capot, c'est un objet de culte pour tout amateur d'automobiles.

The "legend on wheels" stood out for its excellent power-to-weight ratio and its superb handling.

Die „Legende auf Rädern" zeichnet sich durch ein günstiges Leistungsgewicht und exzellente Fahreigenschaften aus.

Cette voiture de légende se distingue par son excellent rapport poids/puissance et une parfaite tenue de route.

Based on the BMW 328, the bodywork designer baron Reinhard of König-Fachsenfeld came up with this streamlined body whose drag coefficient is 0.38, a remarkable figure for those days. The Fachsenfeld design, on the basis of a patent by Paul Jaray, was produced at the Wendler bodywork plant in Reutlingen. Two prototypes were built, one of which can be seen in the Deutsches Museum in Munich, while the other one, illustrated here, is in the hands of a private BMW collector from Nuremberg.

Auf Basis des BMW 328 entwirft der Formgestalter Reinhard Freiherr von König-Fachsenfeld diese Stromlinienkarosserie, deren Luftwiderstandsbeiwert bei 0,38 liegt und für damalige Zeiten recht beachtlich ist. Der Entwurf von Fachsenfeld nach einem Patent von Paul Jaray wird vom Karosseriewerk Wendler in Reutlingen realisiert. Zwei Prototypen werden gebaut, von denen einer im Deutschen Museum in München zu sehen ist. Dieser hier ist im Besitz eines privaten BMW-Sammlers aus Nürnberg.

Sur la plate-forme de la BMW 328, le designer Reinhard, baron de König-Fachsenfeld, dessine cette carrosserie aérodynamique dont le C_x – 0,38 – est vraiment remarquable pour cette époque. Le croquis de Fachsenfeld, selon un brevet de Paul Jaray, est réalisé par le carrossier Wendler, à Reutlingen. Deux prototypes seront construits, dont l'un est exposé au Deutsche Museum de Munich, celui-ci étant la propriété d'un collectionneur privé de Nuremberg.

Fachsenfeld did a huge amount of detail work to get the drag coefficient down, such as the curved windows and the flush door handles. Without the radiator ribs the drag coefficient would have been as low as 0.29.

Zur Reduzierung des Luftwiderstandsbeiwerts leistet Fachsenfeld enorm viel Detailarbeit, zu der abgerundete Scheiben und versenkte Türgriffe gehören. Ohne die Kühlrippen auf der Motorhaube hätte der C_W-Wert sogar nur bei 0,29 gelegen.

Pour obtenir un C_X optimal, Fachsenfeld n'a négligé aucun détail, telles les vitres arrondies et les poignées intégrées aux portières. Sans les ailettes de refroidissement sur le moteur, le C_X aurait été de 0,29 seulement.

BMW 325 Leichter Einheits-Pkw

One people, one Reich, one Führer ... one chassis!" The propaganda slogans of the Third Reich might be extended thus in respect of the passenger vehicle for the German armed forces. The German army procurement office demanded a standard passenger vehicle in three weight classes. With exact instructions regarding the chassis, the order for the light version was awarded to Stoewer, Hanomag, and BMW. No external changes were permitted. Emblems giving any indication of the manufacturer were forbidden.

As well as an engine of the manufacturer's choice—the only requirement was that it should fit under the bonnet and to the transmission—the profile of technical requirements specified permanent all-wheel drive, four limited slip differentials, and selectable, spindle-linked, four-wheel steering. Stoewer started production as early as 1936 and manufactured 7500 examples altogether, although not all of them had four-wheel steering. Hanomag produced 2000 units. BMW production started in April 1937 and carried on until summer 1940 and resulted in somewhere between 3225 and 3259 vehicles being produced, all called BMW 325.

A short wheelbase gave over-sensitive handling. Also, extremely complicated technology, and an unfavorable power-weight ratio, restricted the military usefulness of these vehicles. Transporting the 2.2 tons maximum

permissible weight was hard work even for the strongest engine—BMW used its proven six-cylinders, achieving 50 bhp with two Solex updraft carburetors. The 325 was not suitable for the fabled German Blitzkrieg attacks, hobbled by a fuel tank range of just 150 miles (240 km). These standard specification military vehicles met their "Stalingrad" defeats well before the Russian campaign began. All were withdrawn from the arms supply programs before the winter of 1942.

Today the 325 is a real rarity. Only one roadworthy vehicle is known to exist, one which Udo Beckmann, a motor mechanic from Siegen, has saved from "death in action" by loving restoration. This 325, built in 1939 and supplied to the German army in May 1940, was provided with a large equipment box for communications purposes, in place of one seat and a door. This storage proved useful postwar, thus this 325 served years in Austria with the mountain rescue and fire brigade.

Driving skill is required to handle the all-wheel drive and steering systems, particularly in rough terrain and on winding roads. Beckmann's 325 rolls to the "front" today, without its radio equipment but with spade and searchlight. Then it does not head for the desert, as it did with Rommel, but to a BMW veterans' meeting. Once there, a photo of the Field Marshal in a 325 will be proudly passed around.

Ein Volk, ein Reich, ein Führer ... ein Fahrgestell!" So ließe sich die Propagandaparole des Dritten Reichs hinsichtlich der Personenkraftwagen für die Wehrmacht erweitern, denn das Heereswaffenamt setzt auf Einheits-Pkw, gestaffelt nach drei Gewichtsklassen. Mit genauen Chassis- und Fahrwerksvorgaben geht der Auftrag für die leichte Version an Stoewer, Hanomag und BMW. Äußerliche Abweichungen sind nicht erlaubt. Embleme, die auf den Hersteller schließen lassen, sind verboten.

Das technische Anforderungsprofil sieht neben Motoren eigener Wahl – sie müssen nur unter die Haube und an das Getriebe passen – permanenten Allradantrieb, vier Sperrdifferentiale und eine hinten abstellbare Vierrad-Spindellenkung vor. Stoewer beginnt bereits 1936 mit der Produktion und fertigt insgesamt rund 7500 Wagen, freilich nicht alle mit Vierrad-Lenkung. Hanomag produziert 2000 Einheiten. Bei BMW, wo der Produktionsstart im April 1937 erfolgt und bis zum Sommer 1940 gefertigt wird, entstehen zwischen 3225 und 3259 Wagen, genannt BMW 325.

Zu kurzer Radstand, empfindliche, da sehr aufwändige Technik und ein ungünstiges Leistungsgewicht schränken die Truppentauglichkeit dieses Fahrzeugs ein. Selbst für den stärksten Motor, den BMW-Sechszylinder, der mit zwei Solex-Steigstromvergasern 50 PS leistet, bedeutet

1937

das Bewegen von 2,2 Tonnen zulässigen Gesamtgewichts Schwerstarbeit – nichts für Blitzkriege, zumal der Tank im Gelände nach 240 Kilometern leer ist. So erleben die Einheits-Pkw ihr Stalingrad bereits in der Anfangsphase des Russlandfeldzugs. Noch vor dem Winter 1942 werden sie aus dem Rüstungsprogramm genommen.

Heute ist der 325 eine absolute Rarität. Bekannt ist nur ein fahrtaugliches Exemplar, das Udo Beckmann, ein Kfz-Meister aus Siegen, durch liebevolle Restaurierung vor dem „Heldentod" bewahrt hat. Dieser 325, der 1939 gebaut und im Mai 1940 an die Wehrmacht ausgeliefert wurde, ist für Fernmeldezwecke mit einem großen Gerätekasten bestückt. Dafür fallen ein Sitz und eine Tür weg. Diese Konfiguration ist auch in Friedenszeiten brauchbar, und so dient dieser Wagen noch geraume Zeit in Österreich bei Bergwacht und Feuerwehr.

Fahrerisches Können ist beim Umgang mit dem Allradantriebs- und Lenkungssystem gefordert, besonders im Gelände und auf kurvenreichen Straßen. Wenn Beckmanns 325, ohne Funkgerät zwar, aber versehen mit Feldspaten und Suchscheinwerfer, heute wieder an die „Front" rollt, dann geht's nicht wie bei Rommel in die Wüste, sondern zum BMW-Veteranentreffen, wo dann stolz das Foto des Generalfeldmarschalls in einem 325 herumgereicht wird.

Un peuple, un Reich, un Führer ... et un châssis!» Ainsi pourrait-on résumer la devise du IIIe Reich en matière de voitures particulières pour la Wehrmacht. En effet, le service des achats de l'Armée exige un seul type de voitures particulières dans trois catégories de poids. Avec un cahier des charges précis pour le châssis et les trains roulants, la commande de la version légère est attribuée à Stoewer, Hanomag et BMW. Aucun changement extérieur n'est autorisé. Tout emblème permettant d'identifier le constructeur est interdit.

Outre le moteur, au libre choix du constructeur – pourvu qu'il entre sous le capot et soit compatible avec la boîte de vitesses –, le cahier des charges prévoit une traction intégrale permanente, quatre différentiels autobloquants et une direction à broche sur les quatre roues, les deux roues arrière étant débrayables. Stoewer inaugure la production dès 1936 et fabrique environ 7500 voitures au total, mais toutes ne possèdent pas quatre roues directrices. Hanomag en produit 2000 exemplaires. Chez BMW (où la production débute en avril 1937 et où la fabrication durera jusque durant l'été 1940), entre 3225 et 3259 voitures sont construites, baptisées BMW 325.

Un empattement trop court, une technique peu fiable parce que trop sophistiquée et un rapport poids/puissance défavorable restreignent les possibilités d'utilisation par les troupes. Même pour le moteur le plus puissant – le six-cylindres BMW à deux carburateurs Solex verticaux développant

50 ch –, déplacer un poids total en charge autorisé de 2,2 tonnes représente un effort surhumain. La 325 ne correspond pas à ce que les Allemands attendent pour mener leurs fabuleuses attaques éclairs. D'autant plus que, en tout-terrain, le réservoir est à sec au bout de 240 km. Ainsi ces voitures vivent-elles leur «Stalingrad» avant même que ne soit entamée la campagne de Russie. L'hiver 1942 n'a même pas commencé qu'elles disparaissent du programme des achats militaires.

Aujourd'hui, la 325 est une rareté. On ne connaît qu'un seul exemplaire apte à rouler, celui d'Udo Beckmann, un mécanicien de Siegen, qui l'a préservé de la «mort des héros» en la restaurant avec amour. Cette 325, construite en 1939 et livrée à la Wehrmacht en mai 1940, comporte un grand caisson pour les appareils de télécommunications (pour cela, il a fallu supprimer un siège et une portière). Après-guerre, cette voiture a encore longtemps été utilisée en Autriche par les secours en montagne et les pompiers.

Un certain savoir-faire est nécessaire pour rouler avec la traction intégrale et les quatre roues directrices, en particulier en tout-terrain et sur des routes sinueuses. Lorsque la 325 de Beckmann, sans appareil de transmission, mais avec sa pelle-bêche et son projecteur orientable, roule de nouveau «vers le front» aujourd'hui, elle ne part pas à la rencontre du désert comme au temps de Rommel, mais aux concentrations de vieilles BMW où l'on se passe alors de main en main la photo du maréchal des armées dans une 325.

Required by the German army procurement office: all-wheel drive and steering. The wheel suspension's double wishbone axles are each fitted with two helical springs. The BMW six-cylinder engine generates 50 bhp, which had to struggle to shift a two-tonner such as the version with a telecommunications equipment box shown here. The 325 is a great rarity, and this example is the only roadworthy one still in existence. After the War, it did service in the Austrian mountain rescue and fire departments.

Vom Heereswaffenamt gefordert: Allradantrieb und -lenkung. Die Doppel-Querlenker der Radaufhängungen sind mit je zwei dieser Schraubenfedern versehen. 50 PS leistet der BMW-Sechszylinder. Das bedeutet Schwerstarbeit beim Bewegen eines Zweitonners, der hier in der Ausführung mit einem Gerätekasten für Fernmelder gezeigt wird. Der 325 gilt als absolute Rarität, und fahrbereit ist offenbar nur noch dieses Exemplar, das nach dem Krieg der Bergwacht und Feuerwehr in Österreich gedient hat.

Le cahier des charges de l'armée est exigeant : traction et direction intégrales. Les doubles bras transversaux des suspensions ont chacun deux ressorts hélicoïdaux. Le six-cylindres BMW développe 50 ch. Il est donc à la peine avec cette voiture qui pèse deux tonnes. Ici, un modèle avec la caisse réservée aux équipements de télécommunication. La 325 est un modèle rarissime. Seul cet exemplaire, utilisé par les secours en montagne et les pompiers en Autriche après-guerre, est encore en état de rouler.

BMW 327 1937

Mr Reif from Chemnitz was one of the few fortunate people who were able to purchase the highly attractive BMW 327 convertible during the War. This stylish black design from Eisenach cost 7500 reichsmarks. When Reif received the bill dated 12 May 1941, he could not know that his car, chassis and engine number 87,306, would be the last of its kind to be made by BMW. Number 87,307 was built in 1948 by the Soviet-owned state company "Awtowelo" in a version identical to the 327 built before the War.

The 2+2 seater sports convertible was publicly unveiled in winter 1937. Initially it was difficult to target the right sales groups for the 327. Beauty and elegant lines, the capacity for storing a medium-sized case and a portable typewriter, and a rating of 55bhp were not high priorities for buyers in this price category. Perhaps it was ideal for a traveling journalist with entourage?

Sales were therefore sluggish. When an 80bhp version appeared in 1938 (327/28) to meet demands for performance and sportiness, strangely enough sales for the basic 327 also picked up. A total of 1124 convertibles and 179 coupés were built. In May 1941, the last coupé was supplied to the Brazilian consul general de Louza-Ribeiro in Hamburg.

Like its predecessors, which were also equipped with a 2-liter engine (BMW 320, 321 and 326), the 327 had a low slung box-section chassis, on which car bodies manufactured by Ambi-Budd coachworks in Berlin-Johannisthal were used. Ambi-Budd and Autenrieth in Darmstadt were BMW's largest suppliers of car bodies in the 1930s.

Hurth and ZF supplied the four-speed transmission (with freewheel facility in first and second gear). The drive ratio was identical in both types, and the differences in the individual gears were minor. What was different was how the doors were hinged—at the front in the convertible and at the back in the coupé.

After the dismantling of Ambi-Budd, the BMW chassis tools of the 321, 326 and 327 types went to Awtowelo in East Germany. The Russians and East German successor EMW (Eisenacher Motorenwerk) manufactured 491 BMW 327 descendants between 1952 and 1954. The EMW 327-3, an attractive coupé with a large rear window, was also manufactured.

Just as it had many devotees among the leaders of the Third Reich, the 327 sports convertible became, in its postwar model, a status symbol for loyal and prominent Socialist Party comrades. Fans of veteran BMWs consider the 327 to be one of the most beautiful convertibles of its time.

Herr Reif aus Chemnitz gehört zu den wenigen Glücklichen, die in Kriegszeiten das äußerst attraktive Cabriolet BMW 327 erwerben dürfen. 7500 Reichsmark kostet dieser vornehmlich in Schwarz ausgelieferte Wagen aus Eisenach. Als Reif die am 12. Mai 1941 ausgestellte Rechnung erhält, weiß er noch nicht, dass sein Wagen mit der Fahrgestell- und Motornummer 87306 der letzte aus der dortigen BMW-Produktion ist. Nr. 87307 wird 1948 von der staatlichen (sowjetischen) Gesellschaft „Awtowelo" in unveränderter Vorkriegsausführung gebaut.

Ausgerechnet im Winter 1937 wird das 2+2-sitzige Sport-Cabriolet der Öffentlichkeit vorgestellt. Zunächst findet es nicht die richtige Zielgruppe, denn Schönheit und elegante Linienführung, die Möglichkeit, neben den Passagieren auch noch einen mittelgroßen Koffer und eine Reiseschreibmaschine unterzubringen sowie 55 PS Leistung sind in dieser Preiskategorie weniger gefragt – ideal höchstens für einen Reisejournalisten mit Anhang!

Der Verkauf läuft schleppend an. Als 1938 eine 80-PS-Version (327/28) kommt, um dem Verlangen nach Leistung und Sportlichkeit stattzugeben, beschleunigt sich seltsamerweise auch der Absatz des 327. Insgesamt werden 1124 Cabriolets und 179 Coupés gebaut. Das letzte Coupé wird im Mai 1941 dem brasilianischen Generalkonsul de Louza-Ribeiro in Hamburg ausgehändigt.

Wie seine ebenfalls mit dem 2-Liter-Motor ausgerüsteten Vorgänger (BMW 320, 321 und 326) hat der 327 einen Tiefbett-Kastenrahmen, auf den Karosserien vom Presswerk Ambi-Budd in Berlin-Johannisthal gesetzt werden. Ambi-Budd und Autenrieth in Darmstadt sind in den dreißiger Jahren die größten BMW-Karossiers.

Die Vierganggetriebe liefern Hurth (mit Freilauf im ersten und zweiten Gang) und ZF. Bei beiden ist die Antriebsübersetzung gleich und die Differenz in den einzelnen Gängen nur geringfügig. Unterschiedlich ist allerdings der Anschlag der Türen – beim Cabriolet vorn, beim Coupé hinten.

Awtowelo heißt die Firma, die bei der Demontage von Ambi-Budd den Zuschlag für den Erhalt der BMW-Karosseriewerkzeuge für die Typen 321, 326 und 327 erhält. Die Russen und der DDR-Nachfolgebetrieb EMW (Eisenacher Motorenwerk) fertigen zwischen 1952 und 1954 noch 491 Abkömmlinge des BMW 327. Unter der Bezeichnung EMW 327-3 entsteht auch ein hübsches Coupé mit großem Heckfenster.

Schon bei den Größen des Dritten Reiches beliebt, wird das Nachkriegsmodell des 327 Sport-Cabriolets zum Statussymbol linientreuer SED-Parteifunktionäre. BMW-Veteranen-Freaks gilt der 327 als eines der schönsten Cabriolets seiner Zeit.

Monsieur Reif, de Chemnitz, est l'un des heureux élus qui, durant la guerre, a eu le droit d'acheter une BMW 327, un cabriolet très réussi. Cette voiture fabriquée à Eisenach – livrée presque toujours en noir – coûtait 7500 reichsmarks. Lorsque Reif reçoit la facture le 12 mai 1941, il ignore encore que sa voiture portant le numéro de châssis et de moteur 87306 est la dernière produite sous le label BMW. En 1948, le véhicule 87307 sera construit dans une version d'avant-guerre par la compagnie (soviétique) nationale Awtowelo.

Au cours de l'hiver 1937, le cabriolet sportif 2+2 est présenté au grand public. Mais il ne trouve pas d'emblée sa cible, car sa beauté et l'élégance de ses lignes alliées à la possibilité de transporter, outre les passagers, une valise de taille moyenne et une machine à écrire, et ses 55 ch sous le capot, ne sont pas les caractéristiques recherchées par les acheteurs d'automobiles dans cette catégorie de prix. Peut-être est-elle destinée à un journaliste en voyage ?

C'est pourquoi les ventes ne décollent pas. Lorsque, en 1938, apparaît une version de 80 ch (327/28) qui offre plus de puissance et de sportivité, les ventes de la 327 s'envolent curieusement elles aussi. Au total, 1124 cabriolets et 179 coupés seront construits. Le dernier coupé sera remis, en mai 1941, au consul général brésilien de Louza-Ribeiro à Hambourg.

Comme les BMW 320, 321 et 326 avant elle, également propulsées par un moteur de deux litres, la 327 possède un châssis à caisson surbaissé sur lequel est boulonnée la carrosserie montée par Ambi-Budd (emboutissage), à Berlin-Johannisthal. Durant les années 1930, Ambi-Budd et Autenrieth de Darmstadt seront les deux principaux carrossiers de BMW.

Les boîtes à quatre vitesses sont fournies par Hurth (avec moyeu de roue libre pour la première et la deuxième vitesse) et par ZF. Toutes les deux possèdent la même démultiplication et l'étagement est également assez proche. La différence se situe au niveau des portières – sur le cabriolet, elles sont articulées à l'avant, sur le coupé à l'arrière.

Après le démantèlement d'Ambi-Budd, la fabrication des carrosseries de BMW des versions 321, 326 et 327 est attribuée à Awtowelo en Allemagne de l'Est. De 1952 à 1954, les Russes et l'entreprise est-allemande EMW (Eisenacher Motorenwerk), qui prendra sa succession, créeront encore 491 dérivés de la BMW 327. Sous la dénomination EMW 327-3, ils créeront également un joli coupé avec une grande lunette arrière.

Déjà apprécié par les dirigeants du IIIe Reich, le modèle créé après-guerre pour succéder à la 327 Sport-Cabriolet deviendra un symbole de réussite pour les fonctionnaires du Parti socialiste. Les amoureux des BMW considèrent la 327 comme l'un des plus jolis cabriolets de son époque.

The elegant headlamps, mounted between the wings and the radiator hood, set the tone for the striking appearance of the BMW 327. Enthusiasts regard it as one of the most beautiful convertibles of the 1930s.

Die elegant in den Übergang von Kotflügel zu Kühlerhaube eingebetteten Scheinwerfer unterstreichen die ansprechende Optik des BMW 327. Kenner zählen ihn zu den schönsten Cabriolets der dreißiger Jahre.

Les phares élégamment positionnés à la césure entre les ailes et le capot soulignent l'esthétique réussie de la BMW 327. Les connaisseurs y voient l'un des plus jolis cabriolets des années 1930.

The option of having the 80 bhp engine of the BMW 328 fitted in the 327/28 meant the otherwise somewhat underpowered 327 Cabriolet had plenty of "oomph," and with a top speed of 78 mph (125 kph) it gave motorists a lot of car for their money.

Mit der Option auf den Einbau des 80-PS-Motors des BMW 328 (als 327/28) kommen auch die nicht so stark motorisierten 327 Cabriolets richtig in Fahrt – 125 Stundenkilometer bereiten durchaus Vergnügen.

Avec la possibilité de faire monter le moteur de 80 ch de la BMW 328 dans la 327/28, même les 327 cabriolets moins puissamment motorisés «décoiffent» – 125 km/h suffisent amplement pour se faire plaisir.

The 327 Cabriolet with its 55 bhp, elegant white spoked steering wheel and matching horn ring is stylish rather than sporting.

Eher vornehm als sportlich lassen sich die 55 PS des 327 Cabriolets mit dem eleganten weißen Speichenlenkrad und dem passendem Hupring lenken.

Le fringant volant blanc à trois branches avec son klaxon circulaire incitera plutôt à conduire avec élégance que sur un rythme sportif cette 327 Cabriolet de 55 ch.

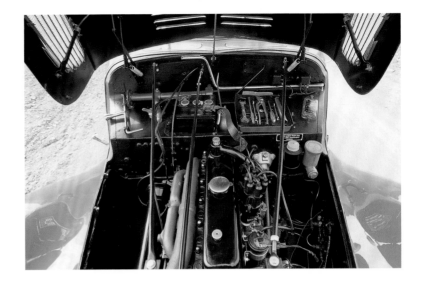

From October 1938 onwards, coupé versions of the 327 and the 327/28 were available.
In contrast to the Cabriolet, the door is hinged at the rear.

Ab Oktober 1938 sind der 327 und der 327/28 auch als Coupé erhältlich. Im Gegensatz
zum Cabriolet ist der Türanschlag beim Coupé hinten.

À partir d'octobre 1938, la 327 et la 327/28 sont également disponibles en version coupé.
Contrairement aux cabriolets, les portes sont articulées à l'arrière.

Captivating lines and timeless beauty: the sweeping tail of the Coupé with a bulge where the spare wheel is housed. Only 179 coupés of the 327 and 86 of the 327/28 were produced by Autenrieth and Ambi-Budd.

Bestechende Linienführung und zeitlos schön: das gestreckte Heck des Coupés mit den spezifischen Rundungen, die sich der Reserveradausbuchtung im Kofferraumdeckel anpassen. Nur 179 Coupés des BMW 327 und 86 des BMW 327/28 wurden insgesamt von Autenrieth und Ambi-Budd gebaut.

Lignes irrésistibles et beauté intemporelle : la poupe élancée et un galbe racé épousent l'emplacement ménagé pour la roue de secours dans le couvercle de la malle. 179 coupés seulement de la 327 et 86 de la 327/28 ont été construits, au total, par Autenrieth et Ambi-Budd.

Available as an option: the 80 bhp straight-six engine
with V-valves and three Solex downdraft carburetors.

Wahlweise erhältlich: der Sechszylinder-Reihenmotor
(80 PS) mit V-förmig hängenden Ventilen und drei
Solex-Fallstromvergasern.

Disponible en option: le six-cylindres en ligne de 80 ch
à soupapes suspendues en V et trois carburateurs
Solex inversés.

With the partial cladding of the rear wheel usually present on the 327/28s removed, the perforated rims can be seen to good effect. The color-contrasted contours of the wings are another pleasing feature.

Ohne die Teil-Hinterradabdeckung, die beim 327/28 eigentlich üblich ist, kommen die Lochfelgen besonders gut zur Geltung. Auch die farblich abgesetzten Kotflügelkonturen treten so besser hervor.

Sans le carénage partiel des roues arrière, normalement utilisé sur les 327/28, les jantes perforées sont particulièrement bien mises en évidence. Les couleurs contrastées utilisées sur le contour des ailes sont une autre caractéristique plaisante de cette voiture.

The 2-liter power unit: a straight-six engine with V-valves, timed by the laterally-mounted camshaft according to a simple principle, three downdraft carburetors and 80 bhp at 5000 rpm.

Die 2-Liter-Kraftquelle: 6 Zylinder in Reihe, V-förmig hängende Ventile, deren Steuerung über die seitlich liegende Nockenwelle nach einem überaus einfachen Prinzip erfolgt, drei Fallstromvergaser und 80 PS bei 5000/min.

Un coup d'œil sous le capot: six-cylindres en ligne de 2 litres, soupapes suspendues en V commandées par l'arbre à cames latéral selon un principe simple, trois carburateurs inversés et 80 ch à 5000 tr/min.

BMW 335 1939

The "cake" consisting of the large cars with three to four liters cubic capacity was apparently already shared out by autumn 1938. A good half of that sales cake went to the Ford V8, whilst Opel received a large portion thanks to its Admiral. Add Daimler-Benz, Auto Union, Borgward and Stoewer to the picture, and the cake was virtually consumed. A small piece of cream was left over for the 140 bhp, extravagantly expensive Maybach SW38.

BMW aimed for their slice of the luxury cake with a 3.5-liter engine. Shortly after the test department moved from Eisenach to Munich, the six-cylinder motors, long-stroke engines displacing 3485cc, were demonstrating the potential to deliver flagship performance of 90 bhp at 3500 rpm.

A mobile experimental lab, which was basically an extended BMW 326, aroused the interest of the Aldington brothers, owners of BMW's British partner and importer, Frazer-Nash. They presented this 335 prototype, equipped with right-hand drive, a lavish leather interior, and the Frazer-Nash BMW emblem, at the London Motor Show in October 1938.

This classy example of automotive technology stole the show from all its competitors, including the roomy US V8 sedans. Overjoyed, the Aldington brothers were able to keep this car, since BMW had already progressed with the

development of the 335 to such an extent that it was ready for launch in volume production. Some adjustments were made to its physical appearance, since larger wheels made it necessary to widen the fenders.

Everything was ready on 17 February 1939. On that date, BMW presented the 335 as a sedan in Berlin, flanked by a convertible and a coupé. The 335 was praised both by experts and the public alike. With a power-to-weight ratio of 42.77lbs (19.44 kg) per bhp—best value in this category—the newcomer was just as accelerative as it was physically appealing.

Before the War forced BMW to change its priorities, just 415 examples of 335 were built. Their variety was astonishing, particularly among the convertibles, for 24 chassis were built with individual designs, mainly by Autenrieth. The Darmstadt company still managed to supply three coupés in 1945. At that time, Ernst Henne had the only works coupé built using Autenrieth components.

What was probably the most beautiful BMW of all was created by the Swiss chassis artist Herrmann Graber: a jewel of a car with a rear elegantly extended. As was Graber practice, this 335 was painted in stylish black and equipped with green leather seats, so this convertible was a BMW enthusiast's dream. The man for whom this dream came true was Dr Bernhard Knöchlein from Franconia, owner of this unique carriage.

Der „Kuchen" der großen Wagen mit drei bis vier Litern Hubraum scheint im Herbst 1938 verteilt zu sein. Die V8 von Ford machen gut die Hälfte aus, Opel sichert sich mit dem Admiral ein großes Stück, und mit Daimler-Benz, Auto Union, Borgward und Stoewer bleibt vom Kuchen so gut wie nichts übrig – nur ein kleines Sahnestück: der 140 PS starke, sündhaft teure Maybach SW38.

In diese PS-Klasse steigt BMW mit seinem 3,5-Liter-Motor ein. Und man beeilt sich. Schon kurz nach dem Umzug der Versuchsabteilung von Eisenach nach München lassen die Sechszylindertriebwerke, Langhuber mit 3485 cm³, ihr Leistungspotential (90 PS bei 3500/min) erahnen.

Ein rollendes Versuchslabor, im Prinzip ein verlängerter BMW 326, erregt das Interesse der Gebrüder Aldington, Herren über den britischen Partner und Importeur Frazer-Nash. Sie präsentieren diesen 335-Prototypen, versehen mit Rechtslenkung, üppigem Lederinterieur und Frazer-Nash-BMW-Emblem, im Oktober 1938 auf der London Motor Show.

Das edle Einzelstück stiehlt allen Konkurrenten, einschließlich den dicken V8-Limousinen aus den USA, die Show. Zu ihrem größten Glück dürfen die Aldington-Brothers diesen Wagen behalten, da BMW mit anderen Versuchsträgern in der Entwicklung des 335 schon zur Serienreife gelangt ist.

Die Optik erfährt noch Korrekturen, da die größeren Räder Kotflügelverbreiterungen erforderlich machen.

Am 17. Februar 1939 ist es soweit. In Berlin stellt BMW den 335 als Limousine vor, flankiert von einem Cabriolet und einem Coupé. Fachwelt und Publikum sind begeistert. Mit seinem Leistungsgewicht von 19,44 Kilo pro PS – Bestwert in dieser Kategorie – glänzt der Neue mit seiner Technik ebenso wie mit dem schwungvollen Äußeren.

Obwohl nur 415 Wagen gebaut werden, ehe der Krieg auch bei BMW andere Prioritäten setzt, ist die Vielfalt – gerade bei den Cabriolets – erstaunlich. Allein 24 Fahrgestelle werden mit Einzelaufbauten, vornehmlich von Autenrieth, versehen. So liefert das Darmstädter Werk noch 1945 drei Coupés aus. Ernst Henne besitzt zu dieser Zeit das einzige Werks-Coupé, aufgebaut mit Teilen von Autenrieth.

Den wohl schönsten BMW überhaupt kreiert der Schweizer Karosseriekünstler Herrmann Graber: eine automobile Preziose mit elegant nach hinten gestrecktem Heck. Vornehm schwarz lackiert und – wie bei Graber üblich – mit grünen Ledersitzen ausgestattet, ist dieses Cabriolet der Traum eines jeden BMW-Enthusiasten. Für einen BMW-Liebhaber ist er Realität: Dr. Bernhard Knöchlein aus Franken ist der Besitzer des einmaligen Gefährts.

À l'automne 1938, le marché des grosses voitures de trois à quatre litres de cylindrée semble être partagé entre les différents acteurs. Les Ford V8 en accaparent largement la moitié; avec l'Admiral, Opel s'assure elle aussi une bonne part du gâteau tandis que Daimler-Benz, Auto Union, Borgward et Stoewer se partagent les miettes. Sans oublier la cerise sur le gâteau: la Maybach SW38 de 140 ch dont le prix est astronomique.

Sans perdre de temps, BMW se lance sur ce marché avec son moteur de 3,5 litres. En effet, peu après que le service des essais a déménagé d'Eisenach à Munich, les six-cylindres, des moteurs à course longue de 3485 cm³, font une première démonstration de leur potentiel (90 ch à 3500 tr/min).

Une voiture expérimentale, en principe une BMW 326 allongée, suscite l'intérêt des frères Aldington, propriétaires du partenaire et importateur britannique Frazer-Nash. Ils présentent ce prototype 335 doté d'une direction à droite avec une superbe sellerie cuir et un emblème Frazer-Nash-BMW au Motor Show de Londres d'octobre 1938.

Cette somptueuse voiture vole la vedette à toutes ses concurrentes, y compris les grosses berlines V8 américaines. Comblés de bonheur, les frères Aldington peuvent même la conserver, car BMW a pratiquement mené à terme le projet de la 335 avec d'autres prototypes. Quelques modifications

d'ordre esthétique auront lieu, notamment parce que les roues de plus grand diamètre exigent des ailes plus larges.

Le 17 février 1939, le jour J est arrivé. BMW présente la 335 en version berline, ainsi qu'un cabriolet et un coupé, à Berlin. Les professionnels et le grand public sont enthousiastes. Outre son rapport poids/puissance de 19,44 kg par cheval (un record dans cette catégorie), la nouvelle venue est aussi puissante que ses lignes sont attrayantes.

Bien que 415 voitures seulement aient été construites chez BMW avant que la guerre n'éclate, leur diversité est étonnante, notamment pour les cabriolets. Pas moins de 24 châssis ont été habillés d'une carrosserie spéciale, le plus souvent signée Autenrieth. Ainsi l'usine de Darmstadt fournira-t-elle encore trois coupés en 1945. Ernst Henne possède, à cette époque, le seul coupé d'usine qui ait été monté à partir de pièces réalisées chez Autenrieth.

C'est incontestablement le carrossier suisse, Herrmann Graber, qui aura signé la plus belle BMW de tous les temps: un véritable bijou avec une poupe élégante aux lignes étirées vers l'arrière. D'une grande distinction avec sa peinture noire et – comme toujours chez Graber – ses sièges en cuir vert, ce cabriolet est le rêve de tous les amoureux de BMW. Il n'y a qu'une personne pour qui il soit une réalité: le Dr Bernhard Knöchlein, de Franconie, qui est le propriétaire de cette voiture unique dans tous les sens du terme.

In 1939 BMW entered the top end of the market with the launch of the 335. This one-off, built by Herrmann Graber in Switzerland, is in a class of its own. It is now in the possession of a German BMW enthusiast. Tilted slightly towards the back for reasons of space is the long 3.5-liter straight-cylinder power unit, with its two vertical staged dual-register carburetors, developed 90 bhp at 3500 rpm.

Mit dem 335 steigt BMW 1939 in die Oberklasse auf. Eine Klasse für sich ist dieses von Herrmann Graber in der Schweiz gefertige Einzelstück, das sich derzeit im Besitz eines deutschen BMW-Enthusiasten befindet. Aus Platzgründen leicht nach hinten geneigt ist das lange 3,5-Liter-Reihentriebwerk, das mit zwei Vertikal-Doppelregistervergasern 90 PS bei 3500/min leistet.

En 1939, avec la luxueuse 335, BMW monte en gamme. Ce spécimen, carrossé en Suisse par Herrmann Graber, est un modèle unique qui appartient actuellement à un Allemand, fanatique de BMW. Par manque de place, le long 3,5 litres en ligne est légèrement incliné vers l'arrière. Avec ses deux doubles carburateurs verticaux à registre, il développe 90 ch à 3500 tr/min.

The 335 dashboard has an extravagant appearance, with its round instruments set in rounded-off rectangular housing. The steering wheel with four spokes instead of three is a new feature.

Extravagant gibt sich das Armaturenbrett des 335. Als ginge es um die Quadratur des Kreises, wurden die Rundinstrumente in abgerundete Rechteckfassungen gesetzt. Neu ist auch das Lenkrad mit vier anstelle von drei Speichen.

Le tableau de bord de la 335 est extravagant. Comme si l'on avait voulu résoudre la quadrature du cercle, les cadrans circulaires sont insérés dans un encadrement carré aux coins arrondis. Autre nouveauté : le volant possède maintenant quatre branches et non plus trois.

BMW 502 1954

Bonjour Madame, please take your seat behind the ivory colored wheel of the 22,000 marks BMW 502 Cabriolet. The advertising brochure for this noble car with the first German V8 engine of the postwar period totally ignored the man's world; only women, catching the admiring glances of men, were shown in this convertible. Indeed, the steering wheel with column shift gear lever, indicator and horn button appeared to be made for delicate hands. The proper signal effect was produced by two Bosch horns behind the front bumper.

The wooden dashboard had a semi-circular speedo, which went up to 180 kph (112 mph), and the arrangement of the instruments gave a relaxed and light impression. The bias was defintely feminine: little levers and buttons below the Becker "Grand Prix" radio, ready to play In the Mood—Glenn Miller inviting the ladies out into the fresh country air. After all, the top was easy for ladies to operate, as the BMW advertising emphasized.

The purring of the 2.6-liter engine was drowned in the sound of the wind. The engine, with light alloy block, wet cylinder liners and five-bearing crankshaft, was thoroughly modern, a 100 bhp power source. The overhead valves were mounted in pairs to be activated by tappets, push rods and rocker arms. The camshaft was driven by a duplex roller chain.

Altogether, Baur in Stuttgart built a little over 130 convertibles and coupés with the 2.6-liter engine. Autenrieth produced some 50 special bodies for the 502, some of them varying significantly and even diverging from the BMW specifications, which earned them no favors with BMW when it came to placing new orders.

The 501 and the 502, the first large postwar BMW sedans, had the unfortunate distinction of being nicknamed the "Bavarian baroque angels", although the rounded lines of these magnificent powerful cars were extremely well-proportioned and, in aerodynamic terms, created relatively little turbulence.

The BMW 502 entered the annals of automotive history with its status of being the first German eight-cylinder car of the postwar era. It was based on the strong box-section frame with the tubular cross beams of the 501, welded to the solid steel body. The main visual difference from the 501 was the large panoramic rear window.

As the most powerful model in the range, the 502 3.2 Liter Super developed 140 bhp thanks to two dualthroat downdraft carburetors. This enabled the heavyweight carriage to attain road speeds of at least 109 mph (175 kph) and accelerate from 0 to 62 mph (0 to 100 kph) in a reported 14.5 seconds.

Undeniably the V8 with its light alloy engine block and wet cylinder lines marked the beginning of a new era of engine technology. Interestingly, the transmission was not directly flanged on to the engine. This resulted in a shorter secondary propshaft to the rear axle. The steering column was also abbreviated and was activated via a bevel gear, which enabled a steering wheel ratio of 3½ turns lock-to-lock; the turning circle equalled that of today's 7 series.

The low numbers of the 3.2 Liter Super sold, which cost 20,000 marks when it was introduced, might have been acceptable on the grounds of prestige, but they were uneconomical. When all of the 502 3.2-liter cars produced between 1955 and 1964 are added together, the total comes to 3840. Not exactly a profitable business.

Bonjour Madame, nehmen Sie Platz hinter dem elfenbeinfarbenen Steuer des 22000 Mark teuren BMW 502 Cabriolets. Die Werbebroschüre des edlen Wagens mit dem ersten deutschen V8-Motor der Nachkriegszeit negiert die Männerwelt völlig. Nur weibliche Personen, die bewundernden Blicke der Männer erhaschend, führen dieses Cabriolet vor. In der Tat sind das Lenkrad mit Gangschaltung, Blinker und Hupring wie geschaffen für zarte Hände. Für die richtige Signalwirkung sorgen zwei Bosch-Fanfaren hinter der vorderen Stoßstange.

Auch das holzgetäfelte Armaturenbrett mit dem halbkreisförmigen Tacho, dessen Anzeige bis zu 180 km/h reicht, und die Verteilung der Instrumente wirken locker und leicht – feminin eben wie auch die Hebelchen und Knöpfchen unterhalb des „Grand Prix"-Radios von Becker, das gerade In the Mood spielt. Glenn Miller lädt die Damen zu einem Open-Air-Ausflug ein. Schließlich ist das Verdeck für Damen leicht zu betätigen, wie es explizit in der BMW-Werbung steht.

Das Surren des 2,6-Liter-Motors geht im Fahrtwind unter. Eine moderne, 100 PS starke Kraftquelle ist dieses Triebwerk mit Leichtmetallblock, nassen Zylinderlaufbüchsen und fünffach gelagerter Kurbelwelle. Die Ventile hängen parallel und werden durch Stößel, Stoßstangen und Kipphebel betätigt. Über eine Duplex-Rollenkette erfolgt der Nockenwellenantrieb.

Insgesamt baut Baur in Stuttgart etwas mehr als 130 Cabriolets und Coupés mit dem 2,6-Liter-Motor. Autenrieth stellt etwa 50 Sonderaufbauten für den 502 her, teilweise recht verschieden und sogar abweichend von den BMW-Vorgaben – nicht gut für ein „Au revoir" bei der Vergabe von Werksaufträgen.

„Bayerische Barockengel", mit dieser volkstümlichen Bezeichnung müssen die ersten großen Nachkriegslimousinen von BMW – die Typen 501 und 502 – leben, obwohl die Rundungen der stattlichen Karossen durchaus gut proportioniert sind und aerodynamisch gesehen relativ wenig Verwirbelungen bilden.

Als erster deutscher Achtzylinderwagen der Nachkriegszeit geht der BMW 502 in die Annalen der Automobilgeschichte ein. Er basiert auf dem äußerst stabilen Kastenrahmen mit Rohrquerträgern des 501, mit dem die Ganzstahlkarosserie verschweißt ist. Vom 501 unterscheidet ihn optisch die große Panoramaheckscheibe.

Als stärkstes Modell der Serie entwickelt der 502 3,2 Liter Super dank zweier Doppel-Fallstromvergaser 140 PS. Damit kommt das schwere Gefährt auf rund 175 Stundenkilometer.

Dem bayerischen V8 mit seinem Leichtmetallblock und nassen Zylinderlaufbüchsen muss attestiert werden, eine neue Ära der Motorentechnik eingeleitet zu haben. Interessanterweise ist das Getriebe nicht direkt an den Motor angeflanscht. Daraus resultiert eine kürzere Kardanwelle zur Hinterachse. Auch die Lenksäule fällt kurz aus und läuft über ein Kegelrad, das dreieinhalb Lenkraddrehungen ermöglicht. Der Wendekreis entspricht dem der heutigen 7er-Serie.

Die Stückzahlen des 3,2 Liter Super, der bei seiner Einführung knapp 20 000 Mark kostet, liegen in einer Größenordnung, die aus Prestigegründen akzeptabel sein mag, sich aber wirtschaftlich nicht rechnet. Die Summe aller von 1955 bis 1964 gebauten 502 3,2-Liter-Wagen beläuft sich auf gerade mal 3840 Fahrzeuge – ein Zuschussgeschäft!

Bonjour madame, prenez donc place derrière le volant couleur ivoire de la BMW 502 Cabriolet qui coûte 22 000 marks.» Le prospectus de la prestigieuse voiture dotée du premier moteur V8 allemand de l'après-guerre fait totalement abstraction du monde masculin : seules de jolies femmes qui attirent les regards admirateurs des hommes conduisent ce cabriolet. De fait, le volant avec levier de changement de vitesses, clignotants et klaxon intégrés est conçu pour des mains de femmes. Deux klaxons Bosch situés près du pare-chocs avant signalent son arrivée à qui veut l'entendre.

Le tableau de bord en bois avec le tachymètre en demi-cercle gradué jusqu'à 180 km/h et la répartition des instruments évoquent, eux aussi, la décontraction et la légèreté. Tout aussi féminins sont les petits leviers et les boutons sous l'autoradio Becker «Grand Prix» qui joue In the Mood. Glenn Miller invite les dames à un concert en plein air. Enfin, la capote est facile à manier par la gent féminine, comme le vante la publicité BMW.

Le ronflement du moteur de 2,6 litres est couvert par le bruit du vent. Ce moteur d'un bloc en alliage léger, chemises humides et vilebrequin à cinq paliers est moderne et puissant (100 ch). Les soupapes suspendues sont parallèles et actionnées par des coupelles, des poussoirs et des culbuteurs. L'arbre à cames est entraîné par une chaîne à rouleaux duplex.

Au total, Baur, à Stuttgart, construit un peu plus de 130 cabriolets et coupés avec le moteur de 2,6 litres. Autenrieth assemble une cinquantaine de carrosseries spéciales de la 502, certaines divergeant fortement ou parfois même totalement des instructions de BMW, ce qui ne

les plaça pas parmi les favoris au moment de passer les nouvelles commandes.

«L'ange baroque de Bavière» est le surnom qu'arborent les premières grandes berlines d'après-guerre de BMW, les 501 et 502, bien que leurs imposantes carrosseries tout en longueur affichent de belles proportions et soient d'une assez grande finesse aérodynamique.

La BMW 502 entrera dans les annales de l'histoire de l'automobile en tant que première huit-cylindres allemande de l'après-guerre. Elle reprend le châssis à caissons, extrêmement solide, à tubes transversaux de la 501 sur lequel la carrosserie en acier est soudée. Elle se distingue de la 501 par la grande lunette arrière panoramique.

Modèle le plus puissant de la série, la 502 3,2 Liter Super développe 140 ch grâce à ses deux carburateurs double corps inversés. Cela permet à la lourde voiture d'atteindre allègrement les 175 km/h et le 0 à 100 km/h en 14,5 secondes.

On doit reconnaître que le V8 bavarois à bloc en alliage léger et chemises humides inaugure une ère nouvelle dans la technique des moteurs. Détail intéressant, la boîte de vitesses n'est pas accolée directement au moteur. Cela se traduit par un arbre de transmission plus court jusqu'à l'essieu arrière. La colonne de direction, elle aussi, est courte et reliée à une roue conique qui autorise trois tours et demi de butée à butée. Le diamètre de braquage est sensiblement identique à celui de la Série 7 d'aujourd'hui.

Le nombre d'exemplaires de la 3,2 Liter Super, qui coûte près de 20 000 marks, est insuffisant pour en assurer la rentabilité malgré son prestige. De 1955 à 1964, 3840 BMW 502 de 3,2 litres ont été construites au total. Une production déficitaire, donc !

The 15'6" (4.7 meter) long convertible is based on a box-section frame with strong tubular cross members. The chassis and body are welded together. It was available in two and four-door models.

Das 4,7 Meter lange Cabriolet ruht auf einem Kastenrahmen mit starken Rohrquerträgern. Chassis und Aufbau sind miteinander verschweißt. Es ist zwei- oder viertürig lieferbar.

Le cabriolet de 4,7 mètres de long possède un châssis à caissons avec de solides poutres transversales. Le châssis et la carrosserie sont soudés l'un à l'autre. Deux versions sont disponibles : en deux ou en quatre portes.

The V proudly displayed on the trunk of this BMW indicates that this is the first German V8 engine of the postwar era. It developed 100 bhp at 4800 rpm.

Stolz trägt dieser BMW das V-Zeichen auf dem Kofferraumdeckel. Es steht für den ersten deutschen V8-Motor der Nachkriegszeit: Leistung 100 PS bei 4800/min.

Cette BMW arbore fièrement un V sur le couvercle de sa malle. Il trahit la présence du premier moteur V8 allemand de l'après-guerre. Puissance: 100 ch à 4800 tr/min.

Ready to pounce: a rarity and an eyecatcher, this 106 mph (170 kph) coupé was manufactured in small numbers by Baur between 1955 and 1958. The coupé roof with the drop-center rim stops short of the steel disk wheels, giving the tail of the car an elongated appearance.

Rarität und deshalb Blickfang: Das wie zum Sprung geduckt wirkende, 170 km/h schnelle Coupé wird von Baur zwischen 1955 und 1958 in kleiner Stückzahl gefertigt. Das noch vor den Stahlscheibenrädern mit Tiefbettfelge auslaufende Coupé-Dach streckt optisch die Heckpartie mit dem umgreifenden Stoßfänger.

Une rareté qui attire immanquablement le regard : ce coupé qui évoque un félin prêt à bondir est capable d'atteindre les 170 km/h et a été construit en nombre limité par Baur de 1955 à 1958. Le toit du coupé, qui se termine avant les roues comportant des jantes ornées d'un disque d'acier, allonge la partie arrière dont les pare-chocs empiètent sur les ailes.

Stylish and contemporary: the white steering wheel and controls, plus a wood-paneled dashboard and leather seats. The engine is fitted with a dual-throat downdraft carburetor and a large air filter. The firing sequence 1-5-4-8-6-3-7-2 is conspicuous on the cylinder head cover.

Vornehm und zeitgemäß: Lenkrad und Bedienelemente in weiß, holz-getäfeltes Armaturenbrett und Ledersitze. Der Motor ist mit einem Doppel-Fallstromvergaser und großem Luftfilter bestückt, auffallend ist die Zündreihenfolge 1-5-4-8-6-3-7-2 auf dem Zylinderkopfdeckel.

Élégants et dans l'air du temps : volant et manettes de commande de couleur blanche, tableau de bord en bois et sièges en cuir. Le moteur est alimenté par un double carburateur inversé doté d'un grand filtre à air. L'ordre d'allumage – 1-5-4-8-6-3-7-2 – est affiché bien lisiblement sur le couvercle de la culasse.

Every porter's dream, the doors of the BMW 502 open at a flick of the wrist. The interior, with its sofa-like rear seat and sumptuously upholstered front seats, conveys the comfortable atmosphere of a cosy living room.

Davon träumt jeder Portier: Der Einstieg zu diesem BMW lässt sich mit einem Handgriff öffnen. Das Interieur mit der couch-ähnlichen Rückbank und den gut gepolsterten Vordersitzen vermittelt eine behagliche Wohnzimmeratmosphäre.

Le rêve de tout voiturier: les portes de la BMW 502 s'ouvrent en un tour de main. L'habitacle, avec le véritable divan à l'arrière et les fauteuils avant aux épais coussins, lui confère une atmosphère de salon douillet.

The top model of the large type 501 and 502 BMW sedans, popularly known as the "Bavarian baroque angels," was the 3.2 Liter Super. The production version of this heavyweight cruiser had a maximum speed of 109 mph (175 kph), while the tuned engine of the sedan illustrated here was capable of 125 mph (200 kph).

Unter den großen BMW-Limousinen der Typen 501 und 502, volkstümlich „bayerische Barockengel" genannt, ist der 3,2 Liter Super das Spitzenmodell. Die Serienversion des schweren Gefährts kommt auf 175 km/h. Die hier gezeigte Limousine mit „frisiertem" Triebwerk erreicht die 200-km/h-Marke.

Parmi les grandes limousines BMW des séries 501 et 502, surnommées les «anges baroques de Bavière», la 3,2 Liter Super est la plus aboutie. La version de série de cette lourde voiture atteint les 175 km/h. La limousine présentée ici, dont le moteur a été préparé, flirte avec les 200 km/h.

The V8 engine, with its twin Zenith 32 NDIX dual-throat downdraft carburetors, developed 140 bhp at 4800 rpm, while this version is capable of 160 bhp at 5600 rpm. Another non-standard feature of the 3.2 Liter Super is the Nardi sports steering wheel with its wooden rim.

Der V8-Motor leistet mit zwei Doppel-Fallstromvergasern der Marke Zenith 32 NDIX 140 PS bei 4800/min, ist aber in dieser Version auf 160 PS bei 5600/min steigerungsfähig. Ebenfalls nicht Standard beim 3,2 Liter Super: das Nardi-Sportlenkrad mit Holzkranz.

Le moteur V8, avec ses deux doubles carburateurs inversés 32 NDIX de marque Zenith, développe 140 ch à 4800 tr/min, mais atteint, dans cette version, jusqu'à 160 ch à 5600 tr/min. Le volant sport Nardi à couronne de bois n'est pas le volant de série de la 3,2 Liter Super.

BMW Isetta 1955

The "cuddle box," as it was nicknamed, was a miniature car to fall in love with, a bench with a cabin on wheels: ideal for lovers! Desired by vintage car fans not just as an easy-to-park funmobile, this mini car with motorbike engine is officially called "Motocoupé Isetta".

Apart from the engine and numerous changes to details, the Isetta 250 outwardly reflected the prototype of the Italian company Iso, from which BMW bought the license plus bodywork tools. The engine already existed and came from the BMW R25 motorcycle, a four-stroke single-cylinder engine offering 12 bhp.

The original version, with wrap-round window at the rear, hinged windows and opening roof, looked like an aircraft cockpit. In 1956 the Isetta 250 was given a big sister with carlike characteristics, the Isetta 300. The figures show the progression in engine size from 245 to 298 cc. This produced a "powerful" jump in performance: just 1 bhp!

The tiny engine chugged and burbled along behind the passenger seat. The capacity of the petrol tank (3.5 gallons or 13 liters) was as modest as the fuel consumption (43 miles per gallon/5.5 liters per 100 km). The rear wheels, only 20 inches (52 cm) apart, were driven by a short transverse propshaft and a duplex chain bathed in oil. A little lever on the left-side panel was available for the driver to poke about mightily in the four-speed transmission: best operated by double declutching, for there was no synchronization.

Road holding—the Isetta was not a car which easily tipped over—was acceptable, and at 53 mph (85 kph) maximum speed, the Isetta could keep up with the traffic flow. A length of just over six feet (2.35 meters), a front-opening door, room for the beer crate in front of the passenger seat, and the shopping bags in the luggage space, are the attributes of this compact car. The Isetta has for more than 50 years been what the current Smart is still trying to attain.

Expectations were still modest in the 1950s. So an Isetta generally served as a car for all seasons: the drive to work as well as the holiday trip over the Alps to the Italian beaches.

As a classic car, the Isetta is still extremely serviceable in everyday use. That is particularly evident in city traffic and its lack of parking spaces. Have you ever tried parking a Corsa, Twingo or Polo at right angles to the traffic flow? Being able to get out forwards directly onto the pavement was also something appreciated by Prince Leopold of Bavaria on ice cream runs with the children. His Royal Highness, whose Isetta is painted in the Bavarian national colors, would not want to be without this midget of a car in his private family car fleet.

More than half of the 136,367 BMW Isettas built in Munich utilized the smaller engine, a question of the category of driver's license in Germany. The British received the Isetta with just a single rear wheel owing to local laws which allowed three wheelers to be driven on a motorcycle license, with no requirement to take a separate car test.

Die „Knutschkugel", so der Volksmund, ist ein Kleinstwagen zum Lieben und Verlieben, eine Bank mit Kabine auf Rädern – ideal für Liebespaare! Das Mini-Auto mit Motorrad-Motor, von Oldtimer-Fans heute nicht nur als parkraumsparendes Spaßmobil gefragt, trägt die offizielle Bezeichnung „Motocoupé Isetta".

Vom Motor und zahlreichen Detailänderungen abgesehen entspricht die Isetta 250 dem Prototyp der italienischen Firma Iso, von der BMW die Nachbaulizenz samt Presswerkzeugen kauft. Der Motor ist ein alter Bekannter und stammt vom BMW-Motorrad R25, ein Viertakt-Einzylinder mit 12 PS.

Die Ur-Version der Isetta mit hinterer Panoramascheibe, Klappfenstern und Faltdach wirkt wie ein Flugzeug-Cockpit. 1956 bekommt die Isetta 250 eine große Schwester mit automobilen Zügen, die Isetta 300. Die Zahlen drücken den Hubraumzuwachs von 245 auf 298 cm³ aus. Damit verbunden ist ein „gewaltiger" Leistungsschub: 1 PS!

Hinter dem Beifahrersitz tuckert und blubbert das kleine Motörchen. Bescheiden wie der Verbrauch (5,5 Liter) ist auch das Tankvolumen (13 Liter). Der Antrieb auf die nur 52 Zentimeter auseinanderstehenden Hinterräder erfolgt über eine quer liegende kurze Gelenkwelle und eine Duplex-Kette, die sich in einem Ölbad suhlt. Mit einem Hebelchen, links an der Seitenwand, darf in dem 4-Gang-Getriebe kräftig herumgerührt werden – am besten mit Zwischengas, denn eine Synchronisation existiert nicht.

Die Straßenlage – kein Umfaller-Wägelchen – ist passabel, und eine Höchstgeschwindigkeit von 85 Stunden-

kilometern reicht zu jenen Zeiten aus, um im Verkehrsfluss mitzuschwimmen. 2,35 Meter Länge, eine sich nach vorn öffnende Tür, Platz für den Bierkasten vor dem Beifahrersitz und die Einkaufsbeutel auf der Ablage sind Attribute eines gelungenen Kompaktfahrzeugs. Was der Smart noch werden will, ist die Isetta schon seit mehr als 50 Jahren.

In den fünfziger Jahren sind die Ansprüche noch bescheiden, und die Isetta dient in den meisten Fällen als Auto für alle Fälle: für die Fahrt zur Arbeit ebenso wie für die Urlaubstour über die Alpen an Italiens Strände.

Als Oldtimer ist die Isetta noch äußerst alltagstauglich. Das zeigt sich besonders im von Parkplatznöten gebeutelten Großstadtverkehr. Versuchen Sie einmal, mit einem Corsa, Twingo oder Polo quer zur Fahrtrichtung einzuparken! Direkt nach vorn auf den Bürgersteig aussteigen zu können, schätzte auch Leopold Prinz von Bayern, wenn er mit seinen Kindern zur Eisdiele fuhr. Königliche Hoheit, dessen Isetta in den bayerischen Landesfarben lackiert ist, möchten den automobilen Winzling in seinem privaten Wittelsbacher Fuhrpark nicht missen.

Mehr als die Hälfte der 136367 in München gebauten BMW Isetta begnügt sich mit dem Motor mit kleinerem Hubraum – in Deutschland eine Frage der Führerscheinklasse. Die Briten hingegen erhielten die Isetta mit nur einem Hinterrad – ebenfalls eine Frage der Führerscheinklasse, denn in Großbritannien darf man die Dreiräder mit dem Motorradführerschein fahren.

Le «pot de yaourt», comme on l'a vite surnommée, est une micro-voiture au charme de laquelle on succombe aisément – un banc avec cabine sur roues, idéal pour les amoureux! La mini-voiture possède un moteur de moto et n'a pas seulement la cote auprès des amateurs de voitures anciennes. Aussi compacte que ludique, elle porte officiellement le titre de «Motocoupé Isetta».

À part le moteur et plusieurs détails techniques, l'Isetta 250 est, extérieurement, identique au prototype fabriqué par la firme italienne Iso, à laquelle BMW rachète la licence de construction et les presses d'emboutissage. Le moteur existe déjà. Il s'agit de celui de la moto BMW R25, un monocylindre à quatre temps de 12 ch.

La version d'origine à lunette arrière panoramique, vitres entrebâillées et son toit ouvrant ressemble à un cockpit d'avion. En 1956, l'Isetta 250 est rejointe par sa «grande sœur» qui ressemble davantage à une véritable voiture, l'Isetta 300. Les chiffres traduisent la hausse de cylindrée de 245 à 298 cm³, laquelle va de pair avec un bond «gigantesque» en terme de puissance: 1 ch!

Le petit moteur ronronne derrière les sièges passagers. La consommation (5,5 litres) est aussi réduite que le volume du réservoir (13 litres). La transmission aux roues arrière, séparées l'une de l'autre par seulement 52 cm, est assurée par un court cardan transversal et une chaîne double immergée dans l'huile. Un petit levier accolé à la paroi latérale gauche permet de sélectionner les quatre rapports: de préférence avec double débrayage, car il n'existe pas de synchronisation.

La tenue de route est correcte – contrairement aux apparences, la voiturette tient la route – et, avec 85 km/h,

l'Isetta se faufile dans la circulation comme un poisson dans l'eau. 2,35 m de long, une porte ouvrant vers l'avant, de la place pour une caisse de bière devant le siège du passager et les sacs de courses sur la plage arrière: telles sont des caractéristiques de cette voiture compacte. Ce que la Smart veut devenir, l'Isetta l'est déjà depuis plus de cinquante ans.

Dans les années 1950, on est encore modeste et l'Isetta sert, dans la majorité des cas, de voiture de tous les jours: pour se rendre au travail aussi bien que pour partir en vacances au-delà des Alpes, sur les plages d'Italie.

Aussi ancienne soit-elle, l'Isetta a encore parfaitement sa place dans la circulation de tous les jours. On le constate particulièrement dans les grandes agglomérations où l'on cherche souvent en vain une place de stationnement. Essayez donc de vous garer perpendiculairement à la circulation avec une Corsa, une Twingo ou une Polo! Le prince Léopold de Bavière apprécie de pouvoir descendre par la porte avant directement sur le trottoir lorsqu'il emmène ses enfants manger une glace. Son Altesse Royale, dont l'Isetta est peinte aux couleurs nationales de la Bavière, ne se séparerait pour rien au monde de cette minuscule automobile qui appartient à son parc privé.

Plus de la moitié des 136367 BMW Isetta qui ont été construites à Munich se contentent du moteur de plus petite cylindrée, ce qui s'explique par la catégorie de permis de conduire en vigueur en Allemagne. Si les Britanniques ne reçoivent l'Isetta qu'avec une seule roue arrière, c'est parce qu'en Grande-Bretagne, il est possible de conduire un véhicule à trois roues avec un permis moto.

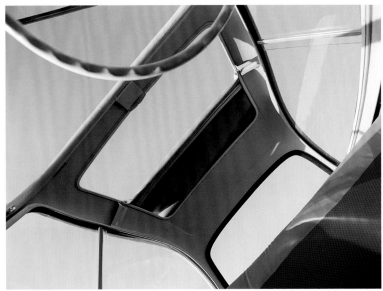

You get into the Isetta with its folding roof from the front. The "dashboard," which consists solely of a speedometer and the ignition lock, swings outwards with the door when it is opened. The gear lever for the four-speed transmission is fitted to the left-hand side wall. Top speed in fourth gear was 53 mph (85 kph), and 0 to 50 mph (0 to 80 kph) took around 40 seconds.

Von vorn erfolgt der Einstieg in die Isetta-Kabine mit Faltdach. Das „Armaturenbrett", lediglich aus Tacho und Zündschloss bestehend, schwenkt mit der Tür mit. Links an der Seitenwand befindet sich der Hebel für die Viergang-Schaltung des Klauengetriebes. Höchstgeschwindigkeit im vierten Gang: 85 Stundenkilometer, Beschleunigung auf 80 Sachen in rund 40 Sekunden!

L'accès à la cabine de l'Isetta à toit ouvrant s'effectue par l'avant. Le «tableau de bord», qui se compose uniquement d'un tachymètre et d'une serrure pour la clé de contact, est solidaire de la porte. À gauche, contre la paroi latérale, se trouve le levier de la boîte à quatre vitesses à crabots. Vitesse maximale en quatrième : 85 km/h, accélération de 0 à 80 km/h en 40 secondes environ.

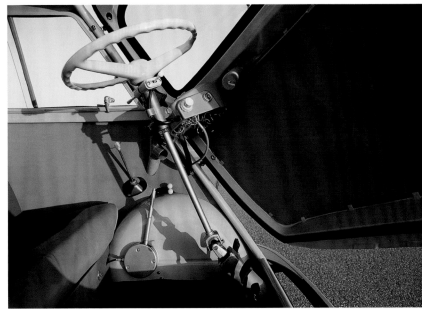

Originally the Isetta had a glass dome, but in 1956 this was replaced by the roof design illustrated, with its sliding windows. The car was also fitted at that time with freestanding headlamps and a modified tail. The "trunk" was externally mounted. The tiny four-stroke, single-cylinder, forced-air-cooled engine in the Isetta 300 developed 13 bhp.

Anfänglich besaß die Isetta noch eine Glaskuppel, die 1956 diesem Dachaufbau mit Schiebefenstern wich. Außerdem erhielt der Wagen freistehende Scheinwerfer und ein modifiziertes Heck. Der „Kofferraum" liegt extern. Das von Gebläseluft gekühlte Viertakt-Einzylindermotörchen der Isetta 300 liefert 13 PS.

À l'origine, l'Isetta possédait un toit en verre qui a fait place, en 1956, à ce type de toit ouvrant coulissant. En outre, la voiture a été dotée de phares proéminents et son arrière a été modifié. Le «coffre» se trouve à l'extérieur. Sous le capot de l'Isetta 300, le petit monocylindre à quatre temps refroidi par turbine délivre 13 ch.

BMW 507 1955

Otto von Schlitz was hereditary marshal of the archdiocese of Fulda in the year 1100. He was also the ancestor of the counts von Schlitz, known as von Goertz, a family who collected assorted honors for more than 800 years. Albrecht Count Goertz added a colorful image to the family history, for he had been resident in the US since 1936 and became a leading international design guru. For BMW's 507, first postwar pure sports car from BMW, creator Goertz built himself a monument.

Externally, the 507 would do honor to any Ferrari: an excitingly beautiful, harmoniously curved body line with an aggressive interpretation of the BMW kidney trademark styling cues, transformed into an appearance like the mouth of a shark. The aluminum skin of the car barely covers its technical elements, so there is nothing surplus to requirements. A small but unmistakable styling element is the grid with cooling slits and BMW symbol on the front wings. This only partly fulfils its task, since it barely covers the wheel.

A strong box frame, which offered excellent protection against side impacts, was the foundation of the Goertz-designed BMWs 507 and 503. The refined V8 engine with two Zenith dual-throat downdraft carburetors produced 150 bhp. Depending on the rear axle transmission ratio, this brought 123 to 138 mph (196 to 220 kph).

Space at the rear of the vehicle was constricted, containing a 29-gallon (110-liter) tank behind the seats. Probably for safety reasons, this large amount of fuel directly behind the backs of the passengers in the car was reduced to a 17-gallon (65-liter) tank surrounding the spare wheel.

"A car to set the pulse racing" was the contemporary comment in the influential magazine *ADAC-Motorwelt* (published by the German automobile club, ADAC). This referred primarily to the looks of the 507, but also covered the small difference between the unladen and the permitted maximum weight—a mere 375 lbs (170 kg). A well-built member of the affluent society with a little luggage was thus forced to find a "light" lady to take along for driving pleasure *à deux* in the 507.

Acceleration from 0 to 62 mph (100 kph), with a driver of normal weight at the wheel, of between 11 and 11.5 seconds is appropriate for a sports car of this caliber. Disk brakes, however, were only enjoyed by the last of the total 254 cars built.

The dream car of the 1950s—Elvis had a 507, too—and on the most wanted lists of classic car freaks today, the 507 could be supplied with a properly fitted hardtop. It could compare with the Mercedes 300 SL, for the latter was just a few marks cheaper in 1956.

A few details can be a nuisance in the 507. The distance of the steering column to the driver can be adjusted telescopically, but it can only be reduced: a blessing for people with short arms, but a nuisance for anyone of elongated build. The arrangement of various push buttons and levers on the dashboard is also far from ergonomic. A small windshield-wiped field and little possibility of adjusting the seats, are items one would put up with—if only one could count oneself among those happy people who can proudly call themselves BMW 507 owners.

Otto von Schlitz, um 1100 Erbmarschall des Hochstiftes Fulda, ist Urahn der Herren von Schlitz, genannt von Goertz, die 800 Jahre lang Meriten aller Art eingeheimst haben. Albrecht Graf Goertz fügt der Familiengeschichte eine farbige Metapher hinzu. Er lebt seit 1936 in den USA und ist Designer. Mit dem ersten Nachkriegssportwagen von BMW, dem 507, setzt sich Goertz ein Denkmal.

Das Äußere des 507 würde jedem Ferrari zu Ehre gereichen: eine aufregend schöne, harmonisch geschwungene Karosserielinie mit einer aggressiv wirkenden Interpretation der BMW-Niere, die eher einem Haifischmaul gleicht. Die Aluminiumschale des Wagens bedeckt so gerade den technischen Kern. Es gibt also keinerlei unnötige Überhänge. Kleines, aber unverwechselbares Stylingelement sind die Gitter mit Kühlschlitzen und BMW-Emblem in den vorderen Kotflügeln. Diese werden ihrer Bestimmung nur teilweise gerecht, da sie das Rad kaum abdecken.

Ein stabiler Kastenrahmen, der viel Schutz gegen seitlichen Aufprall bietet, ist das tragende Element der Goertz-Wagen 507 und 503. 150 PS leistet der kultivierte V8-Motor mit zwei Doppel-Fallstromvergasern von Zenith. Je nach Hinterachsübersetzung resultieren daraus 196 bis 220 Stundenkilometer.

Recht eng geht es im Fahrzeugheck zu, das zunächst ein 110-Liter-Tank hinter den Sitzen füllt. Wohl aus Sicherheitsgründen wird die große Benzinmenge direkt im Rücken der Fahrzeuginsassen zugunsten eines 65-Liter-Tanks, der das Reserverad umschließt, reduziert.

„Ein Herzklopfen erzeugendes Fahrzeug" – dieses eher auf die Optik des 507 bezogene zeitgenössische Statement der *ADAC-Motorwelt* gilt auch für die geringe Differenz zwischen Leer- und zulässigem Gesamtgewicht. Es sind lediglich 170 Kilo. Ein schwergewichtiger Wohlstandsbürger mit etwas Gepäck ist für das Fahrvergnügen zu zweit im 507 quasi gezwungen, eine zarte Frau mitzunehmen.

Die Beschleunigung von 0 auf 100 Stundenkilometer – mit einem normalgewichtigen Menschen am Steuer – zwischen 11 und 11,5 Sekunden, ist angemessen für einen Sportwagen dieses Kalibers. In den Genuss von Scheibenbremsen kommen allerdings nur die letzten der insgesamt 254 gebauten Wagen.

Das Traumauto der fünfziger Jahre (auch Elvis hatte einen 507) und der Oldtimer-Freaks von heute, lieferbar mit einem gelungenen und gut angepassten Hardtop, muss den Vergleich mit dem Mercedes 300 SL nicht scheuen, denn dieser ist 1956 sogar ein paar Mark billiger.

Beim 507 stören lediglich einige Details. So lässt sich der Abstand des Lenkrads zum Fahrer teleskopisch verstellen, aber nur in einem Bereich, der Menschen mit kurzen Armen entgegenkommt, während Fahrer mit großer „Reichweite" keine optimale Sitzposition finden. Auch die Anordnung diverser Zugknöpfe und Hebel des Armaturenbretts ist nicht glücklich gelöst. Kleines Wischerfeld und wenig Sitzverstellmöglichkeiten sind freilich Dinge, an die man sich gewöhnen könnte, würde man zu den Glücklichen gehören, die sich stolz Besitzer eines BMW 507 nennen dürfen.

Otto von Schlitz, qui dirigeait le diocèse de Fulda vers 1100, est l'ancêtre des seigneurs von Schlitz, nommés von Goertz, qui ont accumulé les honneurs en tout genre pendant plus de huit siècles. Le comte Albrecht von Goertz ajoute à la saga de la famille sa touche personnelle: depuis 1936, il vit aux États-Unis où il est designer. Avec le lancement de la première BMW de sport de l'après-guerre, la 507, son créateur, von Goertz, se construit lui-même sa réputation.

Les lignes de la 507 sont dignes d'une Ferrari: une carrosserie de toute beauté, aux galbes harmonieux et une interprétation agressive des naseaux de BMW, une proue qui ressemble plutôt à une gueule de requin. La carrosserie en aluminium de la voiture recouvre à peine sa mécanique. Il n'y a donc pas de superflu. Un élément de style, minuscule mais caractéristique, est la grille située dans l'aile avant, avec des fentes d'aération latérales et l'emblème BMW. Cette aile avant ne remplit d'ailleurs sa tâche qu'à moitié puisqu'elle couvre à peine la roue.

Un solide cadre à caissons, qui offre une bonne protection contre les collisions latérales, est «l'épine dorsale» des 507 et 503 de Goertz. Le velouté V8, à double carburateur inversé Zenith, développe 150 ch. Selon le rapport de pont, la vitesse de pointe oscille entre 196 et 220 km/h.

L'espace est plutôt compté à l'arrière, où un réservoir de 110 litres occupe beaucoup de place. Par sécurité, l'importante quantité d'essence logée directement dans le dos des passagers est réduite et va être stockée dans un réservoir de 65 litres qui encercle la roue de secours.

«Une voiture qui vous donne des battements au cœur»: ce constat de la revue *ADAC-Motorwelt* de cette époque, qui fait surtout allusion à l'esthétique de la 507, vaut aussi pour la faible différence entre le poids à vide et le poids total autorisé – seulement 170 kg! Pour le plaisir de conduire à deux en 507, tout conducteur aisé avec un tant soit peu d'embonpoint et quelques bagages est déjà contraint à emmener avec lui un passager «léger».

Les accélérations de 0 à 100 km/h (avec un conducteur de poids normal au volant) sont dignes d'une voiture de sport de ce calibre puisqu'elles se situent entre 11 et 11,5 secondes. Seules les dernières voitures construites, sur 254 au total, bénéficieront de freins à disques.

La voiture de rêve des années 1950 (Elvis Presley avait lui aussi une 507) et des collectionneurs, qui était livrable avec un *hard-top* esthétique et bien étanche, a toujours été comparée à la Mercedes 300 SL qui, en 1956, coûte même quelques marks de moins.

Seuls quelques détails peuvent être reprochés à la 507. La distance qui sépare la colonne de direction – télescopique – du conducteur est réglable, mais elle peut seulement être diminuée: ce qui est une aubaine pour ceux qui ont de petits bras et un véritable casse-tête pour ceux qui sont dotés de long bras. De même, l'agencement des divers boutons et leviers sur le tableau de bord n'est pas parfaitement ergonomique. Un champ d'action réduit des essuie-glace sur le pare-brise et de faibles possibilités de réglage des sièges sont des détails auxquels on peut s'habituer et auxquels on s'habituerait volontiers – à condition de figurer parmi les heureux propriétaires d'une BMW 507.

The BMW 507, with its harmoniously flowing lines and aggressive version of the BMW kidney grill, is one of Count Goertz's most beautiful designs.

Sicherlich ist der BMW 507 mit seiner harmonisch geschwungenen Karosserielinie einerseits und der aggressiv wirkenden Interpretation der BMW-Niere andererseits eines der schönsten Designs des Grafen Goertz.

La BMW 507, avec sa carrosserie aux galbes élégants d'une part, et l'interprétation quelque peu agressive des naseaux de BMW d'autre part, est sans aucun doute l'une des plus belles réussites du comte von Goertz.

The sports steering wheel later added to the 507 cockpit by the German Nardi importer did nothing to detract from the roadster feeling, while the 4.50 E × 16 steel rims also contributed to the motor sport appearance.

Das nachträglich dem 507-Cockpit zugestandene Sportlenkrad des deutschen Nardi-Importeurs stört das Roadster-Feeling keineswegs. Motorsport-Optik auch bei den 4,50 E × 16 Stahlfelgen.

Le volant sport, concédé ultérieurement au cockpit de la 507 par l'importateur allemand Nardi, ne porte en aucun cas préjudice à son style roadster. Les jantes en acier de 4,50 E × 16 laissent aussi flotter un parfum de compétition.

This classic V8 engine with its light alloy block and twin dual-throat downdraft carburetors developed 150 bhp, rising to 165 bhp in the US version. This allowed top speeds of up to 138 mph (220 kph), depending on the rear axle ratio.

150 PS, in der US-Ausführung sogar 165 PS, leistet der klassische V8-Motor mit einem Leichtmetallblock und zwei Doppel-Fallstromvergasern. Damit sind je nach Hinterachsübersetzung Geschwindigkeiten von bis zu 220 Stundenkilometern möglich.

Le moteur V8 classique à bloc en alliage léger et deux carburateurs double corps inversés développe 150 ch et même 165 ch dans sa version américaine. Il permet de rouler, selon le rapport de pont, jusqu'à 220 km/h.

BMW 503 1955

As well as the 507, Count Albrecht Goertz designed "an elegant luxury travel sports car from the stable of the large BMW eight-cylinder cars" (factory jargon). This design, outstanding owing to its long bonnet and the projecting BMW kidney grill at the front, made its debut as the 503 at the Frankfurt Motor Show during September 1955.

The engine, a light alloy V8 with wet cylinder liners and a separate transmission which was not directly bolted on to the engine, was taken from the 502. The same applied to the descriptive full protection frame. It was not until December 1957 that the transmission, which was situated under the front seats, was bolted to the engine. Then the gear change on the steering column was replaced with a lever on the transmission tunnel.

Convertible and coupé are designed for four passengers, always assuming that those in the rear seats are not too large. "The interior is designed for sporty but comfortable driving," as the 503 brochure put it. Today such coupés are described as having 2+2 seating, offering less accomodation in the rear than a 4-seater.

The 503 convertible folding mechanism was sophisticated. It was the first German automobile to have an electrically operated power-top; cranking the side windows up and down is also completed by electric motors.

The aluminum body, captivating with its neat, snugly-fitting manufacture, limited the weight of the car to 3300 lbs (1500 kg). At this curb weight, 140 bhp manage to produce acceleration of 13 seconds from 0 to 62mph (100 kph) and a top speed of 119mph (190 kph). The petrol tank, situated behind the rear axle and with a space for the spare wheel, held 20 gallons (75 liters), sufficient for approximately 280 miles (450 km).

Like the 507, the last of the 503s enjoyed disk brakes on the front wheels. Also like the 507, the price—29,500 marks for the convertible in 1956—was within range of the Mercedes 300 SL. Only just over 400 of these noble 503 beasts, which needed to be subsidized by BMW, found a buyer. The 503 filled a market niche which was too small to make it economically viable. Today's owners of these flamboyant rarities therefore have all the more reasons to rub their hands together in glee.

Neben dem 507 entwirft Albrecht Graf Goertz „einen eleganten Reisesportwagen aus der Reihe der großen BMW-Achtzylinder" (Werks-Jargon). Dieses Fahrzeug, das durch seine lange Motorhaube und die wulstig nach vorn stehenden BMW-Nieren auffällt, wird als 503 auf der Frankfurter Automobilausstellung im September 1955 vorgestellt.

Das Triebwerk, ein V8 aus Leichtmetall mit nassen Zylinderlaufbüchsen und ein separates, nicht an den Motor angeflanschtes Getriebe, werden aus dem 502 übernommen, ebenso der so genannte Vollschutzrahmen. Erst im Dezember 1957 wird das unter den Vordersitzen liegende Getriebe mit dem Motor verblockt, die Lenkradschaltung von einem Hebel auf dem Kardantunnel abgelöst.

Cabriolet und Coupé sind für vier Passagiere ausgelegt, vorausgesetzt, dass die im Fond sitzenden von kleinerem Wuchs sind. „Der Innenraum ist auf sportliche wie bequeme Fahrweise ausgelegt", so der 503-Prospekt. Aus damaliger Sicht ist dieser Beschreibung nichts hinzuzufügen. Bequem ist sicherlich der Faltmechanismus des Cabrioletverdecks, der erstmalig bei einem deutschen Auto elektrisch betätigt

wird, und auch die Kurbelarbeit zum Heben und Senken der Seitenscheiben übernehmen Elektromotoren.

Dank der Aluminiumkarosserie, die durch ihre saubere und passgenaue Fertigung besticht, kann das Wagengewicht auf 1500 Kilo beschränkt werden. Bei diesem Gewicht erreichen die 140 PS eine Beschleunigung von 0 auf 100 Stundenkilometer in 13 Sekunden und eine Höchstgeschwindigkeit von 190 Stundenkilometern. Der hinter der Hinterachse liegende und mit einer Ausbuchtung für das Reserverad versehene Kraftstofftank fasst 75 Liter. Das genügt für eine Strecke von rund 450 Kilometern.

Wie beim 507 kommen die letzten 503 noch in den Genuss von Scheibenbremsen an den Vorderrädern. Und wie beim 507 rangiert der Preis – 29500 Mark für das Cabriolet 1956 – im Bereich dessen, was man für einen Mercedes 300 SL ausgeben muss. Nur etwas mehr als 400 dieser Edelstücke, bei denen BMW sogar noch ein paar Mark zuschießen muss, finden ihre Käufer. Der 503 füllt eine Marktnische, die zu klein für eine wirtschaftlich rentable Fertigung ist. Umso mehr reiben sich heute die Besitzer dieser extravaganten Rarität die Hände.

Outre la 507, le comte Albrecht von Goertz dessine « une élégante voiture de sport de voyage pour la gamme des grosses BMW huit-cylindres » (dans le jargon de l'usine). Cette voiture qui surprend par son long capot moteur et les proéminents naseaux BMW est présentée sous le nom de 503 au Salon de l'automobile de Francfort en septembre 1955.

Le moteur, un V8 en alliage léger à chemises humides et avec boîte de vitesses séparée non accolée au bloc, est repris de la 502, tout comme le cadre à protection intégrale. Il faudra attendre décembre 1957 pour que la boîte de vitesses placée sous le siège avant rejoigne le moteur et que le sélecteur au volant soit remplacé par un levier sur le tunnel de transmission.

Le cabriolet et le coupé sont prévus pour quatre passagers à condition que les passagers arrière soient de petite taille. « L'habitacle est conçu pour un style de conduite sportif et décontracté », peut-on lire dans le prospectus qui vante la 503.

La commande de la capote, pour la première fois sur une voiture allemande, est électrique et les vitres latérales peuvent être descendues ou remontées grâce à des moteurs électriques.

Avec sa carrosserie en aluminium qui séduit par sa finition et l'exactitude de son montage, le poids de la voiture peut être limité à 1500 kg. Avec un tel poids, les 140 ch permettent des accélérations de 0 à 100 km/h en 13 secondes et une vitesse de pointe de 190 km/h. Le réservoir d'essence placé derrière l'essieu arrière, avec un espace pour la roue de secours, offre une capacité de 75 litres – assez pour parcourir quelque 450 km.

Comme pour la 507, la dernière 503 est équipée, elle aussi, de freins à disques sur les roues avant. Et, comme pour la 507, le prix – 29500 marks pour le cabriolet de 1956 – concurrence celui de la Mercedes 300 SL. Un peu plus de 400 exemplaires de ces superbes voitures, qui coûtent même quelques marks à BMW, trouvent preneur. La 503 se situe sur un marché de niche trop étroit pour être rentable. Aujourd'hui, les propriétaires de cette voiture extravagante s'en frottent d'autant plus les mains.

Designed as a "touring sports car" by the designer and
long-time resident of New York, Albrecht Count Goertz,
the BMW 503 was ready to go on sale in May 1956. Only
273 coupés and 139 convertibles were sold in four years.

Als „Reisesportwagen" von dem lange Zeit in New York
lebenden Designer Albrecht Graf Goertz entworfen,
wird der BMW 503 ab Mai 1956 ausgeliefert. Nur 273
Coupés und 139 Cabriolets werden in vier Jahren gebaut.

Conçue à la fois comme une voiture de sport et de
grand tourisme par le designer allemand Albrecht von
Goertz, qui a longtemps vécu à New York, la BMW 503
est commercialisée en mai 1956. Seulement 273 coupés
et 139 cabriolets seront fabriqués en quatre ans.

The convertible had a top speed of 118 mph (190 kph). Its top was electrically operated—a first among German cars. With a showroom price of just under 30,000 marks in 1956, it was, however, the preserve of an elite class of purchaser.

Das Cabriolet, dessen Verdeck elektrisch betätigt werden kann – übrigens erstmals bei einem deutschen Auto –, erreicht 190 Stundenkilometer. Es ist aber 1956 mit einem Neupreis von knapp 30 000 Mark einer elitären Käuferschicht vorbehalten.

Le cabriolet, dont la capote peut être équipée d'une commande électrique – ce qui est une première sur une voiture allemande –, atteint les 190 km/h. Mais, avec un prix proche de 30 000 marks en 1956, il ne sera à la portée que d'une élite.

There was room for larger pieces of luggage, too, in the rear of the 503. The spare wheel and petrol tank were harmoniously positioned under the floor of the trunk. The tank had been specially shaped to accommodate the wheel. In order to ensure that the round instruments could be seen better, the four spokes of the steering wheel had to move out of the way. Electrically operated windows and adjustable backrests meant additional controls. The V8 engine with two dual-throat downdraft carburetors produced 140 bhp.

Auch größere Gepäckstücke finden im Heck des 503 Platz. Unter dem Kofferraumboden liegen das Reserverad und der Tank einträchtig nebeneinander. Der Tank hat eigens für den Reifen eine Aussparung. Zur besseren visuellen Erfassung der Rundinstrumente müssen die vier Lenkradspeichen zur Seite weichen. Ein elektrischer Fensterheber und die Sitzlehnenverstellung ergänzen die Vielfalt der Bedienelemente. Der V8 mit zwei Doppel-Fallstromvergasern produziert 140 PS.

Le coffre de la 503 ne craint pas les bagages encombrants. Sous son plancher se trouvent la roue de secours et le réservoir. La forme du réservoir a été spécialement conçue pour recevoir la roue. Il a fallu déplacer les quatre branches du volant pour que les cadrans circulaires soient dans le champ de vision du conducteur. Des lève-vitres électriques et des dossiers de siège réglables complètent les multiples manettes de commande. Le moteur V8 à deux carburateurs double corps inversés développe 140 ch.

Wolfgang Denzel, a technically-gifted man who was also a competent racing driver, was hungry for success as BMW's general importer for Austria. He dreamt of a really small, rear-engined BMW car for the middle class. What was so beautiful about the BMW 600 anyway? It was nothing more than a four-seater Isetta.

Denzel submitted his ideas to BMW in November 1957. The ideas received approval from the factory and, since the draft was conscientiously crafted, Denzel was asked that he should create a prototype with the Turin designer Michelotti. A few months later, the beautiful BMW 700 materialized. At the 1959 Frankfurt Motor Show, the 700 made its debut either as the coupé or a two-door sedan.

It caused a sensation and volume production was implemented immediately. The sedan, a value-for-money car designed for use by anyone, achieved a sales total which surpassed 60,000 units in the period 1959–62. Out of almost 30,000 coupés (1959–64), there were 9436 sport and CS versions alone.

The 700 coupé participated in motor racing on an impressively widespread basis. In 1959/60 alone, it had the distinction of winning 67 victories and being second 41 times. Drivers such as Hans Stuck senior (German champion at the age of 60) managed to keep competitors with larger engines at bay with the coupé. A further tuned 700 RS offered 70 bhp and a 125 mph (200 kph) top speed which put an end to the Fiat Abarth's domination of the winning positions in the smallest

capacity classes. No less than 19 of these BMW motor racing open-top designs took victories, mainly at the great hill-climbing events such as Trento-Bondone, Gaisberg, Schauinsland and Roßfeld.

Meanwhile the sedan received a larger interior, achieved by adding 6¼ inches (16 cm) to the wheelbase. BMW extended the rear to accommodate a four-cylinder engine, intended to vault the 700 (with an LS badge suffix) further into the middle class. The overall addition of 12½ inches (32 cm) was of particular benefit to the rear passengers, because the planned change of engine was abandoned, resulting in a cavity between the boxer engine and rear bulkhead. A "workshop-friendly" layout improved access.

However, the proven two-cylinder's power was increased from 30 to 32 bhp in February 1963, although this had little impact on the car's driving performance. The trunk in the nose of the car was divided between the spare wheel—an additional crumple zone behind the bumper—and a 7.9-gallon (30-liter) tank, leaving just enough room for one large suitcase.

The combination of a pleasing interior—an effective dashboard layout with a 2-spoke steering wheel offering a good grip, a sporty gearshift and quality seats—and a tasteful exterior made this car a hit with customers. Great roadholding, 75 mph (120 kph) top speed and reasonable fuel consumption (31.5 miles per gallon of premium/7.5 liters per 100 km) were all contributing factors to its sales success. In three years some 92,416 LS sedans, in addition to 1730 LS coupés, were built.

Wolfgang Denzel – technisch begabt, als Rennfahrer ganz passabel und als BMW-Generalimporteur für Österreich erfolgshungrig – träumt von einem richtigen kleinen BMW-Mittelklassewagen mit Heckmotor. Was ist denn schon der BMW 600? Doch nicht mehr als eine viersitzige Isetta!

Denzel bringt seine eigenen Vorstellungen zu Papier und präsentiert diese im November 1957 im Werk. Den Münchnern ist es recht, und da die Entwürfe Hand und Fuß haben, schlagen sie Denzel vor, zusammen mit dem Turiner Designer Michelotti einen Prototypen auf die Räder zu stellen. Ein bildhübscher Wagen, der BMW 700, entsteht innerhalb weniger Monate. Auf der Frankfurter Automobilausstellung 1959 feiert der 700 als Coupé und zweitürige Limousine Premiere.

Die Resonanz ist gewaltig, und die Serienproduktion läuft sofort an. Die Limousine, ein preiswertes Gefährt für jedermann, wird von 1959 bis 1962 in mehr als 60 000 Einheiten verkauft. Auf knapp 30 000 Coupés (1959–64) kommen allein 9436 Sport- und CS-Ausführungen. Motorsport auf breiter Ebene wird eindrucksvoll praktiziert. Allein 1959/60 feiert das Coupé 67 Siege und 41 zweite Plätze. Fahrer wie Hans Stuck – mit 60 Jahren noch deutscher Meister – hängen mit dem Coupé sogar hubraumstärkere Konkurrenten ab, und mit dem Erscheinen des 700 RS, der mit 70 PS eine Spitzengeschwindigkeit von 200 Stundenkilometern erreicht, bricht BMW in die Domäne der siegesgewohnten

BMW 700 1959

Fiat Abarth ein. Gleich 19 dieser BMW-Rennsport-Spider werden auf die Siegerstraßen, vornehmlich bei großen Bergpreisen wie Trento-Bondone, Gaisberg, Schauinsland und Roßfeld, geschickt.

Mehr Innenraum durch 16 Zentimeter längeren Radstand sowie ein verlängertes Heck zur Aufnahme eines Vierzylindertriebwerks sollen den 700 mit dem Zusatz „LS" in die Mittelklasse heben. Die Gesamtverlängerung von 32 Zentimetern kommt vornehmlich den Fondpassagieren zugute, denn die vorgesehene Ummotorisierung erweist sich als Flop, so dass zwischen Boxermotor und Heckschürze ein Hohlraum entsteht. „Werkstattfreundlich" nennt man das.

Immerhin wird im Februar 1963 die Potenz des Zweizylinders von 30 auf 32 PS angehoben, was sich in den Fahrleistungen allerdings kaum bemerkbar macht. Den Kofferraum im Wagenbug teilen sich das Reserverad – als zusätzliche Knautschzone hinter dem Stoßfänger –, ein 30-Liter-Tank und obendrauf das restliche Volumen für einen großen Koffer.

Ein gefälliges Interieur – ein übersichtliches Armaturenbrett mit griffigem Zweispeichenlenkrad, sportlichem Schaltknüppel und guten Sitzen – sowie das ansprechende Äußere treffen den Geschmack der Kunden. Die ordentliche Straßenlage, eine Spitzengeschwindigkeit von 120 Stundenkilometern und ein vernünftiger Verbrauch (7,5 Liter Super) tragen zum Verkaufserfolg bei. In drei Jahren werden 92416 LS-Limousinen gebaut, zu denen sich noch 1730 LS-Coupés gesellen.

Wolfgang Denzel, génie de la mécanique, bon pilote de course et, en tant qu'importateur exclusif de BMW pour l'Autriche, affamé de succès, rêve d'une vraie petite BMW du segment intermédiaire à moteur arrière. Et il voulait quelque chose de plus beau qu'une BMW 600, qui n'était finalement qu'une Isetta à quatre places.

Denzel réalise quelques croquis de son concept qu'il présente en novembre 1957 à l'usine. Celui-ci est du goût des Munichois et, comme ses plans semblent prometteurs, ils proposent à Denzel de réaliser un prototype conjointement avec le styliste turinois Michelotti. Une très jolie petite voiture, la BMW 700, naît quelques mois plus tard. Son lancement en tant que coupé et berline à deux portes aura lieu au Salon de l'automobile de Francfort de 1959.

Le succès est immense et la production en série débute immédiatement. La berline, un engin à la portée de tous, est produite à plus de 60000 exemplaires de 1959 à 1962. Sur près de 30000 coupés (fabriqués de 1959 à 1964), pas moins de 9436 sont des versions sport et CS. Elles démocratisent en quelque sorte la compétition automobile. Rien qu'en 1959–1960, le coupé engrange 67 victoires et décroche 41 fois la deuxième place. Des pilotes comme Hans Stuck (encore champion d'Allemagne à 60 ans) surclassent même des concurrentes de plus forte cylindrée avec le coupé qui bat en brèche les Fiat Abarth, pourtant abonnées à la victoire jusqu'à l'apparition de la 700 RS (70 ch, 200 km/h en vitesse de pointe). Pas moins de 19 de ces Spider de compétition

BMW remportent des victoires, notamment lors des Grands Prix qui ont lieu sur des routes de montagne comme Trento-Bondone, Gaisberg, Schauinsland et Rossfeld.

Un empattement allongé de 16 cm ainsi qu'une poupe plus longue pour recevoir un moteur à quatre cylindres ont pour objectif de faire accéder la 700, désormais qualifiée de «LS», au segment intermédiaire. Cet allongement total de 32 cm bénéficie en premier lieu aux passagers de la banquette arrière, car le changement de motorisation est un échec. Le boxer original est si petit qu'il n'emplit même pas le compartiment moteur et évite ainsi des contorsions aux mécaniciens lors des révisions.

En février 1963, le deux-cylindres voit sa puissance passer de 30 à 32 ch, ce qui ne change toutefois pratiquement rien à ses performances. La roue de secours – avec un espace supplémentaire prévu derrière le pare-chocs –, un réservoir de 30 litres et assez d'espace pour une grosse valise se partagent le volume du coffre à l'avant.

Un habitacle séduisant (avec un tableau de bord bien agencé et un volant à deux branches, un levier de changement de vitesses sportif au centre et de bons sièges) ainsi que des lignes très réussies sont tout à fait du goût de la clientèle. Une tenue de route correcte, une vitesse de pointe de 120 km/h et une consommation raisonnable (7,5 litres de super aux 100 km) contribuent à son succès commercial. En trois ans, 92416 berlines LS sont construites, auxquelles s'ajoutent encore 1730 coupés LS.

Sober and functional: the cockpit of the 700 LS with its two large round instruments—speedo and clock. The two-cylinder boxer engine with one downdraft carburetor left a lot of space in the rear. The 30 bhp unit was given an additional 2 bhp of performance in 1963.

Nüchtern und funktionell ist das Cockpit des 700 LS mit zwei großen Rundinstrumenten – Tacho und Uhr. Der Zweizylinder-Boxermotor mit einem Fallstromvergaser lässt im Heck viel Platz. 1963 erhält der 30-PS-Triebling einen Leistungszuwachs von 2 PS.

Sobre et fonctionnel : le cockpit de la 700 LS avec ses deux grands cadrans – le tachymètre et l'horloge. Le bicylindre plat à carburateur inversé laisse beaucoup d'espace à l'arrière. En 1963, le petit moteur de 30 ch voit sa puissance augmenter de 2 ch.

When the attractive BMW 700 coupé and sedan were shown at the Frankfurt Motor Show in the autumn of 1959, the response was tremendous. BMW received sufficient advance orders for two whole production years.

Bei der Präsentation des attraktiven BMW 700 Coupé samt Limousine auf der Frankfurter Automobilausstellung im Herbst 1959 ist die Resonanz gewaltig. BMW erhält Vorbestellungen für zwei komplette Produktionsjahre.

Lors de la présentation de l'attrayante BMW 700 coupé aux côtés de la berline, au Salon de l'automobile de Francfort de l'automne 1959, le succès est au rendez-vous. BMW enregistre des commandes correspondant à deux années complètes de production.

BMW 1500 1961

Many motorists waited—the BMW drivers and owners amongst them with true longing—for BMW to build a middle-class car. Suddenly it appeared at the Frankfurt Motor Show in September 1961, as if born of the measures to return the company to profitability, measures which had been introduced so recently. The show BMW was still a prototype—one whose badge number, 1500, reflected the size of the four-cylinder engine in cubic centimeters. It was a plain type designation for a car which BMW described as a "new class."

The public and motoring press immediately placed the newcomer from Bavaria on a pedestal, and it rode back to the factory for fine-tuning on a wave of enthusiasm. It was above all the successful overall technical concept as well as its smart appearance which turned the car into a true alternative to the mid-range cars from American-owned multi-nationals Ford and Opel (GM), based at Cologne and Rüsselsheim.

The engine, initially rated at 75 bhp, had 80 bhp coaxed out of it at 5500 rpm by the time volume production started in October 1962. The small trick here was to raise the compression ratio from 8.2 to 8.8.

"Flexibility at lower engine speeds, phenomenal power at the higher ones," was the promise made by the BMW brochure. They had moved its performance—94 mph (150 kph)

and acceleration from 0 to 62 mph (100 kph) in 16.8 seconds—right into the sports car bracket.

While the Solex downdraft carburetors were changed for a more efficient version from the same manufacturer in 1964, the new transmission with Porsche locking synchronization was a "revelation." One which made the floor gear shift a pleasure to operate.

The beautifully shaped four-door monocoque steel body was based on a chassis which predicted the 4-wheel future at BMW. It was equipped with MacPherson struts and coil springs at the front as well as trailing arms at the back.

Unfortunately the 1500, which was otherwise very solidly built, was prone to occasional technical hiccups. These kind of mechanical gremlins were eliminated in its successor, the BMW 1600.

The bare look behind the wheel—three circular instruments and the space for the radio—was no obstacle to sales. At a purchase price of something less than 9500 marks, the demand was considerably higher than the daily production output of 50 cars. By increasing capacity in 1963, a total of 23,807 cars were produced before the model was discontinued in 1964. By that time, the 1600 was already starting production, and a 1.8-liter model was selling well.

Viele Autofahrer – die markentreuen unter ihnen sogar sehnsüchtig – haben den Bau eines Mittelklassewagens von BMW erwartet. Auf der Frankfurter Automobilausstellung im September 1961 steht er plötzlich da, als sei er der jüngst erfolgten Sanierungsphase der BMW AG frisch entsprungen. Noch ist es ein Prototyp, dessen Zahlenkombination 1500 die Hubraumgröße des Vierzylindermotors widerspiegelt – eine schlichte Typenbezeichnung für ein Auto, das BMW als die „neue Klasse" bezeichnet.

Das Publikum und die Fachpresse heben den Neuling aus bajuwarischen Landen sofort auf einen Sockel, und eine Welle der Begeisterung trägt ihn zum Feinschliff zurück ins Werk. Vor allem das gelungene technische Gesamtkonzept sowie das adrette Erscheinungsbild lassen den 1500 als verlockende Alternative zu den Mittelklassewagen aus Köln und Rüsselsheim erscheinen.

Dem zunächst nur 75 PS starken Triebwerk werden bis zur Serienproduktion im Oktober 1962 80 PS bei 5500 Umdrehungen in der Minute entlockt. Der kleine Trick dabei ist die Anhebung der Verdichtung von 8,2 auf 8,8.

„Elastizität in den niederen, ungestüme Kraft in den oberen Drehzahlbereichen", verheißt der BMW-Prospekt und rückt die Fahrleistungen – 150 Stundenkilometer,

Beschleunigung von 0 auf 100 in 16,8 Sekunden – in den Bereich von Sportwagenwerten.

Während die Solex-Fallstromvergaser 1964 gegen eine effizientere Version dieses Herstellers ausgetauscht werden, ist das neue Getriebe mit Porsche-Sperrsynchronisation eine „Offenbarung", in der man mit dem Mittelschalthebel gern herumrührt. Die formschöne viertürige Pontonkarosserie aus Stahl steht auf einem Fahrwerk, das mit McPherson-Federbeinen und Schraubenfedern vorn sowie Schräglenkern hinten bei BMW die technische Zukunft der rollenden Basis einläutet.

Leider befallen das an sich sehr solide gebaute Fahrzeug ab und zu kleinere technische „Hustenanfälle". Beim Nachfolger, dem 1600, plagen solche inneren Gebrechen den BMW-Fahrer nicht mehr.

Es ist für den Verkauf nicht hinderlich, dass das Armaturenbrett etwas dürftig aussieht – drei Rundinstrumente und die Aussparung für das Radio. Bei etwas weniger als 9500 Mark Kaufpreis ist die Nachfrage ungleich höher als die Produktionszahl von 50 Autos, die pro Tag vom Band rollen. Durch eine Kapazitätserhöhung 1963 werden letztlich bis 1964 23807 Wagen gebaut. Da läuft der 1600 bereits an und das 1,8-Liter-Modell auf Hochtouren.

De nombreux automobilistes attendent – et même ardemment pour les fidèles de la marque – que BMW construise une voiture du segment intermédiaire. Au Salon de l'automobile de Francfort de septembre 1961, elle est soudain là, comme si elle était née à l'issue des mesures prises et appliquées récemment par BMW AG pour renouer avec les profits. Il s'agit encore d'un prototype dont la combinaison de chiffres, 1500, trahit la cylindrée du quatre-cylindres, une dénomination sobre pour une voiture que BMW qualifie de «nouvelle classe».

Le grand public et les professionnels accueillent immédiatement à bras ouverts la nouvelle petite Bavaroise et une vague d'enthousiasme l'accompagne jusqu'à son retour à l'usine pour une ultime mise au point. Le concept technique global réussi, surtout, ainsi que l'élégance de ses lignes en font une authentique alternative à ses concurrentes de Cologne et de Rüsselsheim.

Lors de sa production en série en octobre 1962, le moteur qui ne développait initialement que 75 ch en délivre 80 à 5500 tr/min. Clé de l'énigme : le taux de compression a été majoré de 8,2 à 8,8.

«Souplesse à bas régime, force irrésistible à haut régime», promet le prospectus de BMW qui met en exergue ses performances – 150 km/h, de 0 à 100 km/h en

16,8 secondes – lesquelles la situent dans le segment des voitures de sport.

Alors que les carburateurs inversés Solex disparaissent en 1964 en faveur d'une version plus performante de la même marque, la nouvelle boîte de vitesses à synchronisation Porsche est un chef-d'œuvre que l'on taquine volontiers avec le levier central. La jolie carrosserie ponton à quatre portes en acier trône sur un châssis qui augure, chez BMW, des futures quatre-roues. Elle est équipée des nouvelles plates-formes avec jambes élastiques McPherson et ressorts hélicoïdaux à l'avant ainsi que de bras obliques à l'arrière.

Malheureusement, de petites «quintes de toux» viennent entraver de temps à autre la bonne marche de cette voiture en soi très solide. Avec sa remplaçante, la 1600, ce genre de dysfonctionnement disparaîtra totalement.

Le fait que l'aménagement intérieur soit modeste – trois cadrans circulaires et le réceptacle de l'autoradio – ne fait absolument pas obstacle à son succès commercial. Pour un prix légèrement inférieur à 9500 marks, la demande est très nettement supérieure à la production quotidienne, qui est de 50 voitures. Une augmentation des capacités, en 1963, permet finalement de fabriquer 23807 voitures jusqu'en 1964. Mais, à ce moment-là, la 1600 et la version à moteur de 1,8 litre se vendent déjà très bien.

Its external appearance and four-cylinder engine, just under 1500 cc, as well as a modern chassis, made this car so popular that it exceeded the capacity of the BMW production lines.

Das äußere Erscheinungsbild und der Vierzylindermotor mit knapp 1500 cm³ sowie ein fortschrittliches Fahrwerk machen diesen Wagen so beliebt, dass er die Fließbandkapazitäten von BMW übersteigt.

Son apparence extérieure, son moteur à quatre cylindres de près de 1500 cm³ ainsi que son châssis moderne rendent cette voiture si populaire que BMW doit accroître les capacités de ses chaînes de production.

Spaciousness, comfortable seating and details such as a padded horn button all reflected
the "new class" in the interior of the BMW 1500. The only thing slightly out of character was the
painted dashboard.

Geräumigkeit, Sitzkomfort und Details wie die Hupenknopfpolsterung spiegeln die „neue Klasse"
auch im Interieur des BMW 1500 wider. Lediglich das lackierte Armaturenbrett stört hier ein wenig.

Habitabilité, confort et richesse des détails, comme le capitonnage du bouton de klaxon, reflètent
la «nouvelle classe» également à l'intérieur de la BMW 1500. Seul le tableau de bord peint semble
ici quelque peu déplacé.

The front section, with the headlights and BMW kidney aligned in the grill, made a welcome change from other mid-range sedans. This also applied to the consistent emphasis of the waistline, with a chrome strip around the car integrating door handles and front indicators.

Die Frontpartie mit den im Grill auf einer Ebene liegenden Lampen und BMW-Nieren hebt sich von anderen Mittelklasse-Limousinen wohltuend ab. Das gilt ebenso für die konsequente Betonung der Gürtellinie rundum durch eine Chromleiste mit integrierten Türgriffen und vorderen Blinkern.

La proue, avec les phares et les naseaux BMW intégrés sans cassure dans la calandre, se démarque avec bonheur de l'avant des autres berlines du segment intermédiaire. On peut en dire autant de sa ligne de ceinture, soulignée par un jonc chromé qui intègre les poignées de portières et les clignotants avant.

BMW 3200 CS 1961

All of the designs coming from the pen of motorcar designer Nuccio Bertone were distinguished by timeless and therefore understated elegance. What was so attractive about the Maestro's work was his ability to unite clear lines and technical practicalities. The people in Munich believed that Bertone's reputation enhanced BMW's profile, as would a four-seater coupé, due to replace the slow-selling 503.

When the Italian creation made its debut at the Frankfurt Motor Show in September 1961, it was met with universal acclaim. The sturdiness of the car body was unmistakable and provided yet another example of Bertone's quality workmanship. The cars from Turin started arriving via Munich for sale at the start of 1962.

The fresh wind blowing through the nearby Alps seemed to lend the BMW V8 even more power. With a compression of 9:1, the light alloy engine equipped with two dual-throat downdraft carburetors delivered 160 bhp at 5600 rpm. Despite a corresponding increase in the torque figures, the specific fuel consumption values were more favorable than those of the 140 bhp 3200 L. That meant 15 miles per gallon

(16 liters per 100 km) of premium grade gas fuel consumption in normal use.

The combination of good taste and practicality proved to be just as successful in Bertone's cabin as it had been in the exterior. Large doors and the absence of a B-pillar facilitated access to the rear compartment. In addition to the steering column gear shift—with the scarcely audible meshing of gear teeth underneath the front seats—there was a stick shift for the propshaft center tunnel.

Like the 507, the frame consisted of a box section with tubular cross beams. This provided a strong foundation for Bertone's attractive solid steel body design. The chassis was also identical to the one used in the 507, following the American adage, "If it ain't broke, don't fix it."

Public roads were not graced with many production examples of the 3200 CS. Only 602 coupés were made during the four years of its production run. Only one convertible variant was manufactured. It was intended for the man who wished to make BMW profitable once more—Dr Herbert Quandt, BMW's major shareholder.

Zeitlose und daher eher unauffällige Eleganz schwingt bei allen Entwürfen des Autodesigners Nuccio Bertone mit. Der Maestro besticht durch die klare Linienführung seiner Entwürfe, die sich stets an der Technik orientieren. Bertones Renommee, so findet man in München, steht BMW gut zu Gesicht, und ein viersitziges Coupé, das den schwer verkäuflichen 503 ablösen soll, ebenfalls.

Als die italienische Kreation im September 1961 auf der Frankfurter Automobilausstellung debütiert, erntet sie einhelliges Lob. Die Karosserie strahlt Solidität aus und unterstreicht Bertones Fertigungsqualität. Anfang 1962 treffen die ersten Wagen aus Turin in München ein.

Mit dem frischen Wind, der da über die Alpen weht, wird dem V8-Triebwerk noch mehr Kraft eingehaucht. Mit einer Verdichtung von 9:1 liefert der mit zwei Doppel-Fallstromvergasern bestückte Leichtmetallmotor 160 PS bei 5600 Umdrehungen ab. Trotz Anhebung der Drehmomentkurve fallen die spezifischen Verbrauchswerte günstiger aus als beim 140-PS-Motor des 3200 L, was den Benzinverbrauch von

16 Litern Super auf 100 Kilometern Normalbetrieb jedoch nicht tangiert.

Gediegen und funktionell wie das Äußere präsentiert Bertone den Innenbereich. Große Türen und der Verzicht auf eine B-Säule erleichtern den Zutritt zum Fond. Neben der Lenkradschaltung – die Getriebezähne mahlen kaum hörbar unter den Vordersitzen – wird auch ein Schalthebel auf dem Kardantunnel angeboten.

Wie beim 507 besteht der Rahmen aus einem Kasten mit Rohrquerträgern – eine äußerst stabile Basis, über die Bertone seine hübsche Ganzstahlkarosserie gestülpt hat. Auch das Fahrwerk ist vom 507. Bewährtes soll man nicht neu erfinden!

Was die Produktionszahlen anbelangt, gehört auch der 3200 CS zu den seltenen Erscheinungen im Straßenbild. Nur 602 Coupés entstehen in vier Jahren Bauzeit. Die Produktion einer Cabrioletvariante beschränkt sich auf ein Unikat für den Mann, der BMW wieder schwarze Zahlen bescheren will: BMW-Großaktionär Dr. Herbert Quandt.

Une élégance intemporelle et, donc, plutôt discrète, marque de son sceau toutes les créations du «couturier» automobile Nuccio Bertone. Le maestro est célèbre pour son coup de crayon incisif qui allie lignes pures et prouesses techniques. La renommée de Bertone, estime-t-on à Munich, correspondrait fort bien à BMW, de même qu'un coupé à quatre places qui remplacerait la 503 difficile à vendre.

Lorsque la voiture de création italienne fait ses débuts en septembre 1961, au Salon de l'automobile de Francfort, elle rencontre un succès fou. La carrosserie donne une impression de solidité et témoigne de la qualité des finitions qui a fait la réputation de Bertone. Début 1962, les premières voitures de Turin arrivent à Munich.

Dans son sillage, le moteur V8 gagne lui aussi en puissance. Avec un taux de compression de 9:1, le moteur en alliage léger à deux carburateurs double corps inversés développe 160 ch à 5600 tr/min. Malgré l'amélioration de la valeur de couple, les taux de consommation sont meilleurs que ceux de la 3200 L avec 140 ch, ce qui n'affecte cependant en rien

le prix à payer à la pompe avec 16 litres de super aux 100 km en conduite normale.

Bertone a réalisé un habitacle aussi luxueux et fonctionnel que la carrosserie. De grandes portières et l'absence de pied central facilitent l'accès à l'arrière. Outre le changement de vitesses au volant – presque silencieuse, la boîte se trouve sous les sièges avant – on peut aussi opter pour un levier sur le tunnel de transmission.

Comme pour la 507, le châssis est constitué d'une échelle avec des poutres transversales – une plate-forme d'une extrême solidité que Bertone a coiffée de sa jolie carrosserie tout acier. Les trains roulants, eux aussi, sont ceux de la 507. Pourquoi changer une équipe qui gagne?

Les chiffres de la production font aussi de la 3200 CS un modèle que l'on a rarement l'occasion de croiser sur sa route. 602 coupés seulement seront construits en quatre ans. La production de cabriolets se limite à un spécimen destiné à celui qui veut absolument faire sortir BMW du rouge: Herbert Quandt, l'actionnaire majoritaire de BMW.

Nuccio Bertone designed a four-seater coupé, which was given the designation BMW 3200 CS in accordance with its engine size, as a successor to the 503. This elegant car did not achieve high sales figures either.

Als Nachfolgemodell des 503 entwirft Nuccio Bertone ein viersitziges Coupé, das entsprechend seinem Hubraum als BMW 3200 CS bezeichnet wird. Auch diesem eleganten Wagen sind keine hohen Verkaufszahlen beschieden.

Pour succéder à la 503, Nuccio Bertone dessine un coupé à quatre places baptisé, en raison de sa cylindrée, BMW 3200 CS. Cette élégante voiture ne connaîtra pas, elle non plus, un très grand succès commercial.

For the first time, the company emblem appeared on the C-pillar of a BMW. It represented the circular area of a propeller in the Bavarian state colors. The V8 engine had achieved 160 bhp by 1962. Bertone's all-steel BMW creation—with its lines typical of the maestro—was given large doors and retractable side windows but did not have the B-pillar which can be a nuisance when getting into a car. The attractive coupé had a top speed of 125 mph (200 kph).

Erstmals taucht das Firmenemblem an der C-Säule eines BMW auf. Es stellt eine Propellerkreisfläche in den bayerischen Landesfarben dar. Der V8 ist 1962 bei 160 PS angelangt. Bertones BMW-Kreation aus Ganzstahl – in der Linienführung typisch für den Maestro – verfügt über große Türen und versenkbare Seitenscheiben und verzichtet auf die beim Einsteigen störende B-Säule. 200 Stundenkilometer erreicht das schmucke Coupé.

L'emblème de la marque figure pour la première fois, à l'arrière, sur le montant du toit. Il représente une hélice et les couleurs de la Bavière. En 1962, le V8 délivre 160 ch. La carrosserie tout acier, dessinée par Bertone pour la BMW – dont les lignes trahissent la griffe du maître –, comporte de grandes portières et des vitres latérales descendantes sans montant de toit central, facilitant ainsi l'accès à la voiture. Cet élégant coupé tutoie les 200 km/h.

BMW 3200 S Staatslimousine 1963

After the memorable financial crisis AGM in winter 1959, BMW was well and truly on the road to recovery. The small 700 was selling very well, admittedly with a narrow profit margin, and success seemed to be just round the corner with the new middle-class BMW 1500.

Accompanying that boost in confidence, the company's thoughts turned to the large V8 sedans, whose production had fallen to 661 in 1960. They were due for an update, particularly since the official specifications now prohibited rear doors which opened towards the front.

The BMW chief designer, Wilhelm Hofmeister, implemented his proposed modifications on the solid technical basis of the 160 bhp aluminum V8 3200 S: an extended roof to provide more headroom in the rear compartment, modified rear door hinges, an enlarged boot, and an additional headlamp on the fenders. Rear seat passengers were provided with fresh air by a large steel sunroof, which would become more and more important. However, matters did not progress beyond this prototype, simply because BMW stopped manufacturing large cars.

This car was initially used as a status symbol in the company car fleet. But BMW was soon to enjoy the kudos associated with having built a car for a state official. Alfons Goppel, premier of Bavaria since 1962, occasionally borrowed this flagship. The aforementioned steel sunroof proved to be particularly valuable for state visitors, who only had to stand in front of the rear seats to enjoy spectator applause.

The attempt to intruduce this BMW to the politicians in Bonn proved a failure. Dr Konrad Adenauer's chauffeur was faithful to Mercedes. This also proved to be the case with the second launch in September 1965 in which the 505 was supposed to be BMW's answer to the Adenauer Mercedes 300. No more than two prototypes of this BMW Pullman limousine were manufactured. One of them ended its days in the BMW museum with the 3200 Si prototype, and the other had to endure the indignities of commerce, advertising French fries, before the honor she deserved was restored to her by a BMW vintage car collector.

BMW ist seit der denkwürdigen Hauptversammlung im Winter 1959 auf dem Wege der Sanierung. Der kleine 700er verkauft sich – wenngleich mit geringer Gewinnmarge – recht gut, und mit dem neuen Mittelklassemodell BMW 1500 winkt der Erfolg.

Solchermaßen den Rücken gestärkt, macht sich das Unternehmen Gedanken über die Fortführung der großen V8-Limousinen, deren Stückzahl 1960 auf 661 gesunken ist. Die Modernisierung ist fällig, zumal Änderungen der Zulassungsvorschriften hinten angeschlagene Fondtüren verbieten.

Auf der soliden technischen Basis des 3200 S mit seinem V8-Leichtmetallmotor mit 160 PS verwirklicht BMW-Designchef Wilhelm Hofmeister seine Modifikationsvorschläge: Strecken des Daches, um mehr Kopfraum im Fond zu erzielen, geänderter Türanschlag hinten, Vergrößerung des Kofferraums und Zusatzscheinwerfer in den Kotflügeln. Für die Frischluft auf der Rücksitzbank sorgt ein überdimensionales Stahlschiebedach, das noch Bedeutung erlangt. Es bleibt bei diesem Prototyp, denn BMW stellt die Produktion der großen Wagen ein.

Zunächst dient dieser Wagen zu repräsentativen Zwecken im Werksfuhrpark. Doch dann kann sich BMW den Orden, eine Staatskarosse gebaut zu haben, ans Revers heften. Bayerns Ministerpräsident Alfons Goppel, seit 1962 Landesvater, leiht sich des öfteren dieses einmalige Flaggschiff aus. Besonders bei Staatsbesuchen kommt das bereits erwähnte Stahlschiebedach zur Geltung. Wer auch immer bejubelt werden möchte, kann vor den Rücksitzen stehend die Ovationen entgegennehmen.

Ein Versuch, diesen BMW auch in Bonn zum Einsatz zu bringen, scheitert. Dr. Konrad Adenauers Chauffeur bleibt Mercedes treu. Das bestätigt sich auch beim zweiten Anlauf im September 1965, bei dem BMW mit dem 505 eine weitere Antwort auf den Mercedes 300 von Adenauer geben will. Es bleibt bei zwei Prototypen dieser Pullman-Limousine. Der eine wandert – wie auch der 3200 Si Prototyp – ins BMW-Museum, der andere dient dem schnöden Mammon und wirbt für Pommes frites, ehe er von einem BMW-Oldtimer-Sammler den ihm gebührenden Ehrenplatz zugewiesen bekommt.

Depuis la mémorable assemblée générale de l'hiver 1959, convoquée à la suite d'une crise financière, BMW est de nouveau sur la voie de la guérison. La petite 700 se vend bien – même si elle ne génère pas des bénéfices extraordinaires – et le succès est garanti grâce au nouveau modèle du segment intermédiaire, la BMW 1500.

Maintenant qu'elle a les reins plus solides, l'entreprise songe aux futures grosses berlines V8, qui n'ont été produites qu'à 661 exemplaires en 1960. Une modernisation s'impose, d'autant que les normes bannissent désormais les portières arrière s'ouvrant dans le sens contraire de la marche.

Sur la solide base mécanique de la 3200 S au V8 en alliage léger de 160 ch, le designer en chef de BMW, Wilhelm Hofmeister, concrétise les propositions de modifications qu'il avait faites : allongement du toit pour augmenter l'espace disponible pour la tête à l'arrière, modification des charnières des portières arrière, agrandissement du coffre et phares supplémentaires dans les ailes. Un toit coulissant en acier de grande dimension, qui allait plus tard prendre de l'importance, dégage l'horizon pour les passagers installés à l'arrière. Ce prototype restera un modèle unique, car BMW suspend la production des grosses berlines.

Cette voiture sert d'abord de véhicule de représentation dans la flotte de l'usine. Mais BMW finit, malgré tout, par se distinguer en construisant une limousine destinée aux personnages officiels. Le ministre-président bavarois Alfons Goppel, qui préside depuis 1962 aux destinées du Land, emprunte fréquemment ce navire-amiral exclusif. En particulier lors des visites officielles, où le toit coulissant susmentionné présente des avantages. Quel que soit celui qui veut se faire acclamer, il lui suffit de s'installer à l'arrière et de se lever pour recevoir les ovations du public.

BMW tente aussi de prendre pied à Bonn dans le fief de la marque à l'étoile – en vain. Le chauffeur de Konrad Adenauer est fidèle à Mercedes. La deuxième tentative de BMW, en septembre 1965, de répliquer à la Mercedes 300 d'Adenauer avec la BMW 505 se solde également par un échec. Il n'y aura que deux prototypes de cette limousine Pullman. Comme la 3200 Si, un autre prototype, l'une passera sa retraite au musée BMW et l'autre sera sacrifiée sur l'autel du mercantilisme puisqu'elle fera de la publicité pour une marque de frites avant de reprendre la place qui lui revient, chez un collectionneur de BMW.

The large supplementary headlamps and the pontoon-shaped trunk are striking features. The 160 bhp version of the 3.2-liter V8 engine powers the BMW, taking it up to a top speed of 118 mph (190 kph). Beneath the wood-paneled dashboard we see a large loudspeaker tastefully tucked away—perhaps for playing the national anthems. This car never got beyond a prototype version which saw sporadic service as an official car of the Bavarian State Government.

Auffällig sind die größeren Zusatzscheinwerfer und die Pontonform des Kofferraums. Die 160-PS-Version des 3,2-Liter-V8-Motors bringt das „Flaggschiff" in Schwung und auf 190 km/h. Gediegen ist das holzverkleidete Armaturenbrett, unter dem ein großer Lautsprecher – wohl zum Abspielen der Nationalhymnen – montiert ist. Es bleibt bei diesem Prototypen, der sporadisch der bayerischen Landesregierung dient.

Différences frappantes : des phares d'appoint de plus grand diamètre et un coffre en forme de ponton. La version de 160 ch du V8 de 3,2 litres donne des ailes à ce navire-amiral et lui permet d'atteindre les 190 km/h. Luxueux : le tableau de bord en bois sous lequel se trouve un grand haut-parleur – peut-être prévu pour jouer les hymnes nationaux. Il n'existera que ce prototype, qui sera utilisé de façon sporadique comme voiture officielle par le gouvernement régional de Bavière.

It was in total euphoria that BMW presented its chic coupé in the summer of 1965. This was characterized by its large windows and the absence of a center pillar. It was billed as "the reincarnation of the BMW 327." The most prominent features of the new look BMW were the flat wrap-around head-lamps with integrated indicators. The oval reflectors earned the nickname of "slanted eyes" and were referred to inside BMW as "Asian eyes."

Technically, the coupé seemed to have been a prelude to the 2-liter sedans, which were launched in 1966. The 2000 CS was already equipped with the 1990 cc engine capable of delivering 100 bhp with a single downdraft carburetor and 120 bhp with two double-barrel sidedraft carburetors. The chassis and the two-section propellor shaft were also taken from the sedan.

The majority of the 13,691 coupés leaving the Kar-mann works in Osnabrück over six years were fitted with a manually operated transmission and delivered 120 bhp (2000 CS). The 100 bhp version (2000 C), most of which were equipped with a ZF automatic transmission, was less popular.

To allow the 2-liter to run more smoothly, the chain drive of the overhead camshaft was equipped with sliding rails and an oil damped tensioning fixture. The transmission was also overhauled via wider stronger teeth and an expanding ring synchronizer. Accordingly, the diameter of the clutch was enlarged.

The car's "legs" were equipped with elastic mountings and, as was usual for that time, a special duct was fitted to allow cool air to reach the front brake disks. The dashboard and center console were given a businesslike and functional look. The four electric switches on the center console for window actuation were a nice and unfamiliar luxury toy for contemporary drivers.

Although the 2000 CS was not the sportiest vehicle on the market, since it took 12 seconds to go from 0 to 62 mph (100 kph), but this acceleration figure was in keeping with the performance/weight ratio. The top speed of 115 mph (185 kph) was only slightly lower than that of the 1800 TI/SA with 130 bhp.

The 2000 CS was not expected to become a sporty machine. It was a four-seater which also had enough room for suitcases and bags—an apple for the pragmatist's eye, a medium-sized machine helping its drivers to see and be seen. To put it more simply: quite a lot of car for 17,000 marks.

From February 1966, BMW offered a sporting four-door sedan (the 2000 TI) identical with the 2000 CS in engine, transmission and chassis. The former was replaced as early as 1968 by the tilux, which with its square headlights was compromised for contemporary taste.

Euphorisch präsentiert BMW im Sommer 1965 als „Wie-dergeburt des BMW 327" ein schickes Coupé ohne Mittelpfosten und mit viel Fensterfläche. Auffälligstes Merkmal des neuen BMW-Gesichts sind die flachen, seit-lich herumgezogenen Scheinwerfer mit integrierten Blinkern. Vom Volksmund bald „Schlitzaugen" genannt, findet man für die Ovalreflektoren auch in der werksinternen Terminologie einen sinnentsprechenden Begriff: „Asiatenaugen".

Technisch gesehen stellt das Coupé einen Vorgriff auf die 2-Liter-Limousinen des Jahrgangs 1966 dar. Es hat bereits den 1990-cm³-Motor, der mit einem Fallstromvergaser 100 PS und mit zwei Doppel-Flachstromvergasern 120 PS leistet. Auch das Fahrwerk und die zweigeteilte Kardanwelle werden von der Limousine übernommen.

Von den insgesamt 13691 Coupés, die das Werk von Karmann in Osnabrück innerhalb von sechs Jahren verlassen, haben die meisten ein handgeschaltetes Getriebe und 120 PS (2000 CS). Die 100-PS-Version (2000 C), vornehmlich mit einer ZF-Automatik ausgerüstet, wird weniger gern gekauft.

Um das 2-Liter-Triebwerk zu mehr Laufruhe zu erziehen, wird der Kettenantrieb der oben liegenden Nockenwelle mit Gleitschienen und einer ölgedämpften Spannvorrichtung ver-sehen. Auch das Getriebe mit verbreiterten Zahnrädern wird

BMW 2000 CS 1965

überarbeitet und erhält eine Spreizring-Synchronisierung. Analog fällt der Kupplungsdurchmesser größer aus.

Die „Beine" des Autos bekommen eine elastische Lagerung, und den Scheibenbremsen – wie damals üblich, nur vorn – wird durch einen Kunstgriff Kühlluft zugefächelt. Armaturenbrett und Mittelkonsole wirken aufgeräumt und funktionell. Ein schönes Spielzeug für die Zeitgenossen sind die vier Schalter der elektrischen Fensterheber auf der Mittelkonsole.

Eine Beschleinigung von 0 auf 100 Stundenkilometer in 12 Sekunden entspricht nicht Sprinterwerten, aber dem Leistungsgewicht. Die Endgeschwindigkeit (185 km/h) liegt dagegen nur knapp unter der des 1800 TI/SA mit 130 PS.

Sportliche Ambitionen werden mit dem 2000 CS noch nicht verknüpft. Er ist ein Viersitzer, in dem auch einige Koffer und Taschen Platz finden, ein Beau für Pragmatiker, ein schickes Automobil zum Sehen und Gesehenwerden oder einfacher ausgedrückt – ziemlich viel Auto für 17 000 Mark.

In Motor, Getriebe und Fahrwerk mit dem 2000 CS identisch, offeriert BMW ab Februar 1966 mit dem 2000 TI auch eine sportliche viertürige Limousine. Diese wird bereits 1968 vom tilux – mit seinen Rechteck-Scheinwerfern ein Zugeständnis an den Zeitgeschmack – abgelöst.

Dans l'euphorie, BMW présente durant l'été 1965 la « réincarnation de la BMW 327 », un coupé d'un grand chic sans pied médian et avec de généreuses surfaces vitrées. La caractéristique de style la plus frappante du nouveau visage de la BMW est ses phares allongés qui mordent sur le côté avec leurs clignotants intégrés. Ces derniers sont rapidement surnommés les «yeux bridés» alors que chez BMW, en interne, les réflecteurs ovales possèdent un nom bien à eux: «yeux d'Asiatique».

Sur le plan mécanique, le coupé annonce les berlines de 2 litres du millésime 1966. Il possède déjà un moteur de 1990 cm³ qui développe 100 ch avec un carburateur inversé et 120 ch dans la version à deux carburateurs double corps inversés. Les trains roulants et l'arbre de transmission en deux éléments, aussi, sont repris de la berline.

Sur un total de 13691 coupés qui sortiront de l'usine Karmann à Osnabrück en six ans, la majorité possèdent une boîte manuelle et un moteur de 120 ch (2000 CS). La version de 100 ch (2000 C), la plus souvent équipée d'une boîte automatique ZF, ne fait pas l'unanimité.

Pour accroître la souplesse de fonctionnement du moteur de 2 litres, l'entraînement des chaînes de l'arbre à cames supérieur est assuré par des rails glissants avec un dispositif de tension baignant dans l'huile. La boîte de vitesses à engrenages élargis, elle aussi, est revue et reçoit

une synchronisation à anneaux d'écartement. Logiquement, le diamètre de l'embrayage augmente lui aussi.

Les «jambes» de la voiture possèdent des paliers élastiques et les freins à disques – uniquement à l'avant comme cela était alors la tradition – sont refroidis grâce à une prise d'air spéciale. Le tableau de bord et la console médiane sont bien agencés et fonctionnels. Les quatre commandes des vitres électriques sur la console médiane sont un gadget apprécié des conducteurs de cette époque.

Les 12 secondes pour le 0 à 100 km/h ne constituent pas un record spectaculaire, mais elles reflètent le rapport poids/ puissance. La vitesse de pointe (185 km/h) est, en revanche, proche de celle de la 1800 TI/SA de 130 ch.

La 2000 CS n'a pas encore d'ambitions sportives. Il s'agit d'une quatre-places qui peut aisément emmener quelques valises et quelques sacs – une belle voiture pour conducteurs pragmatiques, un véhicule de taille moyenne destiné à la promenade pour voir et être vu ou, tout simplement, choisi par beaucoup pour son prix de 17 000 marks.

Avec la 2000 TI, identique à la 2000 CS pour le moteur, la boîte de vitesses et le châssis, BMW propose, à partir de février 1966, une sportive berline à quatre portes. Dès 1968, celle-ci sera remplacée par la tilux qui, avec ses phares rectangulaires, fait une concession aux goûts de l'époque.

This coupé, with
its strong appeal to
contemporary taste,
lacking a central pillar
and with a great deal
of window area, stood
out particularly because
of its headlights—also
called "slanted eyes"—
which were wrapped
round to the side to
integrate the indicators.

Das dem Zeitgeschmack
stark angepasste Coupé
ohne Mittelpfosten und
mit viel Fensterfläche
fällt besonders durch
die seitlich herum-
gezogenen Scheinwerfer
– auch „Schlitzaugen"
genannt – auf.

Le coupé, qui reflète
fidèlement le goût
de son époque
avec l'absence de
montant central et ses
généreuses surfaces
vitrées, se distingue
particulièrement par
les phares mordant
sur les côtés.

Dashboard and central console with their sensibly arranged instruments and controls—the four controls for the electrical windows in front of the gear lever could hardly be missed—were appropriate for the outfit of the coupé. The 1990 cc engine anticipated the 1966 2-liter sedan.

Armaturenbrett und Mittelkonsole mit sinnvoll angeordneten Instrumenten und Schaltern – die vier elektrischen Fensterheber vor dem Schaltknüppel sind nicht zu übersehen – passen zum Erscheinungsbild des Coupés. Der 1990-cm³-Motor ist bereits ein Vorgriff auf die 2-Liter-Limousine des Jahrgangs 1966.

Le tableau de bord et la console médiane avec les instruments et manettes agencés ergonomiquement – les quatre lève-vitres électriques devant le levier de vitesses sautent aux yeux – vont avec le style extérieur du coupé. Le moteur de 1990 cm³ annonce déjà la berline de deux litres du millésime 1966.

BMW 02 1966

It requires special skills to cater for almost all tastes with a single model series. To put this ideal into practice, so that the product is also widely accepted, is the art of marketing. This is what happened between 1966 and 1977. BMW stretched the range of their "02 series" to extremes, from a 75 bhp economy model to the powerful 170 bhp turbo 2002. Commercial success proved this policy right: 863,203 cars were sold.

In the middle range there were two models which supplied optimum value for their price: the 1802 (90 bhp, 104 mph/167 kph) for 10,435 marks and the 2002 tii (130 bhp, 119 mph/190 kph) which cost at least 2000 marks more.

The four-cylinder short-stroke engine (with 1766 cc for the 1802 and 1990 cc for the 2002 tii) turned out to be an extremely reliable, lively engine. That the injection engine of the 2002 tii with its 40 extra bhp only consumed slightly more than the carburetor version may have been due to the efficient metering of the Kugelfischer injection pump. Both 02s had good roadholding, although it was worth installing the sway bar in the 1802 which was standard in the 2002 tii.

The 02 series went into the winter of 1973 with pepped-up looks—black radiator grill, rectangular instead of circular rear lights—and with safety equipment such as headrests and

seatbelts. The rear-wheel drive of the tii proved powerful in the snow as was attested by contemporary test reports.

The normal production specification could be uprated in both versions: a sporty five-speed transmission was available as an option. Of course the brakes—disks at the front, drums at the rear—were larger for the 2002 tii, and enlarged HR tires did justice to the greater loads encountered by the tii version.

The tii still had a good advantage over the 1802, sprinting from 0 to 62 mph (100 kph) in just 10 seconds. But that did not particularly worry the typical BMW 1802 buyer who might be lagging behind by two seconds. This was not the sportsman on the road, this was a man who wanted reliability, space and comfort from his vehicle at a reasonable price, whilst being able to keep up with the highway traffic flow.

From September 1973, BMW built larger tanks into the rear of the 1802 and 2002 tii to increase the range. The bonus distance? Approximately 19 miles (30 km). With price increases of 33 per cent in four years, the cars reflected contemporary trends. The economic recession which was beginning to make itself sharply felt did not affect sales. Thus the 1802 achieved 83,351 and the 2002 tii 38,703 units in the sales statistics, benchmarks to stand until the 3 series set new standards in July 1975.

Mit einer Modellreihe fast jeden Geschmack zu treffen, bedarf eines besonderen Riechers. Diese Idee dann so umzusetzen, dass das Produkt auch akzeptiert wird, ist die hohe Kunst des Marketings – so geschehen in den elf Jahren zwischen 1966 und 1977, in denen BMW mit den „02ern" eine Modellreihe in extreme Richtungen ausweitet – vom 75-PS-Sparmobil bis zum 170-PS-Turbo-Kraftpaket. Der Erfolg gibt dieser Modellpolitik recht: 863203 verkaufte Autos.

Mittendrin liegen zwei Modelle, die für ihren Preis einen optimalen Gegenwert liefern: der 1802 (90 PS, 167 km/h) für 10435 Mark und der gut 2000 Mark teurere 2002 tii (130 PS, 190 km/h).

Der Vierzylinder-Kurzhubmotor (mit 1766 cm³ beim 1802 und 1990 cm³ beim 2002 tii) erweist sich als ein äußerst zuverlässiges, temperamentvolles Triebwerk. Dass der 40 PS stärkere Einspritzmotor des 2002 tii nur wenig mehr schluckt als der Vergaser, mag an der guten Dosierung der Kugelfischer-Einspritzpumpe liegen. Gut auf der Straße liegen beide, wobei sich beim 1802 der Einbau von Drehstabstabilisatoren, die beim 2002 tii serienmäßig sind, empfiehlt.

Optisch aufgepäppelt – mit schwarzem Kühlergrill, eckigen statt runden Heckleuchten – und mit Sicherheitskomponenten wie Kopfstützen und Sicherheitsgurten ausgestattet, gehen die 02er in den Winter 1973. Dass auch der Heck-

antrieb des tii die Kraft in den Schnee bringt, attestieren ihm entsprechende Fahrberichte.

Der normale Gang der Dinge lässt sich bei beiden Ausführungen beschleunigen. Gegen Aufpreis gibt es ein sportliches Fünfganggetriebe. Natürlich sind die Bremsen, vorne Scheiben- und hinten Trommelbremsen, beim 2002tii größer dimensioniert, und HR-Reifen werden den größeren Belastungen gerecht.

Beim Sprint aus dem Stand auf 100 Stundenkilometer hat der tii mit 10 Sekunden die Nase vorn. Den typischen Käufer des BMW 1802 stört es aber nicht, dass er da zwei Sekunden hinterherhinkt. Er ist nicht der Sportler auf der Straße, sondern ein Mann, der von seinem Fahrzeug Zuverlässigkeit, Platz und Komfort zu einem günstigen Preis erwartet, und dennoch in der Lage sein will, im Autobahnverkehr gut im Fluss zu bleiben.

Zur Erhöhung der Reichweite stattet BMW ab September 1973 den 1802 und den 2002tii mit größeren Tanks aus. Der Distanzgewinn beträgt rund 30 Kilometer. Mit Preissteigerungen von 33 Prozent in vier Jahren liegen beide Wagen im Trend der Zeit, und die sich andeutende Wirtschaftsrezession tangiert den Absatz offenbar nicht. So bringt es der 1802 auf 83351 und der 2002tii auf immerhin 38703 Einheiten in der Verkaufsstatistik, ehe im Juli 1975 die 3er-Reihe neue Maßstäbe setzt.

Satisfaire tous les goûts avec une seule gamme n'est pas à la portée de tout le monde. Mais réussir ce pari avec un produit qui est largement plébiscité relève du miracle marketing. C'est ce qui s'est passé entre 1966 et 1977, lorsque BMW a, avec les «02», décliné une gamme dans deux directions opposées – du modèle d'appel de 75 ch à la version sportive à moteur turbo de 170 ch. Le succès légitime a posteriori cette politique, puisque BMW en a vendu pas moins de 863203 exemplaires.

Au cœur de cette gamme, il y a deux modèles d'un bon rapport qualité/prix : la 1802 (90 ch, 167 km/h) pour 10435 marks et la 2002tii (130 ch, 190 km/h), qui coûte largement 2000 marks de plus.

Le quatre-cylindres à course courte (de 1766 cm³ pour la 1802 et de 1990 cm³ pour la 2002tii) se révèle être un moteur extrêmement fiable en dépit de son tempérament vif. Si le moteur à injection de la 2002tii, plus puissant de 40 ch, ne consomme qu'un peu plus que la version à carburateur, cela est sans doute dû au bon réglage de la pompe d'injection Kugelfischer. Toutes les deux ont une bonne tenue de route, mais il est recommandé d'équiper la 1802 des barres de torsion stabilisatrices qui figurent en série sur la 2002tii.

Les 02 sont légèrement modifiées esthétiquement au cours de l'hiver 1973 – calandre noire, feux arrière rectangulaires et non plus ronds – et dotée d'éléments de sécurité comme des appuie-tête et des ceintures de sécurité. Les

essais réalisés durant cette saison prouvent que la propulsion arrière de la tii ne connaît pas de problèmes de transmission même sur la neige.

Il est possible d'opter pour des options sur les deux versions : contre supplément, BMW propose une sportive boîte manuelle à cinq vitesses. Naturellement, les freins – à disques à l'avant et à tambours à l'arrière – sont de plus grandes dimensions pour la 2002tii et des pneus HR répondent mieux à plus de sollicitations.

La tii ne perd pas son temps en route puisqu'il lui suffit de dix secondes pour passer de 0 à 100 km/h. La BMW 1802 demande deux secondes de plus, mais cela ne dérange en rien ses acheteurs. Le client type n'est pas un conducteur sportif sur route, mais un homme qui attend de sa voiture fiabilité, habitabilité et confort à un prix intéressant et qui soit malgré tout en mesure d'atteindre aisément la vitesse de circulation sur autoroute.

Pour augmenter l'autonomie de parcours, BMW installe à partir de septembre 1973 des réservoirs de plus grande capacité dans les 1802 et 2002tii. Gain : une trentaine de kilomètres. Avec une hausse du prix de 33% en quatre ans, les deux voitures sont tout à fait dans l'air du temps et la récession économique qui se profile n'affecte en rien les ventes. Ainsi la 1802 se vend à raison de 83351 exemplaires et la 2002tii à 38703 unités, avant que la Série 3 ne vienne ouvrir un nouveau chapitre en juillet 1975.

Outwardly, the two-door 02 series BMW gave a delicate and unassuming effect. But the 130 bhp performance of the 2-liter engine in the 2002 tii, with Kugelfischer fuel injection, was enough to make an impression.

Äußerlich wirken die zweitürigen 02er BMW zierlich und unscheinbar. Aber mit den 130 PS, die der 2-Liter-Motor im 2002 tii mit Kugelfischer-Einspritzpumpe leistet, lässt sich Staat machen.

Extérieurement, les BMW 02 à deux portes n'attirent pas le regard. Mais, avec les 130 ch que délivre le moteur de deux litres de la 2002 tii à injection Kugelfischer, il ne faut pas se fier aux apparences.

A discreet hint of the 2-liter engine under the hood was provided by the radiator grill, black except for two ribs. The designation at the rear specified the model.

Ein dezenter Hinweis auf das 2-Liter-Triebwerk unter der Haube ist der bis auf zwei Rippen geschwärzte Kühlergrill. Die Bezeichnung auf dem Heck gibt den jeweiligen Typ an.

Une allusion discrète au deux-litres qui œuvre sous le capot : la calandre teinte en noir à l'exception de deux rainures chromées. Le logotype à l'arrière indique de quelle version il s'agit.

Of the 863,000 02 series cars which were built, the share in the sales statistics of the 119 mph (190 kph) 2002 tii amounted to 38,703 units.

Von den 863000 gebauten Wagen der 02er Reihe beträgt der Anteil des 190 Stundenkilometer schnellen 2002 tii in der Verkaufsstatistik 38703 Einheiten.

Sur les 863000 exemplaires vendus de la Série 02, 38703 sont des 2002 tii qui flirtent avec les 190 km/h.

BMW 2500 E3 | 1968

BMW wanted an upper mid-range car to invade Mercedes territory. The two new six-cylinder engines were designed accordingly: 2.5 liters at 150 bhp and 2.8 liters at 170 bhp. But equipment, dimensions and pricing were also aimed at their counterparts from Mercedes. "Heavy guns" in the form of a ride level device and a limited slip differential as standard equipment were used by the luxuriously equipped 2800 to go into battle against Mercedes. The battle of material goodies ended in withdrawal by BMW to a less costly position. Nevertheless, the limited slip differential continued to be available—albeit at extra cost.

The 2500 model got off to a better start: between September and Christmas 1968, 2560 of these four-door sedans came off the production line and at the end of the nine-year production period, it was almost 95,000, most of them with manual transmissions. Over 17,000 comfort-conscious BMW customers left the hard work to the ZF automatic transmission with hydraulic torque converter and three-speed planetary gearing.

The new six-cylinder four-stroke in-line engine with a seven-bearing crankshaft and overhead camshaft had a compression ratio of 9:1 and turned out to be extremely refined. It was also an ideal foundation for engine derivatives up to 3.3 liters. It was not easy on the fuel, for the 20.5-gallon (78 liter) tank in the rear was insufficient for 310 miles (500 km), even when driven with fuel economy in mind.

The driving comfort which one expected from a BMW 2500 was taken care of by independent suspension with MacPherson struts having lower control arms at the front and semi-trailing arms at the rear. As befits a luxury car, a servo-assisted hydraulic dual circuit brake system supported disk brakes all round. This spacious sedan was properly equipped: a functional dashboard with circular instruments and a broad central console. There was a manageable steering wheel, comfortable body-shaped seats (from 1973 also height-adjustable, provided with headrests), and sensibly organized compartments for odds and ends or maps.

Another practical detail awaited discovery on opening the trunk. On the inside was a large folding case with 30 tools to cover all eventualities. Whether the three spare spark plugs would have cured any breakdown was never put to the test. The engine was durable and deep-chested: it could accelerate a 2500 with two passengers—a total of around one-and-a-half tons—to 119 mph (190 kph). Not bad for a 1960s sedan.

Mit einem Wagen der gehobenen Mittelklasse will BMW auf Mercedes-Terrain vorstoßen. Entsprechend sind die beiden neuen Sechszylindertriebwerke ausgelegt: 2,5 Liter mit 150 PS und 2,8 Liter mit 170 PS. Aber auch Ausstattung, Abmessungen und das Preis-Leistungs-Verhältnis zielen auf die Pendants mit dem Stern. Mit „schweren Geschützen", nämlich serienmäßiger Niveauregulierung und einem Sperrdifferential, zieht der luxuriös eingerichtete 2800 ins Feld gen Untertürkheim. Die Materialschlacht endet mit dem Rückzug auf eine weniger aufwändige Basis. Immerhin kann das Sperrdifferential, nunmehr gegen Aufpreis, als Extra weiterhin bestellt werden.

Besser läuft die Produktion des 2500 an. Von September bis Weihnachten 1968 gehen 2560 dieser viertürigen Limousinen vom Band, und nach der neunjährigen Produktionszeit sind es nahezu 95 000, vornehmlich mit Schaltgetriebe ausgerüstet. Etwas mehr als 17 000 komfortbewusste BMW-Kunden überlassen die Hebelarbeit der ZF-Automatik mit hydraulischem Wandler und Dreigang-Planetengetriebe.

Der neue Sechszylinder-Viertakt-Reihenmotor mit siebenfach gelagerter Kurbelwelle und oben liegender Nockenwelle ist 9:1 verdichtet und erweist sich als äußerst kultiviert: ein ideales Basistriebwerk für Derivate bis zu

3,3 Litern. Sparsam ist er freilich nicht, denn der 78-Liter-Tank im Heck reicht selbst bei schonender Fahrweise nicht einmal für 500 Kilometer.

Für einen Fahrkomfort, wie man ihn vom BMW 2500 erwartet, sorgen die Einzelradaufhängungen mit Federbeinen – vorn an Quer-, hinten an Schräglenkern. Standesgemäß sorgt eine servounterstützte hydraulische Zweikreisbremse mit vier Scheibenbremsen für angemessene Verzögerung. Die geräumige Limousine ist ordentlich eingerichtet: funktionelles Armaturenbrett mit Rundinstrumenten und breiter Mittelkonsole, griffiges Lenkrad, bequeme, körpergerecht geformte Sitze (ab 1973 auch in der Höhe regulierbar und mit Kopfstützen versehen) und sinnvoll verteilte Ablagen für Kleinigkeiten und Atlanten.

Auch beim Aufklappen des Kofferraumdeckels entdeckt man ein praktisches Detail. An der Innenseite befindet sich ein großes Klapptui mit 30 Werkzeugen für alle Fälle. Ob die drei Reservezündkerzen einen Motorschaden „kurieren" können, ist nie ausprobiert worden. Das Triebwerk erweist sich als standhaft und bringt den Wagen mit zwei Passagieren – zusammen rund anderthalb Tonnen – auf 190 Stundenkilometer: recht passabel für eine Limousine der sechziger Jahre.

BMW veut concurrencer Mercedes avec une voiture du segment intermédiaire supérieur. Les deux nouveaux six-cylindres sont conçus en conséquence: 2,5 litres de 150 ch et 2,8 litres de 170 ch. Leur finition, leurs dimensions et leur rapport qualité/prix rivalisent avec ceux de la marque à l'étoile. D'une grande technicité, à savoir un correcteur d'assiette en série et un différentiel autobloquant, la luxueuse 2800 passe à l'attaque contre la marque d'Untertürkheim. La «bataille» se termine par le retrait de BMW qui opte pour une version moins coûteuse. Le différentiel autobloquant – maintenant proposé en option – est néanmoins toujours disponible.

La 2500 prend, elle, un meilleur départ: de septembre à Noël 1968, 2560 de ces berlines à quatre portes sortent des chaînes et, après neuf ans de production, on en compte 95 000, dont la quasi-totalité possède une boîte manuelle. Un peu plus de 17 000 acheteurs de BMW optent pour la boîte automatique ZF à convertisseur hydraulique et train épicycloïdal à trois rapports.

Le nouveau six-cylindres en ligne à quatre temps avec vilebrequin à sept paliers et arbres à cames en tête affiche un taux de compression de 9:1 et s'avère extrêmement perfectionné. Une excellente base, donc, pour monter en cylindrée jusqu'à 3,3 litres. Il n'est malheureusement pas

économique puisque même le réservoir de 78 litres installé à l'arrière ne permet d'effectuer que 500 kilomètres en conduisant placidement.

Des suspensions indépendantes avec jambes élastiques – avec leviers transversaux à l'avant et bras obliques à l'arrière – garantissent le confort de conduite que l'on est en droit d'attendre d'une BMW 2500. Comme il se doit, le double circuit de freinage à assistance hydraulique est à disques sur les quatre roues. Spacieuse, la berline est parfaitement «aménagée»: un tableau de bord fonctionnel avec des cadrans circulaires et une large console médiane, un volant agréable à manœuvrer, des sièges confortables et ergonomiques (également réglables en hauteur et avec appuie-tête à partir de 1973) et des vide-poches bien placés.

Le couvercle de la malle possède un détail pratique: il comporte une mallette d'outillage intégrée avec une trentaine d'outils pour parer à toutes les éventualités. Quelqu'un aura-t-il jamais réussi à réparer une panne de moteur avec les trois bougies de réserve que l'on y trouve? Le moteur s'avère endurant et, avec deux personnes à bord – soit au total un poids d'environ une tonne et demie –, il propulse cette voiture à 190 km/h, une performance vraiment remarquable pour une berline des années 1960.

The imposing exterior of the 2500, with its double-headlamp front and slightly bulging tail. The car marked a deliberate attempt by BMW to encroach on Mercedes territory.

Wuchtige Doppelscheinwerferfront und ausladendes Heck: Der 2500, mit dem BMW 1968 gezielt auf Mercedes-Terrain vorstößt, hat auch repräsentativen Chrom zu bieten.

Une ligne agressive, des phares doubles et une poupe interminable: la 2500 avec laquelle BMW marche résolument sur les plates-bandes de Mercedes en 1968 ne manque pas d'atouts.

The dashboard, center console and storage shelf are functional and well-designed. The six-cylinder in-line engine, with its block angled 30 degrees to the right, generated 150 bhp.

Klar gegliedert und funktionell angeordnet präsentieren sich Armaturenbrett und Mittelkonsole mit Ablagefach. 150 PS aktiviert der Sechszylinder-Reihenmotor mit einem um 30 Grad zur rechten Seite geneigten Block.

Bien agencés et fonctionnels, telles sont les caractéristiques du tableau de bord et de la console médiane avec vide-poches. Le six-cylindres en ligne, dont le bloc est incliné de 30° sur la droite, développe 150 ch.

Almost 95,000 of this comfortable upper mid-range car were produced by BMW over a nine-year period.

Nahezu 95 000 dieser komfortablen Wagen der gehobenen Mittelklasse werden in neun Jahren bei BMW produziert.

Près de 95 000 de ces confortables voitures du segment supérieur seront produites chez BMW en neuf ans.

BMW CS E9 | 1968

Much admired at the Paris Motor Show in the autumn of 1968, BMW presented the 2800 CS as a commitment to large sporty coupés. The chassis of this slim car without a B-pillar was simply the consistent further development of the 2000 CS and was built by Karmann. Final assembly and the installation of the six-cylinder engine were at Dingolfing, a new BMW site in 1967. Here Hans Glas had failed in the construction of his top-of-the-range coupés and was forced to hand over his factory to BMW. The CS swiftly developed and soon the small "i" behind the CS indicated the transition to an injection engine. Simultaneously, the engine size was increased to 2985 cc—hence the 3.0 badge.

A strong 200 bhp engine catapulted the 3100 lbs (1400 kg) CSi to 135 mph (220 kph). As early as 1972, it was slimmed down by 285 lbs (130 kg) and the engine size was increased to 3003 cc for a special CSL version, the L standing for lightweight. CSL customers were rewarded with a tangible increase in acceleration from 0 to 62 mph (100 kph). The coupé's heart, that highly revving engine, remained refinement personified. But such refinement is expensive: 13.4 miles to the gallon (17.5 liters per 100 km) driven hard made frequent gas station stops inevitable, despite a

18.5-gallon (70-liter) tank. This at a time when European petrol prices rocketed.

Which coupé driver is going to allow an oil crisis to spoil his fun behind the wheel? BMW, believing that it had to respond to a period of economic challenge with a 2.5-liter economy version, produced a flop. The strange calculation of dropping 50 bhp, losing rapid acceleration and the top speed, all to save three quarters of a gallon (three liters) per tankful was hardly worth noting, so there were only 844 buyers. Even savings of about 4000 marks were insufficient. Some options, which came as standard on the CSi, had to be added on.

The opposite trend was indicated. The CSL coupé with huge front spoiler, wind splitters and rear spoiler was aimed at sporting activities, its luxury accessories removed for weight reasons. The sports package was supplemented by gigantic wing structures at the rear of the car and a roof spoiler. This fixed the outline of the racing coupé—except for widening the fenders.

The success story of the coupés (2800 CS from 1968 to 1971, 3.0 CS/CSi from 1971 to 1975) was reflected in healthy production figures. Including 844 "economy" 2.5 coupés, more than 30,000 cars were built, 8142 of them the CSi.

Auf dem Pariser Autosalon im Herbst 1968 viel bestaunt, stellt BMW den 2800 CS als Bekenntnis zu großen sportlichen Coupés vor. Freilich ist die Karosserie des schlanken Wagens ohne B-Säule nichts anderes als eine konsequente Weiterentwicklung des 2000 CS und wird bei Karmann gebaut. Die Endmontage und der Einbau des Sechszylindermotors erfolgen in Dingolfing. Hier ist Hans Glas am Bau solcher Oberklassecoupés gescheitert und hat sein Werk an BMW abtreten müssen. Der CS entwickelt sich rasant, und bald symbolisiert das kleine „i" hinter dem CS den Übergang zum Einspritzmotor. Gleichzeitig wird der Hubraum auf 2985 cm³ vergrößert – deshalb 3.0.

200 PS wuchten den immerhin 1400 Kilo schweren Wagen auf 220 Stundenkilometer. Bereits 1972 wird der CSi um 130 Kilo abgespeckt, und das Triebwerk bekommt 3003 cm³ Hubraum. Diese Ausführung wird CSL genannt. Mit einer deutlich besseren Beschleunigung von 0 auf 100 Stundenkilometer werden die Käufer des Coupés belohnt. Das Herzstück, der drehfreudige Motor, überzeugt durch seine Laufkultur. Aber diese Kultur kostet etwas: 17,5 Liter Super bei allzu scharfer Gangart machen trotz des 70-Liter-Tanks häufige Tankstopps unumgänglich und das bei rapide steigenden Benzinpreisen.

Doch welcher Coupéfahrer lässt sich schon das Fahrvergnügen durch eine sogenannte Ölkrise verderben? Im Glauben, den wirtschaftlich schweren Zeiten mit einer 2,5-Liter-Sparversion begegnen zu müssen, erlebt BMW einen Reinfall. Die Rechnung, auf 50 PS, eindrucksvolle Beschleunigungserlebnisse und Geschwindigkeiten um 220 Stundenkilometer verzichten zu können, um pro Tankfüllung läppische drei Liter zu sparen, begreifen nur 844 Käufer. Selbst die Ersparnis von rund 4000 Mark lockt nicht, da einige Extras, die beim CSi zum Serienumfang gehören, dagegen aufgerechnet werden müssen.

Der Trend geht genau in die andere Richtung. Das CSL-Coupé mit überdimensionalem Frontspoiler, Windsplits und Heckspoiler zielt auf sportliche Aktivitäten, zumal auf Luxusaccessoires aus Gewichtsgründen verzichtet wird. Ein gigantisches Flügelwerk für das Wagenheck und ein Dachspoiler ergänzen das Sportpaket. Damit steht das Outfit des Rennsport-Coupés bereits – bis auf Kotflügelverbreiterungen – fest.

Die Erfolgsstory der Coupés (2800 CS von 1968 bis 1971, 3.0 CS/CSi von 1971 bis 1975) schlägt sich in einer ansehnlichen Produktion nieder. Einschließlich der 844 „Sparbrötchen" werden mehr als 30 000 Wagen gebaut, 8142 davon sind CSi.

Au Salon de l'automobile de Paris, à l'automne 1968, sous les yeux étonnés des nombreux visiteurs, BMW dévoile la 2800 CS, qui se classe parmi les gros coupés sportifs. La carrosserie de l'élégante voiture sans montant central n'est toutefois rien d'autre qu'une juste extrapolation de la 2000 CS. Elle est construite chez Karmann. Le montage final et l'installation du moteur six-cylindres ont lieu à Dingolfing. Dans cette ville, Hans Glas avait fait faillite en voulant construire de tels coupés du segment supérieur et avait dû céder son usine à BMW. La CS connaît un développement rapide et, bientôt, le petit «i» derrière le CS signale la présence d'un moteur à injection. Simultanément, la cylindrée passe à 2985 cm³ – d'où le 3.0.

Pas moins de 200 ch propulsent à 220 km/h cette voiture qui pèse tout de même 1400 kg. Dès 1972, elle est allégée de 130 kg et le moteur a une cylindrée de 3003 cm³. Cette version est appelée CSL. L'acheteur du coupé CSL appréciera, lui, les meilleures accélérations pour le 0 à 100 km/h. Le moteur, par sa spontanéité à monter en régime, séduit par sa perfection. Mais cette perfection a un prix : malgré un réservoir de 70 litres, les 17,5 litres de super consommés à bride abattue imposent des ravitaillements fréquents et ce, alors que le prix de l'essence augmente à vue d'œil.

Mais quel amateur de coupés accepterait de gâcher son plaisir à cause d'un soi-disant choc pétrolier? BMW, croyant répliquer avec une version économique de 2,5 litres en période de crise économique, subit un échec cinglant : seuls 844 acheteurs se laissent séduire – renoncer à 50 ch, à l'ivresse des accélérations et à des vitesses d'environ 220 km/h pour économiser trois malheureux litres par plein d'essence. Même l'économie à l'achat d'environ 4000 marks n'est pas un argument suffisamment convaincant, car il faut y ajouter quelques options qui font partie de l'équipement de série sur la CSi.

La tendance va exactement dans le sens contraire. Le coupé CSL, avec un imposant aileron avant, windsplits et becquet arrière, affiche effrontément sa sportivité, d'autant plus que des accessoires de luxe ont été supprimés pour l'alléger. Le kit sport est complété par un impressionnant becquet arrière et un aileron de toit. Les lignes du coupé compétition sont à la mesure de ses ambitions – à l'exception des élargisseurs d'ailes.

La «success-story» des coupés (2800 CS de 1968 à 1971, 3.0 CS/CSi de 1971 à 1975) s'est traduite par un succès commercial sans précédent – y compris les 844 exemplaires de la «version économique», plus de 30 000 voitures sont construites, dont 8142 CSi.

The type plate on the tailgate makes it abundantly clear that this is a CS with a 3-liter injection engine.

Unübersehbar verkündet das Typenschild auf der Heckklappe, dass es sich hier um einen CS mit dem 3-Liter-Einspritzmotor handelt.

L'inscription sur la malle arrière affiche fièrement qu'il s'agit ici d'une CS à moteur à injection de 3 litres.

Beneath the hood resides a six-cylinder engine with electronically-controlled Bosch fuel injection. It generates 200 bhp at 5300 rpm.

Unter der Haube macht sich ein Sechszylinder mit elektronisch gesteuerter Bosch-Benzineinspritzung breit. Bei 5300 Umdrehungen werden 200 PS frei.

Un six-cylindres à injection électronique Bosch occupe le compartiment moteur. Il délivre 200 ch à 5300 tr/min.

BMW 5 E12 | 1972

The first of a new BMW generation saw the light of an automotive day in September 1972: the 520. It heralded the start of the middleweight 5 series. Although this BMW partially owed its physical appearance to the planned six-cylinder engine, its heart was a four-cylinder engine. And this heartbeat was simply not enough for a vehicle at the top end of the middle class. This fact was only taken into account five years later, when all BMW 520s had a new six-cylinder implant.

The four-cylinder required some automotive surgery. Changing the combustion chambers to what are known as "3-sphere turbulence combustion chambers" prompted a compression ratio increase, therefore optimizing the mixture combustion and increasing both performance and fuel efficiency. More functional changes came for environmental reasons: the new Stromberg downdraft carburetor with automatic start improved emission control, particularly in cold starts.

The only problems encountered were related to the vehicle's performance. A 115 bhp engine required almost 13 seconds to bring a car weighing 2805 lbs (1275 kg) from 0 to 62 mph (100 kph); to make matters worse, there were 44 lbs (20 kg) extra with the automatic. At the top end, speeds of up to 109 mph (175 kph) were attained and the fuel injection car which delivered 130 bhp could reach 114 mph (183 kph).

The addition of longer wheelbases, wider track and anti-roll bars to the tried and tested chassis with MacPherson struts at the front, and a triangulated trailing arm at the rear, was so effective that only a mild "pedicure" was required: fine-tuning the suspension. Helpful cornering characteristics—there were early signals of slight oversteer—and high levels of driving comfort were both 520 plus factors.

The safe chassis with strengthened struts and special beam rigidity in the sub-frame were worthy of special note. Computer calculations predicted what could be crumpled in an accident, and what should remain intact.

High standards were, of course, expected of a car which cost 15,000 marks without any extras in 1972. The efficient interior did not let anyone down. The dashboard lit up in impressive muted orange shades whenever the lights were switched on, but what was most striking was the volume of fresh or heated air which could be displaced every 60 seconds.

The 520 came with either a five-speed or an automatic transmission and options even included the seatbelts. Yet it offered so much for its price that over 45,000 new 5 series were sold in 1973 alone.

Die „Erstgeburt" einer neuen BMW-Generation erblickt im September 1972 das Licht der Autowelt: der 520, mit dem die 5er Reihe anfängt. Auch wenn er sich optisch ein wenig an den großen Sechszylindern orientiert, ist sein Herz ein Vierzylinder. Und das schlägt eigentlich zu schwach für ein Fahrzeug der gehobenen Mittelklasse. Erst fünf Jahre später trägt man diesem Umstand Rechnung und implantiert neue Sechszylinder in den BMW 520.

Einen kleinen „chirurgischen Eingriff" hat sich der Vierzylinder jedoch gefallen lassen müssen. Durch die Umwandlung der Brennräume in sogenannte „3-Kugel-Wirbelwannen" und somit durch die Vergrößerung des Verdichtungsverhältnisses wird die Verbrennung des Gemischs optimiert. Dazu kommt etwas „Umwelt-Kosmetik". Für eine bessere Abgasregulierung – besonders bei Kaltstarts – sorgen die neuen Stromberg-Fallstromvergaser mit Startautomatik.

Trotzdem hapert es bei der Fitness, denn der 115-PS-Motor benötigt nahezu 13 Sekunden, um das stattliche Gewicht von 1275 Kilo (bei der Automatik sind es 20 Kilo zusätzlich) von 0 auf 100 Stundenkilometer zu beschleunigen. Oben heraus geht es bis 175 Stundenkilometer weiter, und der Einspritzer mit 130 PS bringt es immerhin auf 183 km/h.

Verlängerter Radstand, verbreiterte Spur und Drehstab-stabilisatoren kommen dem bewährten Fahrwerk mit McPherson-Federbeinen vorn und einer Schräglenkerachse hinten so entgegen, dass nur noch etwas „Pediküre" notwendig ist, nämlich Feintuning bei der Federungsabstimmung. Gutmütige Kurveneigenschaften – leichtes Übersteuern kündigt sich frühzeitig an – und hoher Fahrkomfort sind Pluspunkte des 520.

Besonderes Augenmerk verdienen die sicheren Chassis mit verstärkten Holmen und besonderen Flankenversteifungen in der Bodengruppe. Computer haben errechnet, was bei einem Unfall geknautscht werden soll und was intakt bleiben muss.

Natürlich werden an einen Wagen, der 1972 ohne Extras knapp 15 000 Mark ab Werk kostet, auch Ansprüche gestellt. In dieser Hinsicht gibt sich das Interieur keine Blöße. Dass die Armaturen bei eingeschaltetem Licht orangefarben leuchten, ist eher nebensächlich. Außergewöhnlich hoch ist das Volumen der Frisch- oder Heizungsluft, die pro Minute bewegt werden kann.

Der Wagen, der auch mit Fünfganggetriebe oder Automatik erhältlich ist, und zu dessen Extras unter anderem Sicherheitsgurte zählen, bietet für seinen Preis offenbar so viel, dass allein 1973 über 45 000 neue 5er verkauft werden.

Une nouvelle génération de BMW voit le jour en septembre 1972. Son premier «rejeton» est la 520. Elle inaugure par la même occasion la Série 5. Même si, sur le plan esthétique, elle s'inspire assez étroitement des grosses six-cylindres, on trouve sous son capot un moteur à quatre-cylindres. Un moteur qui manque d'ailleurs d'un peu de nervosité pour une voiture du segment intermédiaire supérieur. Il faudra attendre cinq ans pour que ce petit défaut disparaisse et que la BMW 520 reçoive un six-cylindres.

Le quatre-cylindres a cependant dû subir bon gré mal gré une petite «intervention chirurgicale». La combustion du mélange est optimisée par des modifications des chambres de combustion appelées «baignoires à tourbillons à trois sphères», ce qui permet d'augmenter le taux de compression. BMW en profite aussi pour faire un geste pour l'environnement. Les nouveaux carburateurs inversés Stromberg avec starter automatique régulent mieux les gaz d'échappement, en particulier lors des démarrages à froid.

Il n'y a que les muscles qui lui fassent défaut. Il faut près de 13 secondes au moteur de 115 ch pour faire passer de 0 à 100 km/h une voiture qui pèse 1275 kg (et même 20 kg supplémentaires dans la version à boîte automatique). La vitesse de pointe se limite à 175 km/h, la version à injection de 130 ch atteignant tout de même 183 km/h.

Un empattement allongé, des sillons plus larges et des barres de torsion stabilisatrices complètent si bien les trains roulants à jambes élastiques McPherson qui ont fait leurs preuves à l'avant tout comme l'essieu arrière à bras obliques qu'il suffit d'affiner les tarages de suspension pour obtenir un comportement parfaitement équilibré. Le comportement sécurisant en virage – le dérapage arrière ne surprend jamais – et le confort dynamique sont des atouts de la 520.

Une attention toute particulière a été apportée à la cellule passagers au niveau de la sécurité avec des longerons renforcés et des flancs plus rigides. Des ordinateurs ont calculé et programmé ce qui doit se déformer ou non en cas de collision.

Naturellement, une voiture qui coûte près de 15 000 marks départ usine sans options en 1972 ne doit pas décevoir. Et, de ce point de vue, le cockpit est assez réussi. Lorsque la lumière est allumée, les cadrans sont illuminés d'une couleur orange, mais ce détail est plutôt secondaire. En revanche, le volume d'air frais ou chaud par minute que brasse l'installation est inhabituellement élevé.

La voiture est disponible au choix avec une boîte manuelle à cinq vitesses ou une transmission automatique. La liste des options comprend même les ceintures de sécurité. Cette voiture en offre tant pour son prix que, rien qu'en 1973, plus de 45 000 nouvelles «cinqs» seront vendues.

The launch of the BMW 520 in 1972 heralded a new generation: the 5 series. Safety, comfort and good handling were the distinguishing characteristics of this automobile, which bears a slight external resemblance to the large BMW six-cylinder.

Mit dem BMW 520 läuft 1972 eine neue Generation an: die 5er Reihe. Sicherheit, Komfort und gutes Fahrverhalten kennzeichnen dieses Fahrzeug, das sich äußerlich leicht an die großen Sechszylinder von BMW anlehnt.

La BMW 520 de 1972 marque l'arrivée d'une nouvelle génération: la Série 5. Sécurité, confort et bonne tenue de route sont les qualités de cette voiture qui, sur le plan esthétique, s'inspire quelque peu des grosses BMW six-cylindres.

Vast quantities of fresh or heated air are forced into the car by the three controls on the center console. However, the car's engine was less impressive, being a four-cylinder affair developing 115 bhp.

Ein enormes Volumen an Frisch- und Heizungsluft wird von den drei Schaltern in der Mittelkonsole des Cockpits bewegt. Den Wagen selbst bewegt allerdings nur ein 115-PS-Vierzylinder.

Les trois commandes sur la console médiane brassent un volume énorme d'air frais ou réchauffé. Pour sa propulsion, la voiture se contente d'un quatre-cylindres de 115 ch.

At first it is just a slight whistling sound at 4000 rpm, which grows into the "sweet roll of thunder" when the performance potential arrives alongside 6400 rpm. In the 2002 turbo, BMW took account of the resolution of the international ruling body of motor sport (FISA = Fédération Internationale du Sport Automobile) in Paris that future rallies would only be open to production cars.

Thus a very powerful machine was presented to the public at the Frankfurt Motor Show in 1973. A specific bhp per liter performance of 85 bhp outdid even the Porsche Carrera RS (80 bhp/liter). The magical letters "turbo" were an incentive to use the accelerator, but for some BMW shareholders, all this extrovert badging was like a red rag to a bull. They demanded that these "unreasonable" letters be removed from the cars, or at least from those supplied in Germany.

Assertive owners of the "turbo" were, of course, inclined to advertise to an even greater extent their four-wheeled power symbol, whose hot exhaust gases caused the vanes of the charger to whiz up to an almost unbelievable speed of 90,000 rpm. But it was not only the stripes of BMW Motorsport GmbH and the standard front spoiler which identified the 2002 turbo as the basis of a sporting car. Massive widening of the fenders and a rear spoiler gave the game away: here was the signal to attack in motor sport.

The interior transmitted a hint of sportiness: bucket seats, leather steering wheel and a speedometer which went to 150 mph (240 kph) with room for even higher speeds. This potential was restricted in the production version, and only really came into play beyond 4500 rpm. Power was shut off after mere moments of glory by a mundane contact breaker that was regulated by centrifugal force.

The understeering performance was a trait that a keen BMW driver, hitherto used to correcting sliding rear wheels during fast cornering, had to practice. However, drivers who were not averse to occasional excursions on to the north loop of the Nürburgring, quickly acclimatized to the effective brakes, which showed little fade. Back in 1973, internally ventilated disks with four-piston calipers at the front and enlarged brake drums at the rear represented state-of-the-art technology. The same praise did not apply to fuel consumption at 12.5 miles per gallon or 19 liters per 100 km. Its thirst for petrol was such that the petrol tank, enlarged to 18.5 gallons (70 liters), was empty after only 250 miles (400 km) of driving.

But anyone who likes to enjoy his driving pleasure to the full, wants to overtake on country roads without difficulty, and gets his kicks from the swing of the turbocharger boost gauge needle will not be too bothered by the dictates of the petrol pump. They sound their horn for the chase—with turbo power.

Erst ist es nur ein leichter Pfeifton bei 4000 Umdrehungen, der sich zu einem „süßen Donnergrollen" erhebt, wenn das Leistungspotential vehement bis auf 6400 Touren ansteigt. Mit dem 2002 turbo hat BMW einem Beschluss der obersten internationalen Automobilsportbehörde FISA (Féderation Internationale du Sport Automobile) in Paris Rechnung getragen, wonach der Rallyesport künftig nur noch mit Serien-Tourenwagen zu bestreiten ist.

Was für ein Kraftpaket, das sich auf der IAA 1973 dem Publikum präsentiert! Mit einer spezifischen Literleistung von knapp 85 PS wird sogar der Porsche Carrera RS (80 PS/Liter) überflügelt. Der magische Schriftzug „turbo" reizt zum Gas geben. Für einige Aktionäre der BMW AG ist der „turbo" eher ein Reizwort. Sie fordern – zumindest für die in Deutschland ausgelieferten Wagen – ein Verbot der „unzumutbaren" Lettern.

Ambitionierte Besitzer des BMW turbo neigen zu noch größerer Plakatierung ihres vierrädrigen Kraftsymbols, dessen heiße Abgase die Schaufeln des Laders in die unglaubliche Rotationsgeschwindigkeit von nahezu 90 000 Umdrehungen pro Minute versetzen. Doch nicht nur das Streifendesign der BMW Motorsport GmbH und der serienmäßige Frontspoiler identifizieren den 2002 turbo als Basissportler. Wuchtige Kotflügelverbreiterungen und ein Heckspoiler verraten, dass hiermit auch im Motorsport zum Angriff geblasen werden soll.

BMW 2002 turbo E20 | 1973

Das Interieur vermittelt einen Hauch von Sportlichkeit: Schalensitze, Lederlenkrad und ein Tacho, der bis 240 km/h reicht – Spielraum für noch mehr Potential. Dieses ist in der Serienversion beschränkt, setzt erst jenseits von 4500 Touren richtig ein und wird nach Momenten der Kraft und Herrlichkeit durch einen banalen fliehkraftgeregelten Unterbrecherkontakt abgeriegelt.

Gewöhnungsbedürftig ist das untersteuernde Fahrverhalten für einen BMW-Fahrer, der bislang gewohnt war, schnellen Kurvenpassagen mit dem Einfangen des Wagenhecks zu begegnen. Schnell gewöhnt sich der Freund gelegentlicher Ausritte auf die Nordschleife des Nürburgrings dagegen an die effektvoll – kaum Fading – arbeitenden Bremsen. Innenbelüftete Scheiben mit Vierkolbensätteln vorn und vergrößerte Bremstrommeln hinten sind 1973 modernster Stand der Technik. Vom Verbrauch (19 Liter bei Vollgas) kann man das weniger behaupten. Der Benzindurst ist so ausgeprägt, dass der auf 70 Liter vergrößerte Treibstofftank bereits nach 400 Kilometern normalen Fahrbetriebs leer ist.

Doch wer den Fahrspaß in vollen Zügen genießen will, auf Landstraßen problemlos überholen kann und sich am Ausschlag der Nadel des Ladedruckanzeigers Adrenalinstöße holt, den interessiert das Diktat der Zapfsäule wenig. Er bläst mit Turbo-Power zum Halali!

On ne perçoit tout d'abord qu'un léger sifflement à 4000 tr/min, qui se mue en un «délicieux coup de tonnerre» à 6400 tr/min lorsque l'on exploite tout le potentiel. Avec la 2002 turbo, BMW a tenu compte d'une résolution prise par la Fédération internationale du sport automobile (FISA), à Paris, qui exige que, désormais, seules les voitures de tourisme de série puissent participer aux rallyes.

Quelle puissante voiture est présentée au public du Salon de l'automobile de Francfort en 1973! Avec une puissance au litre de près de 85 ch, elle bat même la Porsche Carrera RS (80 ch/litre). L'emblème magique «turbo» incite à écraser l'accélérateur. Quelques actionnaires de BMW AG sont choqués et ils exigent, tout au moins pour les voitures livrées en Allemagne, une suppression de cette mention jugée «provocante».

Les propriétaires ambitieux de la «turbo» sont, au contraire, plutôt enclins à afficher encore plus visiblement les performances de leur engin dont les gaz d'échappement brûlants font tourner les ailettes du turbocompresseur au régime incroyable de près de 90000 tr/min. Mais il n'y a pas que les bandes décoratives de la BMW Motorsport GmbH et l'aileron avant de série qui font de la 2002 turbo une excellente voiture pour la course. De massifs élargisseurs d'ailes et un aileron arrière trahissent aussi sa vocation: la compétition automobile.

Le cockpit confirme sa sportivité: baquets, volant cuir et un tachymètre gradué jusqu'à 240 km/h, avec de la marge pour encore plus de potentiel. Celui-ci est limité dans la version de série, qui ne commence vraiment à pousser qu'à partir de 4500 tours et où, après quelques instants de gloire et de splendeur, un banal rupteur actionné par la force centrifuge met un terme à cette débauche de puissance.

Le comportement du véhicule demande une certaine accoutumance de la part des pilotes de BMW, jusqu'ici habitués à franchir rapidement les virages en contrôlant le décrochement de l'arrière. L'amateur de courses folles sur la boucle Nord du Nürburgring s'est vite habitué à l'efficacité des freins pratiquement insensibles au fading: en 1973, les disques ventilés à quatre pistons à l'avant et les tambours de plus grande dimension à l'arrière sont le must. On ne peut pas en dire autant de la consommation (19 litres à plein gaz). Sa soif est telle que le réservoir de carburant agrandi à 70 litres est déjà à sec après 400 kilomètres de conduite normale.

Mais celui qui veut profiter du plaisir de conduire, doubler quand il le souhaite sur les petites routes de campagne et ressentir une poussée d'adrénaline chaque fois que l'aiguille du manomètre de pression atteint la butée ne s'intéresse guère à la facture de la pompe à essence. Il sonne l'hallali – turbo à fond.

From its roof to the tread of its 185/70 HR tires, considered wide at the time, the 2002 turbo provided Bavarian power without compare. Sales were moderate due to the generally bad economic situation. No more than 1670 deliveries were made.

Vom Dach bis hin zur damals als breit geltenden 185/70 HR-Sohle ist der 2002 turbo ein „Kraft-Bayer" sondergleichen. Aufgrund der allgemein schlechten wirtschaftlichen Lage läuft der Verkauf mäßig. Der Wagen wird insgesamt nur 1670 Mal ausgeliefert.

Du toit aux pneus de 185/70 HR, ce qui n'était pas rien à l'époque, la 2002 turbo roule des mécaniques. Mais la conjoncture économique n'est pas favorable aux sportives de cet acabit et cette voiture ne sera, au total, produite qu'à 1670 exemplaires.

Bucket seats, leather steering wheel, speedo up to 150 mph (240 kph) and gauge for the turbocharger: appropriate equipment for this eight-second sprinter from 0 to 62 mph (100 kph). The 2-liter unit unleashed a snarling 170 bhp.

Schalensitze, Lederlenkrad, Tacho bis 240 km/h und Druckanzeige für den Abgasturbolader: Dies sind die standesgemäßen Attribute des 8-Sekunden-Sprinters (von 0 auf 100 km/h). In dem 2-Liter-Aggregat werden 170 PS fauchend entfacht.

Baquets, volant cuir, compteur gradué jusqu'à 240 km/h et affichage de la pression du turbocompresseur, cette sprinteuse qui passe de 0 à 100 km/h en 8 secondes affiche fièrement ses attributs. Le moteur de deux litres délivre 170 ch, qui piaffent d'impatience.

BMW 3 E21 | 1975

With its completely new six-cylinder injection engine, the 323i was the Bavarian muscle in the 3 series, which was launched in May 1975. Two exhaust pipes draw visible and aural attention to the fact that here the monotone of the 3 series palette—from the 316 to the 320—was relieved by the sound of a 143 bhp engine. With inlet manifold fuel injection (Bosch K-Jetronic) the mixture was precisely prepared. The 2.3-liter engine smoothly delivered its power with minimal vibration from a crankshaft held in seven bearings and civilized by a dozen counterweights.

Sheer driving pleasure—not just in a straight line at a top speed of 122 mph (196 kph)—was assisted by strengthened springs and stabilizers. This was a compact car that did not have to be wrestled into corners, for the servo-assisted steering worked with pleasant ease and extreme precision.

Four disk brakes, the front ones internally ventilated, rein in the free-running temperament of the 323i on request. Offering acceleration of just nine seconds from 0 to 62 mph (100 kph) the 323i was a class leader—always assuming efficient use of the five-speed transmission, installed from September 1979 onwards. Those who preferred a little

less sportiness and wished to change gear without hassle were provided with a ZF automatic transmission that featured an hydraulic torque converter and three-speed planetary gears.

Using a relatively high compression ratio of 9.5:1, this 3 series took quite a swig of premium. Yet an average of 17 miles to the gallon (14 liters per 100 km) represented efficient performance in 1978 when compared against the high bhp figure. The competition from Alfa Romeo and Daimler-Benz was thirstier, but after some 260 miles (420 km) the tank of the Bavarian was empty.

The first 3 series (designated E21 for internal use) lived until 1983 and presented the white and blue BMW badge with a result previously thought impossible: 1.36 million cars sold, of which approximately 35 percent featured the six-cylinder engine.

As the top model, the 323i had collected a valuable cross-section of admiring customers: there were drivers with sporting ambitions, casual users of the accelerator, and people who valued reserves of power and effective brakes for everyday use.

Mit einem völlig neuen Sechszylinder-Einspritzmotor ist der 323i der „Kraftbayer" der im Mai 1975 aus der Taufe gehobenen 3er Serie. Zwei Auspuffrohre machen äußerlich, aber auch akustisch darauf aufmerksam, dass hier die „Eintönigkeit" der 3er Palette – beginnend mit dem 316 bis zum 320 – vom Sound eines 143 PS starken Triebwerkes unterbrochen wird. Mit einer Saugrohr-Benzineinspritzung (Bosch-K-Jetronic) wird das Gemisch gut dosiert aufbereitet. Laufruhig entfaltet das 2,3-Liter-Triebwerk seine Leistung: Keine Vibrationen, denn die siebenfach gelagerte Kurbelwelle weist ein Dutzend Gegengewichte auf.

Der Freude am Fahren – nicht nur geradeaus mit einer Spitzengeschwindigkeit von 196 Stundenkilometern – dienen verstärkte Federn und Stabilisatoren. Ein kompaktes Auto, das nicht mit Nachdruck in die Kurven gezogen werden muss, weil die Servolenkung angenehm leicht und äußerst präzise arbeitet.

Vier Scheibenbremsen – die vorderen innenbelüftet – zügeln bei Bedarf das Temperament des 323i, der mit einer Beschleunigung von knapp neun Sekunden von 0 auf 100 Stundenkilometer Primus in der Mittelklasse ist, gute

Schaltarbeit mit dem ab September 1979 eingebauten Fünf-ganggetriebe vorausgesetzt. Wer es weniger sportlich mag und ohne Hakelei in die Gänge kommen will, dem steht eine ZF-Automatik mit hydraulischem Wandler und 3-Gang-Pla-netengetriebe zur Verfügung.

Mit einem relativ hohem Verdichtungsverhältnis von 9,5:1 stemmt dieser 3er eine ordentliche „Maß" Superbenzin. Doch 14 Liter im Schnitt sind 1978 gemessen an der PS-Zahl Best-wert. Die Konkurrenten von Alfa Romeo und Daimler-Benz schlucken mehr Benzin. Nach rund 420 Kilometern ist der Maßkrug des Bajuwaren jedenfalls leer.

Die erste 3er Reihe (werksintern E21 genannt) läuft bis 1983 und beschert der weißblauen Marke ein bis dahin nicht für möglich gehaltenes Ergebnis: 1,36 Millionen Wagen, davon etwa 35 Prozent mit einem Sechszylinder bestückt, werden ausgeliefert.

Als Topmodell dieser Erfolgsreihe schafft sich der 323i einen ansehnlichen Freundeskreis: sportlich ambitionierte Fahrer, lässige Gasgeber und Menschen, die im Alltags-betrieb Kraftreserven und wirksame Bremsen für schnelles und sicheres Vorankommen schätzen.

Avec son nouveau six-cylindres à injection, la 323i est la «Bavaroise musclée» de la nouvelle Série 3 qui voit le jour en mai 1975. Extérieurement, deux pots d'échappement attirent bruyamment l'attention sur le fait que la «monotonie» de la Série 3, qui va de la 316 à la 320, est rompue par ce moteur de 143 ch. L'injection d'essence Bosch K-Jetronic dans les tubulures d'aspiration garantit un bon dosage du mélange. Le 2,3 litres se distingue par une montée en puissance régulière, sans vibration, car le vilebrequin à sept paliers comporte douze contrepoids.

Le plaisir de conduire – et pas seulement en ligne droite à la vitesse de pointe de 196 km/h – est intense grâce à la présence de ressorts et de stabilisateurs renforcés. Une voi-ture compacte qu'il n'est pas nécessaire de pousser dans les virages parce que la direction assistée est agréablement légère et extrêmement précise.

Quatre freins à disques, ventilés à l'avant, jugulent – si besoin est – le tempérament de la 323i, qui est la première de sa classe avec à peine 9 secondes pour les accélérations de 0 à 100 km/h, à condition de bien manier la boîte de cinq vitesses qui l'équipe à partir de septembre 1979. Celui qui

préfère une conduite plus paisible a une excellente alternative avec une boîte automatique ZF à convertisseur hydraulique et train épicycloïdal à trois rapports.

Avec son taux de compression relativement élevé de 9,5:1, cette Série 3 ne dédaigne pas le super. Mais, en 1978, une consommation moyenne de 14 litres aux 100 km est un résultat inégalé compte tenu de la performance. Ses concur-rentes de chez Alfa Romeo et Daimler-Benz consomment davantage. Elle peut parcourir 420 km, avant de rejoindre la pompe à essence.

La première Série 3 (nom de code interne E21) est construite jusqu'en 1983 et permet à la marque à l'hélice bleue et blanche de remporter un succès commercial inédit à ce jour: 1,36 million de voitures vendues, dont un bon tiers de six-cylindres.

Autour de la 323i, se constitue un enviable club d'ama-teurs: les automobilistes férus de conduite sportive, ceux qui aiment rouler vite et décontractés ainsi que ceux qui, dans la vie quotidienne, apprécient d'avoir de la puis-sance en réserve et des freins efficaces pour rouler vite en toute sécurité.

The top model of the new 3 series, designated E21 within the company, is immediately recognizable from the front thanks to the 323i type plate next to the double headlamps. It proved so lively that it was fitted with a five-speed gearbox in September 1979.

Das Top-Modell der werksintern E21 genannten neuen 3er-Reihe, von vorn sofort an dem Typenschild 323i neben den Doppelscheinwerfern erkennbar, versprüht so viel Temperament, dass es im September 1979 mit einem Fünfganggetriebe belohnt wird.

Le top model de la nouvelle Série 3, qui porte le nom de code E21, est reconnaissable immédiatement à l'inscription 323i qui figure à côté des doubles phares. Son tempérament est si débordant qu'il est récompensé, en septembre 1979, par une boîte manuelle à cinq vitesses.

A drive-free continuous fuel injection system supplies the smooth lively six-cylinder in-line engine, which develops 143 bhp, giving this mid-range model a 0 to 62 mph (100 kph) time of just under nine seconds.

Eine antriebslose, kontinuierliche Benzineinspritzung versorgt den drehfreudigen laufruhigen Reihensechszylinder, dessen 143 PS den flotten Mittelklassewagen in knapp neun Sekunden auf 100 Stundenkilometer beschleunigen.

Une injection d'essence continue sans entraînement mécanique alimente le six-cylindres en ligne souple et réactif dont les 143 ch permettent à cette rapide voiture de taille moyenne d'atteindre le 0 à 100 km/h en neuf secondes à peine.

"Don't choose a special car, choose your own standpoint," was the BMW advertisement theme for the 6 series, which could be admired at the Geneva Motor Show in March 1976. The special car (coded E24) turned out to be an elegant coupé for the discriminating. This was a quality guarantee from BMW which its partner Karmann apparently failed to satisfy, since final assembly was transferred early in its production life to the BMW factory at Dingolfing. Karmann was left with the production of the bare body.

Once more it was clear that coupé buyers make sporting comparisons of engine performance. The 630 CS (3-liter carburetor engine) and the 628 CSi (2.8-liter injection engine) sold a total 9642 units between 1971 and 1987. The 633 CSi, whose 3.2-liter unit delivered a more generous 197 bhp, earned 20,234 buyers. Plenty, but nothing when compared to the 635 CSi: 51,564 examples were built with its 3.5-liter engine, rated from 211 bhp (catalytic converter) to 286 bhp (M version). German membership figures of the BMW 6 series club of Germany are correspondingly high.

Externally the CSi appearance was hardly spectacular and characterized more by classical lines, typical for a BMW coupé. Aerodynamic aids such as front and rear spoilers to cut lift at high speeds were probably appearance items, considering the original curb weight of 3290 lbs (1495 kg).

The technical innovations were more convincing, particularly as far as the electronics were concerned. There were digital engine electronics with overrun fuel cutoff down to 1000 rpm. Or there was the option of total electronic control of engine and transmission via a four-speed automatic transmission using electronics and hydraulics. Unfortunately, the entry of electronics to the dashboard could not be avoided either. There was an on-board computer which played along with an "SI Service Interval Indicator" and "EC Energy Control." At 16 miles to the gallon of premium (15 liters per 100 km) this was a joke.

Also mechanically there was progress to report for the CSi of the 6 series. The new coupés eventually combined the advantages of the 7 series' double-jointed transverse control arm front axle and new 13-degree trailing arm angles inherited from the 5 series. For a car of this price class the issue of an ABS system as standard was no longer worthy of comment as early as the 1980s. From 1987 onwards it was supplemented by a rear suspension self-leveling device.

The voluminous coupé proved surprisingly rapid in motor sport, and won the European touring car championships three times (1981, 1983 and 1986) as well as the German national title in 1983. There was no lack of power potential in the racing version of the 3.5-liter engine with two valves per cylinder, peaking at a best of 380 bhp, but frequently having to win against rivals with V12 motors or turbochargers.

"Entscheiden Sie sich nicht nur für ein besonderes Automobil, sondern auch für einen eigenen Standpunkt." Mit diesem Slogan wirbt BMW für die 6er Reihe, deren Vorbote auf dem Genfer Salon im März 1976 zu bestaunen ist. Das „besondere" Auto der Baureihe E24 entpuppt sich als elegantes Coupé für Anspruchsvolle. Für BMW ist dies eine Qualitätsverpflichtung, der Partner Karmann offenbar nicht genügt, denn die Endmontage wird ins BMW-Werk Dingolfing verlegt. Karmann bleibt die Fertigung der Rohkarosse.

Einmal mehr zeigt sich, dass Coupékäufer den Vergleich mit Sportwagen suchen, wenn es um die Triebwerksleistung geht. Der 630 CS mit 3-Liter-Vergasermotor und der 628 CSi mit 2,8-Liter-Einspritzmotor bringen es von 1971 bis 1987 zusammen auf 9642 verkaufte Einheiten. Der 633 CSi, dessen 3,2-Liter-Aggregat mit etwas üppigeren 197 PS aufwartet, findet 20 234 Käufer. Dies sind große Absatzzahlen und doch nichts gegen den 635 CSi: 51 564 dieser Coupés mit 3,5-Liter-Motoren, deren Leistung von 211 PS (mit Kat) bis 286 PS (M-Version) reicht, werden gebaut. Entsprechend hoch ist die Mitgliederzahl im „BMW 6er Club Deutschland e.V."

Das äußere Erscheinungsbild des CSi, kaum spektakulär und eher von klassischer Linienführung geprägt, ist typisch für ein Coupé. Aerodynamische Hilfen wie Front- und Heckspoiler für mehr Abtrieb bei höheren Geschwindigkeiten

BMW 6 E24 | 1976

dürften angesichts von 1495 Kilo Leergewicht in erster Linie der Optik gedient haben.

Überzeugender sind die technischen Innovationen, besonders im Bereich der Elektronik: Digitale Motorelektronik mit Schubabschaltung bis hinunter zu 1000 Touren oder – auf Wunsch – eine elektronische Gesamtsteuerung für Motor und Getriebe durch eine Viergang-Automatik mit elektronisch-hydraulischer Arbeitsweise. Leider lässt sich der Einzug der Elektronik auch ins Armaturenbrett nicht vermeiden. Dort tobt sich ein Bordcomputer mit „SI Service Intervallanzeiger" und „EC Energy Control" aus – bei 15 Litern Super auf 100 Kilometer ein Witz!

Aber auch mechanisch gibt es beim CSi der 6er Reihe Fortschritte zu vermelden. Die neuen Coupés vereinen die Vorteile der Doppelgelenk-Federbeinvorderachse mit denen einer neuen 13-Grad-Schräglenkerhinterachse. Für einen Wagen dieser Preisklasse erübrigt sich schon in den achtziger Jahren die Frage nach einem serienmäßig eingebauten ABS-System. Ab 1987 kommt noch eine Niveauregelung hinzu.

Als erstaunlich wendig erweist sich das voluminöse Coupé im Motorsport. Dreimal immerhin holt es die Tourenwagen-Europameisterschaft (1981, 1983 und 1986) sowie 1983 den nationalen deutschen Titel. An Kraft mangelt es der Rennversion des 3,5-Liter-Motors mit zwei Ventilen pro Zylinder ohnehin nicht: 380 PS bringt er an die Hinterräder.

« Ne choisissez pas une voiture spéciale, choisissez la vôtre », déclare le slogan publicitaire de BMW pour la Série 6 dont on peut admirer le prototype au Salon de Genève en 1976. La voiture « spéciale », nom de code E24, se présente sous les traits d'un élégant coupé pour conducteur exigeant. Pour BMW, qualité oblige – une obligation à laquelle ne répond apparemment pas son partenaire Karmann, car le montage final est transféré à l'usine BMW de Dingolfing, Karmann conservant la fabrication de la carrosserie blanche.

Une fois de plus, on constate que les acheteurs de coupés ont les mêmes critères de jugement que les acheteurs de voitures de sport en ce qui concerne la puissance des moteurs. La 630 CS (moteur à carburateur de 3 litres) et la 628 CSi (moteur à injection de 2,8 litres) ont été vendues à 9642 unités de 1971 à 1987. La 633 CSi, dont le 3,2 litres, plus puissant, développe 197 ch fait 20234 adeptes, ce qui est beaucoup mais peu comparé à la 635 CSi : 51564 de ces coupés à moteur de 3,5 litres, dont la puissance va de 211 ch (avec catalyseur) à 286 ch (version M), seront construits. Comme on peut l'imaginer, le nombre des adhérents au club allemand des BMW Série 6 est élevé.

Rejetant le tape-à-l'œil et plutôt empreinte de classicisme, l'allure extérieure de la CSi est typique d'un coupé. Compte tenu d'un poids à vide de 1495 kg, les composants aérodynamiques tels que les becquets avant et arrière, censés générer la stabilité nécessaire à haute vitesse, n'auraient pas été d'une grande efficacité.

Les innovations techniques sont plus convaincantes, notamment dans le domaine de l'électronique : gestion moteur numérique avec coupure de l'alimentation jusqu'à moins de 1000 tr/min ou, sur demande, une gestion électronique globale du moteur et de la boîte de vitesses grâce à une transmission automatique à quatre rapports avec commande électronique et hydraulique. Malheureusement, l'omniprésence de l'électronique n'épargne pas le tableau de bord. Un ordinateur de bord, avec affichage des périodicités d'entretien et contrôle de la consommation, fait son apparition. À 15 litres de super aux 100 km, c'est une plaisanterie !

Mais, dans le domaine de la mécanique aussi, la version CSi de la Série 6 peut se prévaloir d'avoir fait des progrès. Les nouveaux coupés allient les avantages d'un essieu avant à jambes élastiques à double articulation à ceux d'un nouveau train arrière à bras obliques inclinés de 13 degrés. Pour une voiture de cette catégorie de prix, la présence en série du système ABS dès les années 1980 s'impose. Un correcteur d'assiette s'y ajoute en 1987.

Le volumineux coupé s'avère étonnamment maniable en compétition et remporte trois fois le championnat d'Europe des voitures de tourisme (en 1981, 1983 et 1986) ainsi que le championnat d'Allemagne en 1983. La version course du moteur de 3,5 litres ne manque pas de chevaux avec ses deux soupapes par cylindre : elle a 380 ch sous le capot.

The 3.5-liter power unit generates 218 bhp without the catalytic converter. Including its auxiliaries, the engine fills the 635 CSi's engine space, though leaving sufficient space for the ever-increasing electronics. The age of digital motoring is heralded by such features as total electronic control of engine and transmission.

Das 3,5-Liter-Triebwerk mit 218 PS ohne Kat und seine Nebenaggregate füllen den Motorraum des 635 CSi, lassen aber genügend Platz für die zunehmende Elektronisierung, beginnend bei der digitalen Motorelektronik mit Schubabschaltung bis hin zur elektronischen Gesamtsteuerung von Motor und Getriebe.

Le moteur de 3,5 litres et 218 ch sans catalyseur emplit le compartiment moteur de la 635 CSi avec ses organes, mais laisse assez de place pour l'électronique qui se généralise, de la gestion moteur numérique avec coupure de l'alimentation à la gestion électronique complète du moteur et de la boîte de vitesses.

The M635CSi power unit was borrowed from the M1. The six-cylinder four-valve engine with light alloy cross-flow cylinder heads generates a mighty 286 bhp at 6500 rpm, giving the one-and-a-half ton coupé stunning performance figures, for example 0 to 125 mph (200 kph) in just 30 seconds, a good 10 seconds less than the Mercedes 500 SEC.

Dem M1 entlehnt ist die Kraftquelle des M635CSi. Der Sechszylinder-Vierventiler mit Querstromzylinderkopf aus Leichtmetall mobilisiert bei 6500/min stattliche 286 PS, die dem anderthalb Tonnen schweren Coupé zu beachtlichen Fahrleistungen verhelfen. Von 0 auf 200 km/h benötigt es knapp 30 Sekunden, gut 10 Sekunden weniger als ein Mercedes 500 SEC.

Le moteur de la M635CSi s'inspire de celui de la M1. Le six-cylindres à quatre soupapes avec culasse cross-flow en alliage léger ne développe pas moins de 286 ch à 6500 tr/min qui confèrent de brillantes performances à ce coupé de 1500 kg: à peine 30 secondes pour le 0 à 200 km/h, 10 secondes de moins qu'une Mercedes 500 SEC !

The M635CSi, launched at the 1983 Frankfurt Motor Show, is both sporty and lavishly appointed, as befits a 155 mph (250 kph) coupé costing more than a Porsche S. The variety of accessories is impressive, and ranges from automatic electric controls and firmly-upholstered adjustable leather seats, whose adjustment options include the actual length of the seating surface, to the three-spoke sports steering wheel, also individually adjustable.

Im M635CSi – Premiere auf der IAA 1983 in Frankfurt – geht es sportlich und nobel zu. Schließlich kostet das 250 km/h schnelle Coupé mehr als ein Porsche S. Auffällig sind die vielen Accessoires, die elektrischen Bedienungshilfen und die straff gepolsterten Ledersitze, deren Einstellmöglichkeiten auch die Länge der Sitzfläche einschließen. Ebenfalls individuell einstellbar ist das Dreispeichen-Sportlenkrad.

La M635CSi, dont le lancement a lieu au Salon de l'automobile de Francfort en 1983, est aussi sportive qu'élégante. Ce coupé capable d'atteindre les 250 km/h coûte d'ailleurs plus cher qu'une Porsche S. Il se distingue notamment par ses nombreux accessoires, ses commandes électriques automatiques et des sièges cuir capitonnés et fermes, dont les coussins sont réglables. Le volant sport à trois branches se règle selon les besoins du conducteur.

BMW 7 E23|1977

In accordance with the "law" governing series designations at BMW (3 series from 1975, 5 series from 1972 and 6 series from 1976), the new large sedan which appeared in May 1977 was designated the 7 series—right at the top of the BMW hierarchy. The objective was clear: to gain entry to territory occupied by the Mercedes-Benz S-Class. The 728i in particular, whose six-cylinder engine provided 184 bhp of performance, was unleashed on S-Class buyers in 1979. Its balanced cost-to-performance ratio determined that 33,700 marks had to be forked out for the luxurious one-and-a-half ton car.

The 2.8-liter engine materialized as flexible and willing, barely audible to the passengers. If the car was luxurious under the bonnet, the same was true of the interior with its armchair-like front seats and a back seat "sofa," on which just two headrests indicated that three should not try to squeeze inside. A quality interior and solid workmanship contributed

to the good reputation of the sedan in the same memorable way as its performance.

From 0 to 62 mph (100 kph) with a manual transmission took 9.5 seconds and made the grade as "pretty speedy." The top speed of 125 mph (200 kph) corresponded to rival automotive upper-class standards. Chassis, brakes (disks all round), and the ball and nut type power steering gave this large car an amazing agility even on small country roads.

The 7 series was given six engines (170 to 252 bhp), and in 1984 the equipment was supplemented, as befitted its status, by ABS as standard. Armored 7 series cars for those at risk, and a turbocharged 745i "Executive" for those with "ballistic salaries" concluded the range at the top. The 728 (with Bosch electronic fuel injection from 1979) achieved more than 100,000 units, including production of BMW South Africa. In May 1986, BMW closed the initial and tasty 7 series chapter coded E23.

Nach dem BMW-spezifischen „Gesetz der Serie" (3er ab 1975, 5er ab 1972 und 6er ab 1976) wird die neue große Limousine, die im Mai 1977 erscheint, hierarchisch in der 7er Reihe – also ganz oben – angesiedelt. Die Zielrichtung ist eindeutig. Man will sich mit der S-Klasse von Mercedes Benz messen. Besonders der 728i, dessen Sechszylindermotor 184 PS leistet, geht 1979 mit einem ausgewogenen Preis-Leistungs-Verhältnis auf die S-Klassen-Klientel los. 33 700 Mark sind für den luxuriösen Anderthalbtonner hinzublättern.

Das 2,8-Liter-Triebwerk erweist sich als elastisch und drehfreudig, kaum hörbar für die Passagiere. Kultiviert wie der Antrieb ist auch der Innenraum mit seinen fauteuilartigen Vordersitzen und der sofaähnlichen Rückbank, deren zwei Nackenstützen symbolisch andeuten, dass man sich hier nicht zu dritt hinzwängen sollte. Gediegenes Interieur und solide Verarbeitung tragen zum guten Ruf der Limousine ebenso bei wie die Fahrleistungen.

Die Beschleunigung in 9,5 Sekunden von 0 auf 100 Stunenkilometer (mit Schaltgetriebe) verdienen das Prädikat echt flott". Auch die Spitze von 200 Stundenkilometern ntspricht dem Niveau der automobilen Oberschicht. ahrwerk, Bremsanlage – vorn und hinten Scheiben-remsen – und die Kugelmutter-Hydro-Servolenkung nachen den großen Wagen auch auf kleinen Landstraßen echt beweglich.

Sechs Motoren von 170 bis 252 PS werden der 7er-Reihe pendiert, und 1984 kommt die standesgemäße Ausrüstung nit serienmäßigem ABS hinzu. Gepanzerte 7er für Gefähr-ete und ein 745i Executive für unsinnig hoch Verdienende unden die Palette nach oben ab. Der 728 (ab 1979 mit der elektronischen Benzineinspritzung von Bosch) bringt es ein-chließlich der Produktion von BMW Südafrika auf mehr als 00 000 Einheiten. Im Mai 1986 schließt BMW das erfreuliche Kapitel E23 ab.

Selon la loi des séries chez BMW (Série 3 à partir de 1975, Série 5 à partir de 1972 et Série 6 à partir de 1976), la nouvelle grosse berline qui fait son apparition en mai 1977 se situe, hiérarchiquement, dans la Série 7 – autrement dit dans le haut de la gamme. L'objectif est sans équivoque : concurrencer la Classe S de Mercedes-Benz. En particulier la 728i, dont le six-cylindres développe 184 ch, brigue les faveurs de la clientèle de la Classe S, en 1979, avec un bon rapport qualité/prix. La luxueuse voiture de 1500 kg coûte 33700 marks.

Souple, le moteur de 2,8 litres est friand de hauts régimes et reste pratiquement inaudible pour les passagers. Le «luxe» sous le capot se retrouve également dans l'habitacle avec des sièges avant comparables à des fauteuils et un véritable divan à l'arrière où deux appuie-tête indiquent qu'il est inutile de tenter d'y loger un troisième passager. Un intérieur soigné et une finition de qualité contribuent à asseoir la bonne réputation de la limousine au même titre que ses performances.

Dans cette catégorie, 9,5 secondes pour le 0 à 100 km/h (avec boîte manuelle) est un excellent résultat. La vitesse de pointe de 200 km/h, est, elle aussi, tout à fait à la hauteur dans cette catégorie de véhicules haut de gamme. Trains roulants, circuit de freinage (avec disques à l'avant et à l'arrière) et la direction hydraulique à écrou à billes confèrent une maniabilité inattendue à cette grosse voiture même sur des petites routes de campagne.

Six moteurs (170 à 252 ch) équipent la Série 7 qui voit apparaître, en 1984, le montage en série d'un système ABS «digne de son rang». Une Série 7 blindée pour les hommes politiques et autres personnes en danger ainsi qu'une 745i Executive pour les gros salaires complètent la gamme vers le haut. La 728 (équipée d'une injection électronique Bosch à partir de 1979) est fabriquée à plus de 100 000 exemplaires, y compris la production de BMW Afrique du Sud. En mai 1986, BMW clos le passionnant chapitre E23.

Launched in May 1977, the new BMW 7 series sedans were on an immediate collision course with the Mercedes-Benz S-Class. The 728i, which offered excellent value for money, was particularly successful. After a "learning process" in the 733i, the electronic fuel injection system, indicated on the type plate with the letter "i", was introduced to all 7 series models in 1979.

Die neuen Limousinen von BMW, die im Mai 1977 vom Stapel gelassen und als 7er eingestuft werden, schwimmen auf Kollisionskurs mit der S-Klasse von Mercedes-Benz Besonders erfolgreich, da preiswert, ist der 728i. Die elektronische Benzineinspritzung, äußerlich dokumentiert durch das Kürzel „i" hinter der Typenbezeichnung, wird nach einem Reifeprozess im 733i ab 1979 in alle 7er Modelle implantiert.

Lancées en mai 1977, les nouvelles berlines de BMW, cataloguées Série 7, viennent marcher sur les plates-bandes de la Classe S de Mercedes-Benz. La moins chère, la 728i, est celle qui remporte le plus de succès. L'injection d'essence électronique, dont la présence est signalée par le « i » à l'arrière, équipe toutes les Séries 7 à partir de 1979, après avoir fait ses preuves sur la 733i.

BMW M1 E26 | 1978

Motor sport as a creative platform for engineers and the source of many innovative solutions for the series: that is how BMW Motorsport GmbH, founded in 1972, saw its task, which of course also had its commercial aspects. Ambitious plans, for the BMW personnel in Munich's Preußenstraße wanted more than simply to adapt production cars to the racetrack. With code E26, they certainly succeeded in proving their capabilities through a unique high-tech development.

This internal company code concealed a thoroughbred sports car. To use the car in motor sport, BMW had to prove that 400 road vehicles had been built within a two-year period. And that was their weak point. Due to a lack of capacity of their own, BMW trustingly turned to the sports car manufacturer Lamborghini, a thoroughly competent partner. But Lamborghini was hit by financial problems shortly after the first BMW prototype was completed.

BMW reacted quickly and switched the project to Baur coachworks in Stuttgart. As early as the Paris Motor Show of 1978, the E26 development, designed by Giorgio Guigiaro, was presented to the world as the M1. With the M1, BMW Motorsport GmbH created for itself a hallmark for all subsequent products which utilized the prefix "M".

The M1, a mid-engine sports car without frills, was too functional for its target group. That certain something of a Ferrari was missing, although performance was

adequate: six seconds from 0 to 62mph (100kph) and a top speed of 162mph (260kph). The four-valve M88/1 engine also proved itself durable, offering 277bhp from a volume of 3.5 liters and 495bhp for the racing version. Another technical treat was the chassis with independent suspension for each wheel and internally ventilated disk brakes.

Formula 1 had to provide this piece of BMW sports equipment with an adequate forum. Quickly—as always when the financial conditions are right—the godfather of Grand Prix racing, Bernie Ecclestone, and the BMW sports boss, Jochen Neerpasch, came to an agreement. BMW M1 races were to be held on Saturdays before the Grands Prix in Europe.

It was compulsory for all F1 drivers (except Ferrari and Renault) that the first five in Friday's F1 qualifying participate in the prestigious BMW series, called Procar. This was "huge fun" (said Procar driver Hans-Joachim Stuck), and in 1979 and 1980 sometimes made the pulses of the crowd beat faster than the premier league Grand Prix on Sunday.

Altogether 50 racing versions of the M1 were built, partly with the assistance of Project Four Racing and Osella. Then there was a beefy group 5 version with turbochargers and approximately 900bhp. All in all, the minimum required by the world association was met, but this limited number is probably the reason why the M1 is traded nowadays at higher prices than its new car values back then.

Die 1972 gegründete BMW Motorsport GmbH definiert sich als kreative Bühne für Ingenieure und Ausgangspunkt vieler innovativer Lösungen für die Serie – eine hehre Aufgabe, die natürlich auch kommerzielle Aspekte hat. Die BMW-Mannen in Münchens Preußenstraße wollen mehr als nur Serienwagen die Tauglichkeit für das Rennparkett zu verleihen. Dem selbstgestellten Anspruch, mit eigener High Tech-Entwicklung einen eindrucksvollen Leistungsnachweis zu erbringen, ist die Abteilung mit dem E26 sicherlich gerecht geworden.

Hinter diesem firmeninternen Kürzel verbirgt sich ein reinrassiger Sportwagen. Um diesen im Motorsport einsetzen zu können, muss der Hersteller nachweisen können, dass er innerhalb von zwei Jahren mindestens 400 Straßenfahrzeuge dieses Typs gebaut hat. Und da liegt der Schwachpunkt. Mangels eigener Fertigungskapazitäten wendet sich BMW vertrauensvoll an den Sportwagenhersteller Lamborghini, einen durchaus kompetenten Partner, der jedoch kurz nach Fertigstellung der ersten Prototypen in wirtschaftliche Schwierigkeiten gerät.

BMW schaltet schnell und überträgt der Karosseriefabrik Baur in Stuttgart das Projekt. Bereits auf dem Pariser Autosalon 1978 wird der von Giorgio Guigiaro entworfene Wagen der Weltöffentlichkeit als M1 präsentiert. Mit dem M1 schafft sich die BMW Motorsport GmbH das Aushängeschild für alle Produkte, die sich hinter dem Buchstaben „M" verbergen.

Der M1, ein Mittelmotorsportwagen ohne Schnörkel wirkt auf die Zielgruppe zu funktional. Das gewisse Etwas eines Ferrari fehlt, obwohl die Leistungen adäquat sind:

sechs Sekunden von 0 auf 100 Stundenkilometer und eine Spitze von 260 Stundenkilometern. Auch in puncto Standfestigkeit bewährt sich das Vierventiler-Triebwerk vom Typ M88/1. Aus 3,5 Litern Hubraum werden 277 PS geholt und 495 PS für die Rennversion. Als technischer Leckerbissen erweist sich das Fahrwerk mit Einzelradaufhängungen und innenbelüfteten Scheibenbremsen.

Um diesem Sportgerät das angemessene Forum zu bieten, muss die Formel 1 herhalten. Schnell – wie immer, wenn die finanziellen Konditionen stimmen – werden sich Grand-Prix-Pate Bernie Ecclestone und BMW-Sportchef Jochen Neerpasch einig. An den Samstagen vor den europäischen Grand Prix soll ein BMW-M1-Rennen angesetzt werden. Bei der ohnehin hochkarätig besetzten Serie, genannt Procar, sollen jeweils die fünf Trainingsschnellsten aus dem Freitagstraining der Formel 1 starten. Ausgenommen sind lediglich die Fahrer von Ferrari und Renault. Diese Serie ist eine "Mordsgaudi", so Procar-Pilot Hans-Joachim Stuck, und lässt 1979 und 1980 die Zuschauerherzen manchmal höher schlagen als der am Sonntag folgende Lauf der höchsten Klasse des Motorsports.

50 Rennversionen, teilweise unter Mithilfe von Project Four Racing und Osella, werden gebaut. Dazu kommt eine bullige Gruppe-5-Version mit Turboladern und rund 900 PS. Insgesamt wird das vom Weltverband geforderte Minimum gerade eben erfüllt, und deswegen liegt es wohl an dieser begrenzten Stückzahl, dass der M1 heute zu Preisen gehandelt wird, die weit über seinem damaligen Neuwert liegen.

La compétition automobile est un véritable espace créatif pour les ingénieurs et donne naissance à de nombreuses innovations pour les futures séries : pour la BMW Motorsport GmbH, fondée en 1972, cette stratégie comporte, naturellement, aussi des aspects commerciaux. Les hommes de BMW de la Preussenstrasse veulent plus que conférer à une voiture de série l'aptitude à la compétition. Avec la E26, ils sont assurément parvenus à apporter la preuve de leur savoir-faire avec une débauche de haute technologie.

Derrière ce nom de code se dissimule, en effet, une voiture de sport racée, un véritable pur-sang. Pour pouvoir l'engager en compétition, il faut en avoir construit 400 en version routière sur une période de deux ans. Et c'est là que le bât blesse. Ne possédant pas les capacités de production nécessaires, BMW se tourne en toute confiance vers le constructeur de voitures de sport italien Lamborghini, un partenaire compétent, mais qui, peu après la sortie des premiers prototypes, doit faire face à des difficultés économiques.

BMW n'hésite pas longtemps avant de confier le projet au carrossier Baur, à Stuttgart. Dès le Salon de l'automobile de Paris en 1978, la M1 dessinée par Giorgio Guigiaro est présentée au monde entier. Avec la M1, la BMW Motorsport GmbH s'offre une belle carte de visite pour tous les produits qui arboreront plus tard le « M » magique.

La M1, une voiture de sport à moteur central sans fioritures, est trop fonctionnelle pour ses acheteurs potentiels. Il lui manque le « petit quelque chose en plus » d'une Ferrari bien que ses prestations n'aient rien à lui envier : 6 secondes pour

passer de 0 à 100 km/h et une vitesse de pointe de 260 km/h. En termes de fiabilité, le quatre-soupapes M88/1 est, lui aussi, au-dessus de tout soupçon. Pour une cylindrée de 3,5 litres, il développe 277 ch, et même 495 ch dans la version course. Elle est aussi d'un grand raffinement technique : les trains roulants comportent une suspension à roues indépendantes et des freins à disques ventilés.

La seule scène digne de cette voiture de sport est la Formule 1. Rapidement – comme toujours lorsque les questions d'argent sont réglées –, le parrain de la Formule 1, Bernie Ecclestone, et le directeur de course de BMW, Jochen Neerpasch, se mettent d'accord. Une course de BMW M1 aura lieu le samedi, avant chaque Grand Prix de Formule 1 organisé en Europe. Tous les pilotes (sauf ceux de Ferrari et de Renault) doivent obligatoirement participer à cette course prestigieuse baptisée Procar dès lors qu'ils figurent parmi les cinq premiers des essais du vendredi. Pour le pilote Procar Hans-Joachim Stuck, c'est une « partie de rigolade » et, en 1979 et 1980, cette course fait parfois plus frémir les spectateurs que la catégorie reine de la compétition automobile qui a lieu le dimanche.

Cinquante versions course, dont certaines avec l'aide de Project Four Racing et d'Osella, seront construites – sans compter une puissante version du groupe 5 à turbocompresseurs d'environ 900 ch. En fin de compte, BMW réussit tout juste à respecter les exigences de la Fédération mondiale et c'est bien en raison de ce nombre limité que, aujourd'hui, la M1 affiche une cote plus élevée que son prix de vente en tant que voiture neuve.

Italian bodywork man Giorgio Guigiaro was responsible for the design of the M1. The front of the M1 is reminiscent of Frenchman Paul Bracq's 1972 prototype.

Für das Design des M1 ist der italienische Karosserie-Künstler Giorgio Guigiaro verantwortlich. Die Front des M1 erinnert an den Prototypen des Franzosen Paul Bracq aus dem Jahr 1972.

Le carrossier italien Giorgio Guigiaro signe le design de la M1. L'avant rappelle le prototype du Français Paul Bracq de 1972.

The M1 allowed BMW to show its rivals a clean pair of heels. It provided BMW Motorsport GmbH with a mobile billboard for all its products bearing the letter "M" in their names. The mid-engine automobile is a no-frills machine, with form very much secondary to function. High tech, particularly in the chassis area, and the reliability of the power unit are the dominant factors. The four-valve straight-six M88/1 engine produces 277 bhp (as against the 495 bhp of the racing version). And the cockpit would warm the cockles of any sports car driver. What more could the enthusiast want?

Der Konkurrenz das Heck zu zeigen, ist BMW dank des M1 durchaus gelungen. Mit dem M1 schafft sich die BMW Motorsport GmbH ein Aushängeschild für all ihre Produkte, die sich mit dem „M" schmücken. Der Mittelmotorwagen hat rundum keine Schnörkel, da seine Form der Funktion untergeordnet ist. High-Tech, besonders beim Fahrwerk, und Zuverlässigkeit des Triebwerks dominieren. Der Vierventilmotor, ein Reihensechszylinder des Typs M88/1, aktiviert 277 PS – bei der Rennversion sind es 495 PS. Das Cockpit: Sportfahrer-Herz, was willst Du mehr?

Faire manger la poussière à la concurrence, BMW y est parfaitement arrivée avec la M1. Avec cette voiture, BMW Motorsport GmbH donne du prestige à tous les produits qui arboreront ultérieurement le célèbre « M ». La voiture à moteur central possède une carrosserie sans fioritures, fonctionnelle avant tout. La haute technologie, en particulier pour les trains roulants, et la fiabilité de son moteur sont les éléments prédominants. 277 ch – mais 495 ch pour la version course – sont libérés par le moteur à quatre soupapes, un six-cylindres en ligne du type M88/1. Le cockpit satisfait tous les amoureux de la compétition. Qu'espérer de plus ?

BMW 3 E30|1982

With its touring designation, BMW really presented a station wagon in August 1987: not the blend of coupé with a hatchback, as had been the case for the 1971 touring on an 02 base. The customer demand was there, and thus deliveries started in March 1988 with four engine variants. There was also a 325iX, a designation which was neither secretive nor arbitrarily chosen.

The "X" meant 4-wheel drive (4×4). BMW had previously introduced this 325 name once in their 1939 standard light military vehicle for the German Army. The principle of driving all four wheels, revived by BMW in 1985, made more sense in a station wagon than a sedan—unless, of course, it was for a motor sport application.

Like all touring models, the 325iX was equipped with double-tube shock absorbers, disk brakes all round, headlights with ellipsoid dipped beams and a catalytic converter. The 170 bhp of the six-cylinder engine were sufficient to give the car a top speed of 130 mph (208 kph).

At the core of the four-wheel-drive principle was a central transfer case with planetary differential and visco locks. The additional power to the front axle was transmitted by a side drive, via a sprocket chain, and secondary shaft. A total 63 percent of power went to the rear axle and the remaining 37 percent drove the front wheels.

The 4×4 drive equipment, at about 176 lbs (80 kg), weighed heavily on the purchase price. The "X" cost an additional 8500 marks. Unsurprisingly production of the 4×4 drive

version accounted for less than three percent of the touring output, nevertheless 5273 "X"s were made. This is an indication of the success of the first station wagon from BMW.

In terms of equipment it was anything but your typical workhorse. That is also why a trunk sill directly above the bumper was left off. The rear lights only allowed sufficient opening for, say, golf bags, prams or a collapsible bicycle. Bulky chests, workmen's tools or building materials should kindly be transported by other means. That, at least, is how those who love this car see it—the speedy "three".

It was only in 1990—the new E36 3 series was poised on the brink of volume production—that the 318i was accompanied by a convertible version. The 318i with the new four-cylinder engine had a three-way catalytic converter and a lambda oxygen sensor. This was a sensible solution, particularly since the 113 bhp seemed to be perfectly capable of running for 21.5 miles on a gallon of regular lead-free petrol (11 liters per 100 km).

The price (less than 50,000 marks, back in 1993) was also attractive for those convertibles fans for whom a 325i was simply out of reach. The pleasure to be gained from driving under an open sky was never clouded with the fourcylinder engine. Employing the five-speed manual gearbox, acceleration from 0 to 62 mph (100 kph) came in just under 11 seconds, and with a top speed of 119 mph (190 kph), it was quite enough to lift your spirits without blowing your head off. Models with automatic transmission were almost as fast.

Mit dem touring stellt BMW im August 1987 einen echten Kombi vor, kein Verschnitt aus Coupé mit Heckklappe und Kombilimousine wie das gleichnamige Fahrzeug von 1971. Die entsprechende Nachfrage besteht, und so läuft im März 1988 die Auslieferung mit vier Motorvarianten an. Es gibt auch einen 325iX, eine Bezeichnung, die weder geheimnisvoll, noch x-beliebig gewählt worden ist.

Das „X" steht für Allradantrieb. Den hatte es bei BMW schon einmal gegeben: 1939 und ebenfalls bei einem 325er, dem leichten Einheits-Pkw für die Wehrmacht. Das von BMW 1985 wieder aufgegriffene Prinzip des Vierradantriebs macht bei einem Kombi eher Sinn als bei einer Limousine, es sei denn, man will diese im Motorsport einsetzen.

Wie alle Touringmodelle ist der 325iX mit Doppelrohr-Gasdruckdämpfern, Scheibenbremsen rundum, Scheinwerfern mit Ellipsoid-Abblendlicht und einem Katalysator ausgerüstet. Die 170 PS des Sechszylindertriebwerks reichen aus, um dem Wagen eine Spitzengeschwindigkeit von 208 Stundenkilometern zu verleihen.

Kernpunkt des Allradprinzips ist ein zentrales Verteilergetriebe mit Planetendifferential und Visco-Sperren. Der zusätzliche Antrieb zur Vorderachse wird durch einen Seitentrieb über Zahnkette und Nebenwelle erreicht. Zu 63 Prozent geht die Kraft an die Hinterachse, die restlichen 37 Prozent treiben die Vorderräder an.

Die rund 80 Kilo Allradtechnik liegen dem Käufer im wahrsten Sinne des Wortes schwer auf der Tasche: 8500 Mark Aufpreis kostet das „X". Kein Wunder also, dass der

Produktionsanteil der Allradler unter den Tourings keine drei Prozent ausmacht. Absolut gesehen sind es immerhin 5273 „X". Daran lässt sich ermessen, wie erfolgreich der erste Kombi von BMW insgesamt ist.

Der Ausstattung nach ist er alles andere als ein typischer Lastesel. Und deshalb wurde auch auf eine Ladekante direkt über der Stoßstange verzichtet. Die Heckleuchten lassen nur eine Durchreiche frei, etwa für Golfbags, Kinderwagen oder ein Klappfahrrad. Sperrige Kisten, Handwerkerzubehör oder Baumaterialien sollen gefälligst mit anderen Transportmitteln befördert werden. So sehen es jedenfalls diejenigen, die ihn lieben – den „flotten 3er".

Erst 1990 – die neuen 3er der Baureihe E36 stehen bereits kurz vor der Serienreife – gesellt sich dem 318i ebenfalls ein Cabriolet zu. Der 318i mit dem neuen Vierzylindermotor verfügt über einen Dreiwegekatalysator und eine Lambda-Sonde – eine vernünftige Lösung, zumal sich die 113 PS mit knapp 11 Litern normaler bleifreier Flüssignahrung zufriedengeben.

Attraktiv ist auch der Preis für die Cabriolet-Fans, denen der 325i ein zu „starkes Stück" ist, kostet der 318i doch selbst 1993 noch unter 50 000 Mark. Auch mit dem Vierzylindertriebwerk bietet der offene 3er ungetrübten Fahrspaß unter freiem Himmel. Mit dem Fünfgang-Schaltgetriebe ist eine Beschleunigung von 0 auf 100 Stundenkilometer in knapp 11 Sekunden möglich, und die Spitzengeschwindigkeit von 190 Stundenkilometer genügt für viel Kopffreiheit. Nur geringfügig langsamer geht es mit der Automatik voran.

BMW dévoile en août 1987 un authentique break : qui ne ressemble en rien à la première voiture du même nom présentée en 1971. Les commandes ne se font pas attendre et c'est ainsi que la commercialisation commence en mars 1988 avec quatre motorisations différentes. Il existe aussi une 325iX, une dénomination qui n'est pas fortuite.

Le « X » signifie traction intégrale. BMW avait déjà utilisé ce numéro 325 en 1939 pour une voiture militaire légère destinée à l'armée allemande. Reprendre, en 1985, le principe des quatre roues motrices a plus de sens avec un break qu'avec une berline, à moins que l'on ne veuille engager celle-ci en compétition.

Comme toutes les touring, la 325iX possède des amortisseurs à gaz bitube, des freins à disques sur les quatre roues, des feux de croisement ellipsoïdaux et un pot catalytique. Les 170 ch du six-cylindres suffisent pour donner à la voiture une vitesse de pointe de 208 km/h.

La clé de voûte de la traction intégrale est une boîte de distribution centrale avec différentiel universel et viscocoupleurs. La prise de force supplémentaire pour l'essieu avant s'effectue sur le côté à l'aide d'une chaîne dentée et d'un arbre secondaire. 63% de la puissance dégagée sont dirigés vers l'essieu arrière, les 37% restants entraînant les roues avant.

Les quelque 80 kg de traction intégrale pèsent aussi sur le prix d'achat : la « X » coûte 8500 marks de plus que la version normale. Rien d'étonnant, donc, à ce que les ventes de quatre roues motrices parmi les touring ne dépassent pas

3%, ce qui se traduit tout de même par 5273 « X » vendues. Ces chiffres indiquent le succès remporté par le premier break de BMW.

Son aménagement est tout sauf banal. Et c'est d'ailleurs la raison pour laquelle on renonce au seuil de chargement placé directement au-dessus du pare-chocs. Les optiques arrière n'autorisent en effet qu'une découpe de coffre limitée – par exemple pour un équipement de golf, une poussette ou un vélo pliant. Pour le transport d'objets encombrants, vous choisirez un autre véhicule. Telle est en tout cas la philosophie de ceux qui l'adorent, cette rapide Série 3.

Ce n'est qu'en 1990 – alors que la nouvelle Série 3 de la gamme E36 va bientôt être dévoilée au grand public – que l'on voit également apparaître un cabriolet 318i. Cette 318i propulsée par un nouveau moteur à quatre-cylindres possède un catalyseur trois voies et une sonde lambda. Une solution raisonnable, d'autant plus que les 113 ch se contentent d'à peine 11 litres aux 100 km d'essence ordinaire sans plomb.

Le prix est aussi attrayant pour les amateurs de cabriolets (en 1993, inférieur à 50 000 marks) pour lesquels une 325i est hors de portée. Avec le quatre-cylindres sous le capot, rouler cheveux au vent sous les rayons du soleil est un aussi grand plaisir. La boîte manuelle à cinq vitesses permet d'accélérer de 0 à 100 km/h en 11 secondes à peine et la vitesse de pointe de 190 km/h est tout à fait suffisante pour vous libérer l'esprit sans vous arracher la tête. La version à boîte automatique est quasiment aussi rapide.

The convertible version of the 318i first arrived on the market in 1990. It is a highly economical convertible, its four-cylinder engine with three-way catalytic converter and lambda sensor having a fuel consumption of around 21.5 miles per gallon (11 liters per 100 km).

Erst 1990 kommt der 318i auch „oben ohne" auf den Markt: ein äußerst preiswertes Cabriolet, dessen Vierzylindermotor mit Dreiwegekatalysator und Lambda-Sonde knapp 11 Liter Normalbenzin verbraucht.

Il faut attendre 1990 pour voir une 318i décapotable apparaître sur le marché: il s'agit d'un cabriolet au prix extrêmement intéressant, dont le quatre-cylindres à catalyseur trois voies et sonde à oxygène se contente de 11 litres d'essence ordinaire aux 100 km.

BMW identified a market niche and, to fill it, constructed a pure estate car based on the 3 series. The 325iX touring is driven by a 170 bhp engine and a transfer gear providing power to all axles. The harmonious parallel roof and belt line give the touring an interesting appearance, while the BBS design alloy wheels lend a sporty note. The design of the tailgate adds to the torsional rigidity, but is a nuisance when it comes to loading the trunk.

Eine Marktlücke: BMW baut, basierend auf dem 3er, einen reinen Kombi. Der 325iX touring wird von 170 PS über ein zentrales Verteilergetriebe an allen Achsen angetrieben. Der harmonische „Parallelschwung" aus Dach- und Gürtellinie macht den touring auch optisch interessant, wobei die Leichtmetallräder im BBS-Design eine sportliche Note hinzufügen. Das Heck, dessen Rücklichter wie bei der Limousine angeordnet sind, dient der Verwindungssteifigkeit, ist beim Beladen aber eher hinderlich.

BMW découvre un marché de niche et, sur la base de la Série 3, construit un authentique break: la 325iX touring de 170 ch possède une traction intégrale avec boîte de distribution centrale. Les lignes harmonieuses du toit et de la carrosserie donnent à la touring une esthétique intéressante, tandis que les jantes en alliage BBS lui confèrent une touche de sportivité. La découpe du coffre est favorable à la rigidité torsionnelle, mais n'est guère pratique.

The road version of the M3 Sport Evolution has
impressive handling and performance, with a top
speed of 155 mph (248 kph) and a 0 to 62 mph (100 kph)
time of 6.3 seconds. The racing version won more than
1500 races and captured 50 international titles over a
six-year period.

Die „zivile" Version des M3 Sport Evolution beeindruckt
durch ihr Handling und ihre Leistung: 248 km/h Spitze,
in 6,3 Sekunden von 0 auf 100 km/h. In der Rennversion
bringt es der M3 innerhalb von sechs Jahren auf
1500 Siege und 50 internationale Titel.

La version Sport Evolution pour la route de la M3
stupéfait par sa maniabilité et ses performances :
248 km/h en vitesse de pointe, 0 à 100 km/h en
6,3 secondes. Dans la version course, la M3 remporte
en six ans 1500 victoires et 50 titres internationaux.

The chassis beneath the "plump cheeks" of the M3, which is equipped to take wide tires in a variety of sizes, had three electronically-adjustable suspension settings: a stiff sporty set-up, normal or comfortable.

Das Fahrwerk unter den „dicken Backen" des M3, der für Breitreifen unterschiedlicher Dimensionen gerüstet ist, lässt sich via Elektronik sportlich straff oder komfortabel einstellen. Dazwischen liegt noch die Stufe „Normal".

Sous les «ailes joufflues» de la M3 conçue pour recevoir des pneus larges de différentes dimensions, le châssis peut être réglé électroniquement. Trois niveaux au choix: «Sport», «Normal» ou «Confort».

Aerodynamic features such as spoilers with manually adjustable lips to increase downforce, so vital in motor sport, were here introduced into the small production run of 500 M3s—thus the name Sport Evolution. The super-functional cockpit features leather bucket seats with guide mechanisms for harness belts (though these do not come with the car) and a sports steering wheel with a suede grip area. Tests reveal a power output of 238 bhp at 7000 rpm for the four-valve four-cylinder engine with electronic fuel injection and a three-way catalytic converter.

Die im Motorsport erforderlichen aerodynamischen Attribute, wie Spoiler mit manuell verstellbarer Lippe für mehr Abtrieb, halten in der Kleinserie der 500 M3 Einzug – darum der Name Sport Evolution. In dem äußerst funktionellen Cockpit fallen die Lederschalensitze mit Führungen für Hosenträgergurte (die freilich nicht mitgeliefert werden) und das Sportlenkrad mit Wildleder-Griffzone auf. Das Power-Stenogramm des Vierventil-Vierzylinders mit elektronischer Benzineinspritzung und geregeltem Dreiwegekatalysator lautet 238 PS bei 7000/min.

Des accessoires aérodynamiques indispensables en compétition, comme l'aileron à arête réglable à la main pour obtenir plus de stabilité, font leur apparition dans la petite série de la M3 produite à 500 exemplaires et qui porte le nom de Sport Evolution. Dans l'habitacle extrêmement fonctionnel, on remarque les baquets en cuir avec ouvertures pour le harnais six points (qui n'est toutefois pas livré avec la voiture) et le volant sport partiellement gainé de daim. La puissance du quatre-cylindres à quatre soupapes à injection électronique et catalyseur réglé à trois voies culmine à 238 ch à 7000 tr/min.

BMW 7 E32 | 1986

Count Hans von der Goltz, supervisory board chairman of BMW AG, and his equally blue-blooded managing director, Dr Eberhard von Kuenheim, know what is right: *"Noblesse oblige."* BMW was to be among those who set the future tone in the highest sedan society, echoing Maybach in the 1930s. Expensive handbuilt labor, little high-tech and incredibly high prices handicapped the noble British conveyance of aristocracy, Rolls-Royce. They were no competition for BMW—except that the name has that ring of royalty about it. The real competition in terms of numbers of cars registered was the S-Class from Mercedes-Benz. Stuttgart was convinced the S-Class would not lose any buyers to Munich.

Wrong! The new 750i—the first German twelve-cylinder luxury car since the Second World War—overtook the S-Class in new cars registered in Germany as early as May 1987. It was almost unheard-of that the Bavarians should steal the show from Stuttgart's Swabians in the luxury class. The only sound from Rolls was a surprised whisper. One was clearly "not amused."

This miracle of Bavarian engine technology had a block and twelve cylinder heads made of aluminium. That is why the 2500 or so refined engine parts together did not weigh more than 530 lbs (240 kg). The crankshaft of the V-engine had seven bearings. Since the two halves of the V had their own drive units and catalytic converters, total engine failure was almost unthinkable.

The 5-liter engine could only be heard when it delivered all 300 bhp—something which happened at an engine speed of 5200 rpm, so it was nobly restrained but powerful. Simply majestic. The most modern engine management and four-speed automatic transmission with drive programs "Sport" and "Economy" belonged to the magnificent and splendid Bavarian aristocrat. The 1.8 tons of unladen weight could be accelerated to 62 mph (100 kph) in less than eight seconds, and BMW was content to limit top speed electronically to 155 mph (250 kph). Higher speeds than that would reduce driving comfort. This, in any case, was equivalent to being carried in a sedan-chair due to automatic stabilization and electronic shock absorber controls.

Luxury reigned in the cabin, with five comfortable seats of the finest leather. And however hard you looked, not even the smallest technical refinement invented to make cars more comfortable was missing. Anyone wanting a drinks cabinet or a television would be advised to choose the 4 inches (11 cm) longer 750iL. In 1987 the 750i still cost a "modest" 102,000 marks, the stretched (L-badged) version demanded 17,000 marks more. The refined pleasure of being able to afford this ultimate sedan was enjoyed by almost 20,000 obviously well-heeled people in 1987/88.

Hans Graf von der Goltz, Aufsichtsratsvorsitzender der BMW AG, und sein ebenfalls blaublütiger Vorstand Dr.-Ing. h.c. Eberhard von Kuenheim wissen, was sich gehört: „Noblesse oblige!" BMW soll auch in der High society der Nobelkarossen künftig mit den Ton angeben – so wie Maybach in den dreißiger Jahren. Viel Handarbeit, wenig High-Tech und zu hohe Preise sind das Handicap der britischen Hochadels-Kutsche Rolls-Royce. Für BMW ist dieser Hersteller kein Konkurrent – nur der Name ist eben unvergleichlich vornehm. Die eigentliche Konkurrenz in der Zulassungsstatistik ist die S-Klasse von Mercedes-Benz. Und von der, so ist man zumindest in Stuttgart überzeugt, wird kein Käufer nach München abwandern.

Irrtum! Der neue BMW 750i – der erste deutsche Zwölfzylinder-Luxuswagen nach dem Zweiten Weltkrieg – überholt bereits im Mai 1987 die S-Klasse bei den Fahrzeugzulassungen in Deutschland. Ein unerhörter Vorgang, dass die Bayern in der Luxusklasse den Schwaben die Show stehlen! Von Rolls-Royce hört man nur erstauntes Raunen: Man ist sichtlich „not amused".

Motorblock und Zylinderköpfe dieses Wunderwerks bayerischer Motorenbaukunst bestehen aus Aluminium, und deshalb wiegen die rund 2500 edlen Motorenteile zusammengenommen nicht mehr als 240 Kilo. Die Kurbelwelle des V-Motors ist siebenfach gelagert, und da die beiden Sechszylinder, aus denen er sich zusammensetzt, ihre eigenen Antriebsaggregate und Katalysatoren aufweisen, ist ein völliger Motorausfall kaum denkbar.

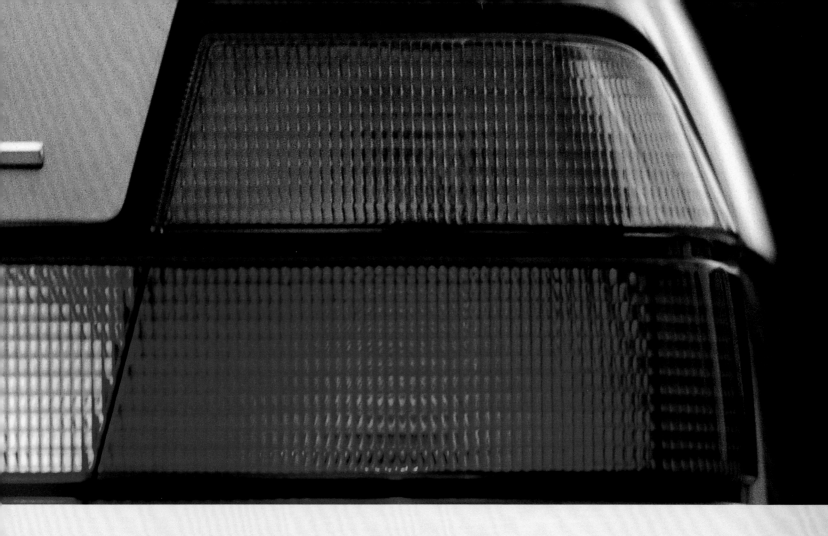

Erst wenn dieses 5-Liter-Triebwerk die vollen 300 PS entfaltet – und das geschieht bei 5200 Umdrehungen pro Minute – ist auch der Sound vernehmbar: vornehm zurückhaltend, aber kraftvoll – majestätisch eben. Modernstes Motormanagement und eine Viergangautomatik mit den Fahrprogrammen „Sport" und „Economy" gehören zur Standardausstattung dieses bayerischen Prunkstücks, und wenn dessen Fahrer es wünscht, katapultiert die Urgewalt dieses Motors die 1,8 Tonnen Leergewicht in weniger als acht Sekunden auf 100 Stundenkilometer. Um den Fahrkomfort nicht zu schmälern, beliebt man werkseitig die Höchstgeschwindigkeit elektronisch auf 250 Stundenkilometer zu begrenzen. Mehr soll es nicht sein. Dieser Fahrkomfort wird ohnehin durch eine automatische Stabilisierung und eine elektronische Dämpferkontrolle auf Sänftenniveau gehalten.

In der „Sänfte" mit fünf komfortablen Sesseln aus feinstem Leder regiert der Luxus, und solange man auch sucht, es fehlt nicht die geringste jener vielen technischen Raffinessen, die für die Bequemlichkeit von Fahrzeuginsassen erfunden worden sind. Wer den Einbau einer Bordbar oder eines Fernsehers wünscht, sollte sich für den 11 Zentimeter längeren 750iL entscheiden.

1987 kostet der 750i noch „bescheidene" 102 000 Mark, die Langversion 17 000 Mark mehr. Das hochnoble Vergnügen, dieses Nonplusultra einer Limousine zu fahren – oder standesgemäß fahren zu lassen – gönnen sich 1987/88 fast 20 000 entsprechend betuchte Menschen.

Le comte Hans von der Goltz, président du conseil de surveillance de BMW, et son collègue Eberhard von Kuenheim, noble lui aussi, docteur *honoris causa* en ingénierie, savent ce qu'il faut faire : «Noblesse oblige!» À l'avenir, BMW donnera le ton sur le marché des limousines de très grand luxe – comme Maybach dans les années 1930. Beaucoup de travail encore réalisé à la main, peu de haute technologie et des prix trop élevés sont les handicaps de Rolls-Royce, cette noble marque de l'industrie automobile britannique : pour BMW, ce n'est pas un concurrent – seul son nom lui donne une connotation royale. Sa concurrente directe, selon les statistiques d'immatriculations, c'est la Classe S de Mercedes-Benz. Et, à Stuttgart, chacun est convaincu que celle-ci ne perdra aucun acheteur. Ces derniers ne passeront pas dans le camp de Munich.

C'est une erreur! La nouvelle BMW 750i – la première douze-cylindres de luxe allemande depuis la Seconde Guerre mondiale – double la Classe S en termes d'immatriculations de voitures neuves en Allemagne dès mai 1987. Il est absolument stupéfiant que les Bavarois volent la vedette aux Souabes dans la catégorie des voitures de grand luxe. Rolls-Royce s'en étonne et n'est manifestement pas *amused*.

Le bijou de la technique bavaroise en termes de moteur possède un bloc et des culasses en aluminium. Ce qui explique que les quelque 2500 prestigieuses pièces du moteur ne pèsent pas plus de 240 kg. Le vilebrequin du moteur en V est à sept paliers. Comme chacun des deux «six-cylindres»

du moteur comporte son propre groupe de transmission, il est pratiquement exclu que le moteur tombe totalement en panne.

Il faut que ce moteur de 5 litres libère la totalité de ses 300 ch – ce qu'il fait dès 5200 tr/min – pour que l'on en perçoive la présence, il est d'une retenue discrète mais vigoureux. Majestueux, tout simplement. Une gestion moteur ultramoderne et une boîte automatique à quatre rapports avec comme programmes «Sport» et «Économique» équipent ce pur-sang digne des haras des rois de Bavière. Côté performance, il est tout à fait possible de catapulter les 1,8 tonne à vide de la voiture en moins de 8 secondes de 0 à 100 km/h et la vitesse maximum limitée électroniquement à 250 km/h laisse planer une ombre sur les possibilités réelles de la voiture. Cela suffit pour que l'on puisse profiter pleinement du confort. Grâce à un contrôle automatique de la stabilisation et électronique des amortisseurs, on a de toute façon l'impression de rouler sur un nuage.

Le luxe règne en maître dans ce carrosse aux cinq fauteuils en cuir confortables. Et même en cherchant bien, il ne manque aucun gadget technique inventé pour le confort des passagers. Celui qui souhaite faire installer un bar ou un téléviseur devra opter pour la version 750iL allongée de 11 cm.

En 1987, la 750i coûte encore la «modique» somme de 102 000 marks, ajoutez 17 000 marks pour la version à empattement long. En 1987–1988, 20 000 personnes peuvent se payer le luxe incomparable de posséder ce *nec plus ultra* de la technique automobile.

Four and a half inches (11 cm) more legroom than the 750i: triple world champion Niki Lauda enjoys the unaccustomed comfort of the back seat. Barely audible is the noise of the 300 bhp engine, whose two cylinder banks have their own separate aggregate running from the injection unit to the catalytic converter. Boeing pilot Lauda samples the sumptuous driver area of the 7 series.

11 Zentimeter mehr Beinfreiheit als im 750i: Dem dreifachen Weltmeister, der hier Fondpassagier ist, behagt dieser Komfort. Kaum hörbar ist die „12-Ton-Musik" des 300-PS-Triebwerks, dessen zwei Zylinderreihen von der Einspritzanlage bis zum Kat beide über eigene Aggregate verfügen. Dem Boeing-Piloten Lauda ist das Cockpit des 7ers eine Laudatio wert.

Onze cm de plus pour les jambes que dans la 750i : le triple champion du monde, installé sur la banquette arrière, apprécie ce confort. Le V12 de 300 ch est très silencieux ; de l'injection aux catalyseurs, chaque banc de cylindres possède son groupe de transmission. Lauda, le pilote de Boeing, ne tarit pas d'éloges sur l'habitacle de la Série 7.

BMW 5 E34 | 1988

Just eight months after the launch of the 5 series (E34), the sporting version arrived in August 1988. It concealed, as always with BMW, massive performance behind a tiny abbreviation: M5. Externally, only the restrained aerodynamic aids on the lower body, the ventilated light alloy wheels and the badge indicated the M5. The power of the engine (315 bhp; from 1992 upped to 340 bhp) remained hidden.

Well then, raise the hood. "BMW M Power" stamped boldly on the valve cover could not be overlooked, and neither could the long funnels of the inlet tract with the unusual air intake. An electronically controlled flap was activated here in such an ingenious way that enhanced torque and performance were achieved right back in the intake area. "Resonance-tuned intake pressure charging" was BMW's name for this process.

Also at the back there were tell-tale signs that this engine was a powerful unit. After the catalytic converter, the exhaust gases exited by two mighty tail pipes. It is hardly necessary to mention that optimum combustion was achieved in the six cylinders with a total of 24 valves, and that the crankshaft with 12 counterweights was a metal-forging masterpiece.

A 25 bhp increase in power in 1992 boosted maximum torque from 360 Nm to 400 Nm (266–295 lb-ft) at 4750 rpm, but had no effect on acceleration. This was powerful enough as it was, at 6.5 seconds from 0 to 62 mph (100 kph). That leaves the question of top speed. Not really relevant, for at 155 mph (250 kph) the Bosch Motronic intervened and prohibited further speed. This Motronic, initially the M1.2, and from 1992 the M3.3, managed the engine and regulated the catalytic converter.

The M5 sat ¾ inches (20 mm) lower than its brothers in the 5 series. Yet little adjustment was required to adapt the chassis to cope with the enhanced performance. Electronic shock absorber ride adjustment and hydropneumatic leveling were the magic technical words. As in the 750i, they stood for impressive roadholding and cornering, giving pleasure to those occupying the sporty and elegant cockpit. Whether a light inside the gearshift knob for the sporty five-speed transmission was really necessary is debatable.

In 1992, the year in which the M5 was upgraded again, including hot five-spoke star wheels, BMW also supplied its "M5 bullet" in a touring derivative. This sporting wagon cost 127,650 marks, and had particularly wide rear tires (255/40 ZR 17).

To blow away a Porsche or a Chevy Corvette on the highway with a four-door station wagon is most certainly not part of any driving test. But—leaving all morals aside—this might well be an uplifting moment.

Nur acht Monate nach der Vorstellung der 5er-Reihe (E34) folgt im August 1988 das „Muskelpaket". Und dieses verbirgt, wie bei BMW üblich, seine große Leistung hinter einem kleinen Kürzel: M5. Äußerlich deuten nur dezente aerodynamische Hilfen im unteren Karosseriebereich, die Leichtmetallräder mit Lüftereinsatz und das Kürzel auf den M5 hin. Die Kraft (315 PS, ab 1992 sogar 340 PS) liegt im Verborgenen.

Also Haube auf! „BMW M Power" steht unübersehbar auf dem Zylinderkopfdeckel. Unübersehbar auch die langen Trichter des Ansaugtrakts mit dem ungewöhnlichen Luftmengensammler, in dem eine elektronisch gesteuerte Klappe derart geschickt arbeitet, dass sie schon im Ansaugbereich für mehr Drehmoment und Leistung sorgt. „Resonanzaufladung" nennt BMW diesen Vorgang. Auch am hinteren Ende gibt es verräterische Anzeichen dafür, dass es sich bei diesem Motor um ein Kraftwerk handelt. Nach Passieren des Katalysators entweichen die Auspuffgase durch zwei gewaltige Endrohre. Dass in den sechs Zylindern mit insgesamt 24 Ventilen eine optimale Verbrennung erzielt wird und die Kurbelwelle mit 12 Gegengewichten ein Meisterstück der Schmiedekunst ist, braucht wohl nicht erwähnt zu werden.

Die Potenzsteigerung um 25 PS im Jahre 1992 hebt zwar das maximale Drehmoment von 360 Nm auf 400 Nm bei 4750 Touren, wirkt sich aber nicht auf die Beschleunigung aus, die mit knapp 6,5 Sekunden von 0 auf 100 Stundenkilometer

ohnehin jenseits von Gut und Böse ist. Auch die Frage nach der Endgeschwindigkeit erübrigt sich, denn bei 250 Stundenkilometern greift die Bosch Motronic ein und untersagt weiteres „Speeding". Diese Motronic – zunächst die M1.2, ab 1992 die M3.3 – steuert den Motor und regelt den Katalysator.

Der M5 liegt 20 Millimeter tiefer als die Serienbrüder der 5er-Reihe. Doch sind für die Anpassung des Fahrwerks an das neue Kräfteverhältnis nur geringe Einstellarbeiten erforderlich. Wie schon beim 750i heißen die technischen Zauberworte für gute Straßen- und Kurvenlage elektronische Dämpferkraftverstellung und hydropneumatische Niveauregulierung – zur Freude der Fahrer, die sich in dem sportlich-eleganten Cockpit betätigen dürfen. Über den Sinn des von innen angestrahlten Schaltknopfes des sportlich abgestimmten Fünfganggetriebes lässt sich streiten.

1992, im Jahre der nochmaligen Aufrüstung des M5, unter anderem mit „heißen" Fünfstern-Rädern, liefert BMW das M5-Geschoss auch als Touring aus. Dieser 127650 Mark teure Wagen steht hinten auf besonders breiten Sohlen (255/40 ZR17).

Mit einem viertürigen Kombi auf der Autobahn einen Porsche oder eine Chevy-Corvette zu „verblasen", gehört gewiss nicht zur Reifeprüfung eines Autofahrers, dürfte aber – mal ganz unpädagogisch betrachtet – ein erhebender Moment sein.

Huit mois seulement après la présentation de la Série 5 (E34), BMW en dévoile, en août 1988, la version «musclée». Et, comme cela est la tradition chez BMW, celle-ci dissimule son immense potentiel derrière une simple abréviation : M5. Extérieurement, seuls de discrets artifices aérodynamiques le long des bas de caisse, des jantes en alliage léger ressemblant à des ailettes de turbine et l'abréviation indiquent qu'il s'agit bien de la M5. La puissance du moteur (315 ch et même 340 à partir de 1992) ne saute pas aux yeux.

Alors, ouvrons le capot! «BMW M Power» peut-on lire en grandes lettres sur la culasse et les longues tubulures du collecteur d'aspiration avec l'immense boîtier du filtre à air. On sait tout de suite à qui on a affaire. Dans ce boîtier, une soupape à commande électronique agit avec tant d'ingéniosité qu'elle génère plus de couple et de puissance dès le collecteur d'aspiration. C'est ce que BMW appelle la «suralimentation par résonance».

À l'arrière aussi, certains signes trahissent que ce moteur n'est pas d'un gabarit courant. Après avoir franchi le catalyseur, les gaz brûlés s'échappent par deux énormes pots d'échappement. Point n'est besoin de signaler à ce propos qu'une combustion optimale est garantie dans les six-cylindres avec, au total, 24 soupapes et que le vilebrequin à 12 contrepoids est un chef-d'œuvre. L'augmentation de puissance de 25 ch en 1992 fait passer le couple maximum de 360 Nm à 400 Nm à 4750 tr/min, mais reste sans effet sur l'accélération : avec

6,5 secondes à peine pour le 0 à 100 km/h, elle est de toute façon suffisante. Reste la question de la vitesse de pointe. Elle n'est pas capitale. En effet, à 250 km/h, la gestion Bosch Motronic intervient et jugule efficacement les autres accélérations. Cette Motronic, tout d'abord la M1.2, puis la M3.3 à partir de 1992, gère le moteur et le catalyseur.

La M5 est surbaissée de 20 millimètres par rapport aux autre modèles de la Série 5. Mais peu de réglages sont nécessaires pour adapter les trains roulants au nouveau rapport de forces. Des amortisseurs à réglage électronique et un correcteur d'assiette hydropneumatique comme pour la 750i sont la formule magique qui garantit une tenue de route à toute épreuve en ligne droite et dans les courbes, pour le plus grand plaisir de celui qui a l'opportunité et le bonheur de se glisser au volant. Les avis sont partagés quant au bien-fondé de l'éclairage intérieur du pommeau de changement de vitesses de la boîte manuelle à cinq rapports.

En 1992, année de la montée en puissance de la M5 – notamment avec de spectaculaires jantes en étoile à cinq rayons –, BMW commercialise également sa «bombe M5» en une version touring. Ce break de 127650 marks est monté sur des pneus particulièrement larges à l'arrière (255/40 ZR17).

Donner la réplique sur autoroute à une Porsche ou à une Chevrolet Corvette au volant d'un break à quatre portes n'est pas à la portée de tous les automobilistes, mais – faisons pour une fois abstraction de toute morale – ceci est sans aucun doute un moment inoubliable.

The extensively equipped cockpit of the M5 reflects well on this exclusive car. Its M Power means that a worthy "opponent" rarely appears in the aerodynamically shaped rear-view mirror.

So manchem Nobelgefährt zur Ehre gereicht das reichhaltig ausgestattete M5-Cockpit. Dank der M-Power taucht nur selten ein ebenbürtiger „Gegner" im aerodynamischen Rückspiegel auf.

L'habitacle richement équipé de la M5 est digne d'une voiture de sport de prestige. Avec le moteur M Power, peu de véhicules sont capables de rivaliser avec ses performances.

With the M5, the power—315 bhp to begin with, then 340 bhp from 1992—and the brilliance of a sports car are contained in a spacious sedan. The M5 touring perfectly combines a load capacity of 1058 lbs (480 kg) with extreme performance: a top speed of 155 mph (250 kph) and from 0 to 62 mph (100 kph) in 6.5 seconds. The discreet spoilers in the lower body area are essential because of the wide tires and emphasize the aerodynamic shape of the car.

Beim M5 stecken die Kraft – zunächst 315 PS, ab 1992 dann 340 PS – und die Herrlichkeit eines Sportwagens in einer geräumigen Limousine. Der M5 touring kombiniert perfekt eine Transportkapazität von 480 Kilo mit extremen Fahrleistungen: 250 km/h Spitze und von 0 auf 100 km/h in 6,5 Sekunden. Das dezente Spoilerwerk im unteren Karosseriebereich ist wegen der Breitreifen unabdingbar und unterstreicht die aerodynamische Form des Fahrzeugs.

Avec la M5, le ramage – tout d'abord 315 ch, puis 340 ch à partir de 1992 – vaut le plumage, une fougueuse voiture de sport se cache sous les traits d'une spacieuse familiale. La M5 touring combine à la perfection une capacité de transport de 480 kg à des performances extrêmes : une vitesse de pointe de 250 km/h et le 0 à 100 km/h en 6,5 secondes. Les discrets artifices aérodynamiques le long du soubassement sont indispensables en raison de la largeur des pneus et soulignent la forme aérodynamique de la voiture.

BMW 8 E31|1989

In the 8 series coupé, BMW once and for all invaded the territory of the Mercedes-Benz luxury class. Launched in the autumn of 1989, it contained a synthesis of sportiness and comfort, advanced technology and all that is good and expensive. Opinions diverge as to whether this new upper-class car was exciting or just beautiful. Either way, it combined several styling elements which are typical of BMW.

Because of the extremely slim nose of the 850i, the BMW kidney grills were made wider rather than high to remind us of the 1972 BMW Turbo study by Paul Bracq. The prominent lines of the fenders were borrowed from the M3 (E30), but both shape and height of the stub rear end are like those of other contemporary BMWs. Four exhaust pipes under a lip predict the power and splendor of a twelve-cylinder engine.

This V12 motor, shared by the 750i with aluminum engine block and cylinder heads, produced 300 bhp. That was increased in the 850 CSi (from 1992 on) by a rise in cubic capacity from 4988 to 5578 cc to produce 380 bhp. The six-speed transmission is less popular than the optional automatic: a classic choice by the wealthy buyers of this coupé in favor of comfort. For sporty drivers, there are more agile models in the BMW range than this heavy coupé.

As far as maneuverability was concerned, the CSi entered a new dimension, for the wider rear tire treads (265/40 ZR 17) and unique rear axle were responsive to steering inputs. The cost-benefit calculation for these expensive, active rear axle kinematics was a matter of debate. Yet expensive things—particularly when they concern electronics—have their enthusiastic supporters. Measured against the sales figures (before the introduction of the Ci and CSi in 1992, some 16,000 coupés were sold), the price was probably not important. The CSi sold at 180,000 marks and more, but the demand was somewhat restrained.

The alarm bells rang immediately in BMW's marketing department: in 1993 the 840 Ci appeared with a 286 bhp V8 engine, five-speed transmission and fewer electronics for 129,000 marks. This model did without the usual speed-limiting device at 155 mph (250 kph), for that was the actual top speed.

The sensual pleasure which BMW promises when driving the 8 series coupé is produced just by looking at the functional and extremely tasteful interior. It is quite simply "upper class," and the safety belts integrated into the seats are "safety first."

Eine Synthese aus Sportlichkeit und Komfort, Technik auf höchstem Niveau und allem, was gut und teuer ist, steckt im 8er Coupé, mit dem BMW im Herbst 1989 endgültig in die Pfründe der Mercedes-Benz-Luxusklasse eindringt. Die Meinungen darüber, ob das neue Nobelmobil aufregend oder nur schön ist, gehen auseinander. Immerhin vereint es mehrere BMW-typische Stylingelemente.

So erinnert die extrem flache Schnauze des 850i, dessen BMW-Nieren eher breit als hoch ausfallen, an die Turbo-Studie Paul Bracqs von 1972. Die ausladende Linienführung der Kotflügel ist dem M3 (E30) entlehnt, Form und Höhe der Abrisskante des Hecks gleichen den anderen Modellreihen. Vier wuchtige Auspuffrohre unter einer Lippe verkünden die Kraft und die Herrlichkeit eines Zwölfzylinders.

Dieses auch im 750i verwendete Kraftwerk mit Motorblock und Zylinderköpfen aus Aluminium bringt 300 PS und wird beim 850 CSi ab 1992 durch eine Hubraumvergrößerung von 4988 cm³ auf 5578 cm³ auf 380 PS gesteigert. Das Sechsgang-Schaltgetriebe findet weniger Anklang als die wahlweise erhältliche Automatik – ein unmissverständliches Bekenntnis der wohlhabenden Käuferschicht dieses Coupés zum Komfort. Für eher sportliche

Fahrer gibt es im Hause BMW wendigere Mobile als das schwere Coupé.

Das Thema Wendigkeit allerdings erfährt beim CSi eine neue Dimension, denn die breiten hinteren Sohlen (265/40 ZR 17) lassen sich lenken. Über die Kosten-Nutzen-Rechnung dieser aufwändigen aktiven Hinterachskinematik lässt sich freilich streiten. Dennoch findet Aufwändiges, besonders im Bereich Elektronik, Liebhaber. Angesichts der Verkaufszahlen – vor Einführung des Ci und CSi 1992 wurden mehr als 16 000 Coupés verkauft – scheint in dieser Fahrzeugkategorie der Preis keine entscheidende Rolle zu spielen. Der CSi für 180 000 Mark ohne Extras findet ebenfalls Käufer, aber der Absatz ist verhalten.

In der Marketingabteilung läuten die Alarmglocken. 1993 erscheint der 840 Ci mit 286-PS-V8-Motor, Fünfganggetriebe und etwas weniger Elektronik für 129 000 Mark. Dieses Modell benötigt keine Abriegelung bei 250 Stundenkilometern: Es ist seine Spitzengeschwindigkeit.

Der sinnliche Genuss, den BMW beim Fahren des 8er Coupés verheißt, kommt zumindest bei einem Blick auf das funktionelle, äußerst geschmackvoll gestaltete Interieur auf. Dieses ist einfach „upper class", und die in den Sitzen integrierten Sicherheitsgurte „safety first".

Une synthèse de sportivité et de confort, un summum de technicité et tout ce qui est bon et cher se dissimulent dans le coupé de la Série 8 avec lequel BMW veut, à l'automne 1989, marcher définitivement sur les plates-bandes de la luxueuse Mercedes-Benz. Cette nouvelle voiture de prestige est-elle sensationnelle ou simplement belle ? Les avis sont partagés. Elle réunit toutefois plusieurs éléments de style typiques de BMW.

Ainsi le mufle extrêmement plat de la 850i, dont les naseaux BMW sont plus larges que hauts, rappelle-il le prototype qu'était la BMW Turbo de Paul Bracq en 1972. L'ample galbe des ailes s'inspire de la M3 (E30) tandis que la forme et la hauteur de l'arête de décrochement à l'arrière sont identiques à celles des autres gammes. Quatre imposants pots d'échappement sous un becquet trahissent la puissance débordante et la magnificence d'un douze-cylindres.

Ce moteur à bloc et culasses en aluminium aussi utilisé pour la 750i développe 300 ch et voit sa cylindrée passer, pour la 850 CSi (à partir de 1992), de 4988 à 5578 cm³ pour une puissance de 380 ch. La boîte manuelle à six vitesses remporte moins de succès que la transmission automatique proposée comme une alternative : un choix classique de la part des acheteurs aisés de ce coupé en faveur du confort. Pour les amateurs épris de conduite sportive, il y

a, chez BMW des engins autrement plus maniables que ce lourd coupé.

Le thème de la maniabilité prend une dimension nouvelle avec la CSi, car les larges pneus arrière (265/40 ZR 17) braquent. On peut toutefois se perdre en conjecture sur le rapport coût/utilité de cette sophistiquée cinématique d'essieu arrière actif.

La complexité, notamment dans le domaine de l'électronique, fait cependant des adeptes. Par rapport aux chiffres de ventes (avant le lancement de la Ci et de la CSi en 1992, le nombre de coupés avait déjà dépassé 16000), le prix n'a apparemment aucune incidence. Et c'est ainsi que la CSi trouve preneur même à 180000 marks et plus, mais la demande s'affaiblit quelque peu.

L'alarme se déclenche immédiatement chez les spécialistes du marketing : en 1993, BMW lance l'840 Ci à moteur V8 de 286 ch, boîte manuelle à 5 vitesses et un peu moins d'électronique pour 129000 marks. Ce modèle n'a pas besoin de rupteur à 250 km/h : c'est sa vitesse de pointe.

Le plaisir que BMW promet aux conducteurs des coupés de la Série 8 transparaît rien qu'en jetant un coup d'œil sur l'habitacle fonctionnel, de bon goût. Il est tout simplement haut de gamme, et les ceintures intégrées aux sièges assurent une totale sécurité.

Beneath the hood of the 850i we see a familiar sight: as in the 750i, a mighty 5-liter V12 engine does the business. The dashboard is restrained, but well-illuminated and ergonomic, and the center console features a trip computer and air-conditioning system as well as the radio.

Unter der Haube des 850i bietet sich ein vertrautes Bild: Wie beim 750i verrichtet hier der starke 5-Liter-V12 seine Arbeit. Nüchtern, gut beleuchtet und im Blickfeld: Die übersichtlichen Armaturen und die Mittelkonsole mit Bordcomputer, Radio und Klimaanlage.

Sous le capot de la 850i se trouve une «vieille connaissance»: le puissant V12 de 5 litres de la 750i. Sobre mais bien éclairé: le tableau de bord est bien agencé, il se prolonge par la console médiane avec ordinateur de bord, autoradio et climatisation.

The 850i's retractable headlights incorporate low beam and fog lamps. The parking lights and high beam are integrated into the fender area. The trunk has ample space for two people's baggage. The tail of the coupé conceals a novelty: thanks to a suspension system with five wheel suspension arms, the multi-link suspension, the wide rear wheels steer along with the driver, so to speak.

Die „Schlafaugen" des 850i: Klappscheinwerfer mit Abblend- und Nebellampen. Stand- und Fernlicht erstrahlen aus dem Stoßfänger. Für das Gepäck von zwei Personen gut bemessen ist der Kofferraum. Das Coupé wartet mit einer Besonderheit im Heck auf. Dank einer räumlich wirkenden Radaufhängung mit fünf Lenkern, der Integralachse, lenken die breiten Hinterräder sozusagen mit.

Les phares escamotables de la 850i renferment les feux de route et de croisement. Les feux de position et les longues portées se trouvent dans le pare-chocs. Le coffre est suffisamment grand pour loger les bagages de deux personnes. Grâce à une suspension agissant comme un essieu intégral, les larges roues arrière ont un effet directionnel.

BMW Z1 1989

"The roadster is focused, it embodies the core qualities of a BMW directly and unmistakably," was the comment of Dr Wolfgang Reitzle on the return of the BMW roadster in its most modern form. The Z1 was the surprise at the 1987 Frankfurt Motor Show. Pleasure could also be seen on the face of the rather distinguished and reticent BMW director for development and production as he invited the journalists for a test drive. Relaxed Reitzle wore a turtleneck pullover and a broad grin: "It might not be the most sensible car, but it's great fun."

This piece of fun was to cost more than 80,000 marks and was not originally planned as a production car, for it was designed and built as a high-technology demonstration vehicle for BMW Technik GmbH. So customer demand was all the more surprising. When the first Z1s went to the dealers, there were already 5000 orders. Assumed buyers' interest led to doubled and tripled production, reaching up to 18 Z1s per day. That was too much for a limited market. The Z1 could only be made affordable to roadster fans with discounts, and production ceased at 8000 cars in June 1991.

The marketing and pricing principle is missing from the Z1, and that was the crux of a roadster which was to serve as a test bed for new axles and trend-setting processed plastics in automotive construction. A galvanized sheet steel frame encloses the vehicle floor made of epoxy resin and PV

plastics which were reinforced with glass fiber. This monocoque structure carried the external skin made of various thermoplastic compounds, and the relatively central front engine from the BMW 325i.

Virgin territory was entered with the doors: they retracted downwards. In view of the high sill, it is not easy for non-sporty people to get into the Z1, particularly when the folding top is closed. But anyone not of a sporty disposition has the wrong vehicle with the roadster anyway. Perfect handling, even with extreme load changes, is due to the chassis with independent suspension and the Z-axle at the rear. The "Z" signifies a "centrally articulated, spherical double wishbone axle" in German. Got that?

That the Z1 did without the usual spoilers, was due to the turbulence-free underbody, and a diffuser which—together with a lip on the trunk—ensured sufficient downward aerodynamic air pressure, even at a top speed of 141 mph (225 kph).

Just as Reitzle said, the maneuverability and easy handling of this roadster, which is less than 13 feet long (4 meters), makes it incredible fun to drive. It can only be fully enjoyed when the top is folded down, even if this increases the drag coefficient from 0.36 to 0.43. The irrationality of this car is due less to the fact that there is insufficient luggage space for longer journeys, or that it offers drivers with sporting ambitions a meager 170 bhp, than to its price. 10,000 marks less and the Z1 would have been a big seller for a decade.

"Der Roadster bringt die Sache auf den Punkt. Er verkörpert die Kerneigenschaften eines BMW direkt und unmissverständlich", so kommentiert Dr.-Ing. Wolfgang Reitzle die Rückkehr zum Roadster, wenngleich modernster Prägung. Der Z1 ist die Überraschung auf der IAA 1987. Und man merkt dem eher vornehm zurückhaltenden BMW-Vorstandsmitglied für Entwicklung und Produktion die Freude über den gelungenen Coup an, als er die Journalisten zu Testfahrten bittet. Reitzle mit Rollkragenpullover und breitem Lausbuben-Grinsen: „Er ist vielleicht etwas unvernünftig, aber er macht ungemein Spaß."

Der Spaß soll mehr als 80 000 Mark kosten und war ursprünglich nicht für die Serie vorgesehen, sondern konzipiert und gebaut als Technologieträger der BMW Technik GmbH. Umso mehr überrascht die Nachfrage. In der Phase der Erstauslieferungen an die Händler liegen bereits 5000 Bestellungen vor. Spekulatives Käuferinteresse führt zur Verdoppelung und Verdreifachung der Produktion – bis zu 18 Z1 werden pro Tag gefertigt. Zuviel für einen begrenzten Markt. Nur mit Rabatten ist der Z1 letztlich an den Roadster-Fan zu bringen, und nach 8000 gebauten Wagen wird im Juni 1991 die Fertigung eingestellt.

Die Komponenten Marketing und Preispolitik haben bei der Konzipierung des Z1 keine Rolle gespielt, und das ist die Crux dieses Roadsters, der ursprünglich frei von Produktionszwängen zur Erprobung neuer Achsen und richtungsweisender Kunststoffverarbeitungsverfahren im Automobilbau dienen sollte. Ein Stahlblechgerüst, natürlich verzinkt, umschließt

den Fahrzeugboden aus glasfaserverstärktem Epoxidharz und PV. Dieses „Monocoque" trägt die aus verschiedenen Thermoplast-Verbindungen bestehende Außenhaut und den relativ zentrierten Frontmotor des BMW 325i.

Bei den Türen werden neue Wege beschritten: Sie sind nach unten versenkbar. Angesichts der hohen Schwelle bietet der Z1 unsportlichen Menschen keinen leichten Einstieg, besonders bei geschlossenem Verdeck. Aber für Unsportliche ist der Roadster sowieso nicht das richtige Auto. Sein perfektes Handling selbst bei extremen Lastwechseln verdankt der Z1 dem Fahrwerk mit Einzelradaufhängungen und der Z-Achse hinten. Das „Z" steht für eine „zentralpunktgeführte sphärische Doppel-Querlenkerachse". Alles klar?

Dass der Z1 ohne das übliche Spoilerwerk auskommt, verdankt er dem verwirbelungsfrei gestalteten Unterboden und einem Diffusor, der zusammen mit einer Lippe auf dem Kofferraum für genügend Anpressdruck auch bei einer Höchstgeschwindigkeit von 225 Stundenkilometern sorgt.

Wendigkeit und Handlichkeit des nicht einmal vier Meter langen Roadsters machen, wie Reitzle richtig feststellt, wirklich ungemein Spaß – ein Vergnügen, das erst bei offenem Verdeck voll zu genießen ist, auch wenn dadurch der Luftwiderstandsbeiwert von 0,36 auf 0,43 steigt. Die Unvernunft des Wagens liegt weniger darin, dass er für längere Reisen nicht genügend Gepäckraum bereithält und sportlich ambitionierten Fahrern nur magere 170 PS bietet, sondern in seinem Preis. 10 000 Mark günstiger, und der Z1 wäre ein Renner für ein Jahrzehnt geworden.

Le roadster met les points sur les i, il incarne à la perfection les caractéristiques d'une BMW, de façon claire et nette », déclare l'ingénieur Wolfgang Reitzle pour commenter le retour du roadster dans sa version ultramoderne. La Z1 est «la» surprise du Salon de l'automobile de Francfort en 1987. Reitzle, plutôt discret et réservé membre du directoire de BMW, au titre du développement et de la production, ne peut s'en cacher lorsqu'il invite les journalistes à essayer la voiture. Vêtu d'un pull à col roulé et arborant un large sourire, il déclare : «Ce n'est peut-être pas raisonnable, mais c'est un véritable plaisir. »

Le plaisir est censé coûter plus de 80 000 marks et n'était, à l'origine, pas prévu pour la série : il a été conçu et construit au départ pour servir de vitrine technologique à la BMW Technik GmbH. La demande des acheteurs est d'autant plus surprenante. Durant la phase des premières livraisons aux concessionnaires, 5000 commandes ont déjà été passées. La spéculation fait doubler puis tripler la production – jusqu'à 18 Z1 par jour sortent des chaînes de production. Ce qui est beaucoup trop pour un marché restreint. Au final, la Z1 ne trouve preneur parmi les fanas du roadster qu'avec une réduction de son prix et la production est suspendue en juin 1991 avec 8000 voitures sorties des chaînes.

Les composantes marketing et une stratégie commerciale font défaut à la Z1. C'est là le problème pour un roadster, libéré des contraintes de la production pour la mise à l'essai de nouveaux essieux et de matières plastiques novatrices dans la construction automobile. Un squelette d'acier, naturellement galvanisé, enserre la plate-forme en résine époxyde

et PVC renforcés de fibre de verre. Cette «monocoque» est dotée d'une carrosserie en matériaux composites et matière thermoplastique et héberge le moteur avant de la BMW 325i en position presque centrale.

Innovation également pour les portières : elles sont escamotables vers le bas. Compte tenu de sa hauteur, l'accès n'est pas aisé pour un conducteur non sportif, a fortiori quand la capote est fermée. De toute façon, ceux pour qui le sport est un vain mot n'ont pas leur place dans le roadster. La Z1 doit son comportement parfait, même lors d'importants changements de charges, à son châssis à suspension à roue indépendante et à son essieu en Z à l'arrière. Le «Z» signifie «double essieu transversal sphérique à guidage central». Tout est clair ?

Si la Z1 peut se passer des ailerons traditionnels, elle le doit à son soubassement qui ne provoque aucun tourbillon et à un diffuseur qui, conjointement avec une lèvre sur le couvercle du coffre, génère suffisamment de stabilité même à la vitesse maximum de 225 km/h.

La vivacité et la maniabilité de ce petit roadster de moins de quatre mètres de long sont, comme le disait Reitzle, vraiment amusantes et le plaisir est encore plus grand en décapotable même si, alors, le C_X passe de 0,36 à 0,43. Le caractère déraisonnable de la voiture, c'est son prix plutôt que le fait qu'il n'y ait pas suffisamment de place pour les bagages ou encore qu'avec 170 ch, elle ne peut guère satisfaire les pilotes amateurs de conduite sportive. Dix mille marks de moins, et la Z1 aurait été la vedette d'une décennie entière.

For the roadster fan, the Z1 with its 170 bhp and retractable doors represents pure motoring fun. For BMW, its main purpose was to test new technology. The Z1 tail is fitted with a diffuser whose airstream is directed over a reverse airfoil fitted between the flat exhaust pipes.

Für den Roadster-Fan ist der Z1 mit seinen 170 PS und den versenkbaren Türen ein „Spaßmobil". Für BMW ist er primär ein Technologieträger. Das Z1-Heck verfügt über einen Diffusor, dessen Luftstrom über ein umgekehrtes Flügelprofil zwischen den flachen Auspuffrohren abgeführt wird.

Pour les fanas du roadster, la Z1 de 170 ch aux portières escamotables est une véritable voiture d'agrément. Pour BMW, il s'agit surtout d'une vitrine technologique. L'arrière de la Z1 comporte, en effet, un diffuseur dont le courant d'air est canalisé par un profil d'aile inversé entre les pots d'échappement aplatis.

Even more elegant than its predecessor and full of technological gems, the E36 BMW 3 series convertible was unveiled in 1993. The aerodynamic wedge shape underlined the classic look of the open-top BMW which, according to its creators, was joy incarnated. From 1994, the advent of the 318i made this pleasure available to those with a more modest budget.

This tried and tested engine could deliver 115 bhp along with a few other innovations. For example, the maximum torque of 124 lb-ft (168 Nm) could now be achieved at 3900 rpm. "DISA" was the name given by BMW to a new, high-tech component: the variable air intake unit controlled by the complex Digital Motor Electronics (DME). This unit delivered enhanced torque characteristics over the entire torque range by creating long intake tracts at low engine speeds, shortening as engine speed rises to develop full power at optimum revs.

When BMW recalled old virtues in 1994, seeking its lost target customer group with the 318ti compact, those potential customers had largely swapped over to Volkswagen's Golf GTI. With spirited engine performance

and driving manners, BMW became involved in the market of the GTI which was 1000 marks cheaper. Truly, the looks of the Bavarian with the short rear end compensated for the 7mph (11kph) missing at the top compared with the GTI.

Compared to other 3 series, 9 inches (23cm) are missing from the rear end, but the large tailgate and individually folding rear seats provide excellent versatility on the inside. Those for whom this is not enough can allow themselves the open air variant—an electrically-operated fabric top, stretching the whole length of the roof.

The 3 series "touring" of the E36 generation, which was described by BMW as an "automobile for people who value individuality and have a mobile dynamic lifestyle," is more than a refined example of a four-door station wagon.

The 320i, one of seven different engine configurations, has the now classic BMW format of the six-cylinder in-line 1991cc engine. This power source with a three-way catalytic converter and a lambda sensor can deliver 150 bhp—exactly what could be expected from this "high-class beast of burden," which can take a load of half a ton.

Noch eleganter als der Vorgänger und vollgepackt mit technischen Leckerbissen stellt sich 1993 das Cabrio der 3er Reihe (E36) vor. Die aerodynamisch günstige Keilform unterstreicht den Chic des offenen BMW, den seine Schöpfer als ein Stück Lebensfreude anpreisen. Diese ist ab 1994 auch weniger Betuchten in Form des 318i zugänglich.

115 PS leistet inzwischen das bewährte Triebwerk, das mit einigen Innovationen aufwarten kann. So wird das maximale Drehmoment von 168 Nm schon bei 3900 Umdrehungen pro Minute erreicht. „DISA" nennt BMW eine neue High-Tech-Komponente: die differenzierte Sauganlage, gesteuert durch eine komplexe digitale Motorelektronik. Sie gewährleistet einen verbesserten Drehmomentverlauf über das gesamte Drehzahlspektrum durch lange Ansaugwege bei niedrigen Touren und kurze zur vollen Leistungsausbeute im Bereich der Höchstdrehzahl.

BMW besinnt sich 1994 wieder auf alte Tugenden und sucht mit dem 318ti compact die verlorene Zielgruppe, die in der Zwischenzeit größtenteils auf den Golf GTI umgestiegen ist. Mit temperamentvoller Motorleistung und Fahrkultur mischt sich BMW in das Segment des 1000 Mark günstigeren

BMW 3 E36 | 1990

GTI. Und gewiss macht die Optik des Kurzheck-Bayern die gegenüber dem GTI um 11 Stundenkilometer geringere Spitzengeschwindigkeit wett.

Gegenüber den anderen 3ern fehlen am „Hintern" 23 Zentimeter, doch durch die große Hecktür und die einzeln umklappbaren Fondsitze ist eine gewisse Innenraumvariabilität gegeben. Wem diese nicht ausreicht, der kann sich die Open-Air-Variante genehmigen – ein Stoffverdeck, das elektrisch über die ganze Dachlänge geöffnet werden kann.

Der 3er touring der E36-Generation, von den Werbestrategen als „Automobil für Menschen, die auf Individualität Wert legen und einen mobilen dynamischen Lebensstil haben" beschrieben, ist mehr als ein viertüriger Kombi der besseren Art.

Der 320i, eine von sieben verschiedenen Triebwerkskonfigurationen, hat den mittlerweile schon klassischen Sechszylinder-Reihenmotor mit 1991 cm³ Hubraum. Diese Kraftquelle mit Dreiwegekatalysator und Lambda-Sonde leistet 150 PS, genau das Richtige für einen Edel-Lastesel, dem eine halbe Tonne Zuladung aufgebürdet werden kann.

Plus élégant encore que celui de la génération précédente et truffé de détails techniques, le cabriolet de la Série 3 (E36) apparaît en 1993. Ses lignes aérodynamiques mettent en évidence le chic de la BMW décapotable qui, pour ses créateurs, contribue à voir la vie en rose. Pour les portefeuilles moins bien garnis, cette voiture est disponible également, à partir de 1994, sous la forme d'une 318i.

Le moteur testé qui bénéficie de quelques innovations développe entre-temps 115 ch. Le couple maximum de 168 Nm est ainsi disponible dès 3900 tr/min. BMW a baptisé «DISA» un nouveau dispositif à haute technologie: le système d'aspiration différencié commandé par le complexe moteur électronique (Digital Motor Electronics). Il garantit une meilleure valeur de couple dans tous les régimes grâce à des tubulures d'aspiration longues à bas régime, mais plus courtes à haut régime pour exploiter totalement le potentiel.

Lorsque BMW en prend conscience en 1994 et cherche à reconquérir sa clientèle cible qu'elle a perdu en lui proposant la 318ti compact, ses acheteurs potentiels ont, en majorité, rejoint sans tambour ni trompette le camp de la Golf GTI. Avec une motorisation qui a du tempérament et qui

se conduit en douceur, BMW offre un véhicule de la catégorie des GTI, moins cher de 1000 marks. Et, assurément, l'esthétique de la BMW à l'arrière tronqué compense un peu les 11 km/h de vitesse de pointe qui lui manque face à la GTI.

Par rapport aux autres Séries 3, elle a raccourci de 23 cm à l'arrière, mais le grand hayon et la banquette arrière fractionnée et rabattable lui permettent d'offrir une grande souplesse d'utilisation. Celui à qui cela ne suffit pas peut opter pour la variante «open air» – avec une capote électrique s'ouvrant sur toute la longueur du toit.

La Série 3 touring de la génération E36 de BMW, que Munich qualifie d'«automobile pour les conducteurs qui ont une personnalité et qui sont dynamiques», est un bel exemplaire d'un break à quatre portes.

La 320i, l'une de sept configurations de moteur différentes, possède le six-cylindres de 1991 cm³ qui est, entre-temps, devenu un grand classique. Ce propulseur à catalyseur trois voies et à sonde à oxygène développe 150 ch, juste ce qu'il convient pour une «bête de somme prestigieuse» qui peut transporter une demi-tonne de bagages.

The 318i Cabrio is visually very pleasing with its elegant and harmonious lines from the flat hood to the relatively low rear. It has 115 bhp at its disposal.

Das 318i Cabrio ist wegen der eleganten und harmonischen Linienführung von der flachen Motorhaube bis zu dem relativ niedrigen Heck optisch äußerst ansprechend. Es verfügt über 115 PS.

La 318i Cabrio est une très grande réussite esthétique en raison de l'élégance et de l'harmonie de ses lignes qui partent du capot moteur plat à l'arrière relativement bas. Elle est propulsée par un moteur de 115 ch.

The fuel efficiency of the proven four-cylinder engine does nothing to reduce the feeling that there are no "constraints."

Der sparsame Benzinverbrauch des bewährten Vierzylinders mindert gewiss nicht das Gefühl der grenzenlosen Freiheit.

Les économies prouvées de consommation du quatre-cylindres ne minorent en rien la sensation de liberté.

Younger buyers in particular value this compact zippy BMW without a "rear," which is 9 inches (23 cm) shorter than the other 3 series cars. The space in the two-door hatchback is quite acceptable. 930 lbs (422 kg) of additional load are allowed.

Besonders jüngere Käuferschichten schätzen den kompakten spritzigen BMW ohne „Hintern", der 23 Zentimeter kürzer ist als die anderen 3er. Das Platzangebot in der zweitürigen Schrägheck-Limousine ist durchaus akzeptabel. 422 Kilo Zuladung sind erlaubt.

Les jeunes acheteurs, en particulier, apprécient la compacte et nerveuse BMW dont l'arrière mesure 23 cm de moins que les autres Séries 3. L'habitacle de la berline trois portes est tout à fait acceptable. Elle peut transporter jusqu'à 422 kg.

Until 1996, the 318ti compact was powered by the 140 bhp four-valve four-cylinder engine of the 318ti coupé. Smart: the steering wheel with leather grip.

Bis 1996 wird der 318ti compact vom Vierventil-Vierzylinder mit 140 PS des 318ti coupé angetrieben. Schick ist das Lenkrad mit Ledergriffzone.

Jusqu'en 1996, la 318ti compact est propulsée par le quatre-cylindres à quatre soupapes de 140 ch de la 318ti coupé. Très chic : le volant en cuir.

The 320i touring is well equipped with the 150 bhp 2-liter six-cylinder engine which can easily carry the burden of an extra half-ton load.

Mit dem 150 PS starken 2-Liter-Sechszylindermotor ist der 320i touring, dem ohne weiteres eine halbe Tonne Zuladung aufgebürdet werden kann, bestens ausgestattet.

Avec le six-cylindres de 2 litres et 150 ch, la 320i touring, qui peut transporter sans difficulté une demi-tonne, dispose d'un propulseur idéal.

The 286 bhp 3-liter engine of the M3 was replaced in 1995 by a 3.2-liter engine with 321 bhp. It was based on the aluminum six-cylinder engine of the 328i. As the basis for motor sport, the coupé is the "racer" in the M3 family. The appropriate wheel design for the road is also supplied.

Der 3-Liter-Motor des M3 mit 286 PS wird 1995 von einem 3,2-Liter-Triebwerk mit 321 PS abgelöst. Er basiert auf dem Aluminium-Sechszylinder des 328i. Als Basisfahrzeug für den Motorsport ist das Coupé der „Renner" in der M3-Familie. Das passende Raddesign für die Straße wird mitgeliefert.

Le moteur de 3 litres de la M3, qui développe 286 ch, est remplacé par un 3,2 litres de 321 ch en 1995. Il s'est inspiré du six-cylindres en aluminium de la 328i. Comme voiture de base pour la compétition, le coupé est «la fusée» dans la famille des M3. Le design des jantes pour la route est à l'unisson.

With acceleration almost as fast as the M3 coupé, the M3 convertible accelerates from a standing start to 62 mph (100 kph) in 5.5 seconds, turning a drive with the top down into an exceptional experience.

Fast so sprintstark wie das M3 Coupé beschleunigt das M3 Cabrio in 5,5 Sekunden aus dem Stand auf 100 Stundenkilometer und lässt das Fahren mit offenem Verdeck zu einem besonderen Erlebnis werden.

Avec presque d'aussi bonnes reprises que le coupé M3, la M3 Cabriolet abat le 0 à 100 km/h en 5,5 secondes. Dans cette voiture, rouler en décapotable fait éprouver des sensations exceptionnelles.

The large air intake on the M3 front spoiler is
unmistakable; it ensures the necessary pressure at
high speeds.

Unverkennbar ist der große Kühllufteinlass des
M3-Frontspoilers, der in den hohen Geschwindigkeits-
bereichen für den nötigen Anpressdruck sorgt.

Reconnaissable entre mille: la grande prise d'air de
refroidissement dans l'imposant aileron avant de la M3
lui confère l'appui indispensable à haute vitesse.

This large BMW contains a multitude of useful small items with which BMW has done an excellent job. The 740i is a regal representative of the automotive upper class: technically perfect, luxuriously appointed, functionally thought through down to the smallest switch. Powered by the satin-smooth performance of the 4.4-liter V8 engine, whose long stroke characteristics mean the maximum torque peak for pulling power arrives at a remarkably low 3900 rpm.

What characterizes this latest generation of BMW eight-cylinder engines is not enhanced performance—286 bhp does that job—but smoothness, a broad torque range and improved fuel economy. In figures, acceleration from 0 to 62 mph (100 kph) in 6.6 seconds says as much for the 740i as average fuel consumption of just 19 miles to the gallon of unleaded premium (12.5 liters per 100 km). As usual for many bigger BMWs, top speed is electronically limited to 155 mph (250 kph).

In the manual transmission model, a sixth gear was added to the fifth to serve as an overdrive ratio, reducing engine revs

by 17 percent and thus saving fuel. Anyone who loves luxury sedans will want to avoid straining his clutch foot, particularly as BMW offers an electro-hydraulically controlled five-speed automatic transmission as a popular optional extra. This is provided with technical refinements such as adaptive transmission control and Steptronic.

The BMW technical dictionary, which forms part of every 7 series brochure, reads at first sight like the manual for a space shuttle. There is reference to "Check Control," "Multi-Information Display (MID)," "On-Board Computer," "On-Board Diagnostics," and the optionally available satellite navigation system which calculates the car's position through the "Global Positioning System (GPS)."

It is no doubt reassuring for the normal car user to know that the 740i (like all new 5 and 7 series cars) is equipped as standard with a head airbag, which has been fitted into the roof frame and usefully supplements the effect of the side airbag in the door. Naturally this system of tubed bags also has a catchy designation: "Inflatable Tubular Structure (ITS)."

Im großen BMW steckt eine Fülle nützlicher Kleinigkeiten, bei denen BMW Großartiges geleistet hat. Der 740i ist ein souveräner Vertreter der Oberschicht unter den Automobilen: technisch perfekt, luxuriös im Interieur und funktionell durchdacht bis zum kleinsten Schalter. Er verwöhnt seine Passagiere mit der samtweichen Laufkultur des V8-Motors mit knapp 4,4 Litern Hubraum. Dank der langhubigen Auslegung dieses Triebwerks wird das maximale Drehmoment bereits bei 3900 Umdrehungen pro Minute erreicht.

Die jüngste Generation der BMW-Achtzylinder kennzeichnet nicht mehr brachiale Kraft und Leistung – 286 PS genügen –, sondern Laufkultur, breiterer Drehmomentverlauf und gleichzeitige Senkung des Kraftstoffverbrauchs. In Zahlen ausgedrückt spricht eine Beschleunigung von 0 auf 100 Stundenkilometer in nur 6,6 Sekunden ebenso für den 740i wie ein durchschnittlicher Benzinverbrauch von 12,5 Litern Super. Wie bei BMW Usus, ist die Höchstgeschwindigkeit elektronisch auf 250 Stundenkilometer beschränkt.

Beim Schaltgetriebe wurde auf den fünften Gang noch ein sechster gesetzt – als Schongang, der die Motordrehzahl

BMW 7 E38 | 1994

um 17 Prozent senkt und somit den Benzinverbrauch reduziert. Wer Luxuslimousinen liebt, schont meist den Kupplungsfuß, zumal BMW im Sonderausstattungspaket ein elektronisch-hydraulisch gesteuertes Fünfgang-Automatikgetriebe anbietet. Dieses ist natürlich mit technischen Raffinessen wie adaptiver Getriebesteuerung und Steptronic versehen.

Das BMW-Techniklexikon, Bestandteil jedes 7er-Prospekts, liest sich auf den ersten Blick wie das Handbuch eines Spaceshuttles. Da ist die Rede von „Check Control", „Multi-Informations-Display" (MID), „Bordcomputer", „On-Bord-Diagnose" und dem auf Wunsch erhältlichen Navigationssystem, das mit Hilfe des „Global Positioning System" (GPS) den jeweiligen Aufenthaltsort des Fahrzeugs errechnet.

Für den Normalverbraucher ist sicherlich beruhigend, dass der 740i (wie alle neuen 5er und 7er) serienmäßig mit einem Kopf-Airbag ausgerüstet ist, der, im Dachrahmen integriert, die Wirkung des in der Tür befindlichen Seiten-Airbags sinnvoll ergänzt. Natürlich trägt auch dieses Schlauchsystem eine werbewirksame Bezeichnung in unaussprechlichem Technikerslang: „Inflatable Tubular Structure" (ITS).

La grosse BMW regorge de multiples petits détails pour lesquels BMW n'a pas regardé à la dépense. La 740i incarne la voiture de luxe par excellence qui prend soin de ses passagers : parfaite sur le plan mécanique, avec un habitacle luxueux, fonctionnelle jusqu'au bout des manettes et animée d'un moteur V8 de 4,4 litres de cylindrée. Sa course longue permet à ce propulseur de délivrer son couple maximum dès 3900 tr/min.

Ce qui caractérise la dernière génération des huit-cylindres BMW n'est pas une débauche de puissance – 286 ch suffisent. Ses points forts sont en réalité la souplesse, la plage de couples et, simultanément, une moindre consommation de carburant. En chiffres, cela se traduit par des accélérations de 0 à 100 km/h en 6,6 secondes seulement ainsi que par une consommation moyenne de 12,5 litres de super aux 100 km. Comme il est de coutume chez BMW, la vitesse maximum est régulée électroniquement à 250 km/h.

La boîte manuelle a vu sa cinquième vitesse complétée par un sixième rapport – une démultipliée qui fait retomber le régime moteur de 17 % et donc aussi la consommation. Le

véritable amateur de berlines de luxe ne manie pas volontiers l'embrayage, d'autant que, dans la liste des options, BMW propose une boîte automatique à cinq vitesses à commande électronico-hydraulique. Celle-ci comporte naturellement divers détails techniques comme une gestion adaptative et une commande Steptronic.

La notice de la mécanique d'une BMW, qui fait partie intégrante de tout prospectus de Série 7, évoque à la première lecture le mode d'emploi d'une navette spatiale. On y parle de «Check Control», de «Multi-Information Display» (MID), d'«ordinateur de bord», d'«On-Board Diagnostics» et du système de navigation proposé en option, qui indique l'endroit où l'on se trouve à l'aide du «Global Positioning System» (GPS).

Pour l'automobiliste lambda, il est assurément tranquillisant de savoir que la 740i (comme toutes les Séries 5 et 7) comporte en série un airbag spécial intégré pour protéger la tête, complétant efficacement les airbags latéraux se trouvant dans les portières. Ce système de coussins gonflables porte le nom d'«Inflatable Tubular Structure» (ITS).

The aesthetics of top-of-the-range cars find expression in the elegant lines of the 740i:
a refined atmosphere with functional dashboard inside and a powerful eight-cylinder
engine under the hood.

Die Ästhetik der „Oberschicht unter den Automobilen" drückt sich in der eleganten
Linienführung des 740i aus: ein edles Ambiente mit funktionellem Armaturenbrett im
Inneren und einem kraftvollen Achtzylinder unter der Haube.

Le «grand chic automobile» se retrouve dans l'élégance des lignes de la 740i: le luxe
avec un tableau de bord fonctionnel à l'intérieur et un puissant huit-cylindres sous
le capot.

As flagship of the fourth generation of the 5 series (E39), which entered the automotive spring of 1997 with seven engine options, the 540i has been given a beefy but very modern 4.4-liter unit. This V8 aluminum engine with electronic engine management develops 310 lb-ft (420 Nm) torque at a remarkably low 3900 rpm and even at very low engine revs it is surprisingly flexible. The 286 bhp provides acceleration of 6.2 seconds from 0 to 62 mph (100 kph) and a top speed of 155 mph (250 kph).

With reasonably restrained driving, not always easy given the premium road holding, the 540i does a good 19.2 miles to the gallon of premium (12.3 liters per 100 km). With the touring model, the higher weight of 3737 lbs (1695 kg) instead of 3494 lbs (1585 kg) becomes apparent with additional consumption of four percent. A carefully calculated six-speed manual transmission is designed for drivers who like to use the gears. Those who do not are happier with the modern adaptively controlled automatic transmission with five gears.

This new member of the 5 series stands out by ist lightweight construction; thus the rigidity of the body shell has been considerably increased while maintaining the same weight as the previous model. The lightweight construction chassis components, mostly of aluminum, were a world first for a production model. Aluminum wheels were also standard on the 540i.

The first press photos of the new BMW M5 were of symbolic character: they showed a miracle in blue—one available to drive from November 1998, at 400 bhp, 370 lb-ft (500 Nm)

torque and offering acceleration of 5.3 seconds from 0 to 62 mph (100 kph)!

The "ultimate performance machine" from Munich is outwardly unassuming. It is distinguished subtly from the usual 5 series by a larger air intake, oval fog lights, aerodynamically designed external mirrors which can be folded away, shiny chrome light alloy wheels with fat tires (245/40 ZR 18 and 275/35 ZR 18) and the four stainless steel exhausts of the eight-cylinder engine.

A special Bosch Motronic manages the throttle flaps, the temperature-sensitive lubrication oil supply, and fully automatic variable timing of the intake and exhaust camshafts. This increases torque at lower and middle engine speeds. As well as this double VANOS system, patented by BMW M GmbH, the accelerator action can also be electronically adjusted. Power with an instant "blast" or a comfortable power surge: the press of a button is all it takes.

Clever aerodynamic design of the subframe and a taut sporty chassis enable the M5 to achieve lateral acceleration loads of 1.2 g. When the color drains from drivers' faces in fast bends, the engine oil also experiences an unhealthy centrifugal force. Instead of a racing dry sump system, the M5 counters such oil surges with a lubrication system that reacts to lateral force.

Compound disk brakes, which BMW uses in motor racing, ensure better heat diffusion when braking through their "floating" construction. In addition, they are longer lasting than normal brakes. The conventional six-speed transmission has short precise shifts.

Als Flaggschiff der vierten Generation der 5er Reihe (E39), die mit sieben Motorisierungsoptionen in den Autofrühling 1997 startet, ist der 540i mit einem bulligen, aber hochmodernen 4,4-Liter-Aggregat bestückt. Dieses V8-Aluminiumtriebwerk mit elektronischem Motormanagement entwickelt bereits bei 3900 Touren ein Drehmoment von 420 Newtonmetern und ist selbst bei ganz niedrigen Drehzahlen erstaunlich elastisch. Die 286 PS ermöglichen eine Beschleunigung von 0 auf 100 Stundenkilometer in 6,2 Sekunden und eine Spitzengeschwindigkeit von 250 Sachen.

Bei nicht allzu forcierter Fahrweise, die sich angesichts der optimalen Straßenlage allerdings gern aufdrängt, schlürft der 540i lediglich 12,3 Liter Super. Beim Touring macht sich das höhere Gewicht von 1695 (statt 1585) Kilo mit einem Mehrverbrauch von knapp einem halben Liter bemerkbar. Ein sorgsam abgestimmtes Sechsgang-Getriebe kommt schaltfreudigen Fahrern entgegen. Schaltfaule freuen sich über das moderne, adaptiv gesteuerte Automatikgetriebe mit fünf Gängen.

Der neue 5er glänzt durch seine Leichtbauweise. So kann die Steifigkeit der Rohkarosse bei gleichem Gewicht gegenüber dem Vorgängermodell erheblich vergrößert werden. Weltpremiere bei einem Serienmodell feiert das weitgehend aus Aluminium gefertigte Leichtbaufahrwerk. Da ist es nur sinnvoll, dass auch die Alufelgen zur Serienausstattung des 540i gehören.

Die ersten Pressefotos des neuen BMW M5 haben Symbolcharakter: Zu sehen ist ein blaues Wunder, und das kann man seit November 1998 auch erleben – bei 400 PS, 500 Newtonmetern Drehmoment und einer Beschleunigung von 0 auf Tempo 100 in 5,3 Sekunden!

BMW 5 E39 | 1995

Das „ultimative Kraftpaket" aus München gibt sich äußerlich unaufdringlich. Vom normalen 5er unterscheidet es sich nur durch einen größeren Kühllufteinlass, ovale Nebelscheinwerfer, aerodynamisch gestaltete und elektrisch wegklappbare Außenspiegel, chromglänzende Leichtmetallräder mit dicken Puschen (245/40 ZR 18 und 275/35 ZR 18) und die vier Edelstahl-Auspuffrohre des Achtzylinders.

Eine spezielle Mototronic regelt die Drosselklappen, den thermischen Ölniveau-Geber und die vollautomatische Spreizung der Ein- und Auslassnockenwellen zur Drehmomentsteigerung im unteren und mittleren Drehzahlbereich. Neben diesem von der BMW M GmbH patentierten Doppel-VANOS-System lässt sich auch das Gaspedal elektronisch beeinflussen. Ob plötzliche Kraftentfaltung oder komfortables Anschwellen der motorischen Leistung – ein Druck auf den Schalter genügt!

Geschickte aerodynamische Gestaltung des Unterbodens und ein straffes sportliches Fahrwerk erlauben dem M5 Querbeschleunigungen von 1,2 g. Wenn einem Fahrer in schnellen Kurven die Farbe aus dem Gesicht weicht, verspürt auch das Motoröl den ungesunden Drang nach außen. Statt mit einem Trockensumpf begegnet der M5 solchen Strömungen mit einem querkraftgesteuerten Schmierungssystem.

Sogenannte „Compound-Scheibenbremsen", wie sie BMW im Motorsport verwendet, sorgen durch ihre „schwimmende" Bauweise für eine bessere Ableitung der Reibungswärme. Außerdem sind sie haltbarer als die üblichen Bremsen. Eher konventionell ist das Sechsganggetriebe mit kurzen präzisen Schaltwegen.

En tant que navire-amiral de la quatrième génération de la Série 5 (E39) qui inaugure le printemps automobile 1997 avec une gamme de sept moteurs, la 540i est propulsée par un vigoureux et ultramoderne 4,4 litres. Ce V8 en aluminium à gestion moteur électronique développe déjà un couple de 420 Nm à 3900 tr/min; même à bas régime, il fait preuve d'une souplesse étonnante. Les 286 ch lui permettent d'accélérer de 0 à 100 km/h en 6,2 secondes et d'atteindre allégrement les 250 km/h.

Avec une conduite décontractée, qui ne met pas à contribution sa tenue de route exceptionnelle, la 540i consomme seulement 12,3 litres de super aux 100 km. Dans la version touring, le poids de 1695 kg, au lieu de 1585, se traduit par un supplément de consommation d'un demi-litre à peine. Une boîte à six vitesses bien étagée séduira les virtuoses du pommeau. Les adeptes de la boîte automatique se féliciteront de la moderne transmission automatique à cinq vitesses et de la commande adaptative.

La nouvelle Série 5 brille par la légèreté de sa construction: ainsi la carrosserie blanche offre-t-elle, à poids identique, une bien plus grande rigidité torsionnelle que l'ancien modèle. Les trains roulants en alliage léger, pratiquement tout en aluminium, sont une première mondiale sur une voiture de série. Sur la 540i, les jantes alliage sont également de série.

Les premières photos parues dans la presse de la nouvelle BMW M5 sont symboliques: au diapason de la couleur de la carrosserie, du sang bleu coule dans les veines de cette voiture. C'est un cocktail détonant que l'on peut déguster depuis novembre 1998: une puissance de 400 ch, un couple de 500 Nm et 5,3 secondes pour les accélérations de 0 à 100 km/h!

Extérieurement, la «nouvelle reine de la Bavière» est presque trop discrète. De la Série 5 «normale» elle ne se distingue que par de plus grandes prises d'air, des phares antibrouillard ovales, des rétroviseurs extérieurs électriques plus fins, aérodynamiques et rabattables, des jantes alliage chromées avec des pneus larges (245/40 ZR 18 et 275/35 ZR 18) et les quatre sorties du pot d'échappement chromées du huit-cylindres.

Une gestion Mototronic spéciale orchestre la symphonie des papillons des gaz, du capteur de niveau d'huile thermique et de la distribution variable automatique des arbres à cames d'admission et d'échappement aux régimes inférieurs et intermédiaires qui augmente le couple. Outre ce système breveté par BMW M GmbH sous le nom de «double VANOS», elle régule aussi l'accélérateur électronique. Montée en puissance instantanée ou envol progressif et régulier de la performance: pour choisir, il suffit d'appuyer sur un bouton.

Une juste configuration aérodynamique du soubassement et un châssis sportif d'une fermeté de bonne qualité permettent à la M5 d'encaisser des accélérations transversales de 1,2 g. Quand le visage du conducteur commence à changer de couleur dans les virages, l'huile moteur a, elle aussi, la propension «malsaine» à succomber aux effets de la force centrifuge. En alternative à la lubrification à carter sec, la M5 combat un tel afflux d'essence avec un système de lubrification commandé par la force transversale.

Grâce à leur montage «flottant», les freins à disques en composites, utilisés par BMW en compétition, garantissent une meilleure évacuation de la chaleur de friction, ce qui leur donne accessoirement beaucoup plus d'endurance que les freins traditionnels. La boîte à six vitesses est, quant à elle, plutôt conventionnelle avec ses changements courts et précis.

The monitor for on-board computer, navigation system and TV has been cleverly integrated into the central console of the stylishly thoroughbred 5 series.

Geschickt ist der TV-taugliche Monitor für Bordcomputer und Navigationssystem in die Mittelkonsole des schnittigen Edel-5ers integriert.

L'écran de l'ordinateur de bord, du système de navigation et de la télévision est parfaitement intégré dans la console médiane de la rapide Série 5 de prestige.

Tremendous power, discreetly packaged, speedy light alloy wheels, M sports seats and a well-built interior: the 400 bhp M5 is a high-performance sedan of that special type which sets new standards.

Gewaltige Power, diskret verpackt, rasante Leichtmetallräder, M-Sportsitze und ein gediegenes Interieur: Der 400-PS-M5 ist eine Hochleistungs-Limousine der besonderen Art, die neue Maßstäbe setzt.

Une puissance pléthorique, une allure de paisible familiale, de saisissantes jantes en alliage léger, des sièges sport M et un habitacle soigné: la M5 de 400 ch est une berline racée à hautes performances. Elle fera date, incontestablement.

BMW Z3 E36/7 E36/8 | 1996

Based on such beautiful two-seaters as the 328 and the postwar 507 and Z1 models, the first drawings for a new road sports car were created in Munich during 1989. It was to be a roadster, though not quite as spartan as in the originals. Modern technology, packaged in a sporting dress, with a touch of traditional BMW fashion at an affordable price: that is the profile of design priorities.

However, it is not in Bavaria's 1972 Olympic City, but near the site of the 1996 Olympic Games that the Z3 roadster begins to depart a production line. The newest BMW factory in America's Spartanburg, South Carolina, adjacent to Interstate 85 to Atlanta, offers the Z3 with various engines: 115 bhp 1.8-liter four-cylinder, 140 bhp 1.9-liter four-cylinder and the 192 bhp 2.8-liter six-cylinder.

Real roadster driving required even more power. This was acquired around the BMW resources that ring Munich's river, the Isar. Thus the M model with 3.2 liters and 321 bhp (as for the European M3) was developed for the "ultimate driving experience," as BMW put it. But the M roadster has to power 265 lbs (120 kg) less than the M3. This difference does not, however, show up in the enormous acceleration from 0 to 62 mph (100 kph): recorded 5.4 seconds for both.

A slightly longer wheelbase and a wider track at the front and rear, as well as significantly wider tire dimensions differentiate the M roadster from the Z3, as do discreet spoilers. At the end of the side cooling grills—surely a reminder of the 507—the "M" badge of speed is displayed proudly, instead of the BMW roundel.

A roadster aura is also transmitted by the round chrome instruments for the clock, external temperature and oil temperature on the wide transmission tunnel, under which a five-ratio gearbox, geared like the Z3 2.8, does its duty. Dashboard and rich leather interior provide evidence of design imagination.

There is no spare wheel. The special shape of the light-alloy wheels is designed to prevent the tires coming off if there is a flat. Should a puncture occur, the driver operates an "M Mobility System" comprising a mini-compressor and quick sealant. If that does not help, nothing for it but a phone rescue: BMW breakdown service is famous for its good organization.

The electro-hydraulic activation of the fabric top comes as standard on the M, and as an extra on the four-cylinder models. The tonneau fabric must be manually buttoned over the folded top for that real roadster feeling.

The expensive chassis is not harsh, but well adjusted. Even under high acceleration this sports car dips only slightly. Performance, especially along roads with many bends and steering load changes, is a pleasure, for the steering stays precise. The vehicle amiably covers loose ground. The stunts which Pierce "James Bond" Brosnan did with the Z3 in the film *Golden Eye* do not require the driving skills of a Finnish rally star such as Rauno Aaltonen.

Given its enormous potential, the M roadster must have large-diameter ventilated disk brakes, measuring 12⅜ inches (315 mm) front; the rears are 12¼ inches (312 mm). ABS braking and anti-dive mechanisms are BMW virtues of the 1990s.

Anknüpfend an so schöne Zweisitzer wie den 328 und die Nachkriegsmodelle 507 und Z1 entstehen 1989 in München erste Zeichnungen für einen neuen Straßensportwagen – ein Roadster, wenngleich die Ausstattung weniger spartanisch sein soll. Moderne Technik in sportlichem Anzug mit einem Hauch traditioneller BMW-Mode, dazu ein erschwinglicher Preis – so lautet das Anforderungsprofil.

Doch nicht in Bayerns Olympiastadt, sondern in der Nähe des Austragungsortes der Spiele von 1996 geht der Z3-Roadster vom Band. Das jüngste BMW-Werk in Spartanburg, South Carolina (USA) ganz in der Nähe des Interstate Highway 85 nach Atlanta, bietet den Z3 in unterschiedlichen Motorisierungsvarianten an: 1,8-Liter-Vierzylinder mit 115 PS, 1,9-Liter-Vierzylinder mit 140 PS und 2,8-Liter-Sechszylinder mit 192 PS.

Richtiges Roadster-Running erfordert noch mehr Power, und die ist wiederum an der Isar zu haben. Dort gibt es für das „ultimative Fahrerlebnis", so BMW, die Variante „M" mit 3,2 Litern und 321 PS – analog zum M3. Allerdings wiegt der M roadster 120 Kilo weniger als der M3, was bei diesem Kraftpotential allerdings keine Rolle mehr spielt. In unglaublichen 5,4 Sekunden beschleunigen beide von 0 auf 100 Stundenkilometer.

Geringfügig längerer Radstand und die breite Spur vorn und hinten sowie wesentlich breitere Reifen und der dezente Spoiler unterscheiden den „M" vom „Z". Am Ende der seitlichen Kühlschlitze – sicherlich eine Reminiszenz an den 507 – prangt stolz statt des BMW-Emblems das „schnelle M".

Roadster-Feeling vermitteln auch die in Chrom gefassten Rundinstrumente für Uhrzeit, Außen- und Öltemperatur

auf dem breiten Getriebetunnel, unter dem eine Fünfgang-Schaltung, abgestuft wie beim Z3 2.8, ihren Dienst verrichtet. Armaturenbrett und reichlich Lederinterieur zeugen von Einfallsreichtum.

Diesen vermisst man hingegen beim Reserverad – es gibt keines! Die spezielle Form der Leichtmetallfelgen soll ein Abspringen des Reifens im Falle eines „Platten" verhindern. Kommt es doch dazu, greift der Fahrer zum „M Mobility System", einem Kleinkompressor und Schnelldichtmittel. Hilft das nicht, muss der BMW-Notdienst anrücken, der bekanntlich gut organisiert ist.

Die elektrohydraulische Betätigung des Stoffverdecks gehört beim „M" zum Standard, bei den Vierzylindermodellen zu den Extras. Hier muss die Persenning von Hand über das zusammengefaltete Verdeck geknöpft werden – ein Rest von Roadster-Feeling.

Keineswegs hart, sondern gut abgestimmt ist das aufwändige Fahrwerk. Selbst bei hoher Querbeschleunigung neigt sich dieser Sportwagen nur geringfügig. Das Fahrverhalten ist eine Wonne, besonders auf kurvenreicher Strecke mit vielen Lastwechseln; die Lenkung ist präzise. Gutmütig bewegt sich dieses Fahrzeug selbst auf lockerem Untergrund. Was James-Bond-Darsteller Pierce Brosnan im Film *Golden Eye* mit dem Z3 anstellt, bedarf nicht der Fahrkünste eines Rauno Aaltonen.

Angesichts des enormen Leistungspotentials kann der M roadster auf belüftete Scheibenbremsen großen Durchmessers – vorn 315, hinten 312 Millimeter – nicht verzichten. ABS, Brems- und Anfahrnickausgleich gehören zu den BMW-Ausstattungsmerkmalen der neunziger Jahre.

C'est dans la tradition des jolies biplaces telles que la 328 et les 507 et Z1 d'après-guerre que sont réalisées, en 1989 à Munich, les premières esquisses pour une nouvelle sportive de route. Ce sera un roadster, mais pas aussi modeste que les originaux. Technicité et modernisme, une allure sportive et les arguments esthétiques traditionnels de BMW, un prix attrayant – tel est le cahier des charges.

Ce n'est pas dans la ville olympique bavaroise, mais à proximité du site des jeux Olympiques de 1996 que la Z3 roadster sort des chaînes. La toute nouvelle usine de BMW à Spartanburg, en Caroline du Sud (États-Unis), près de l'Interstate Highway 85 qui mène à Atlanta, propose la Z3 avec trois motorisations : le quatre-cylindres de 1,8 litre et 115 ch, le quatre-cylindres de 1,9 litre et 140 ch, et le six-cylindres de 2,8 litres et 192 ch.

Mais pour obtenir un roadster digne de ce nom, il faut encore plus de puissance et le savoir-faire des équipes de Munich. C'est là qu'est assemblée, pour conduire «avec un maximum de plaisir» dit BMW, la variante «M» avec ce même moteur de 3,2 litres et 321 ch qui propulse la M3. La M roadster pèse 120 kg de moins que la M3. Mais cela n'a aucune incidence sur les fantastiques accélérations de 0 à 100 km/h : 5,4 secondes pour toutes les deux.

Un empattement légèrement plus long et des voies plus larges à l'avant et à l'arrière, des pneus nettement plus volumineux et de discrets ailerons distinguent la «M» de la «Z». À l'extrémité des ouïes de refroidissement latérales – une réminiscence de la 507 – s'affiche fièrement, à la place de l'emblème BMW, le «rapide M».

Les cadrans circulaires cernés de chrome pour la montre, le thermomètre affichant la température extérieure et le thermomètre à huile sur le large tunnel de transmission sous lequel se trouve une boîte à cinq vitesses avec même étagement que pour la Z3 2.8 contribuent à faire de ce véhicule un authentique roadster. Le tableau de bord et le cuir à profusion dans l'habitacle sont le fruit de l'imagination des ingénieurs.

Ne cherchez pas la roue de secours – il n'y en a pas. La forme particulière des jantes en alliage est censée empêcher le pneu de se dégonfler en cas de crevaison. Si toutefois cela se produit, le conducteur dispose du «M Mobility System», un mini-compresseur et une bombe anti-crevaison. Si cela ne suffit pas, un appel téléphonique et le service de dépannage de BMW est toujours là, bien organisé.

La commande électro-hydraulique de la capote est de série pour la M et en option pour les quatre-cylindres. Le couvre-capote doit être fixé manuellement. N'est pas roadster qui veut !

Sophistiqués, les trains roulants sont souples, mais bien réglés. Même en cas de fortes accélérations transversales, cette voiture de sport ne prend pratiquement pas de roulis. Le comportement, notamment sur routes sinueuses avec de nombreux transferts de charges, est un délice et la direction est précise. Même sur revêtement peu adhérent, cette voiture ne perd rien de son tempérament. Pour ressembler à Pierce Brosnan qui a incarné James Bond dans le film *Golden Eye* au volant de la Z3, il n'est pas nécessaire d'être un virtuose du volant comme le pilote finlandais Rauno Aaltonen.

Vu son énorme potentiel, la M roadster ne peut pas se passer de disques ventilés de grand diamètre (315 mm à l'avant, 312 mm à l'arrière). ABS et dispositif antiplongée au freinage et à l'accélération font partie des avantages des BMW des années 1990.

Open or closed, the driving characteristics of the M roadster with its sporty chassis and a power to weight ratio of 9.7 lbs (4.4 kg) per bhp are so convincing that many competitors see nothing but the rear end of the car.

Ob offen oder geschlossen: Die Fahreigenschaften des M roadsters sind angesichts des sportlichen Fahrwerks und einem Leistungsgewicht von 4,4 Kilo pro PS so überzeugend, dass viele Konkurrenten nur noch das Heck des Wagens sehen.

Que la capote soit ouverte ou fermée les performances de la M roadster sont si exceptionnelles, compte tenu du châssis sport et d'un rapport poids/puissance de 4,4 kg par ch, que beaucoup de ses rivales ne voient cette voiture que de l'arrière.

The 3.2-liter in-line six-cylinder engine with 24 valves provides a convincing display of power with a torque of 350 Nm, which is achieved at a speed as low as 3250 rpm.

Der 3,2-Liter-Reihensechszylinder mit 24 Ventilen überzeugt neben seiner Kraft durch ein Drehmoment von 350 Newtonmetern, das bereits bei 3250 Umdrehungen pro Minute erreicht wird.

Outre sa puissance, le six-cylindres en ligne de 3,2 litres convainc aussi par son couple de 350 Nm déjà délivré à 3250 tr/min.

Success through performance! Together with the BMW emblem, the M symbol not only stands for success on the racetrack, but also on the road. The leather and chrome trim makes an essential contribution to the design of the cockpit, as can be seen on the wide central console above the five-speed transmission tunnel.

Erfolg durch Leistung! In Verbindung mit dem BMW-Emblem steht das M-Symbol nicht nur für Erfolg auf der Rennpiste, sondern auch auf der Straße. Dass Leder und Chromblenden zur Gestaltung des Cockpits wesentlich beitragen, zeigt die breite Mittelkonsole über dem Tunnel des Fünfgang-Schaltgetriebes.

Conjointement avec le logo BMW, le M emblématique est un symbole de succès tant sur les pistes des circuits que sur la route. La large console médiane sur la colonne hébergeant la boîte manuelle à cinq vitesses témoigne de ce que le cuir et les applications de chrome contribuent joliment à la sportivité de l'habitacle.

The coupé body, with its echoes of a station wagon and its large hatch, is particularly striking from the rear. The 2.8-liter engine with 192 bhp gives the Z3 coupé a top speed of 144 mph (231 kph)—the ideal transport for golfers in a hurry offers enough space for two complete sets of golf equipment.

Der einem Kombi ähnliche und mit einer großen Ladeklappe versehene Coupé-Aufbau wirkt von hinten besonders markant. Der 2,8-Liter-Motor mit 192 PS beschert dem Z3 coupé eine Spitzengeschwindigkeit von 231 Stundenkilometern. Eigentlich ein ideales Gefährt für Golfer in Eile, da der Kofferraum für zwei vollständige Golfausrüstungen Raum bietet.

La version coupé, qui rappelle un break avec son grand hayon, est très caractéristique vue de l'arrière. Le moteur de 2,8 litres et 192 ch permet au coupé Z3 d'atteindre une vitesse de pointe de 231 km/h. C'est l'engin idéal, donc, pour les joueurs de golf pressés puisqu'il peut même héberger deux équipements de golf complets.

"Errors are the rungs on the ladder to success. The trick is to detect them at an early stage of the design process, to eliminate them and to learn from them." That is what the American BMW design chief Christopher E. Bangle had to say about the development of the new 3 series. Five and a half years had elapsed between the first draft design and the car's market launch in April 1998.

Some 2.6 million working hours were invested in the E46, as it was referred to in-house. Over 2400 parts were completely redesigned and 130 prototypes handmade. The new model was to meet the highest standards of excellence right down to the last detail. The "small BMW" embodies the achievement of these exacting objectives.

"Corporate design" meant that this model had to bear at least some resemblance to the 5 series car, but on closer inspection, you can see that Chris Bangle has achieved stylistic high-precision work. The striking face of this car is characterized by the extended kidney-shaped grill on the hood, and the individually framed double round headlights. A harmonious effect is also created by the rear section, its rear lights wrapping around the trunk lid, surmounted by a wedge-shaped spoiler acting as an aerodynamic highlight.

Despite the high trunk compartment and the bulky appearance of the wide track body, the car does not seem to be out of proportion thanks to finely detailed artistic touches. For example, the elegant roof and beltlines are supported by horizontal grooves, lips and rubber strips all round—stylish elements which also have a function.

This wonderful outline conceals an optimum use of space and, most importantly, a great deal of technology. With 193 bhp, the 328i is the most powerful of the five engine variants with which the E46 BMW 3 series begins. The torque characteristics of this in-line six-cylinder engine—already silky smooth anyway—have been enhanced still further. "Double VANOS" is the latest entry in BMW's technical dictionary, stating: "Depending on the accelerator's position and the engine speed, the valve activation times of the intake and exhaust camshafts are adapted to the operating conditions of the engine in an infinitely variable manner." The electromechanical control of the throttle valve allows the engine to idle tranquilly, and ensures power is delivered in a smooth surge during acceleration.

"Putting your foot down" with the new 328i is always a pleasure because the 62mph (100 kph) mark is reached by the high-precision speedo after a mere 7 seconds, and top speeds of 150mph (240kph) are not too bad either. Hans-Joachim Stuck put it in a nutshell in the BMW magazine: "The roadholding and power are phenomenal." As for the statement of his racing partner Johnny Cecotto, no one could have summarized the aesthetically-pleasing harmonious lines any better: "There is a unique synthesis of sportiness and elegance and the standard of active and passive safety is no less impressive. It is wonderful that so many familiar developments from larger BMW models have been incorporated into the new 3 series sedan, and that they are not only reserved for people who can afford larger models. All in all, the very comfortable driving characteristics, despite the car's enormous power capacity, mean that it is a truly charismatic drive."

„Fehler sind die Sprossen auf der Leiter zum Erfolg. Die Kunst ist es, sie beim Designprozess frühzeitig zu erkennen, auszumerzen und aus Ihnen zu lernen", so BMW-Chefdesigner Christopher E. Bangle über die Entwicklungsphase des neuen 3ers. Zwischen dem ersten Entwurf und der Markteinführung im April 1998 sind fünfeinhalb Jahre vergangen.

2,6 Millionen Arbeitsstunden werden in den E46, wie er firmenintern heißt, investiert. 2400 Teile werden völlig neu konzipiert und 130 Prototypen von Hand gefertigt. Höchsten Qualitätsansprüchen soll der Neue genügen, und diese erfordern Perfektion bis ins letzte Detail. Dafür ist der „kleine BMW" ein Musterbeispiel.

Zwar verlangt das Corporate Design nach einer gewissen Ähnlichkeit zum 5er, aber bei näherer Betrachtung stellt sich heraus, dass Christopher Bangle stilistische Feinarbeit geleistet hat. Die verlängerte Nierennase der Motorhaube und die Doppelscheinwerfer mit den Augenringen prägen das markante Gesicht. Harmonisch wirkt auch die Heckpartie mit den in den Kofferraumdeckel gezogenen Heckleuchten, über denen sich eine Abrisskante als aerodynamisches Attribut wölbt.

Trotz des hohen Kofferraums und der wuchtigen Wirkung des Breitfahrwerks stimmen die Proportionen dank kleiner, aber gelungener Kunstgriffe. So unterstützen horizontale Sicken, Lippen und rundum geführte Gummileisten die elegante Dach- und Gürtellinienführung – Stylingelemente, die auch eine Funktion erfüllen.

BMW 3 E46 | 1998

Unter dieser Silhouette verbirgt sich eine optimale Raumausnutzung und vor allem viel Technik. Unter den fünf Antriebsvarianten, mit denen die Baureihe startet, ist der 328i mit 193 PS die kraftvollste. Der Drehmomentverlauf dieses ohnehin seidenweichen Reihensechszylinders ist nochmals verbessert worden. „Doppel-VANOS" heißt der jüngste Eintrag ins BMW-Techniklexikon: „Die Ventilsteuerzeiten sowohl der Einlass- als auch der Auslassnockenwelle werden abhängig von der Gaspedalstellung und der Motordrehzahl stufenlos den Betriebsbedingungen des Motors angepasst." Eine elektromechanische Drosselklappensteuerung sorgt für einen butterweichen Leerlauf und sanftes Ansprechverhalten.

Es macht Spaß, beim neuen 328i zu beschleunigen, denn bereits nach 7 Sekunden zeigt der präzise Tacho 100 km/h an, und eine Spitzengeschwindigkeit von 240 Stundenkilometer lassen keine Wünsche offen. Hans-Joachim Stuck bringt es im *BMW Magazin* auf den Punkt: „Straßenlage und Power sind phänomenal". Dem Statement seines Rennfahrer-Kollegen Johnny Cecotto ist wohl nichts mehr hinzuzufügen, wenn er diesem 3er ästhetische Harmonie bescheinigt und zusammenfasst: „Die Synthese von Sportlichkeit und Eleganz ist einzigartig, der Standard der aktiven und passiven Sicherheit eindrucksvoll. Es ist toll, dass viele aus größeren Baureihen bekannte Entwicklungen in die neue 3er Limousine einfließen und nicht Menschen vorbehalten bleiben, die sich größere Modelle leisten können. Mein Fazit: Das trotz der Power sehr komfortable Fahrverhalten macht das Fahrzeug zu einem richtig sympathischen Wegbegleiter."

C'est en forgeant que l'on devient forgeron. L'art consiste à reconnaître ses erreurs à temps, lors du processus de design, à les éliminer et à en tirer les enseignements », déclare Christopher E. Bangle, chef styliste chez BMW, en évoquant les phases de développement de la nouvelle Série 3. Avant sa commercialisation en avril 1998, cinq ans et demi se sont écoulés depuis le premier coup de crayon.

Quelque 2,6 millions d'heures de travail sont investies dans la E46, comme on l'appelle au sein de l'entreprise. 2400 pièces sont conçues à partir d'une feuille blanche et 130 prototypes sont fabriqués à la main. La nouvelle voiture doit satisfaire aux exigences de qualité les plus strictes et cela implique la perfection jusque dans les moindres détails. La « petite BMW » en est un exemple.

Certes, le *corporate design* exige une certaine similitude avec la Série 5, mais, à y regarder de près, on constate que Christopher Bangle a réalisé un excellent travail esthétique. Le léger prolongement du mufle caractéristique de BMW et les phares doubles avec les « valises » sous les yeux lui donnent une allure caractéristique. Tout aussi harmonieuse est la poupe avec les phares empiétant sur le couvercle du coffre qui se termine sur un léger décrochement aérodynamique.

Malgré la hauteur du coffre et l'effet massif des larges trains roulants, les proportions sont parfaites grâce à des astuces à peine perceptibles, mais efficaces: des rainures horizontales, des arêtes et les bandeaux de caoutchouc cernant la voiture mettent en exergue l'élégance des lignes de toit et de ceinture – des éléments de style qui sont fonctionnels.

Sous cette silhouette magnifique se dissimule une utilisation optimale de l'espace disponible et surtout beaucoup

de technique. Des cinq Série 3 qui sont lancées, la 328i est la plus puissante avec ses 193 ch. La courbe de couple de ce six-cylindres en ligne déjà réputé pour sa souplesse a encore été améliorée. « Double VANOS » est le nom de la dernière entrée au lexique de BMW: « Ce système permet d'adapter en continu la distribution des soupapes, aussi bien pour l'arbre à cames d'admission que pour l'arbre à cames d'échappement, en fonction de la position de l'accélérateur et du régime moteur et selon l'état de charge du moteur. » Une commande électromécanique de la vis papillon garantit un ralenti régulier et des réactions spontanées à l'accélérateur.

Quel plaisir à appuyer sur l'accélérateur de la nouvelle 328i, dont le tachymètre très précis indique 100 km/h au bout de seulement 7 secondes, et qui satisfait tout à fait avec une vitesse de pointe de 240 km/h. Dans le magazine de BMW, le verdict de Hans-Joachim Stuck tombe comme un couperet: « Tenue de route et puissance sont phénoménales. » Il n'est pas nécessaire d'ajouter le moindre commentaire à la déclaration de son collègue, le pilote de course Johnny Cecotto, qui confère à cette Série 3 une harmonie esthétique qu'il résume ainsi: « La synthèse de sportivité et d'élégance est unique au monde; le niveau de sécurité active et passive est impressionnant. Il est intéressant de voir que de nombreuses innovations apparues avec les gammes supérieures soient reprises par la nouvelle BMW de la Série 3 et ne soient pas réservées aux conducteurs qui peuvent s'offrir les modèles haut de gamme. Pour conclure: le comportement très confortable malgré la puissance disponible fait de cette voiture un compagnon de route bien sympathique. »

A typical feature of the new face of the 3 series is the flat hood pulled down around the BMW kidney, with a space left for the flanking double headlights.

Typisch für das neue Gesicht der 3er Reihe ist die flache, über die BMW-Niere heruntergezogene Motorhaube, flankiert von Doppelscheinwerfern mit nach unten ausgesparten Masken.

Le capot moteur aplati descendant au-delà des naseaux BMW et cerné par les phares doubles avec découpe inférieure est caractéristique du nouveau visage de la Série 3.

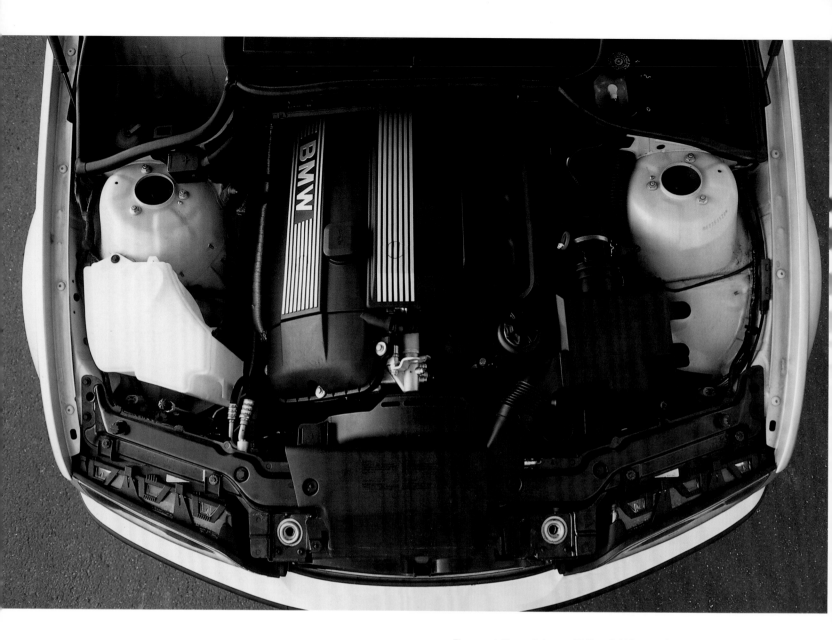

The coupé-like roof shape with the slight lip over the trunk is part of an overall aerodynamic concept which allows the 328i to achieve a top speed of 150 mph (240 kph) with 193 bhp.

Die Coupé-ähnliche Dachform mit leicht angedeuteter Abrisskante über dem Kofferraum ist Teil eines aerodynamischen Gesamtkonzepts, das den 328i mit 193 PS auf 240 Stundenkilometer bringt.

Le toit de style coupé, avec arête de décrochement légèrement esquissée au-dessus du coffre, fait partie d'un concept aérodynamique général qui permet à la 328i de 193 ch d'atteindre les 240 km/h.

The 360 bhp-strong six-cylinder with its carbon-fiber intake stroke is embedded from top to bottom in the light-construction concept. Above it arches a front suspension brace. The cockpit is also sporty: the most important instrumentation lays, framed in matt black, and in full field of view between the rocker switches.

In das Leichtbau-Konzept vom Scheitel bis zur Sohle ist ein 360 PS starker Sechszylinder mit Kohlefaser-Ansaugtrakt eingebettet. Darüber wölbt sich eine Domstrebe. Sportlich auch das Cockpit: Genau im Blickwinkel zwischen den Schaltwippen liegen, mattschwarz eingerahmt, die wichtigsten Armaturen.

Un six-cylindres de 360 ch avec collecteur d'aspiration en fibre de carbone fait partie intégrante du concept de construction allégée poussée au paroxysme. Une barre antirapprochement se tend au-dessus du moteur. Le cockpit est lui aussi sportif: les cadrans les plus importants, cernés d'un noir mat, se trouvent exactement dans le champ de vision, entre les basculeurs.

BMW X5 E53 | 1999

Although it was built in Spartanburg, South Carolina, it was a German car that was the highlight of the North American International Auto Show 1999, right in the Mecca of the US automobile industry, Detroit. The search for new market niches produced the so-called SAV (Sports Activity Vehicle) segment, resulting in the BMW X5.

The X5 was neither intended as competition for the Range Rover within the BMW group, nor represented a "tuned" 5 series Touring. On the sidelines at the debut of the X5 BMW announced: "Like other BMW automobiles, the X5 is defined by well-known classic BMW characteristics, such as aesthetics, dynamism and safety. But the X5 in addition places great emphasis on a completely new feel for the driver, produced in particular through the high seating and the excellent road-holding on all the highways and byways of this world."

The most modern all-wheel drive technology with anti-skid regulation by brake action, as well as some BMW high-tech goodies such as automatic and dynamic stability control, lend the X5 on-road qualities which allow for an emphatically sporty drive. But off-road the X5 also makes a strong impression – a powerful mountaineer which has no difficulties with returning to earth due to "hill descent control".

The range of engines for the X5 contains not only the well-known eight-cylinder V-engines, but also offers six-cylinder inline petrol and diesel engines with direct fuel injection.

On the subject of safety, BMW powers ahead too with its "F.I.R.S.T." safety package. Strong beams, well-designed crumple zones, and up to ten airbags provide protection in a crash.

As far as equipment and driver comfort is concerned, the range stretches from a sports package via a multi-function steering wheel to a great many items that are electrically controlled, plus diverse seating "furniture" alternatives on to a navigation system and practical roof and rear rack storage systems.

There is enough space between the beefy 19-inch wheels for excursions into uneven countryside. On the other hand there is calculated ground clearance to prevent aerobatics during cornering. As the 23/1998 issue of *auto motor und sport* stated, this BMW, in meeting the dynamic requirements for this brand of car, was designed to lap the north loop of the Nürburgring in less than nine minutes.

At the Frankfurt IAA in 2003, the X5 presents itself thoroughly revamped, optically and technically, and in possession of three new engines. The off-road sportsman from Spartanburg achieves a top speed of 153 mph (246 kph) when fitted with the 4.4-liter V8, and its 320 bhp.

The "xDrive" four-wheel drive, that enables a stepless and variable distribution of driving power between the front and rear axles at incredible speed, is also new.

Ausgerechnet ein deutsches Auto, wenngleich in Spartanburg, South Carolina, gebaut, ist das Highlight der North American International Auto Show 1999" im US-Automobil-Mekka Detroit. Das Entdecken neuer Marktnischen brachte das sogenannte SAV-Segment (Sports Activity Vehicle) hervor und resultiert im BMW X5.

Am Rande der Premiere dieses Wagens, der weder innerhalb des Konzerns dem Range Rover Konkurrenz machen soll, noch einen „aufgebockten" 5er Touring darstellt, lässt BMW verlauten: „Der X5 definiert sich wie die anderen BMW-Automobile über die bekannten klassischen BMW-Eigenschaften wie Ästhetik, Dynamik und Sicherheit. Im Falle des X5 ist darüber hinaus ein völlig neues Fahrgefühl, insbesondere durch die hohe Sitzposition und das exzellente Fahrverhalten auf allen Straßen und Wegen dieser Welt stark ausgeprägt."

Modernste Allradtechnologie mit Schlupfregelung durch Bremseingriff sowie einige High-Tech-„Bonbons", zu denen auch eine automatische und dynamische Stabilitätskontrolle gehört, verleihen dem X5 On-Road-Qualitäten, die eine durchaus sportliche Fahrweise ermöglichen. Aber auch im Off-Road-Betrieb hinterläßt der X5 einen starken Eindruck – ein kräftiger Bergsteiger, dem der Abstieg dank „hill descent control" leicht gemacht wird.

Die Motorenpalette für den X5 sieht nicht nur die bekannten Achtzylinder-V-Motoren vor, sondern umfasst auch den

Reihensechszylinder als Benziner und als Diesel mit Direkt-einspritzung. Auch beim Thema Sicherheit rüstet BMW mit dem „F.I.R.S.T."-Safety-Paket auf. Starke Holme, gut ange-legte Knautschzonen und bis zu zehn Airbags bieten bei einem Crash Schutz.

Hinsichtlich Ausstattung und Fahrkomfort reicht das Angebot vom Sportpaket über ein Multifunktionslenkrad, vielen elektrisch verstellbaren Komponenten und diversen Sitzmöbeln bis zum Navigationssystem oder praktischen Dach- und Heck-Trägersystemen.

Zwischen den bulligen 19-Zoll-Rädern befindet sich genügend Freiraum für Exkursionen in unebene Botanik. Andererseits reicht der Bodenabstand noch aus, um in Kurven nicht abzuheben. Denn – so auto motor und sport 23/1998 – sollte dieser BMW in Erfüllung markentypischer Dynamikanforderungen in der Lage sein, die Nordschleife des Nürburgrings in weniger als neun Minuten zu umrunden.

Bei der IAA 2003 in Frankfurt präsentiert sich der X5 optisch und technisch gründlich überarbeitet und erhält drei neue Motoren. Mit dem 4,4-Liter-V8, der 320 PS leistet, erzielt der Offroad-Sportler aus Spartanburg eine Spitzen-geschwindigkeit von 246 Stundenkilometern.

Neu ist auch das Allradsystem „xDrive", das eine stu-fenlose und variable Verteilung der Antriebskräfte zwischen Vorder- und Hinterachse in unglaublicher Schnelligkeit ermöglicht.

C'est le monde à l'envers: c'est une voiture alle-mande, construite à Spartanburg, en Caroline du Sud, qui est la vedette du North American Interna-tional Auto Show 1999 à Detroit, la capitale nord-américaine de l'automobile. Le segment des SAV (Sports Activity Vehi-cle) a permis de découvrir de nouvelles niches. Le résultat en est la BMW X5.

En marge du lancement de cette voiture, qui n'est pas appelée à concurrencer le Range Rover au sein du groupe et n'est pas non plus une touring série 5, BMW déclare: «La X5 se définit, au même titre que les autres automobiles de BMW, par les caractéristiques classiques bien connues de BMW, telles l'esthétique, la dynamique et la sécurité. Dans le cas de la X5, les sensations de conduite sont absolument diffé-rentes, caractérisées, en particulier, par la position élevée du conducteur et son excellent comportement sur la totalité des routes et des chemins du monde.»

Une technologie de traction intégrale ultramoderne avec régulation antipatinage par intervention sur les freins ainsi que quelques perfectionnements dus à la haute technologie, chère à BMW, parmi lesquels figure également un contrôle automatique et dynamique de la stabilité, confèrent à la X5 des qualités qui autorisent parfaitement un style de conduite sportif. Mais, en tout-chemin aussi, la X5 fait forte impression. C'est un véritable «chamois», qui n'a pas de problèmes dans les descentes grâce au «hill descent control».

La gamme de moteurs pour la X5 ne comporte pas seulement les huit-cylindres en V bien connus, mais aussi le six-cylindres en ligne en version essence et diesel à injec-tion directe. Sur le plan de la sécurité, BMW ne lésine pas avec son pack de sécurité «F.I.R.S.T.». De solides longerons, des zones de déformation programmée bien calculées et jusqu'à dix airbags offrent une protection optimale en cas de collision.

Dans le registre de l'aménagement et du confort, on n'a que l'embarras du choix: du pack sport au système de navi-gation ou aux systèmes de portage sur le toit et à l'arrière en passant par un volant multifonctions, de nombreux acces-soires électriques et un choix de fauteuils.

Entre les larges roues de 19 pouces, on dispose de suffisamment de marge pour sortir des sentiers battus. D'un autre côté, l'adhérence est suffisante pour conserver sa stabilité dans les virages. En effet, comme le constate le numéro 23/1998 d'auto motor und sport, cette BMW, pour respecter les propriétés dynamiques typiques de sa caté-gorie, devrait être en mesure de couvrir la boucle Nord du Nürburgring en moins de neuf minutes. Moins de huit minutes, c'est le temps que mettra sans aucun doute le nouveau roadster Z7 que BMW a dévoilé à l'automne 2000.

Pour les habitants de Spartanburg, la X5 est, après la Z3, une deuxième bonne nouvelle: les capacités de l'usine ont été multipliées par deux et les effectifs majorés de 50% en janvier 1999. Avec cet engagement aux États-Unis, BMW considère avoir franchi une nouvelle étape en consolidant la position du groupe dans le monde grâce à sa politique de globalisation.

An extensive range of equipment with up to ten airbags and many extras is as much a part of the X5's SAV (Sports Activity Vehicle) segment as are the BMW engines for the different markets. The X5 performs well on dirt tracks due to its ultra-modern four-wheel drive technology. It is exemplary with regard to driving dynamics and safety.

Eine reichhaltige Ausstattung mit bis zu zehn Airbags und viele Extras gehören ebenso zum SAV-Segment (Sports Activity Vehicle) des X5 wie die BMW-Motoren für die jeweiligen Märkte. Auf unbefestigtem Untergrund macht der X5 dank modernster Allradtechnologie eine gute Figur. Hinsichtlich der Komponenten Fahrdynamik und Sicherheit ist er vorbildlich.

Un équipement presque parfait avec jusqu'à dix airbags et de nombreuses options qui caractérisent le segment de la SAV (Sports Activity Vehicle) auquel appartient la X5, au même titre que les moteurs BMW sur ses marchés respectifs. Sortie des sentiers battus, la X5 fait bonne figure grâce à la technologie ultramoderne de sa traction intégrale. Elle est une référence en termes de dynamique et de sécurité.

BMW Z8 E52 2000

The Bavarian vehicle producer presented the Z07 sports car study in distant Tokyo in October 1997 as a conceptional homage to one of the most beautiful vehicles ever built, the BMW 507 of 1956, and harvested much applause. The length and height is almost identical to that of the dream vehicle of the 1950s, and also the sheer endless front construction, the flat BMW kidneys, as well as the side air intakes pick up the design of Count Goertz once again. The pleasing outer skin with short overhangs consists of high stability structured aluminum plates, which fill in the space between the ribs of the extruded profile. This construction of the Dingolfing aluminum experts, a unitized body space frame, bestows upon the roadster the rigidity and torsion stability necessary for high speed driving. 1999 the retro design went into production as the Z8—almost unchanged.

As with the 507, under the hood beats a V8 engine, positioned so far behind the front axle that the weight ratio to the rear axle lies by a balanced 50:50. The 400 bhp at 6600 rpm and the maximum torque of 370 lb-ft (500 Nm) at 3800 rpm is standard for the sporty two-seater. Variable valve control and an induction tract with electronically controlled individual throttle valves bestow a relatively high torque at low engine speed. The engine management MSS 52 can process more than a million control commands per second. But of what use are these giddying dimensions, which we are well used to from Formula 1, when the power and the glory of the engine is suddenly emasculated at 155 mph (250 kph)? At least there is joy to be had with the precise switching of the six gear transmission on sprinting to 62 mph (100 kph) in 4.7 seconds, and opening up a distance a kilometer in only 23.5 seconds.

There is also joy to be had in straining the sporty chassis—at the front completely aluminum, at the rear partially—especially on stretches with a lot of cornering. Especially here is one thankful for the special braking aid CBC (Cornering Brake Control). The power assisted rack-and-pinion steering reacts immediately and directly—as one would expect of a sports car of this caliber—to the classical spoke steering wheel fitted with an airbag. If a slight understeering should creep in despite the dynamic stability control, one has taken the corners a little too vigorously. The Z8 driver is not immobilized by a flat tire: the "run-flat" tires, 245/45 R 18 W at the front, 275/40 R 18 W at the rear, have emergency running characteristics that allow a further 185 miles (300 km) of driving at a speed of up to 50 mph (80 kph). For this reason, it is pointless to look for a spare wheel in the trunk.

The cockpit's appearance is factual, almost sober, in which leather and lacquered aluminum dominate. The instrumentation is reduced to the bare essentials, whereby the positioning of the round instruments above the center console—that is, not in the same field of vision as the steering wheel—needs some getting used to and can be irritating when driving more forcefully. A semiautomatic soft top with power-assisted closing mechanism or the aluminum hard top delivered as a Z8 standard can be used according to the time of year and weather conditions prevailing. This coupé top, at the time without a heated rear window, was also available for the 507—more filigree in design and so harmoniously integrated by Goertz that he still prefers today the closed version to the open-air model.

Als konzeptionelle Verbeugung vor einem der schönsten jemals gebauten Autos, dem BMW 507 von 1956, präsentiert der bajuwarische Fahrzeughersteller im Oktober 1997 im fernen Tokio erstmals die Sportwagen-Studie Z07 und erntet viel Beifall. Länge und Höhe sind nahezu identisch mit dem Traumauto der fünfziger Jahre, und auch der schier endlos lange Vorderbau, die flachen BMW-Nieren sowie die seitlichen Lufteinlässe greifen den Entwurf des Grafen Goertz wieder auf. Die gefällige Außenhaut mit kurzen Überhängen besteht aus hochfesten Aluminium-Strukturblechen, die die Räume zwischen dem Gerippe aus Strangpress-Profilen füllen. Dieser Aufbau der Dingolfinger Alu-Experten, ein selbsttragender Spaceframe, verleiht dem Roadster die nötige Steifheit und Verwindungs-Stabilität selbst für rasanten Fahrbetrieb. 1999 geht das Retro-Design – nahezu unverändert – als Z8 in Serie.

Wie beim 507 pulsiert unter der Haube ein V8-Triebwerk, das so weit hinter der Vorderachse positioniert ist, dass die Gewichtsverteilung zur Hinterachse in einem ausgeglichenen Verhältnis von 50:50 ausfällt. Standesgemäß für den sportlichen Zweisitzer sind die 400 PS bei 6600/min und das maximale Drehmoment von 500 Newtonmetern bei 3800/min. Variable Nockenwellenverstellung und ein Ansaugtrakt mit elektronisch gesteuerten Einzel-Drosselklappen bescheren schon im unteren Drehzahlbereich ein relativ hohes Drehmoment. Mehr als eine Million Steuerkommandos kann das Motormanagement MSS 52 pro Sekunde umsetzen. Doch was nützen diese schwindelerregenden Dimensionen, die man ja aus der Formel 1 kennt, wenn Kraft und Herrlichkeit des Motors bei 250 Stundenkilometern „einen auf den Deckel" bekommen. Zumindest macht das Beschleunigen

mit dem präzise schaltbaren 6-Gang-Getriebe Spaß, denn in 4,7 Sekunden wird auf Tempo 100 gesprintet und nach 23,5 Sekunden ist bereits ein Kilometer zurückgelegt.

Auch beim Strapazieren des sportlichen Fahrwerks – vorn ganz, hinten teilweise aus Aluminium – kommt Freude auf, besonders auf kurvenreichen Straßen. Gerade hier ist man für die spezielle Bremshilfe CBC (Cornering Brake Control) dankbar. Auf Lenkeinschläge des klassischen Speichen-Volants, in dem sogar ein Airbag untergebracht ist, reagiert die servo-unterstützte Zahnstangenlenkung direkt und genau – wie man es von einem Sportwagen dieses Kalibers erwartet. Sollte sich freilich trotz der dynamischen Stabilitäts-Kontrolle ein leichtes Untersteuern einschleichen, ist man in der Kurve wohl zu forsch unterwegs. Immer noch unterwegs ist der Z8-Fahrer nach einer Reifenpanne: die „Run-flat"-Reifen, vorn 245/45 R18W, hinten 275/40 R18W, besitzen Notlauf-Eigenschaften, die bei gemäßigter Geschwindigkeit bis zu 80 km/h noch für eine 300-Kilometer-Distanz reichen.

Sachlich, fast ernüchternd wirkt das Cockpit, in dem Leder und lackiertes Aluminium dominieren. Das Instrumentarium beschränkt sich auf das Wesentliche, wobei die Positionierung der Rundinstrumente über der Mittelkonsole – also nicht in Blickrichtung Lenkrad – gewöhnungsbedürftig ist. Je nach Jahreszeit und Wetterlage bedient man sich beim Z8 eines halbautomatischen Stoffverdecks mit einem servo-unterstützten Schließmechanismus oder des serienmäßig mitgelieferten Aluminium-Hardtops. Diesen Coupé-Aufsatz, seinerzeit ohne Heckscheiben-Beheizung, gab es auch beim 507 – filigraner gestaltet und von Goertz so harmonisch integriert, dass ihm noch heute die geschlossene Version besser als die offene gefällt.

Pour rendre hommage à l'une des plus belles voitures jamais construites, la BMW 507 de 1956, BMW présente en première mondiale, en octobre 1997, à Tokyo, une étude de style de voiture de sport, la Z07. Le succès est immédiat. Sa longueur et sa hauteur sont pratiquement identiques à celles de la voiture mythique des années 1950 et son capot avant semble ne jamais vouloir finir. Les naseaux BMW à l'horizontale ainsi que les sorties d'air latérales sont une réminiscence de l'esquisse réalisée par le comte von Goertz. La gracile carrosserie aux courts porte-à-faux consiste en tôles d'aluminium structurelles à grande résistance qui habillent avec élégance le squelette en profilés extrudés. Cette robe réalisée par les spécialistes de l'aluminium de Dingolfing, une carrosserie *spaceframe* autoporteuse, confère au roadster la rigidité nécessaire et la stabilité torsionnelle indispensable pour rouler à grande vitesse. Et c'est bien là, *a priori*, sa mission d'origine quand le modèle au design néo-rétro est fabriqué en série – pratiquement sans changements – en 1999 sous l'appellation Z8.

Comme avec la 507, un V8 palpite sous le capot, mais placé si loin derrière le train avant que la répartition du poids est parfaitement équilibrée à raison de 50% pour chaque essieu. La puissance de la sportive biplace est digne de son rang avec 400 ch à 6600 tr/min pour un couple maximum de 500 Nm à 3800 tr/min. Les arbres à cames à distribution variable et un collecteur d'aspiration avec six vis papillons individuelles à commande électronique garantissent déjà un couple relativement élevé à bas régime. La gestion moteur MSS52 est capable de répondre à plus d'un million d'instructions par seconde. Au moins appréciera-t-on les accélérations avec la précise boîte manuelle à six vitesses, car la Z8 bondit en 4,7 secondes de 0 à 100 km/h et abat le kilomètre départ arrêté en 23,5 secondes seulement.

Même si l'on pousse dans ses derniers retranchements le châssis sportif – tout en aluminium à l'avant et partiellement à l'arrière –, le plaisir est toujours au rendez-vous, en particulier sur routes sinueuses. C'est là, précisément, que l'on apprécie l'assistance de freinage CBC (*Cornering Brake Control*) spéciale. La direction à crémaillère assistée réagit avec spontanéité et précision aux ordres de braquage que transmet le volant classique, qui héberge même un airbag – comme on est en droit de l'attendre d'une voiture de sport de ce calibre. Un léger sous-virage s'est-il manifesté malgré le contrôle de stabilité dynamique? Cela signifie que vous avez abordé la courbe trop rapidement. Et ce n'est pas une crevaison qui contraindra le conducteur de Z8 à l'arrêt: les pneus «run-flat», de 245/45 R18W à l'avant et 275/40 R18W à l'arrière possèdent un dispositif anti-crevaison qui permet, à la vitesse modérée de 80 km/h au maximum, de couvrir encore 300 km.

Le cockpit, où dominent le cuir et l'aluminium vernis, est sobre et presque spartiate. L'instrumentation se limite à l'essentiel. Selon la saison et le temps, on peut ouvrir la capote en tissu semi-automatique de la Z8 avec un mécanisme à assistance ou la coiffer du hard-top en aluminium livré en série. Ce toit coupé, mais alors sans lunette dégivrante, était aussi proposé pour la 507. Plus mince, le comte von Goertz l'avait intégré si harmonieusement qu'aujourd'hui encore, la version fermée lui plaît davantage que son homologue décapotée.

The retro-design of the Z8 is reminiscent of Count Goertz's BMW 507, a homage to one of the most beautiful of sports cars. The flat BMW kidneys are not to be forgotten, neither are the side air vents.

Das Retro-Design des Z8 erinnert an den BMW 507 des Grafen Goertz, Hommage an einen der schönsten Sportwagen. Da dürfen die flachen BMW-Nieren ebenso wenig fehlen wie die seitlichen Lüftungsschlitze.

Le design néo-rétro de la Z8 rappelle la BMW 507 du comte von Goertz – ce qui n'est pas fortuit, mais un hommage à l'une des plus belles voitures de sport de tous les temps. Bien évidemment, les plats naseaux de BMW ne doivent pas briller par leur absence, aussi peu que les fentes d'aération latérales.

The classical side profile of the Z8 embodies the BMW roadster tradition. The V8 with 400 bhp is positioned behind the front axle.

Das klassische Seitenprofil des Z8 verkörpert die BMW-Roadster-Tradition. Hinter der Vorderachse positioniert ist der V8 mit 400 PS.

Le profil latéral classique de la Z8 incarne à la perfection la tradition du roadster selon BMW. Le V8 de 400 ch est positionné à l'arrière du train avant.

BMW 7 E65 | 2001

Although the form language of BMW designer Christopher Bangle takes some getting used to, and especially the rear of the BMW 7 of 2001 has heartily rubbed conservative esthetes up the wrong way, the top class sedan convinces skeptics by its exceedingly good engine technology, dynamism, and many driving comforts. The extent of BMW's involvement in this luxury segment of the market is demonstrated by the 5½-inch (14-centimeter) longer Li version with its feudal rear seating area presented at the same time at the 2001 IAA, and the announcement that a 12-cylinder 760 would be on offer from 2002. In 2003, every 18th BMW bought in China was a 760 Li; possessing almost everything that is to be had, cost what it may, as a standard fitting. That the abbreviation "Li"—previously "iL"—sounds Chinese is pure coincidence.

The upper crust 7 from BMW has a choice of six engines. The unusual running characteristics of the great V8 engine (333 bhp) has not been left to chance, as all the relevant parameters—such as engine valve timing, valve stroke, and intake pipe length—are regulated in a stepless manner. Due to the fully variable intake system, the throttle valve is no longer needed, for a longer intake enables a greater torque at lower rpm, and reciprocally, a shorter intake enables an extra burst of power at higher rpm levels. The 445-bhp V12 can make do without an intake pipe fitted as it is with valvetronic and direct gas injection.

Before the world's first standard 6-gear automatic transmission with electrical switching, in short "Drive-by-wire," can transfer power to the rear axle a somewhat tedious start procedure must be carried out. Instead of simply turning the ignition key, the remote control must first be placed in

the ignition, and only then can the start button be pressed. The automatic can be activated in the usual manner ("D" for drive) by using the gear stick, or, alternatively, the Steptronic switches on the upper section of the steering wheel can be used. Manual switching is rewarded with better acceleration: from 0 to 62 mph (100 kph) in only 6.3 instead of 7.5 seconds.

That one simply glides along in the 7 is certainly only secondarily due to the lavishly upholstered seating. The extravagant aluminum chassis with a bi-articulated telescopic-legged front axle and an integrated rear axle ensure comfort per se. Help is given by the level adjustment—ensuring a constant distance to the road surface irrespective of load—and, available as an extra on payment of a surcharge, the electronic shock absorber control. Thanks to "Dynamic Drive"—only available as a standard in the 760, as is the case with the pneumatic suspension—wobble during cornering can be reduced to a minimum. Despite the long version of the 7's massive appearance its road handling is exemplary, a plus point for the whole range.

Also intended as a plus point but unfortunately not well accepted, is the "benchmark" (BMW's favorite word) in driver orientation and comfort, the "i-Drive" concept. To bring together in a round switch eight main computer menus, arranged compass-like, with over 700 subsidiary functions, is definitely a masterly performance, but one that also completely overstretches the driver when driving. Luckily the really important elements needed for driving, such as blinkers, headlights, and windshield wipers can be operated by the usual switches on the steering wheel. Simple functionality can also be a "benchmark"!

Wenn auch die progressive Formensprache von BMW-Designer Christopher Bangle gewöhnungsbedürftig ist und besonders das Heck des 7er-BMW, Jahrgang 2001, bei konservativen Automobil-Ästheten kräftig aneckt, überzeugt die Oberklassen-Limousine durch souveräne Motorentechnik, Dynamik und sehr viel Fahrkomfort. Wie weit dieses Luxus-Segment bei BMW reicht, demonstriert auf der IAA 2001 auch die gleichzeitig vorgestellte, 14 Zentimeter längere Li-Version mit einem feudalen Fondbereich und die Ankündigung, ab 2002 einen 760 mit 12-Zylinder-Motor anzubieten. 2003 ist jeder 18. in China verkaufte BMW ein 760 Li, bei dem so ziemlich alles, was gut und teuer ist, zur Serienausstattung gehört. Dass das Kürzel „Li" – früher „iL" – chinesisch klingt, ist reiner Zufall.

Insgesamt stehen der 7er-Hautevolee von BMW sechs Motoren zur Auswahl. Nicht von ungefähr kommt die außergewöhnliche Laufkultur dieses Triebwerkes (333 PS), da alle relevanten Parameter – wie Ventil-Steuerzeiten, Ventilhub und Saugrohrlängen – stufenlos reguliert werden. Durch die vollvariable Sauganlage entfällt die Drosselklappe, denn ein langer Ansaugweg ermöglicht ein hohes Drehmoment bei niedrigen Drehzahlen, und reziprok sorgt ein kürzerer Ansaugweg für einen Leistungsschub auch im oberen Drehzahlbereich. Positiver Nebeneffekt: geringerer Treibstoff-Verbrauch und weniger Emissionen. Ohne Saugrohre kommt der 445-PS-V12 aus, da er mit einer Valvetronic und einer Benzin-Direkteinspritzung versehen ist.

Ehe das erste serienmäßige 6-Gang-Automatik-Getriebe der Welt mit elektrischer Schaltung, kurz und präzise (Drive-by-wire) den Krafttransfer zur Hinterachse übernehmen kann, muss die etwas umständliche Startprozedur eingeleitet

werden. Statt einer simplen Zündschlüssel-Drehung steckt man zunächst die Funkfernbedienung in die Zündanlass-Buchse, und dann erst darf der Startknopf gedrückt werden. Über einen Lenkstockschalter kann die Automatik im herkömmlichen Verfahren („D" wie Drive) aktiviert werden, oder man schaltet über die Steptronic-Tasten am oberen Lederlenkradkranz. Das manuelle Schaltvergnügen wird mit besserer Beschleunigung belohnt: Von 0 auf 100 Stundenkilometer sind es 6,3 statt 7,5 Sekunden.

Dass man im 7er wie in einer Sänfte dahingleitet, liegt sicherlich nur sekundär an den üppig gepolsterten Sitzmöbeln. Das aufwändige Aluminium-Fahrwerk mit einer Doppelgelenk-Federbein-Vorderachse und einer Integral-Hinterachse bietet Fahrkomfort per se. Hilfestellung leisten die Niveauregulierung – gleich gleibender Bodenabstand unabhängig von der Beladung – und, gegen Aufpreis, die elektronische Dämpfer-Kontrolle. Dank „Dynamic Drive" – wie die Luftfederung nur im 760 serienmäßig – können Wankbewegungen bei Kurvenfahrten auf ein Minimum reduziert werden. So wuchtig gerade die Lang-Version des 7er wirken mag, ihr Fahrverhalten ist vorbildlich, ein Pluspunkt der gesamten Reihe.

Als Pluspunkt gescheitert ist die „Benchmark" (was bei BMW so viel wie Messlatte heißt) in Fahrerorientierung und Komfort, das „i-Drive"-Konzept. Acht Hauptmenüs eines Computers mit über 700 Nebenfunktionen in einem runden Schaltknopf zu vereinen, ist technisch gewiss eine Meisterleistung, überfordert aber den Autofahrer völlig. Zum Glück sind wirklich wichtige Elemente wie Blinker, Licht und Scheibenwischer noch über herkömmliche Schalter am Lenkrad zu bedienen. Einfache Funktionalität kann auch eine „Benchmark" sein!

Même s'il faut être habitué au langage formel très autoritaire de Christopher Bangle, le styliste en chef de BMW, même si la poupe de la BMW Série 7 millésime 2001 a choqué certains esthètes de l'automobile à l'esprit conservateur, la limousine de luxe du constructeur bavarois séduit par sa motorisation souveraine, son dynamisme et son remarquable confort de conduite. Ce segment du luxe est très large chez BMW. Preuve en est lorsque le constructeur présente aussi, à l'IAA 2001, la version Li, dévoilée simultanément, avec un empattement allongé de 14 centimètres et des fauteuils arrière au confort somptueux. Mais, surtout, BMW annonce la commercialisation, en 2002, d'une 760 à moteur V12.

Au total, la luxueuse Série 7 de BMW est proposée avec un choix de six moteurs. Mais l'exceptionnelle souplesse de fonctionnement de ce moteur (V8, 333 ch) n'a, elle, rien à voir avec le hasard. En effet, tous ses paramètres importants – par exemple la distribution et la course des soupapes ou la longueur des tubulures d'aspiration – sont régulés en continu. Le collecteur d'aspiration à longueur variable dans son intégralité rend superflues les vis papillons : une longue tubulure d'aspiration engendre, en effet, un couple élevé à bas régime et, inversement, une courte tubulure d'aspiration, un pic de puissance à haut régime.

Avant que la première – courte et précise (Drive-by-wire) – boîte automatique à six rapports avec commande électrique commercialisée dans le monde puisse assurer le transfert du couple au train arrière, il faut bien s'imprégner de la procédure de démarrage, il est vrai un peu complexe. Au lieu de se contenter de tourner la clé de contact, il faut tout d'abord insérer la télécommande-radio dans la prise de

l'allumage et, ensuite seulement, on peut appuyer sur le starter. Le levier sur la colonne de direction permet d'actionner la transmission automatique selon la procédure usuelle (« D » pour Drive), à moins que l'on ne veuille changer soi-même de vitesse avec les touches Steptronic sur le haut du volant gainé de cuir. La procédure de changement de vitesse à la main est récompensée par de meilleures accélérations : 6,3 secondes au lieu de 7,5 secondes pour le 0 à 100 km/h.

Si, dans la Série 7, on a l'impression de planer sur un nuage, ceci n'est assurément pas dû au seul capitonnage très généreux des fauteuils. Très sophistiquées, les liaisons au sol en aluminium avec un train avant à jambes élastiques à double articulation et un essieu arrière intégral offrent un confort de conduite difficile à égaler. Grâce au « Dynamic Drive » – comme la suspension pneumatique, offerte en série uniquement sur la 760 –, la prise de roulis est réduite au strict minimum.

Ce qui était considéré comme l'un de ses grands avantages et n'a, pourtant, malheureusement pas reçu l'accueil escompté, c'est le « benchmark » (terme de prédilection de BMW qui signifie aune) pour l'information du conducteur et le confort avec le concept « i-Drive ». Combiner huit menus principaux d'ordinateur, à plus de 700 fonctions secondaires dans un bouton de commande circulaire est assurément une prouesse technique. Mais l'utiliser en conduisant excède la capacité de concentration de tout automobiliste.

Par bonheur, on continue de manier les éléments réellement importants pour la conduite, par exemple les clignotants, les phares et les essuie-glaces, à l'aide de commandes conventionnelles. Une fonctionnalité toute simple peut aussi être un « benchmark » !

BMW turns to a new direction in automobile architecture with the design of the 7 series: unusual and innovative, but the rear section takes some getting used to.

Eine neue Auto-Architekturrichtung schlägt BMW mit dem Design des 7er ein: außergewöhnlich und innovativ, aber auch gewöhnungsbedürftig, was die hintere Region angeht.

Avec le design de la Série 7, BMW s'est engagée dans une nouvelle direction de l'architecture automobile: sortant de l'ordinateur et novatrice, elle demande aussi une certaine accoutumance, notamment en ce qui concerne la poupe.

A challenge: the rear of the 7 range and central control of the i-Drive, a dial and button combination between the comfortable seating. The source of power: a refined V8 with 333bhp.

Herausforderungen: das 7er-Heck und das zentrale i-Drive-Eingabe-Element, ein Dreh- und Druckknopf zwischen den komfortablen Sitzen. Kraftquelle: kultivierter V8 mit 333 PS.

Défis: la poupe de la Série 7 et le *joystick* de commande centrale du i-Drive, un bouton que l'on fait tourner et sur lequel on appuie entre les confortables sièges. Propulsion: un V8 très raffiné de 333 ch.

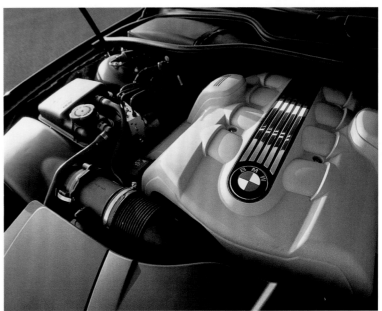

The spiritual father of the Mini, Sir Alexander Arnold Constantino Issigonis, the son of a Greek father and Bavarian mother, would definitely have been greatly pleased by the rebirth of his already legendary cult vehicle. The BMW Group has produced the successor to the original Mini in Oxford since 2001—as an autonomous and unmistakable mark. As was the case with its predecessor, the Mini is characterized by its long wheelbase with extremely short wheel overhangs, while the wheels together with their typical small wing extensions form the corner stone, as it were. The roof contour and the wide stocky rear, under which the trunk nestles, are also reminiscent of the Mini of 1959. A modern stylistic contrast: with all struts and beams concealed behind glass, the green toned window surface of this two-door vehicle gives the impression of a continuous glass band around the automobile.

The Cooper and its powerful S version's option for roof and exterior mirrors to be in black or white irrespective of the body color distinguish it optically from the normal Mini. Alloy wheels, front spoiler lip, roof spoiler, and the air inlet on the hood, all belong to the deportment of a vehicle whose predecessors have won no less than 19 major international rally events between 1962 and 1967—including three times the "Monte."

The basis of the modern Mini's motorization is provided by BMW's and Chrysler's jointly designed "Pentagon" standard engine with its 1.6-liter capacity, an engine that needs neither secondary air injection nor exhaust gas recirculation. Correspondingly modest is the starting potential of the Mini One with 90 bhp and of the Mini Cooper with 115 bhp. A

supercharger was needed. As the Mini Cooper S it brings 163 bhp to the front wheels, and since 2004 it even achieves 170 bhp. One is served well by the sprint time of 0 to 62 mph (100 kph) in 7.2 rather than in 7.4 seconds and a top speed in the meantime of 141 mph (227 kph), even though the engine is somehow lacking the right bite. This is present in the "Works" edition with modified supercharger that brings the power of 200 horses into play.

Unusual for its class are the technically advanced common denominators of all Mini models: 6-gear transmission, MacPherson struts, drive shafts of equal length that ensure a symmetrical feedback effect of the driven front wheels to the steering on cornering, acceleration, and braking, and a multi-link rear suspension with an additional stabilizer. The standard fittings of the Mini Cooper S, already lowered at the factory, also include the "Automatic Stability Control + Traction" (ASC+T) system, a central double-piped exhaust system, and alloy wheels fitted with the 195 "run-flat"-tires.

The large round display over the center console, flanked by two amply dimensioned ventilation vents, dominate the cockpit of the Cooper S. The rev counter and speedometer stare out of the dashboard, well in view of the driver, but with a somewhat forlorn appearance. The adjustable height and good grip of the steering wheel, foot pedals and rests in stainless steel, in addition to the various interior elements with aluminum patina, impart a hint of a sporting atmosphere. However, the interior is not without a certain pep, corresponding to the general impression of the Mini. This has already been enriched by the Mini Design Studio, Munich, with a racy cabriolet, further evolution, also in detail, is being prepared.

Der geistige Vater des Mini, Sir Alexander Arnold Constantino Issigonis, Spross eines griechischen Vaters und einer bayerischen Mutter, hätte an der Wiedergeburt seines mittlerweile schon legendären Kult-Autos gewiss seine Freude gehabt. Seit 2001 lässt die BMW Group den Nachfolger des Ur-Mini in Oxford produzieren – als eigenständige, da unverwechselbare Marke. Wie sein Vorgänger wird der Mini von einem langen Radstand mit extrem kurzen Überhängen geprägt, und die Räder samt ihren typischen kleinen Kotflügel-Verbreiterungen bilden sozusagen die Eckpfeiler. Auch die Dachkontur und das breite, gedrungene Heck, unter dem sich das Kofferräumchen einigelt, erinnern an den Mini von 1959. Neuzeitlicher stilistischer Kontrast: Die grün getönten Fensterflächen des Zweitürers vermitteln den Eindruck eines durchgehenden Glasbandes rund ums Auto, denn alle Säulen sind hinter Glas verborgen.

Optisch unverwechselbar mit dem Normal-Mini macht den Cooper und seine kraftvolle S-Version die Option, Dach und Außenspiegel unabhängig von der Wagenfarbe in Schwarz oder Weiß erhalten zu können. Leichtmetallräder, Frontspoiler-Lippe, Dachspoiler und der Luftschacht auf der Motorhaube gehören zum sportlichen Gehabe eines Fahrzeugs, dessen Vorfahren zwischen 1962 und 1967 nicht weniger als 19 große internationale Rallye-Veranstaltungen – darunter dreimal die „Monte" – gewonnen haben.

Basis der neuzeitlichen Mini-Motorisierung ist der von BMW und Chrysler gemeinsam entwickelte „Pentagon"-Grundmotor mit 1,6 Litern Hubraum, ein Triebwerk, das weder Sekundärluft-Zufuhr noch eine Abgas-Rückführung nötig hat. Entsprechend bescheiden ist das Anfangspotential mit 90 PS für den Mini One und 115 PS für den Mini Cooper, und deshalb

Mini | 2001

musste ein Kompressor her. Als Mini Cooper S bringt er 163 PS und seit 2004 sogar 170 PS auf die Vorderräder. Mit 7,2 statt 7,4 Sekunden von 0 auf 100 und einer Spitzengeschwindigkeit von inzwischen 227 km/h ist man gut bedient, wenngleich dem Triebwerk irgendwie der richtige Biss fehlt. Diesen hat die „Works"-Ausgabe mit modifiziertem Kompressor, der 200 Pferdestärken aktiviert. Klassen-unüblich ist der technisch hochangesiedelte gemeinsame Nenner aller Mini-Modelle: 6-Gang-Getriebe, McPherson-Federbeine und gleich lange Achsschwellen, die für einen symmetrischen Rückkopplungseffekt der angetriebenen Vorderräder auf die Lenkung beim Kurvenfahren, Beschleunigen oder Bremsen sorgen, und eine Multilenker-Hinterachse mit zusätzlichem Stabilisator. Beim Mini Cooper S, von Haus aus tiefer gelegt, umfasst die Serienausstattung auch die „Automatische Stabilitäts-Control + Traktion" (ASC+T), eine zentrale Doppelrohr-Auspuffanlage und Leichtmetallräder mit 195er „Run-flat"-Reifen.

Im Cockpit des Cooper S dominiert das große Runddisplay über der Mittelkonsole, flankiert von zwei wohldimensionierten Belüftungs-Düsen. Gut im Blickfeld des Fahrers, aber etwas verloren wirkend, äugen Drehzahlmesser und Tacho aus dem Armaturenbrett. Griffiges, höhenverstellbares Leder-Volant, Pedalerie und Fußstütze in Edelstahl sowie Interieur-Elemente mit Alu-Patina vermitteln auch im Innenraum einen Hauch von Sportlichkeit, was man von den in der Seitenführung laschen Sitzen nicht behaupten kann. Dennoch mangelt es dem Interieur nicht an einem gewissen Pep, passend zum gesamten Erscheinungsbild des Mini. Dieses hat das Mini-Design-Studio, München, bereits um ein flottes Cabrio bereichert und bereitet weitere Evolutionen – auch im Detail – vor.

Le père spirituel de la Mini, Sir Alexander Arnold Constantino Issigonis, fils d'un père grec et d'une mère bavaroise, aurait sans aucun doute été ravi de voir la voiture de légende qu'il a créée renaître avec le statut de voiture culte. Depuis 2001, le BMW Group assemble, à Oxford, l'héritière de la mythique Mini – qui est maintenant une marque indépendante et, donc, plus unique que jamais. Comme son ancêtre, la Mini se distingue par un empattement long avec des porte-à-faux extrêmement courts et des roues repoussées, avec leurs typiques petits élargisseurs d'aile, aux quatre coins de la voiture. De même, les contours du toit et la poupe large et râblée sous laquelle se dissimule un petit coffre modulable rappellent, eux aussi, la Mini de 1959. Les jantes en alliage léger, la lèvre d'aileron avant, le becquet de toit et la prise d'air sur le capot moteur sont les attributs sportifs justifiés d'un modèle dont les ancêtres ont remporté pas moins de dix-neuf grands rallyes internationaux – dont le «Monte» à trois reprises – entre 1962 et 1967.

La motorisation de base de la Mini des temps modernes est le moteur «Pentagon» de 1,6 litre de cylindrée mis au point conjointement par BMW et Chrysler, qui respecte d'emblée la norme de dépollution UE4 et n'a besoin ni d'une alimentation en air secondaire ni d'un recyclage des gaz d'échappement. Il ne faut donc pas s'attendre à une puissance exubérante avec 90 ch pour la Mini One et 115 ch pour la Mini Cooper. Un peu plus de cavalerie s'imposait donc, raison pour laquelle BMW a décidé de lui greffer un compresseur. En version Mini Cooper S, elle développe 163 ch et, depuis 2004, même 170 ch, qui entraînent les roues avant. Avec 7,2 secondes au lieu de 7,4 secondes pour le 0 à 100 km/h et une vitesse de pointe d'entre-temps de 227 km/h, on n'a plus aucune raison de se plaindre, même si le moteur donne bizarrement

l'impression de manquer de punch. La version «Works», avec un compresseur modifié qui libère 200 chevaux, pallie ce défaut.

La dotation technique de toutes les versions de la Mini, déjà très relevée, est inhabituelle dans cette catégorie: boîte manuelle à six vitesses, jambes élastiques McPherson et demi-arbres de longueur identique garantissant une remontée de couple symétrique des roues avant motrices à la direction dans les courbes ainsi qu'à l'accélération et au freinage, sans oublier un essieu arrière multibras avec barre anti-roulis supplémentaire. Dans le cas de la Mini Cooper S, à l'assiette abaissée départ usine, la dotation de série s'enrichit du dispositif de «Traction + Contrôle de Stabilité Automatique» (ASC+T), d'une sortie d'échappement centrale à double pot et de jantes en alliage léger chaussées de pneus «run-flat» de 195.

Dans le cockpit de la Cooper S, le premier rôle est joué par le grand écran circulaire, flanqué de deux aérateurs bien proportionnés, au-dessus de la console médiane. Le compte-tours et le compteur de vitesse sont placés directement dans le champ visuel du conducteur mais semblent un peu perdus sur le tableau de bord. Le volant cuir ergonomique et réglable en hauteur, le pédalier et le repose-pied en acier inoxydable ainsi que d'autres éléments de cockpit en aluminium brossé diffusent, dans l'habitacle aussi, une aura de sportivité à laquelle on ne s'attend pas au vu des sièges un peu lâches sur les côtés. Mais l'intérieur possède bel et bien une incontestable originalité qui s'inscrit dans le droit-fil de la généalogie de la Mini. Le studio de design munichois de la Mini lui a déjà donné un petit frère, un élégant cabriolet dont le succès est assuré et qui annonce d'autres évolutions – également au niveau des finitions.

The charm and compactness of the original Mini is also expressed in the design lines of the new edition. The sporting attributes of the Mini Cooper S: air scoop, roof spoiler, light alloy wheels under the widened fenders, and double exhaust pipe.

Charme und Kompaktheit des Ur-Mini drücken sich auch in der Linienführung des neuen Mini aus. Sportliche Attribute des Mini Cooper S: Lufthutze, Dachspoiler, Leichtmetallräder unter den Kotflügelverbreiterungen und Doppelrohr-Auspuff.

Le charme et la compacité de la Mini originelle s'expriment aussi au travers des lignes de la nouvelle Mini. Ingrédients sportifs de la Mini Cooper S : prise d'air sur le capot, aileron de toit, jantes alliage sous de volumineux élargisseurs d'ailes et double sortie d'échappement.

The Mini Cooper S's supercharger engine produces
170 bhp. Classical round instrumentation: rev counter
and speedometer. Elliptical forms: The interior door
paneling with a handle combination in anthracite,
and the rearview mirrors. Stainless steel entree: the
entry baseboard.

170 PS produziert der Kompressor-Motor des
Mini Cooper S. Klassische Rundinstrumente:
Drehzahlmesser und Tacho. Elliptische Gebilde: Die
Türinnenverkleidungen mit einer Griffkombination
in Anthrazit und die Außenspiegel. Edelstahl-Entree:
die Einstiegsleiste.

170 chevaux piaffent sous le capot du moteur à
compresseur de la Mini Cooper S. Cadrans circulaires
classiques : compte-tours et tachymètre. Coup de griffe
en ellipse : contre-porte avec combinaison de poignée
anthracite et rétroviseur extérieur. Entrée en beauté :
enjoliveur de seuil de portière chromé.

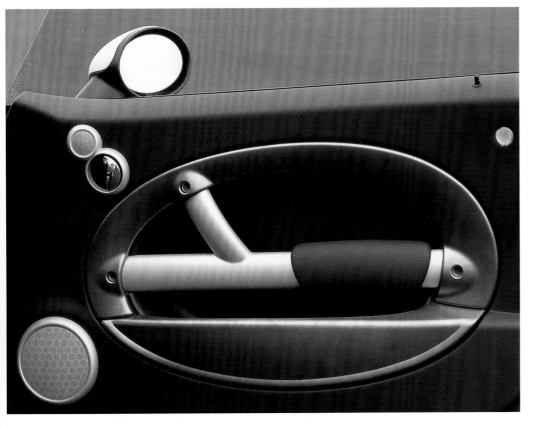

The wide-opening split door sections at the back and on the passenger side of the Clubman are perfect for driving fun with bags and baggage.

Zwei gegenläufig sperrangelweit zu öffnende Türhälften im Kombi-Heck und auf der Beifahrerseite des Clubman laden förmlich zum Fahrvergnügen mit Sack und Pack ein.

Les deux portes battantes antagonistes ouvrant en grand sur le coffre et du côté passager de la Clubman invitent dans les formes à un plaisir de conduire avec armes et bagages.

The small, transversely fitted 1.6-liter turbo engine produces 175 bhp in the Cooper S, and 211 bhp in the John Cooper Works. Well-rounded: the instrument panel with the large speedometer in the middle.

Der kleine quer eingebaute 1,6-Liter-Turbo-Motor entwickelt 175 PS beim Cooper S und deren 211 im John Cooper Works. Eine wirklich runde Sache: das Instrumentarium mit dem großen, zentralen Tacho.

Le petit moteur turbo 1,6 litre transversal développe 175 ch sur la Cooper S et 211 ch sur la John Cooper Works. Les équipements intérieurs avec le grand compteur de vitesses central se présentent tout en rondeurs.

The Mini Roadster promises open-air driving pleasure for two—pictured here is the most powerful John Cooper Works version, which speeds up to 147 mph.

Offenes Fahrvergnügen zu zweit verheißt der Mini Roadster, hier in seiner stärksten Version, John Cooper Works, die 237 km/h erreicht.

Le Mini Roadster promet du plaisir de conduire à ciel ouvert pour deux. Il est présenté ici dans sa version la plus puissante, John Cooper Works, qui atteint 237 km/h.

Large circular instruments, 211 bhp under the hood, a unique look with roll bars, sills and alloy wheels: pure Mini Cooper.

Große Rundinstrumente, 211 PS unter der Haube, unverwechselbare Optik mit Überrollbügeln, Schwellern und Leichtmetallrädern: ganz Mini Cooper.

Grands instruments ronds, 211 ch sous le capot, un look inimitable avec arceaux, bas de caisse et jantes en alliage léger: très Mini Cooper.

2015 sees a Mini being made into a Maxi-Mini, when the third generation (F56) of this five-door vehicle is stretched to an impressive 13 feet. New electro-mechanical power steering, essential for the optional parking assistant, and optimized brakes encourage Mini drivers in the densest city traffic. And in the Cooper S, or the Cooper Works version with 231 bhp, they are "King of the Road".

Aus einem Mini wird 2015 ein Maxi-Mini, denn der Fünftürer der dritten Generation (F56) wartet mit statt-lichen 3,98 Metern auf. Eine neue elektromechanische Servolenkung, Voraussetzung für einen optionalen Parkassistenten, und optimierte Bremsen machen dem Mini-Fahrer auch im dichtesten Stadtverkehrsgetümmel Mut. Und mit dem Cooper S oder dessen Cooper-Works-Variante mit 231 PS ist er „King of the Road".

La Mini devient maxi en 2015, car cette cinq-portes de troisième génération (F56) en impose avec ses 3,98 mètres de long. Une nouvelle direction assistée électromécanique, condition préalable pour le système d'aide au stationnement en option, et des freins optimisés donnent du courage au conducteur de Mini, même dans la mêlée du trafic citadin. Et avec la Cooper S ou sa variante la Cooper Works de 231 ch, il est couronné «King of the Road».

One should imagine a large "Z," swinging over the front wing of a classical sports car with a long hood, falling downward at an angle at the A-pillar, and carrying the door threshold contour with it gently upward at the rear. This is how to describe the unconventional design of the Z4's flanks through to the rear wheels. On looking the front of the Z4 deep in the slit eyes of its headlights, the brave form innovation of BMW's chief designer Chris Bangle even appears beautiful. It is only at the rear that the harmony of style once again falls by the wayside. Actually, a repetition of the finely beveled swage line of the lower fender area readily presents itself for the trunk lid, instead of which one is confronted with a "duck's tail" à la Marcos for the integrated additional rear lighting. There can be no aerodynamic grounds for this stunted trailing end.

Since the 2003 IAA, a smaller and less expensive 2.2-liter engine has been added to the tried and tested 6-cylinder in-line engines with their 2.5 and 3-liter capacities. It produces 170 bhp, enough to accelerate to a speed of 62 mph (100 kph) in 7.7 seconds. The 3.0i with its 231 bhp on the other hand, thunders past this mark in only 5.9 seconds, and is only electronically tamed when it reaches its supposed top speed of 155 mph (250 kph). Irrespective of whether fitted with an automatic or the standard 6-gear switching transmission, the power of the 3.0i provides endless driving enjoyment. It is only when faced with bumps and ruts that the sporty chassis behaves like an ill-mannered clumsy oaf. As so beautifully put in the Z4 brochure: "Never before has one had the impression of experiencing the road so directly." The Z4 hardly notices a quick change of load. The wide chassis (front track width

4 ft 10 in, rear 5 ft, 1473 mm and 1523 mm), the low center of gravity, and the almost optimal weight distribution between front and rear axles of 50.6 and 49.4 percent, turn the vehicle into easily controlled instrument of joy, helped by many various driving aids.

Maximal safety in case of overturning is ensured by the two steel roll bars behind the headrests—connected to an extremely stabile frame crossbeam—and a bar running through the A-pillar and windshield frame. The airbags react independently according to direction of impact and passenger seat occupancy. The powerful ventilated disk brakes, supported by a very sensitive Anti-locking Brake System, deserve special praise. As with the Z8, emergency running tires make the carrying of a spare tire in the luggage compartment superfluous, allowing 8.5 cu.ft (240 liters) of luggage space with folded top, or 9.2 cu.ft (260 liters) without.

The dashboard and instrument panels of the Z4's interior appear almost modest—in view of the large aluminum trim—and yet are both orderly and functionally laid out. The sports' steering wheel equipped with multifunctional or with switches for the sequential manual transmission (SMG)—for an additional 1250 euros—lies comfortably in the hand. The seating is also above all criticism, leather upholstery being the standard for the 3.0i. Optional extras such as heated seats, or the luxury of electrical seat adjustment with memory function for the passenger seat, let the BMW cash registers ring. If a professional navigation system, whose display folds up from the dashboard at the press of a button, is also desired, then the Z4's price reaches the 50,000 euro mark.

Man stelle sich ein großes „Z" vor, schwinge es über den vorderen Kotflügel eines klassischen Sportwagens mit langer Motorhaube, lasse es in Verlängerung der A-Säule schräg nach unten fallen und ziehe es mitsamt Türschwellen-Kontur sanft nach hinten hoch. So lässt sich das eigenwillige Design des Z4-Flanken-Verlaufs bis zu den Hinterrädern beschreiben. Der Z4-Front tief in die Schlitzaugen der Scheinwerfer geschaut, wirkt das mutige Linienspiel von BMW-Chefdesigner Chris Bangle sogar schön. Nur beim Heck bleibt die Harmonie des Stylings einmal mehr auf der Strecke. Eigentlich bietet sich eine Wiederholung der fein gewölbten Sicke im unteren Stoßfänger-Bereich auf dem Kofferraumdeckel an, doch stattdessen sieht man sich mit einem „Entenbürzel" à la Marcos für die integrierte Heck-Zusatzleuchte konfrontiert. Aerodynamische Zwänge für diese verkümmerte Abrisskante gibt es wohl kaum.

Neben den bewährten 6-Zylinder-Reihen-Motoren mit 2,5 und knapp drei Litern ist seit der IAA 2003 eine kleinere, preiswertere Motorisierungsstufe mit 2,2 Litern dazugekommen. Sie bringt es auf 170 PS, genug für eine Beschleunigung auf Tempo 100 in 7,7 Sekunden. Der 3.0i hingegen donnert mit seinen 231 PS in 5,9 Sekunden bis zu dieser Marke und wird erst bei seiner Soll-Spitzengeschwindigkeit von 250 km/h elektronisch gebändigt. Ganz gleich, ob mit einer Automatik oder dem serienmäßigen 6-Gang-Schaltgetriebe ausgerüstet, bereitet die Kraft des 3.0i unendliches Fahrvergnügen. Nur bei unangenehmen Bodenwellen oder Spurrillen gebärdet sich das sportliche Fahrwerk wie ein ungezogenes Trampeltier. Wie heißt es doch so schön im Z4-Prospekt: „Noch nie hatte man den Eindruck, eine Straße so unmittelbar zu erfahren." Schnelle Lastwechsel nimmt der Z4 kaum zur

BMW Z4 E85 | 2002

Kenntnis. Das breite Fahrwerk (Spur vorn 1473 mm, hinten 1523 mm), der niedrige Schwerpunkt und die fast optimale Gewichtsbalance von 50,6 und 49,4 Prozent, verteilt auf Vorder- und Hinterräder, machen ihn zu einem leicht beherrschbaren Instrument der Freude.

Im Falle aller Fälle gewährten die zwei Stahl-Überrollbügel hinter den Nackenstützen – verbunden mit einem äußerst stabilen Karosserie-Querträger – sowie ein Bügel, der sich durch A-Säulen und Windschutzscheiben-Rahmen zieht, maximale Sicherheit bei einem Überschlag. Die Airbags reagieren einzeln, je nach Aufprallrichtung und Belegung des Beifahrersitzes. Besonderes Lob verdienen die innenbelüfteten Scheibenbremsen, die kräftig zupacken können und von einem sehr sensiblen Antiblockier-System unterstützt werden. Wie schon beim Z8 erübrigen Reifen mit Notlaufeigenschaften das Mitführen eines Reserverades im Gepäckraum, der mit versenktem Verdeck 240, ansonsten 260 Liter fasst.

Fast bescheiden – angesichts einer großen Aluminium-Blende –, doch aufgeräumt und funktionell gut gegliedert geben sich Armaturenbrett und Bedienelemente im Innenraum des Z4. Das Sportlenkrad, ob nun multifunktional oder mit Wippen für das sequenzielle manuelle Getriebe (SMG) - für zusätzlich 1250 Euro – bestückt, liegt gut in der Hand. Auch die Sitze, beim 3.0i serienmäßig mit Leder überzogen, sind über jede Kritik erhaben. Sitzheizung oder elektrische Sitzverstellung mit Memory-Funktion für den Beifahrersitz lassen die BMW-Kasse zusätzlich klingeln. Will man dann vielleicht sogar ein professionelles Navigationssystem, dessen Monitor auf Knopfdruck aus der Armaturentafel klappt, ist der Z4 3.0i in einer Preisregion von 50 000 Euro angelangt.

Imaginez-vous un immense «Z». Gravez-le sur les ailes avant d'une voiture de sport classique avec un long capot moteur. Modelez, avec ce «Z», les flancs de la voiture en lui donnant une légère ascendance vers l'arrière. Ainsi peut-on décrire le design, très original, des flancs de la Z4 jusqu'aux roues arrière. Si l'on regarde l'avant de la Z4 aux yeux bridés, on en vient même à concéder une certaine beauté au jeu courageux des lignes auquel se prête Chris Bangle, le chef designer de BMW. Il n'y a que pour l'arrière que, une fois de plus, l'harmonie du style n'échappe pas à toute critique. Alors que l'on s'attendait, en effet, à une poursuite du coup de crayon au galbe élégant dans l'entourage du pare-chocs, on découvre au contraire un arrière tronqué à la Marcos avec un troisième feu de frein intégré au becquet. Pourtant, aucune contrainte aérodynamique ne semble justifier une poupe aussi torturée.

Outre les six-cylindres en ligne éprouvés de 2,5 et 3 litres de cylindrée, BMW propose, depuis l'IAA 2003, une motorisation plus modeste et moins coûteuse de 2,2 litres. Elle développe 170 ch, suffisamment pour couvrir le 0 à 100 km/h en 7,7 secondes. Avec ses 231 ch, la 3.0i accomplit, en revanche, cette discipline en 5,9 secondes et ne voit son élan jugulé électroniquement qu'à une vitesse de pointe de 250 km/h. Que l'on ait opté pour la transmission automatique ou la boîte manuelle à six vitesses de série, la montée en puissance de la 3.0i procure un agrément de conduite infini. Il n'y a que sur mauvaise route ou en présence d'ornières que le châssis sportif se comporte comme un mauvais garçon. Les transferts de charge rapides laissent la Z4 de marbre. Les larges liaisons au sol (voies de 1473 mm à l'avant et de 1523 mm à l'arrière), le centre de gravité très bas et la répartition presque optimale du poids de respectivement 50,6 % et de 49,4 % pour les trains avant et arrière font d'elle un instrument de plaisir qu'il est toujours facile de maîtriser.

En cas de tonneau, les deux arceaux de sécurité en acier derrière les appuie-tête – qui sont reliés à une poutre transversale extrêmement solide – ainsi que les renforts de la baie de pare-brise offrent une sécurité maximum. Les airbags réagissent individuellement en fonction du sens de la collision et de l'occupation du siège passager. Les freins à disque ventilés méritent des éloges : ils attaquent avec beaucoup de mordant et ils sont soutenus par un système d'antiblocage très sensible. À l'instar de la Z8, des pneus anti-crevaison rendent superflue toute roue de secours dans le coffre, qui, lorsque la capote est repliée, offre une capacité de 240 litres contre 260 litres capote fermée.

Le tableau de bord et les manettes de commande dans le cockpit de la Z4 frisent la sobriété – malgré un vaste panneau en aluminium – mais ils sont bien agencés et d'une grande fonctionnalité. Le volant sport, qu'il soit multifonctionnel ou comporte les palettes de la boîte de vitesses manuelle séquentielle (SMG) – pour un supplément de 1250 euros – tombe bien en mains. Les sièges aussi, gainés de cuir en série dans le cas de la 3.0i, sont au-dessus des critiques. Le chauffage des sièges ou le luxe d'un réglage des sièges avec fonction «Memory» pour le passager font tomber quelques billets supplémentaires dans l'escarcelle de BMW. Si on le souhaite même, on peut se procurer un système de navigation professionnel, dont l'écran sort du tableau de bord en appuyant sur un bouton : la Z4 3.0i flirte alors avec les 50 000 euros.

The cockpit of the roadster concentrates on the essential. The BMW emblem is the focal point of the curvaceous "Z" contour. Well braced: the tidy engine compartment of the 6-cylinder in-line engine.

Auf das Wesentliche beschränkt sich das Cockpit dieses Roadsters. Das BMW-Emblem ist der zentrale Punkt der geschwungenen „Z"-Kontur. Gut verstrebt: der aufgeräumte Motorraum des 6-Zylinder-Reihenmotors.

Le cockpit de ce roadster se limite à l'essentiel. L'emblème BMW est le point central de la griffe en Z. Bien renforcé : le compartiment moteur du six-cylindres en ligne.

The double launch of the Z4 Coupé and the M version in January 2006 was intended to add new, sporty impulses. By the time this project was halted in August 2008, an impressive 17,000 units of this "beefy" vehicle had been built; seen here: the 3.0 si of 265 bhp.

Neue sportliche Impulse sollte die gleichzeitige Einführung von Z4 Coupé und seiner M-Version im Januar 2006 bringen. Immerhin wurden bis zur Einstellung dieses Projektes im August 2008 17 000 Einheiten dieses bullig wirkenden Wagens gebaut – hier der 3.0 si mit 265 PS.

L'introduction simultanée du coupé Z4 et de sa version M en janvier 2006 devait insuffler un nouveau souffle de sportivité. 17 000 exemplaires de cette voiture à l'allure imposante ont été construits jusqu'à l'arrêt du projet en août 2008 – ici la 3.0 si de 265 ch.

BMW 5 E60 | 2003

An entirely new 5 series BMW was due in 2003; the four previous generations (E12, E28, E34, and E39) had needed an average production time of seven and a half years, which in itself is evidence of their qualities. The "representative of the dynamic business class," as BMW called the fifth offspring of the 5 series (referred to internally as the E60), came with plenty of variety. As well as the 530d with 235 bhp—top speed 155 mph (250 kph)—there were three other diesel variants ranging from 177 to 286 bhp. The weakest link in this 5 series chain proved also to be the most economical, with a fuel consumption of 46 miles to the gallon (5.1 liters per 100 kilometers) in the European Union test cycle, burdening the environment with just 219 grams per mile (136 g/km) of emitted CO_2. Against it were six gasoline versions ranging from 170 (520i) to 367 (550i) bhp. Even the 4.8-liter V8 version, the one with the most powerful engine, propels the 1.9 short tons (1.7 tonnes) to 62 mph (100 kph) in an astonishing 6.1 seconds.

For it to perform like this, the E60 was put on a strict diet to bring its weight to below that of its "father," the E39. The entire front section, including side panels and hood, are made of aluminum, and even the double-cardan universal joint telescopic front axle and the integral rear axle, are made of

this non-rusting light metal. The balance between aluminum and high-strength steel is expressed in the 5 series by the optimum 50:50 axle load distribution, which is evident in the vehicle's excellent handling. Since 2005, in addition to this "business class" BMW, the M5, described as a "business airplane on wheels," has also been available to over-stressed manager types. Its naturally aspirated 10-cylinder engine activates 507 bhp at 7750 rpm, and gets the 2-ton (1885-kg) sedan to 62 mph (100 kph) in just 4.7 seconds. The sequential 7-gear M gearbox assists in the highly efficient generation of power. Gear-change times are measured in milliseconds here.

The M5 touring had to carry an additional 220 pounds (100 kg). And this workhorse performs this task like a racing steed, namely 4.8 seconds to 62 mph (100 kph) and just 22.9 seconds to the 124 mph (200 kph) mark. Like all the M vehicles, the touring also proved its sporting abilities on what is probably the best test track in the world: the Nordschleife of the Nürburgring. Up the Quiddelbacher Höhe at 164 mph (200 kph) and down the Fuchsröhre; through the banked corners of the Carousel with ease; and then towards the Antoniusbuche, albeit with the engine not quite at the cut-off point. So the driver of the M5 touring curses the electronic cut-off, which is a reminder of its everyday use.

Im Jahre 2003 war wieder einmal ein völlig neuer 5er-BMW fällig, denn seine vier Vorgänger-Generationen (E12, E28, E34 und E39) hatten es auf eine durchschnittliche Produktionszeit von siebeneinhalb Jahren gebracht, was ganz für ihre Qualitäten spricht. Der „Repräsentant der dynamischen Business-Klasse", wie BMW den fünften Spross des 5ers (werksintern E60) bezeichnet, gibt sich äußerst variantenreich. So scharen sich um den 530d mit 235 PS – Spitzengeschwindigkeit 250 km/h – noch drei weitere Dieselvarianten von 177 bis 286 PS, wobei sich das schwächste Glied in dieser 5er-Reihe mit einem Verbrauch von 5,1 Litern auf 100 Kilometer im EU-Testzyklus als besonders sparsam erweist und die Umwelt mit lediglich 136 g/km CO_2 belastet. Sechs Benziner – von 170 PS (520i) bis 367 PS (550i) – stehen dagegen. Mit den 4,8-Liter-V8-Motor, also dem stärksten Triebwerk, beschleunigt selbst dieser 1,7-Tonner wieselflink in 6,1 Sekunden auf hundert Stundenkilometer.

Um derart glänzen zu können, ist das Gewicht des E60 gegenüber seinem „Vater", dem E39, einer gründlichen Diät unterzogen worden. So besteht der gesamte Vorderbau einschließlich Seitenwänden und Motorhaube aus Aluminium, und auch Doppelgelenk-Federbein-Vorderachse und Integral-Hinterachse sind aus diesem nichtrostenden Leichtmetall gefertigt. Die Ausgewogenheit zwischen Aluminium

und hochfestem Stahl drückt sich beim 5er durch eine optimale Achslastverteilung von 50:50 aus, was sich letztendlich in hervorragendem Handling bemerkbar macht. Ab 2005 steht neben dieser „Business-Class" von BMW für besonders eilige Manager-Typen auch ein „Geschäftsflugzeug auf Rädern" zur Verfügung: der M5. Dessen 10-Zylinder-Saugmotor aktiviert 507 PS bei 7750/min und erlaubt der 1855 Kilo schweren Limousine einen Vortrieb in lediglich 4,7 Sekunden auf Tempo 100. Bei der effizienten Kraftentfaltung assistiert das sequenzielle 7-Gang-M-Getriebe. Die Schaltzeiten sind hier im Millisekunden-Bereich angesiedelt.

Als „Renn-Kombi" entpuppt sich der M5 touring, der weitere 100 Kilo, insgesamt 1955, in Bewegung setzen muss. Und diese Arbeit verrichtet dieser Lastesel wie ein Rennpferd, nämlich in 4,8 Sekunden auf 100 km/h und lediglich 22,9 Sekunden bis zur 200-km/h-Marke. Wie alle M-Mobile erhielt auch der Touring seine sportliche Fahrwerksabstimmung auf der wahrscheinlich idealen Teststrecke: der Nordschleife des Nürburgrings. Mit 200 Stundenkilometern die Quiddelbacher Höhe hinauf und die Fuchsröhre hinunter, locker über die Fahrbahnrillen des Karussells und mit leider nicht voll ausgedrehtem Triebwerk in Richtung Antoniusbuche: Da verflucht der Lenker des M5 Touring den elektronischen Geschwindigkeitsbegrenzer, der an den Alltagsgebrauch erinnern soll.

L'année 2003 vit le lancement d'une toute nouvelle Série 5 BMW, les quatre générations précédentes (E12, E28, E34 et E39) ayant atteint une durée de production moyenne de sept ans et demi, gage incontestable de leurs nombreuses qualités. La « représentante d'une classe business dynamique », pour désigner la cinquième Série 5 (appelée E60 en interne) selon les termes de BMW, existe en une multitude de versions. Ainsi la 530d de 235 ch, avec une vitesse de pointe de 250 km/h, est accompagnée de trois autres variantes diesel de 177 à 286 ch, le modèle le moins puissant de cette Série 5 s'avérant particulièrement frugal avec une consommation de 5,1 litres dans le cycle de tests de l'UE sur 100 km pour un taux d'émission de CO_2 de seulement 136 g/km. Six moteurs essence, de 170 ch (520i) à 367 ch (550i), sont autant d'alternatives au diesel. Avec le moteur le plus puissant de tous, le V8 4,8 litres, cette voiture de 1,7 tonne passe comme une flèche de 0 à 100 km/h en 6,1 secondes.

Pour obtenir d'aussi bons résultats, la E60 a été soumise à un régime draconien par rapport à la précédente, la E39. Les parois latérales du châssis avant et le capot moteur sont exclusivement composés d'aluminium, le train avant à double articulation des pivots de fusée et l'essieu arrière intégral sont également fabriqués dans ce métal léger inoxydable. L'équilibre entre aluminium et acier haute résistance

s'exprime sur la Série 5 par une répartition optimale de la charge par essieu de 50:50 ce qui se traduit par une exceptionnelle maniabilité. Depuis 2005, BMW propose, aux côtés de cette voiture « business class », un véritable « jet sur roues » pour managers pressés : la M5. Son moteur atmosphérique dix-cylindres développe 507 ch à 7750 tr/min et lui permet malgré ses 1855 kg de passer de 0 à 100 km/h en seulement 4,7 secondes. La boîte de vitesses séquentielle 7 rapports participe au déploiement efficace de cette puissance. La durée du passage entre les rapports se compte en millisecondes.

La M5 touring, qui doit mettre en mouvement 100 kg de plus, soit 1955 kg en tout, se révèle être un véritable « break de course ». Cette « bête de somme » effectue d'ailleurs cette tâche avec le même talent qu'un cheval de course en passant de 0 à 100 km/h en 4,8 secondes avant d'atteindre les 200 km/h en 22,9 secondes. Comme toutes les voitures M, la touring a fait ses premiers essais sportifs sur le meilleur circuit du monde : la boucle nord du Nürburgring. À 200 km/h, elle franchit la bosse de Quiddelbach et descend le Fuchsröhre, roule avec souplesse sur les rainures de la chaussée du Carrousel et se dirige, malheureusement pas à plein régime, vers l'Antoniusbuche : le conducteur maudit alors le limiteur électronique de vitesse de la M5 touring, cruel rappel du quotidien au volant de son bolide.

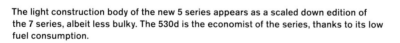

The light construction body of the new 5 series appears as a scaled down edition of the 7 series, albeit less bulky. The 530d is the economist of the series, thanks to its low fuel consumption.

Äußerlich wie eine verkleinerte Ausgabe des 7er – aber weniger massig – wirkt die Leichtbau-Karosse des neuen 5er. Dank seines niedrigen Verbrauchs ist der 530d der Ökonom seiner Baureihe.

Extérieurement, on dirait une copie conforme – raccourcie, mais moins massive – de la Série 7 : la carrosserie en construction allégée de la nouvelle Série 5. Grâce à sa faible consommation, la 530d est la championne de l'économie dans sa gamme.

Internally, the 530d convinces by means of its modern cockpit containing a reworked i-Drive with reduced functions, and by an extraordinary smooth running common-rail diesel engine that deploys 218 bhp.

Innerlich überzeugt der 530d durch sein modernes Cockpit mit einem überarbeitetem i-Drive, dessen Funktionen reduziert wurden, und durch einen ungemein laufruhigen Common-Rail-Dieselmotor, der 218 PS entfaltet.

Intérieurement, la 530d séduit par son cockpit moderne avec un i-Drive revu et corrigé, dont le nombre des fonctions a été revu à la baisse, et par un moteur diesel à rampe commune étonnamment soyeux qui développe 218 ch.

The M5 is the world's first series sedan to have a 507-bhp V10 engine at its disposal, whose 8250 rpm verge on the engine speed of motor sport. New: a 7-gear SMG switching transmission with extremely short switching times as in Formula 1. A further superlative: the performance to weight ratio is about only 7.7 lbs (3.5 kilograms) per bhp.

Als erste Serien-Limousine der Welt verfügt der M5 über ein 507-PS-V10-Triebwerk, das mit 8250 Touren in die Drehzahlregionen von Rennmotoren vorstößt. Neu: ein 7-Gang-SMG-Schaltgetriebe mit extrem kurzen Schaltzeiten wie in der Formel 1. Und noch ein Superlativ: das Leistungsgewicht liegt bei nur 3,5 Kilo pro PS.

La M5 est la première berline de série au monde à être propulsée par un V10, en l'occurrence de 507 ch, qui atteint des régimes de moteur de course: la zone rouge débute à 8250 tours. Nouveauté: la boîte manuelle SMG à sept vitesses avec changements de rapports aussi rapides qu'en Formule 1. Et encore un superlatif: le rapport poids/puissance n'est que de 3,5 kg par ch.

Combination of classy racehorse and pack mule: the powerful V10 of the M5 Touring transports the two-ton vehicle to 62mph (100kph) in less than five seconds. Gears are shifted either using rocker switches on the steering wheel or a shift on the center console.

Symbiose von rassigem Rennpferd und Lastesel: Der kraftvolle V10 des M5 Touring beschleunigt den Zweitonner in weniger als fünf Sekunden aus dem Stand auf Tempo 100. Geschaltet wird entweder mit Wippen am Lenkrad oder über Wählhebel auf der Mittelkonsole.

Symbiose parfaite entre un étalon de course et mulet : le puissant V10 fait passer la M5 Touring de 0 à 100 km/h en moins 5 secondes pour un poids de 2 tonnes. Les vitesses se passent soit par des palettes au volant soit par un levier sur la console centrale.

BMW 6 E63|2003

A picture-book beauty that has been with us since 2003, the BMW 645Ci coupé has a long engine hood and elongated roof contour, and the cabriolet has a conventional fabric cover that—also at low speeds—packs away inside the rear in less than 25 seconds. The side struts of the closed top, called "fins" by BMW, cleverly echo the coupé's silhouette. BMW also demonstrates its passion for practical details with the vertical rear window, which can be retracted independently or, if necessary, used as a wind blocker for rear passengers.

A golf-playing couple might be happy with the 333bhp of the 4.4-liter engine under the hood of the 645Ci—the trunk is practically designed for two stuffed golf bags—but any lover of beautiful cars who is of a more sporting bent will judge a car by its power. And BMW offers that in the M6—in the first place as a coupé that can easily hold its own in comparison with a purebred sports car, since its uncharged engine provides 507bhp at 7750rpm. Lightweight, carbon fiber-reinforced plastic for the roof, front fender with a distinct spoiler lip, and the rear with the diffuser, plus the plentiful use of aluminum have made the M6 coupé several pounds lighter. Next to the compact V10, a work of art in aluminum, gray iron, and light metal alloys, the 19-inch wheels developed specifically for the M6 also deserve recognition for the part they play

in helping it to "lose weight safely." The saving is just under four pounds (1.8kg) per wheel—and thus a reduction in the unsprung mass. Nothing more to say, since all in all, the M6 with its 3927lbs (1585kg) dutifully undercuts the M5.

The ten-cylinder engine that really comes into its own once it gets above 8250rpm is accompanied, of course, by the seven-gear transmission that shifts sequentially—or automatically for those who prefer it. The sprint record amounts to 4.6 seconds and, thanks to Launch Control, it can make it to 62mph (100kph) in 4.2 seconds. The engine double clutches when shifting down, which the four tailpipes announce with an excited staccato, adding to the already masterful sound composition. So the engine control with more than a thousand components is joined by a "musical engine management" by highly paid acoustic specialists: the appropriate accompaniment for the growing energy level. As the speedometer goes up to 210mph (330kph), an experienced M6 driver will not want to be told what to do. By paying an appropriate fee, he can be released from the manufacturer's self-imposed limiter and put his abilities to the test on a speed-driving course. Which is probably a very good idea when faced with the temptation of 190mph (300kph). It's also wonderful to be able to see the sky, made possible for the first time in June 2006 in an M6 Cabrio.

Bildhübsch präsentiert sich seit 2003 der BMW 645Ci als Coupé mit langer Motorhaube und gestreckter Dachkontur sowie als Cabriolet mit konventionellem Stoffverdeck, das sich – sogar bei langsamer Fahrt – in knapp 25 Sekunden in sein Heckabteil versenken lässt. Die Seitenteile des geschlossenen Verdecks, von BMW als „Finnen" bezeichnet, greifen die Coupé-Silhouette gekonnt auf. Auch mit der senkrecht angeordneten Heckscheibe, die separat eingefahren werden kann oder notfalls auch als Windschott für Fondpassagiere dient, demonstriert BMW die Liebe zu praktischen Details.

Mit den 333 PS des 4,4-Liter-Motors unter der Haube des 645Ci ist vielleicht das Golfer-Ehepaar – der Kofferraum ist für zwei komplette Ausrüstungen geradezu prädestiniert – zufrieden, doch der sportlich angehauchte Freak schöner Automobile beurteilt diese nach ihrer Power. Die offeriert BMW mit dem M6 – zunächst als Coupé, das den Vergleich mit reinrassigen Sportwagen nicht zu scheuen braucht, denn sein „Super-Sauger" entfesselt bei 7750 Umdrehungen 507 PS. Leichter, kohlefaserverstärkter Kunststoff bei Dach, vorderem Stoßfänger mit ausgeprägter Spoiler-Lippe und Hinterteil mit Diffusor sowie der reichliche Gebrauch von Aluminium erleichtern das M6 Coupé um etliche Kilos. Neben dem kompakten V10, einem Material-Kunstwerk aus Aluminium, Grauguss und Leichtmetall-Legierungen, gebührt auch den speziell für den M6 entwickelten 19-Zoll-

Alu-Schmiederädern Anerkennung fürs „Abspecken ohne Risiken": Gewichtsersparnis pro Rad 1,8 Kilo und damit eine Reduzierung der ungefederten Massen. Keine Marginalien, denn insgesamt unterbietet der M6 mit 1785 Kilo pflichtgemäß den M5.

Zur Zehnzylinder-Kraftquelle, die erst jenseits von 8250 Touren versiegt, gehört natürlich das Siebengang-Getriebe, sequenziell zu schalten oder mit automatischer Gangwahl für Schaltfaule. Der Sprintwert schlägt mit 4,6 Sekunden zu Buche, und dank Launch Control sind sogar 4,2 Sekunden bis 100 km/h möglich. Das Zwischengas beim Runterschalten übernimmt der Motor selbst, was die vier Auspuffrohre mit erregten Staccati in der per se meisterhaften Sound-Komposition quittieren. Zur Motorsteuerung mit mehr als tausend Bauteilen gesellt sich also ein „musikalisches Motorenmanagement" hochbezahlter Akustik-Spezialisten: angemessene Begleitmusik für das sich entfaltende Potenzial. Da der Tacho bis 330 km/h ausgelegt ist, möchte ein versierter M6-Fahrer nicht in die Schranken gewiesen werden. Gegen Zahlung eines angemessenen Obolus kann er sich von der selbstauferlegten Beschränkung des Herstellers entbinden lassen und darf sein Können in einem Schnellfahr-Kurs unter Beweis stellen. Das ist wohl auch sinnvoll, wenn Tempo 300 lockt. Verlockend ist auch, wenn der Himmel zu Füßen liegt. Diese Perspektive eröffnet seit Juni 2006 das M6 Cabrio.

La très jolie BMW 645 Ci s'affiche depuis 2003 en version coupé avec un long capot moteur et un toit aux contours étirés et en version cabriolet avec capote traditionnelle qui s'escamote en à peine 25 secondes, même lorsque l'on roule lentement, dans le logement prévu à cet effet. Les pans latéraux de la capote fermée, appelés « nageoires » chez BMW, reprennent avec maestria la silhouette du coupé. Avec la custode verticale amovible faisant le cas échéant office de pare-vent pour les passagers arrière, BMW donne une nouvelle preuve de son penchant pour les détails pratiques.

Les 333 ch du moteur 4,4 litres dissimulé sous le capot de la 645 Ci feront peut-être le bonheur d'un couple de golfeurs – le coffre est prévu pour deux équipements de golf complets – mais les amateurs de conduite sportive jugent plus les belles voitures sur leur puissance. BMW leur offre précisément sur un plateau avec la M6, d'abord en version coupé qui n'a pas à craindre la comparaison avec les voitures de sport pur jus puisque son « super moteur » délivre 507 ch à 7750 tours. Des matières plastiques renforcées de fibres de carbone pour le toit, un pare-chocs avant à l'arête prononcée, un arrière avec diffuseur ainsi que l'utilisation généreuse d'aluminium allègent la M6 coupé de quelques kilos. En plus du compact V10, véritable œuvre d'art en aluminium, fonte grise et alliages de métaux légers, les jantes forgées en aluminium 19 pouces développées spécialement pour la M6 sont elles aussi responsables de ce « régime forcé sans risque ». Économie de poids de 1,8 kg par roue et ainsi réduction des masses en mouvement ! Aucun effet secondaire car, avec ses 1785 kg, la M6 bat dans l'ensemble et « comme il se doit » la M5.

Le moteur dix-cylindres, qui n'abdique qu'au-delà 8250 tours, s'accompagne naturellement d'une boîte à sept vitesses séquentielle ou avec sélection de rapport automatisée pour les paresseux du levier. Départ arrêté, elle atteint les 100 km/h en 4,6 secondes, ce temps pouvant même être réduit à 4,2 secondes grâce au Launch Control. Le double-débrayage au rétrogradage est assuré automatiquement par le moteur, manœuvre à laquelle les quatre pots d'échappement répondent par un grondement vif dans la composition sonore intrinsèquement magistrale. Le contrôle du moteur mettant en jeu plus de 1000 pièces s'assortit donc d'une « gestion musicale » orchestrée par des spécialistes en acoustique très bien rémunérés : une musique d'accompagnement adaptée au potentiel déployé. Comme le compteur est prévu jusqu'à 330 km/h, les conducteurs les plus chevronnés devraient y trouver leur compte. Pour un prix raisonnable, ils peuvent même s'affranchir de la limite auto-imposée par le constructeur et mettre leurs aptitudes à l'épreuve lors d'un stage de conduite rapide qui peut s'avérer judicieux pour tous ceux tentés par les 300 km/h. Tentant également d'avoir le ciel à ses pieds : cette perspective s'ouvre depuis juin 2006 avec la M6 cabriolet.

A picture of beauty: the elongated roof contour leaves only a horizontal air trailing edge remaining of the trunk lid. The cockpit presents itself as sporty and luxurious. Powerful: the V8 engine of the 645 Ci.

Bildhübsch: die lang gestreckte Dachkontur lässt vom Kofferraumdeckel nur noch eine waagerechte Luft-Abrisskante übrig. Sportlich und luxuriös präsentiert sich das Cockpit. Kraftvoll: der V8-Motor des 645 Ci.

Beauté sculpturale : les contours étirés du toit ne laissent plus place, à hauteur du couvercle de malle, qu'à une arête de décrochement horizontale. Sportif et luxueux : le cockpit. Puissant : le moteur V8 de la 645 Ci.

The long, gently falling-away hood of the vehicle's weight-reduced aluminum front flows into a kidney-shaped configuration set with aperture covers whose lines are continued in the upper glazing of the headlights.

Die lange, sanft abfallende Haube des gewichts-reduzierten Vorderwagens aus Aluminium mündet in einer Nieren-Konfiguration mit aufgesetzten Blenden, deren Linienführung sich in der oberen Scheinwerfer-Verglasung fortsetzt.

Le long capot moteur légèrement plongeant selon les principes de la construction allégée en aluminium débouche sur des naseaux surmontés par un jonc chromé dont la ligne se poursuit, tel un sourcil, au-dessus des phares.

The cabriolet fans of this four-seater are not encased by a collapsible coupé roof, but rather by a thermal material lid, fully retractable in 25 seconds, with a separately operable rear windshield.

Kein zusammenklappbares Coupé-Dach, sondern ein in 25 Sekunden voll versenkbares Thermo-Stoffverdeck mit separat bedienbarer Heckscheibe erschließt die Cabrio-Freuden dieses Viersitzers.

Ce n'est pas un toit coupé repliable, mais une capote parfaitement isolée qui s'escamote en 25 secondes, avec une lunette arrière à commande séparée permettant aux passagers de cette quatre-places de profiter sans regrets des joies du cabriolet.

The M6 revealed itself to be a powerful "Bavarian" with a pleasingly company 5-liter V10 high rev engine. The interior is a combination of sporty attributes and elegant fittings, with lots of leather and classy wood trims.

Als „Kraft-Bayer" gebärdet sich der M6, dessen 5-Liter-V10-Hochdrehzahl-Triebwerk recht kompakt ausfällt. Im Interieur begegnen sich sportliche Attribute und noble Ausstattung – mit viel Leder und dezenten Holztäfelungen.

La M6, dont le moteur V10 5 litres au régime élevé semble très compact, se comporte comme un véritable concentré de puissance. Dans l'habitacle, les attributs sportifs se marient avec des équipements élégants, alliant le cuir à profusion aux boiseries raffinées.

BMW X3 E83|2003

The smaller brother of the X5 is not that much smaller: only four inches (ten centimeters) difference in length, and a mere ¾ inch (two centimeters) in width. X5 and X3 are not separated by their technology but rather by geography, for the X3 is not produced parallel to the X5 in Spartanburg, SC. It is constructed by Magna Steyr, Graz, where BMW has had engines built since 1982. As with Steyr-Daimler-Puch AG, the home of the Mercedes G, Germans and Austrians have successfully moved jointly into terrain known in the case of the X3 only by the American term "Sports Activity Vehicle" (SAV). At first glance, this multi-purpose vehicle for road and, when necessary, off-road driving, only differs from the X5 by a bend. This stylistic element which slightly bevels the rearmost side windows is known by BMW internally as the "Hofmeister kink" and has appeared occasionally since the 1970s—for example the M1 designed by Giugiaro. The reversible plastic fenders, fixed to the bodywork at different heights, are not completely in unison with the homogeneity of double kidney headlight section and curved roof contour. This slight deficit in design integration, to which the positioning of the fog lights also belongs, is of less weight when one considers the potential of the X3.

The "xDrive" (BMW's spelling) of this beefy four-wheel drive vehicle sets new standards. It enables a smoothly variable distribution of the propulsion between the powered axles by means of a multi-plate clutch. The system reacts immediately to changes in the road and ground surface conditions, transferring propulsion force to the axle that has the best ground contact at the time. "xDrive" is especially welcome by

snow and ice, but it also limits the on-road tendency to over- or understeer when cornering at speed. The "Hill Descent Control" (HDC) springs into action should a steep descent occur when off-road, gliding the X3 and its passengers slowly and safely to the bottom at a speed of between 4 and 16 mph (6 and 25 kph) depending on the button pressed. The HDC only takes its leave after the gas pedal has been operated.

Additional security on all surfaces is naturally provided by the tried and tested BMW dynamic stability control, which includes all previously presented regulatory aids such as Anti-lock Braking System, dynamic and cornering brake control, and the automatic differential lock. In order to achieve a relative low center of gravity despite the 8 inch (201 millimeter) ground clearance—measured with only the driver onboard— the drive shaft for the front wheels runs through the oil pan.

The 3.0i engine's four-valve technology with double variable valve timing control mobilizing 231 bhp at 5900 rpm, is a BMW standard. With it the X3 can accelerate from 0 to 62 mph (100 kph) in 7.8 seconds like a roadrunner, while the top speed of 130 mph (210 kph)—or even 139 mph (224 kph) with the sport package—is remarkable for an SAV. In contrast to the 3.0d diesel variation with 204 bhp, the EU4 exhaust category 3-liter engine develops a considerable thirst for fuel when driven in a mixture of freeway and city conditions. In open country a little extra gas is in order, for here too the X3 proves its capabilities: it manages mud to a depth of 20 inches (50 centimeters) at 4.5 mph (7 kph), masters diverse gradients, and has an enormous climbing capability where many of its competitors would simply give up and overturn.

Viel fehlt ihm nicht, dem kleinen Bruder des X5: nur zehn Zentimeter Differenz in der Länge und lediglich deren zwei in der Breite. X5 und X3 trennen keine technischen Welten, sondern geographische, denn der X3 läuft nicht parallel zum X5 in Spartanburg, USA, vom Band. Ihn fertigt Magna Steyr, Graz, wo BMW schon seit 1982 Motoren bauen lässt. Wie bei der Steyr-Daimler-Puch AG, Heimstätte des Mercedes G, begeben sich Deutsche und Österreicher gemeinsam erfolgreich auf ein Terrain, das im Falle des X3 nur die amerikanische Bezeichnung „Sports Activity Vehicle" (SAV) kennt. Dieses Mehrzweck-Mobil für befestigte und – wenn es sein muss – auch unbefestigte Pfade unterscheidet sich vom X5 auf den ersten Blick nur durch einen Knick. Dieses stilistische Element, das die hinterste Seitenscheibe leicht abschrägt, wird BMW-intern „Hofmeisterknick" genannt und taucht schon seit den sechziger Jahren auf – sogar beim von Giugiaro entworfenen M1. Nicht ganz im Einklang zur Homogenität von Doppelniere und Scheinwerfer-Partie und der geschwungenen Dachkontur einschließlich Spoiler stehen die reversiblen Kunststoff-Stoßfänger, in unterschiedlicher Höhe an die Karosserie angeflanscht. Diese Marginalien mangelnder gestalterischer Integration, zu der auch die Positionierung der Nebelscheinwerfer gehört, fallen angesichts des X3-Potentials weniger ins Gewicht.

Bei dem bulligen Allradler setzt „xDrive" (so die BMW-Schreibweise) neue Maßstäbe. Es ermöglicht eine stufenlos variable Verteilung der Antriebskräfte zwischen den angetriebenen Achsen durch eine Lamellenkupplung. Das System reagiert sofort auf wechselnde Straßen- und Gelände-Gegebenheiten und überträgt das Antriebsmoment auf die Achse, die gerade die beste Haftung findet. Besonders positiv macht

sich „xDrive" bei Schnee und Eis bemerkbar, aber auch bei schnellen Kurvenfahrten im Onroad-Betrieb minimiert es die Tendenz zum Unter- oder Übersteuern. Geht es im Off-road-Bereich einmal steil bergab, springt die „Hill Descent Control" (HDC) ein und geleitet den X3 samt Passagieren langsam und sicher zu Tal – je nach Tastendruck zwischen 6 und 25 km/h. Erst wenn man auf das Bremspedal tritt, verabschiedet sich HDC.

Zusätzliche Geborgenheit auf allen Pfaden vermittelt natürlich die bei BMW erprobte dynamische Stabilitätskontrolle, die alle vorgelagerten Regulative wie Anti-Blockier-System, dynamische sowie Kurven-Bremskontrolle oder die automatische Differenzialsperre mit einbezieht. Um trotz 201 Millimetern Bodenfreiheit – gemessen nur mit dem Fahrer an Bord – einen relativ niedrigen Schwerpunkt erzielen zu können, führen die Antriebswellen für die Vorderräder durch die Ölwanne.

Die Vierventil-Technik mit doppelt variabler Nockenwellensteuerung des 3.0i-Triebwerkes, das bei 5900/min 231 PS mobilisiert, ist BMW-Standard. Damit beschleunigt der X3 in 7,8 Sekunden von 0 auf 100 Stundenkilometer wie ein Roadrunner, und auch die Spitze von 210 km/h – mit Sportpaket sogar 224 km/h – ist beachtlich für einen SAV. Im Gegensatz zur Diesel-Variante, 3.0d mit 204 PS, entwickelt das in der Schadstoffklasse EU4 angesiedelte 3-Liter-Aggregat ziemlich viel Spritdurst im gemischten Fahrbetrieb von Stadt und Autobahn. Im Gelände darf es ein Schluck Benzin zusätzlich sein, denn auch hier stellt der X3 sein Können unter Beweis: 50 Zentimeter Wattiefe bei 7 km/h, das Meistern von diversen Böschungswinkeln und eine enorme Steigfähigkeit, bei der so mancher Konkurrent andächtig nach hinten kippen würde.

I ne lui manque pas grand-chose à la petite sœur de la X5 : dix centimètres de différence en longueur et seulement deux en largeur. Ce n'est pas un monde mécanique, mais géographique qui sépare la X5 de la X3. En effet, la X3 n'est pas construite sur les mêmes chaînes que la X5 à Spartanburg, aux États-Unis. Elle est, en effet, fabriquée par Magna Steyr, à Graz, où BMW fait déjà assembler les moteurs depuis 1982. Comme avec la société Steyr-Daimler-Puch AG, le berceau de la Mercedes G, Allemands et Autrichiens s'engagent conjointement, et avec succès, sur un terrain qui, dans le cas de la X3, ne connaît que la désignation américaine « Sports Activity Vehicle » (SAV). Au premier coup d'œil, cette voiture polyvalente, pouvant très bien rouler hors des sentiers battus s'il le faut, ne se distingue de la X5 que par un pli. Cet élément stylistique, le retour vers l'avant de la ligne des vitres arrière, est appelé « pli Hofmeister » chez BMW et apparaît depuis les années 1960, notamment sur la M1 dessinée par Giugiaro.

Avec ce tout-terrain musclé, la transmission « xDrive » (selon la logique de BMW) pose de nouveaux jalons. Elle permet une répartition variable en continu du couple entre les essieux moteurs grâce à un embrayage à lamelles. Le système réagit immédiatement aux changements de la route et selon la nature du terrain, transmettant de manière optimale le couple à l'essieu qui a respectivement la meilleure adhérence. La transmission « xDrive » s'avère particulièrement efficace sur la neige et le verglas, mais lors des virages franchis rapidement sur route asphaltée elle aussi réprime la tendance au sous-virage ou au survirage. Au moment d'aborder une pente escarpée en tout-terrain, le « Hill Descent Control »

(HDC) intervient, garantissant à la X3 et à ses passagers une descente lente et en toute sécurité. Il suffit ensuite de donner un léger coup de frein pour que le HDC se déconnecte.

Un confort et une sécurité supplémentaires dans toutes les situations sont, naturellement, garantis par le contrôle dynamique de stabilité, qui a fait ses preuves chez BMW et intègre toutes les assistances à la conduite, telles que le système d'antiblocage, le contrôle dynamique du freinage et en courbe ou le différentiel autobloquant. Afin d'obtenir un centre de gravité relativement bas malgré une garde au sol de 201 millimètres – mesurée uniquement avec le conducteur à bord –, l'arbre de transmission menant aux roues avant franchit de part en part le carter d'huile.

La technique de culasse à quatre soupapes avec la distribution variable des arbres à cames double-Vanos du moteur 3.0i développant 231 ch à 5900 tr/min est standard pour cette BMW. Avec ce moteur, la X3 réalise le temps flatteur de 7,8 secondes pour le 0 à 100 km/h et atteint une vitesse maximum de 210 km/h – et même de 224 km/h avec le pack Sport – chiffre remarquable pour un SAV. Contrairement à la version Diesel, 3.0d de 204 ch, le moteur à combustion de 3 litres qui respecte la norme de dépollution UE4 s'avère plutôt glouton en consommation mixte (ville et autoroute). En tout-terrain, il s'octroie même une gorgée d'essence supplémentaire. En effet, ici aussi, la X3 administre la preuve de son savoir-faire : avec une guéabilité de 50 centimètres à 7 km/h, la maîtrise d'angles d'attaque et de fuite importants ainsi qu'un angle de rampe si remarquable que certains de ses concurrents risqueraient de faire la galipette.

The dominant figure among the compact all-rounders is the BMW X3 produced in Austria, a multi-purpose vehicle that feels at home on the road or in open country. Unfortunately, the very functional cockpit is somewhat soberly designed.

Platzhirsch unter den kompakten Allroundern ist der in Österreich gefertigte BMW X3, ein Mehrzweck-Mobil, das sich auf der Straße und im Gelände wohl fühlt. Leider ist das zwar sehr funktionelle Cockpit etwas nüchtern ausgefallen.

Le seigneur parmi les SUV compacts polyvalents est le BMW X3 fabriqué en Autriche, qui se sent aussi bien sur la route qu'en tout-terrain. Malheureusement, le cockpit certes très fonctionnel s'avère un peu sobre.

Reversible plastic bumpers encase the under section of the X3 with a ground clearance of 8 inches (20 centimeters) and fording capability of 20 inches (50 centimeters). The four-wheel drive system enables a smoothly variable dispersion of propulsion power.

Reversible Kunststoff-Stoßfänger umschließen das Unterteil des X3 mit 20 Zentimetern Bodenfreiheit und einer Wattiefe von 50 Zentimetern. Das Allrad-System ermöglicht eine stufenlos variable Verteilung der Antriebskräfte.

Les pare-chocs réversibles en matière plastique cernent la partie inférieure de la X3, dont la garde au sol est de 20 centimètres et qui offre une guéabilité de 50 centimètres. Le système de traction intégrale permet de répartir le couple en continu entre les deux essieux.

BMW 1 E81, E82, E87, E88 | 2004

The newcomer in 2004, the 1 series BMW, proved that it has what it takes to become top of the hotly contested compact class. It has interesting looks as well as sophisticated technology. A long wheelbase, short overhangs, and no high build; instead a car that, with a drag coefficient of 0.29, is aerodynamically a sports car. The trunk capacity, which ranges from 11.5 to 40.5 cu.ft (330 to 1150 liters) depending on the position of the rear seat, is rather low for a five-door car, but that really is its only weak point. When it was launched on the market, the 120i had the most powerful motor of all the 1 series cars: 150 bhp from a four-cylinder with variable valve train and continuously variable camshaft adjustment. The result: 0 to 62 mph (100 kph) in 8.7 seconds, and a top speed of 135 mph (217 kph).

In 2007, BMW responded to the trend towards greater efficiency, economy, and low emissions with a 143-bhp diesel engine with an impressive mileage of 52.3 mpg (4.5 liters per 100 km), and produced less than 193 grams per mile (120 g/km) of CO_2. The world's first all-aluminum diesel engine followed for the 2008 model, and had the latest common-rail technology and a variable twin turbo.

BMW introduced the 1 series coupé in the fall of 2007, available as a turbodiesel in two variants, and a lightning-fast

135i with a twin turbo that boosted the straight six-cylinder engine, borrowed from the 3 series, to 306 bhp. This turned the pretty little coupé into a "wolf in sheep's clothing" that had to be tamed electronically at 155 mph (250 kph). The acceleration time to 62 mph (100 kph) of 5.3 seconds also speaks for itself.

With this much power, the call for the appropriate passive safety features could not be ignored. These are concealed behind a chassis structure that has achieved excellent results in international consumer safety tests. Crash-optimized front seats and headrests also reduce the risk of injury in the event of rear collisions. It goes without saying that the impressive engine's dynamic stability and traction control, as well as an efficient braking system, are also included among the safety components.

Another 1 series BMW with two large, frameless doors followed just a few months after the coupé with the striking silhouette: the convertible was introduced with a choice of five engines. In addition, its appearance at the Detroit Motor Show in 2008 was celebrated with a further highlight: the electrohydraulic soft top was also available with silver threads worked into the fabric. They reflected the sunlight and created iridescent effects. What a show!

In der heiß umkämpften Kompaktklasse beweist der Neueinsteiger von 2004, der 1er-BMW, dass er das Zeug zum Klassenprimus hat. Neben aufwendiger Technik bietet er eine interessante Optik: Langer Radstand, kurze Überhänge und kein Hochbau, sondern ein Fahrzeug, das mit einem Luftwiderstandsbeiwert von 0,29 aerodynamisch schon zu den Sportwagen zählt. Mit einem Gepäckraum-Volumen, das je nach Rückbank-Positionierung zwischen 330 und 1150 Litern variiert, ist der Fünftürer zwar nur Mittelmaß, doch damit wäre der einzige Schwachpunkt bereits abgehakt. Bei Markteinführung stellt der 120i die stärkste Motorisierung dar: 150 PS aus einem Vierzylinder mit variablen Ventiltrieb und stufenloser Nockenwellen-Verstellung. Resultat: 8,7 Sekunden von 0 auf 100 km/h und eine Spitze von 217 km/h.

Auf den Trend zu Sparsamkeit und günstigen Emissionen reagiert BMW 2007 mit einem 143-PS-Dieselmotor, der nur 4,5 Liter schluckt und im CO_2-Ausstoß unter 120 Gramm pro Kilometer liegt. Für das Modelljahr 2008 folgt der weltweit erste Vollaluminium-Dieselmotor mit modernster Common-Rail-Technologie und variablem Twin-Turbo.

Im Herbst 2007 stellt BMW das 1er-Coupé vor, als Turbodiesel in zwei Varianten und auch als einen blitzschnellen 135i,

in dem ebenfalls ein Twin-Turbo den aus der 3er-Reihe ent- lehnten Sechszylinder-Reihenmotor auf 306 PS anheizt. Damit mutiert das hübsche kleine Coupé zum Wolf im Schafspelz und muss bei 250 km/h elektronisch gebändigt werden. Eine deutliche Sprache spricht auch der Beschleunigungswert von 5,3 Sekunden. Bei soviel Kraft wird natürlich auch der Ruf nach entsprechender passiver Sicherheit laut. Diese ver- birgt sich hinter einer Karosseriestruktur, die bei weltweiten Testreihen hervorragend abschneidet. Außerdem reduzieren crashoptimierte vordere Sitzlehnen und Kopfstützen das Verletzungsrisiko bei Auffahrunfällen. Dass das aufwendige Fahrwerk mit dynamischer Stabilitäts- und Traktionskontrolle sowie ein effizientes Bremssystem weitere Sicherheitskom- ponenten beitragen, versteht sich von selbst.

Nur wenige Monate nach dem Coupé mit der prägnanten Silhouette folgt ein weiterer 1er-BMW mit zwei großen Türen: das Cabrio mit fünf Motoren zum Einstand. Und dieser Akt wird bei der Detroit Motor Show im Januar 2008 gefeiert – mit einem weiteren Glanzpunkt: Optional kann das elektro- hydraulisch betätigte Softtop mit eingewirkten Silberfäden bestellt werden. Diese erzeugen bei Sonnenlichteinstrahlung changierende Glanzeffekte. What a show!

Dans la catégorie très disputée des voitures compactes, la nouvelle venue de BMW en 2004, la Série 1, prouve qu'elle a l'étoffe d'une première de la classe. En plus d'une débauche de technologies, son allure même suscite l'intérêt : empattement allongé, porte-à-faux réduit et pas de surélévation mais une voiture, qui avec un coefficient de traî- née de 0,29, compte déjà, d'un point de vue aérodynamique, parmi les voitures de sport. Avec un volume de coffre qui varie entre 330 et 1150 litres selon la position de la banquette arrière, cette cinq portes n'est certes que de taille moyenne mais ce serait bien là son seul point faible. Pour son lance- ment sur le marché, la 120i est dotée de la motorisation la plus puissante : 150 ch délivrés par un quatre-cylindres à distribu- tion variable et système de calage en continu des arbres à cames. Résultat : 0 à 100 km/h en 8,7 secondes et une vitesse de pointe de 217 km/h. Par souci d'économie et pour réduire le taux d'émission de CO_2, BMW réagit en 2007 avec un moteur diesel de 143 ch qui ne consomme que 4,5 litres pour un taux de rejet inférieur à 120 g/km. Suit en 2008 le premier moteur au monde entièrement en aluminium avec injection à rampe commune dernière génération et double turbo variable.

À l'automne 2007, BMW présente la Série 1 Coupé, pro- posée en deux versions turbo-diesel mais aussi sous une forme « ultrarapide », baptisée 135i, dans laquelle un Twin Turbo vient « doper » le moteur six-cylindres en ligne emprunté à la Série 3 lui permettant de développer 306 ch. Le joli petit coupé prend ainsi des airs de « loup déguisé en agneau » et doit être bridé électroniquement à une vitesse maximale de 250 km/h. L'accélération de 0 à 100 km/h en 5,3 secondes en dit long. Autant de puissance appelle naturellement un niveau adéquat de sécurité passive. On le retrouve derrière une structure de carrosserie qui excelle dans les tests inter- nationaux menés par des organismes indépendants. Les dos- siers et les appuie-têtes des sièges avant optimisés en cas de crash réduisent le risque de blessure en cas de collision par l'arrière. Il va de soi que d'autres composants de sécu- rité complètent le châssis à système de contrôle dynamique de stabilité et de motricité ainsi que le système de freinage haute performance.

Une autre BMW Série 1 munie de deux grandes portières sans montant est présentée quelques mois après le coupé à la silhouette si particulière : le cabriolet, proposé avec cinq versions de moteur. Cet événement est célébré au salon de l'automobile de Détroit en janvier 2008, avec une autre sur- prise : en option, la capote électrique en toile peut être tissée de fils d'argent qui chatoient au soleil. Quel spectacle !

Smiling, BMW design boss Christopher Bangle justified the relatively low 4'8"- (1.43-meter-) height of the compact 1 series BMW in an interview with the renowned specialist publication *auto motor und sport:* "After all, one is not supposed to stand in the vehicle."

Dass der kompakte 1er-BMW mit 1,43 Metern relativ niedrig ausgefallen ist, begründet BMW-Design-Chef Christopher Bangle in einem Interview mit der renommierten Fachpublikation *auto motor und sport* lächelnd: „Man soll in dem Auto schließlich nicht stehen."

Si la compacte BMW Série 1 est, avec 1,43 mètre, relativement basse, Christopher Bangle, le chef du design chez BMW, l'explique dans un sourire lors d'une interview accordée à la fameuse revue spécialisée *auto motor und sport :* « Il n'est pas prévu de rester debout dans la voiture. »

Special requests such as for leather seating are met promptly. The journey from supplier to incorporation at the Regensburg works takes only a few hours. One searches for the oil-level dipstick in the engine compartment in vain, for the oil level is recorded by an electronic sensor.

Sonderwünsche wie Ledersitze werden prompt erledigt. Der Weg vom Lieferanten bis zum Einbau im Werk Regensburg dauert nur wenige Stunden. Vergeblich wird man im Motorraum den Öl-Messstab suchen, denn den Pegelstand erfasst ein elektronischer Sensor.

Des options telles qu'une sellerie cuir sont disponibles presque instantanément. Le trajet entre le fournisseur et l'usine de montage de Ratisbonne ne prend que quelques heures. C'est en vain que l'on recherchera une jauge à huile dans le compartiment moteur, car le contrôle est désormais assuré par un capteur électronique.

This compact convertible has a conventional fabric cover. It opens and closes electro-hydraulically in just 22 seconds, and weighs a mere 264 lbs (120 kg) more than the 1 series Coupé. Neat, clearly structured, and always pleasing: the cockpit.

Mit klassischem Stoffverdeck präsentiert sich dieses Cabrio der Kompaktklasse. Es lässt sich elektro-hydraulisch binnen 22 Sekunden öffnen und schließen. Gegenüber dem 1er Coupé bringt es lediglich 120 Kilo mehr auf die Waage. Aufgeräumt, klar gegliedert und stets gut temporiert: das Cockpit.

Ce cabriolet compact est équipé d'une capote en tissu classique. Elle s'ouvre en 22 secondes grâce à un système hydroélectrique. Cette voiture ne pèse que 120 kg de plus que la Série 1 Coupé. L'habitacle reste clair, bien segmenté et toujours équilibré.

BMW 3 E90, E91, E92, E93 | 2006

April 2006 saw the arrival of the most powerful of four engine options at the debut of the 3 series Coupé, referred to internally as the E92: a twin-turbo straight six producing 306 bhp. Two sporty diesel engines add to the potential of this technology. The general impression of a coupé is generally determined by the side view. This BMW creation, with its flat, elongated roof with the traditional "Hofmeister kink," and the high beltline, is a clear indication of the independence of this design from the 3 series sedan (E90). The long wheelbase and passenger cell that is shifted to the rear further reinforce this impression. The front and rear aprons plus the door sills are early indicators of this vehicle's sporting ambitions.

This is also confirmed by the new turbo engine, celebrated by BMW as a world first. The six-cylinder with an all-aluminum housing boasts high precision injection in addition to the turbochargers. The 306 bhp and a maximum torque of 295 lb-ft (400 Nm) that can be achieved very quickly—and within a range of 1300 to 5000 rpm—are impressive. However, it will rev much higher, and is automatically cut off electronically at 155 mph (250 kph). The 335i

Coupé will happily sprint to 62 mph (100 kph) in 5.5 seconds, although the 6.1 seconds needed by the 330i with 272 bhp are also sprightly.

The turbochargers of the 330d deliver 231 bhp. This coupé achieves the sprint to 62 mph (100 kph) in 6.6 seconds, and also has to contend with the electronic cut-off at top speed. On the other hand, with an average consumption of just 36 mpg (6.5 liters per 100 km), it more than compensates with economy. More power was added with the update of 2008. With the optimum 50/50 weight distribution over the front and rear axles, double-pivot type suspension at the front, and a five-link axle at the rear, this coupé has a deluxe running gear that is further enhanced by dynamic stability control. The ABS is supported by two brake control systems. A continuous wear display informs the driver of the condition of the brake pads. And last but not least, dynamic traction control fuels the urge for sportier driving. The elegant interior—available with "M" facets on request—emphasizes the independence of this two-door car, the back seat of which has been lowered slightly so that rather than having to stoop, the occupants feel as comfortable as those in the front.

Mit einem Twin-Turbo-Reihensechszylinder, der 306 PS leistet, präsentiert sich im April 2006 die stärkste von vier Motoren-Varianten zur Premiere des 3er-Coupés, werksintern als E92 verzeichnet. Aber auch zwei sportliche Dieselmotoren untermauern das Potenzial dieser Technologie. Der Charakter eines Coupés wird generell von seiner Seitenansicht geprägt. Diese BMW-Kreation signalisiert mit ihrem flachen, gestreckt nach hinten fließendem Dach – mit dem traditionellen „Hofmeister-Knick" – und der hohen Gürtellinie die Eigenständigkeit des Designs gegenüber der 3er-Limousine (E90) deutlich. Langer Radstand und die nach hinten versetzte Fahrgastzelle verstärken diesen Eindruck nachhaltig. Front- und Heckschürze sowie die Seitenschweller verraten, dass dieser Wagen sportliche Ambitionen schon in der Einführungsphase hegt.

Das dokumentiert auch das neue Turbo-Triebwerk, von BMW als Weltpremiere gefeiert. Dieser Sechszylinder mit einem Vollaluminiumgehäuse verfügt neben den Ladern über eine so genannte High Precision Injection. 306 PS und das maximale Drehmoment von 400 Newtonmetern, ohne spürbare Verzögerung aufgebaut und einen Bereich von 1300 bis 5000 Touren abdeckend, sind beeindruckend. Doch der PS-Spender dreht noch wesentlich höher und wird bei 250 km/h elektronisch in seine Schranken gewiesen. 5,5 Sekunden

benötigt das 335i Coupé im Sprint auf 100 km/h, aber auch der 330i mit 272 PS gibt sich mit 6,1 Sekunden recht munter.

Die Turbolader des 330d entfachen immerhin noch 231 PS. Dieses Coupé schafft den Sprint in 6,6 Sekunden und muss sich bei der Topspeed ebenfalls die elektronische Begrenzung gefallen lassen. Andererseits setzt es mit einem durchschnittlichen Verbrauch von nur 6,5 Litern neue Akzente in puncto Sparsamkeit. Beim Facelift 2008 wurde zusätzliche Power aktiviert. Mit einer optimalen Gewichtsverteilung von 50 zu 50 Prozent auf Vorder- und Hinterachse, Doppelgelenk-Zugstrebenachsen mit Federbein vorn und einer Fünflenkerachse hinten bietet dieses Coupé ein Fahrwerk der Extraklasse, das von einer dynamischen Stabilitätskontrolle unterstützt wird. Gleich zwei Bremskontrollsysteme stehen dem ABS zur Seite. Eine Verschleißanzeige informiert den Fahrer kontinuierlich über den Bremsbelag-Zustand. Last, but not least schürt eine dynamische Traktionskontrolle die Lust auf eine sportlich orientierte Fahrweise. Das edle Interieur – auf Wunsch auch mit M-Facetten – unterstreicht die Eigenständigkeit des Zweitürers, dessen hintere Sitzbank ein wenig nach unten versenkt wurde, damit die „Hinterbänkler" nicht den Kopf einziehen müssen, sondern sich komfortabel wie in der ersten Reihe fühlen dürfen.

Le six-cylindres en ligne technologie double turbo de 306 ch, le plus puissant des quatre moteurs proposés, a été présenté en avril 2006 lors de la grande première de la Série 3 Coupé, appelée E92 en interne. Deux moteurs diesel sportifs complètent également le potentiel de cette technologie. Le caractère d'un coupé est en général signalé par son profil. Avec sa ligne de toit basse filant jusqu'à l'arrière, avec le traditionnel « pli Hofmeister », et sa ceinture de caisse haute, cette création BMW proclame haut et fort l'indépendance de son design par rapport à la Série 3 berline (E90). L'empattement long et un habitacle très en recul renforcent efficacement cette impression. Les tabliers avant et arrière ainsi que les bas de caisse révèlent que cette voiture possède déjà dès son lancement des ambitions sportives.

Impressions confirmées par le nouveau moteur turbo, célébré par BMW comme une première mondiale. Ce six-cylindres au carter entièrement en aluminium dispose, en plus des turbocompresseurs, de la technologie High Precision Injection. Les 306 ch, le couple maximal de 400 Nm sans interruption notable du transfert de la puissance motrice et une plage de régimes allant de 1300 à 5000 tours, sont impressionnants. Cependant, le régime moteur est considérablement plus élevé, mais la vitesse est bridée électroniquement

à 250 km/h. Il faut 5,5 secondes au coupé 335i pour passer de 0 à 100 km/h, mais le 330i avec ses 272 ch s'avère déjà très alerte avec un temps de 6,1 secondes.

Les turbocompresseurs de la 330d développent tout de même 231 ch. Ce coupé passe ainsi de 0 à 100 km/h en 6,6 secondes et doit lui aussi se plier à la limitation électronique de la vitesse maximale. Par ailleurs, avec une consommation moyenne de seulement 6,5 litres, il marque des points nouveaux en matière d'économie. Lors de son lifting en 2008, une puissance supplémentaire a été débridée. Avec une répartition optimale de la charge par essieu à 50:50, un essieu avant à double articulation des pivots de fusée et un essieu arrière à cinq bras, ce coupé possède un châssis de toute première classe, soutenu par un système de contrôle dynamique de stabilité. Deux systèmes de contrôle du freinage secondent l'ABS. Une indication continue d'usure informe le conducteur sur l'état des plaquettes de frein. Enfin et non des moindres, un système de contrôle dynamique de motricité attise le plaisir d'une conduite sportive. L'intérieur raffiné, en version M en option, souligne le caractère unique de cette deux portes dont la banquette arrière a été un peu descendue pour que les passagers n'aient pas à rentrer la tête dans les épaules pour se sentir aussi à l'aise que sur les sièges avant.

Less "fancy" than its predecessor, this 3 series (E92) is the successful continuation of the tradition of 2-door BMW coupés. Another treat for the eyes: the "powerhouse" and interior architecture.

Schnörkelloser als sein Vorgänger setzt dieser 3er (Baureihe E92) die Tradition zweitüriger BMW-Coupés erfolgreich fort. Ebenfalls eine Augenweide: das „Kraftwerk" und die Innenraum-Architektur.

Moins tarabiscotée que son prédécesseur, cette Série 3 (E92) perpétue la tradition des coupés BMW 2 portes de manière très réussie. Véritable plaisir pour les yeux : le moteur et l'architecture de l'habitacle.

The "Powerdome" on the hood of the M3—seen here: the cabrio—conceals a modern lightweight V8 of 420 bhp. Decidedly conservative: the stick shift for manual insertion of the six gears, ideally with double clutching.

Unter dem „Powerdome" auf der Haube des M3 – hier seine Cabrio-Version – verbirgt sich ein moderner Leichtbau-V8 mit 420 PS. Geradezu konservativ: der Schaltknüppel zum manuellen Einlegen der sechs Gänge – am besten mit Zwischengas.

Le «powerdome» du capot de la M3, ici en version cabriolet, dissimule un V8 moderne de construction légère qui développe 420 ch. Très classique: le levier de changement de vitesses pour passer manuellement les six vitesses, idéalement avec double embrayage.

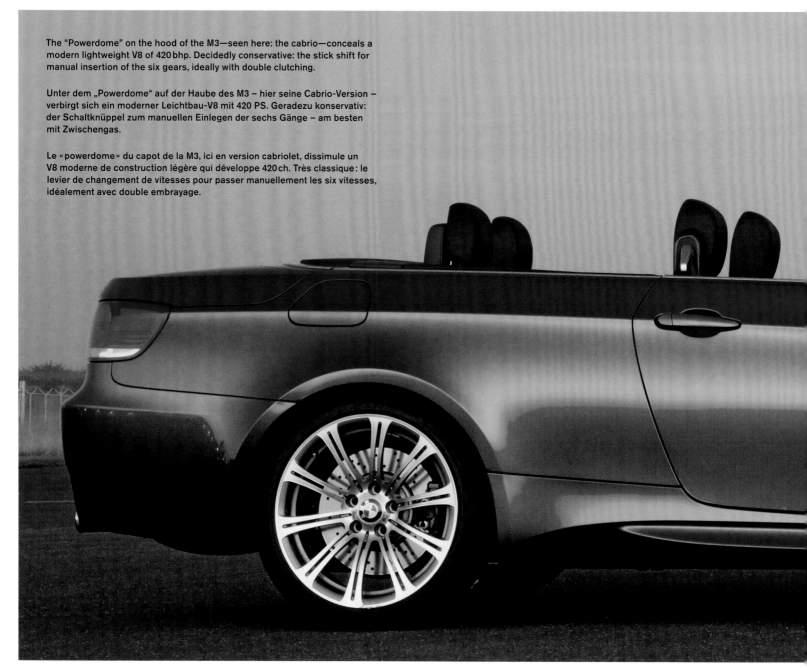

The editorial for the X5 brochure, tacked onto the X5 xDrive 40d is almost a laudation. Despite its ebullience, however, it captures the spirit of this SAV from Spartanburg, South Carolina: "In spite of its size, elegance and versatility, the X5 oozes a dignified restraint. It boasts outstanding harmony of power, dynamism and economy, thanks to the latest BMW EfficientDynamics technology."

The fact that the BMW diesel engines in the X5—three inline six-cylinder engines with 245 bhp (30d), 306 bhp (40d) and 381 bhp (M50d)—achieve high torques even at low speeds, despite only drawing off the diesel tank, is thanks to the single (30d), twin (40d) or triple (M50d) turbochargers and the common-rail diesel injection.

The X5 M50d is the latest craze in the second X5 generation, with enough M power and torque—546 lb-ft—to make its driver feel like the king of the road, even in the city and on the highway. Its 4905 lbs accelerate from 0 to 62 mph in 5.4 seconds, and at 155 mph the driver of the M50d speeds into sports car territory on the 20-inch double-spoke type 333M aluminum alloy wheels.

As an alternative to diesel, BMW also offer two engines from the gasoline portfolio: the 35i with 306 bhp and the 50i with 407 bhp. With these systems, the X5's natural racecar qualities still shine through, too: 6.6 seconds for the 35i and 5.5 for the turbo-V8 of the 50i. No matter what's under the hood, the X5's chic look and classy interior show that this is no off-roader. Its rigid chassis structure is designed primarily as protection in case of a collision, not to deal with the untamed countryside.

Thanks to its air vent control, the sensors of which shorten the engine's warm-up phase and provide support for the cooling system, large fluctuations in temperature are no problem for the X5. Its downhill control is great for getting down alpine passes; the fording depth of about 19 inches and the slope angles or ground clearance make no difference.

However, it much prefers stealing the limelight as an imposing SAV, with a matt aluminum undershield that likes to keep its distance from rocks and boulders. It is more at home on the boulevard than on overgrown forest trails, though the X5 requires neither the M Sport package nor the cornucopia of BMW's Individual range for the latter.

Das Editorial zum X5-Prospekt, aufgehängt am X5 xDrive 40d, gleicht einer Laudatio, die zwar etwas überschwänglich formuliert ist, doch den Kern dieses SAV aus Spartanburg in South Carolina trifft: „Trotz seiner Größe, Eleganz und Variabilität pflegt der X5 eine vornehme Zurückhaltung. Bemerkenswert ist der Dreiklang aus Kraft, Dynamik und Sparsamkeit. Dafür sorgt der neueste Stand der BMW-Efficient-Dynamics-Technologie."

Dass die BMW-Dieselmotoren im X5 – drei Reihensechszylinder mit 245 PS (30d), 306 PS (40d) und 381 PS (M50d) – ein hohes Drehmoment bereits im niedrigen Drehzahlbereich erzielen und dennoch nur aus dem Dieseltank nippen, liegt an den ein (30d), zwei (40d) oder drei (M50d) Turboladern und der Common-Rail-Direkteinspritzung.

Der X5 M50d ist der letzte Schrei der zweiten X5-Generation. Mit derart viel M-Power und einem Drehmoment von 740 Newtonmetern ist man auch im Straßenverkehr und auf Autobahnen ein „King of the Road". 2225 Kilo werden hier aus dem Stand in 5,4 Sekunden auf 100 km/h beschleunigt, und mit 250 km/h schwingt sich der M50d-Lenker auf seinen 20-Zoll-Leichtmetallrädern, Typ 333M mit Doppelspeichen, in sportliche Bereiche auf.

BMW X5, X6 E70, E71|2006

Als Alternative zu den Dieselmotoren bietet BMW zwei Triebwerke aus den Benziner-Regalen an: den 35i mit 306 PS und den 50i mit 407 PS. Auch mit diesen Aggregaten sind dem schweren X5 Sprinterqualitäten in die Wiege gelegt: 6,6 Sekunden für den 35i und 5,5 Sekunden für den Turbo-V8 des 50i. Dass der X5, ganz gleich, wie motorisiert, nicht fürs Gelände gedacht ist, verraten schon seine schicke Gewandung und das noble Interieur. Seine steife Karosserie-Struktur soll primär eher Schutz bei Unfällen gewährleisten und nicht den Unwegsamkeiten der Natur trotzen müssen.

Dank seiner Luftklappensteuerung, deren Sensor die Warmlaufphase des Motors verkürzt, beziehungsweise seine Kühlung unterstützt, machen große Temperaturunterschiede dem X5 nichts aus. Seine Bergabfahrkontrolle mag gut für die Abfahrten von Alpenpässen sein. Die Wattiefe von immerhin knapp 50 Zentimetern sowie Böschungs- und Rampenwinkel spielen bei ihm keine Rolle.

Viel lieber steht er im Rampenlicht als imposanter SAV, dessen Unterfahrschutz in Alu-Mattlack nie mit Gesteinsbrocken Bekanntschaft machen möchte. Sein Auftritt gehört eher den Boulevards als verwucherten Waldwegen. Für letztere bräuchte ein X5 weder ein M-Sportpaket noch das Füllhorn des BMW-Individual-Angebots.

Le texte de la brochure de la X5, basé sur la X5 xDrive 40d, est on ne peut plus dithyrambique, mais malgré son exubérance, il saisit assez fidèlement l'esprit de ce SUV sportif produit à Spartanburg, en Caroline du Sud: «Malgré ses dimensions, son élégance et sa polyvalence, la X5 cultive l'art de la retenue. Elle offre un accord parfait de puissance, de dynamisme et d'économie grâce à la dernière technologie EfficientDynamics de BMW.»

Si les moteurs diesel de la X5 – trois moteurs six cylindres en ligne de 245 ch (30d), 306 ch (40d) et 381 ch (M50d) – atteignent un couple élevé dès les basses vitesses, en ne tirant que sur le réservoir diesel, c'est grâce aux turbocompresseurs (un dans la 30d, deux dans la 40d et trois dans la M50d) et à l'injection directe à rampe commune.

La X5 M50d est le joyau de la deuxième génération des X5, avec assez de puissance «M» et de couple (740 Nm) pour que prendre place derrière son volant transforme quiconque en «roi du bitume», aussi bien en ville que sur autoroute. Ses 2225 kilos accélèrent de 0 à 100 km/h en 5,4 secondes, et à 250 km/h, le conducteur de la M50d s'engouffre sur le terrain des voitures de sport sur ses jantes en alliage léger 20 pouces type 333M à rayons doubles.

Comme solution de rechange au diesel, BMW propose aussi deux moteurs à essence: le 35i avec 306 ch et le 50i avec 407 ch. Même avec ces systèmes, les qualités de sprinter de la X5 restent évidentes: 6,6 secondes pour la 35i et 5,5 secondes pour le V8 turbo de la 50i. Peu importe la motorisation, les beaux atours de la X5 et son intérieur noble indiquent bien qu'elle n'est pas faite pour les chemins de terre. La structure rigide de son châssis est conçue principalement pour protéger en cas de collision, et non pour se mesurer à la nature sauvage.

Grâce à son système de commande des volets d'aération, dont le capteur raccourcit la phase de chauffage du moteur et assiste le refroidissement, les fluctuations de température ne sont pas un problème pour la X5. Son contrôle de motricité en descente est parfait lorsqu'on revient de la montagne. La profondeur guéable de presque 50 centimètres et l'angle de la pente ne font aucune différence.

Ce SUV sportif imposant est plus à l'aise sur les boulevards que sur les pistes de forêt embroussaillées et son dispositif anti-encastrement en aluminium mat préfère rester à une distance prudente des chemins pierreux. À la campagne, la X5 ne saurait que faire d'une finition M Sport ou de l'abondance d'options BMW Individual.

Though more at home on the boulevard than in open country, the X5 xDrive 40d always cuts a fine pose. Its turbo-diesel and common-rail diesel injection give the wheels 306 bhp.

Eine gute Figur, wenngleich eher auf einem Boulevard als im Gelände, macht der X5 xDrive 40d, dessen Turbodiesel mit Common-Rail-Einspritzung 306 PS auf die Räder bringt.

Plus à l'aise sur les avenues que sur terrain accidenté, la X5 xDrive 40d est photogénique en diable. Son moteur turbo-diesel avec injection à rampe commune développe 306 ch.

Below the belt, this is a chunky four-wheel SUV; above, a very pretty coupé: BMW became the first automobile manufacturer to break into a new vehicle category with the X6. The company invented the genre name "Sports Activity Coupé" for this unusual combination of boulevard stallion and multi-purpose vehicle.

Unter der Gürtellinie ein stämmiger Allradler aus dem so genannten SUV-Segment und oben herum ein hübsches Coupé: Mit dem X6 stößt BMW als erster Automobilhersteller in eine neue Fahrzeugkategorie vor. Für diese ungewöhnliche Symbiose aus Boulevard-Hengst und Crossover-Muli erfand BMW die Genre-Bezeichnung „Sports Activity Coupé".

Sous la ceinture de caisse un tout-terrain robuste de la gamme SUV, au-dessus un joli coupé: avec la X6, BMW est le premier constructeur à tenter sa chance dans une nouvelle catégorie de véhicules. La marque a décidé de baptiser ce nouveau genre, inhabituelle symbiose entre un cheval de course citadin et un mulet crossover, «Sports Activity Coupé».

Anyone getting into the new flagship of the Munich marque will find themselves in seventh heaven: the fifth generation of the 7 series—with smoother lines than its predecessor—embodies a new interpretation of luxury and high-tech together under the same roof. Lightweight construction, dynamic driving characteristics, comfort, and an innovative engine design are key features of this beautiful automobile. However, its launch during a period that saw the most serious financial catastrophe since the Wall Street Crash of 1929 meant that it was confronted with a somewhat smaller clientele. Still, this clientele was offered a choice of three interesting engines to mark the debut of the 2008 7 series: a 3-liter aluminum turbodiesel; its gasoline counterpart, also to be found in the 335i, with two turbochargers; and—last but not least—the 4.4-liter twin turbo with 407 bhp. A hybrid version of the latter, the 750i, added to the competition, reducing consumption by an impressive 15 percent for the sake of the environment—a BMW message that now also included the luxury end of the market.

Unlimited Internet access; a sound system with DVD player; hard disk memory for audio files and navigation system;

speed limit display; and front seats with integrated screens, also available for TV reception—the interior boasted a wide range of technical delights. Another was the "iDrive" with its many and versatile programs, and menu button ideally situated in the vicinity of the electronic gear shift on the center console. The array of control elements made up of many individual items blended harmoniously with the tasteful interior. With full air-conditioning reaching to the farthest corner, the 7 positively tempted the potential customer to climb aboard and make themselves comfortable. If desired, the rear seats operate a clever massage cycle of wave-like movements to relax the muscles in a tense manager's back—from neck to lumbar region.

Even those who are more sports-minded will thoroughly enjoy this spacious sedan once they get behind the wheel. The chassis has a number of stabilizing systems to provide a safe and pleasurable driving experience, even when cornering at speed. When accelerating, the 740i gets to the 62 mph (100 kph) point in just 5.9 seconds—definitely a thoroughbred stallion! Radar sensors monitor the oncoming traffic and, once they have checked the blind spot, indicate when it is safe to overtake.

Auf Wolke Sieben darf schweben, wer das neue Flaggschiff der Münchener Marke besteigt. Die fünfte Generation der 7er-Reihe – mit geglätteter Linienführung gegenüber dem Vorgänger – verkörpert eine neue Interpretation von Luxus und Hightech unter einem Dach. Leichtbau, dynamische Fahreigenschaften, Komfort und ein innovatives Motorenangebot kennzeichnen diesen Beau. Doch dessen Markteinführung, just in einer Zeit, die von der gewaltigsten Finanzmisere seit dem „schwarzen Freitag" 1929 gebeutelt wird, sieht sich einer geschrumpften Klientel konfrontiert. Dieser werden zum Einstand des 7ers, Baujahr 2008, drei interessante Antriebseinheiten angeboten: ein Dreiliter-Turbodiesel aus Aluminium, dessen Benziner-Pendant, das auch im 335i mit zwei Turboladern arbeitet und *last but not least* der 4,4-Liter-V8 Biturbo mit 407 PS. Letzterer, als 750i apostrophiert, soll auch als Hybrid-Bomber in den Kampf um die Kundengunst ziehen. Den Verbrauch um satte 15 Prozent senken – der Umwelt zuliebe: Diese BMW-Botschaft kommt auch im Luxussegment an.

Unbeschränkter Internet-Zugang, Soundsystem mit DVD-Laufwerk, Festplattenspeicher für Audiodateien und Navigationssystem, Speed-Limit-Anzeige sowie Vordersitze

BMW 7 F01, F02 | 2008

mit integrierten Bildschirmen, optional auch für den TV-Empfang: Das Cockpit wartet mit technischen Leckereien auf, zu denen sich noch die vielfältigen Programme des „iDrives" gesellen. Der entsprechende Menü-Knopf ruht direkt in der Nachbarschaft des elektronischen Gangwahlschalters auf der Mittelkonsole. Das aus vielen Teilen bestehende Puzzle der Bedieneinheiten fügt sich harmonisch in das geschmackvolle Interieur ein. Vollklimatisiert bis in den letzten Winkel, laden die üppigen Fauteuils des 7ers zum Platznehmen ein. Auf Wunsch vermitteln die Sitze im Fond einen ausgeklügelten Massage-Zyklus mit wellenartigen Bewegungen zur Lockerung der Muskulatur vom Thorax- bis zum Lendenbereich eines verspannten Manager-Rückens.

Aber auch sportlich orientierten Menschen hinterm Volant dürfte diese große Limousine gefallen. Das mit mehreren Stabilitätssystemen bestückte Fahrwerk bereitet selbst in schnellen Kurvenpassagen sicheren Fahrgenuss. Beim „Aufgalopp" des 740i ist die 100-km/h-Marke bereits nach 5,9 Sekunden erreicht – ein „Vollbluthengst"! Fahrerlebnis ohne Hindernisse: Radarsensoren überwachen den Gegenverkehr und geben, nachdem sie den toten Winkel abgetastet haben, den Weg zum souveränen Überholen frei.

Le nouveau vaisseau amiral de la marque munichoise accède au «7e ciel». La cinquième génération de la Série 7, aux lignes adoucies par rapport à ses prédécesseurs, incarne une nouvelle interprétation du luxe et du high-tech sous un même toit. Construction légère, conduite dynamique, confort et offre de moteurs innovante caractérisent cette merveille. Pourtant, son introduction sur le marché, à une époque menacée par la plus grande crise financière depuis le «vendredi noir» de 1929, se voit confrontée à une clientèle réduite. Au lancement de la Série 7, millésime 2008, trois unités motrices intéressantes sont proposées: un diesel 3 litres turbo en aluminium, l'équivalent à essence à deux turbocompresseurs qui propulse aussi la 335i et, «last but not least», le V8 4,4 litres bi-turbo de 407 ch. Ce dernier, baptisé 750i, doit également attaquer le marché avec un modèle hybride. Consommation réduite de 15%, plus grand respect de l'environnement: BMW dispense aussi ce message dans le segment du luxe.

Accès Internet illimité, système audio avec lecteur DVD, disque dur pour les données audio et le système de navigation, indication des limitations de vitesse et sièges avant avec écrans intégrés et réception TV en option: l'habitacle

propose donc un certain nombre de raffinements techniques auxquels viennent s'ajouter les divers programmes de l'«iDrive». La molette du menu du système est situé directement à côté du levier électronique de vitesses sur la console centrale. Le puzzle à quatre pièces des unités de commande s'intègre harmonieusement dans l'habitacle très élégant. Avec la climatisation automatique 4 zones, les fauteuils plus que confortables de la Série 7 invitent à prendre place dans la voiture. En option, les sièges effectuent un cycle de massages aux mouvements ondulatoires pour relaxer, du thorax aux lombaires, les muscles tendus du dos des managers.

Cette grande berline devrait cependant aussi plaire aux conducteurs avides de sensations sportives. Le châssis équipé de plusieurs systèmes de stabilité offre un grand plaisir de conduite en toute sécurité même à vitesse élevée dans les trajectoires en courbe. Départ arrêté, la 740i passe la barre des 100 km/h en 5,9 secondes – un vrai cheval de course! Une expérience de conduite dénuée de tout obstacle: des capteurs radar contrôlent la circulation en sens inverse et indiquent, après avoir vérifié l'angle mort, que la voie est libre pour un dépassement parfaitement maîtrisé.

The 7 series BMW of 2008 radiates sophistication and elegance. As the 740i, the luxurious sedan has the popular 6-cylinder in-line engine that produces 320 bhp.

Souveränität und Eleganz strahlt der 7er BMW, Jahrgang 2008, aus. Als 740i verfügt die luxuriöse Limousine über den bewährten 6-Zylinder-Reihenmotor, der 320 PS entfaltet.

La Série 7 millésime 2008 de BMW rayonne de majesté et d'élégance. La version 740i de cette luxueuse berline est équipée d'un moteur 6 cylindres en ligne qui développe 320 ch.

It's time to bid farewell to the classic roadster fabric cover; to update the Bangle design swage that printed a Zorro-style "Z" on the current Z4 flank; to elongate the "duck's tail" into a harmonious trailing end to the trunk, into which a two-part hardtop now disappears in 20 seconds; and include an aggressive, flat BMW kidney grille that tapers in a V shape. The new Z4 is sporty, magnificent, and this time from Bavaria—unlike its predecessors, it is made in Regensburg and not in Spartanburg, SC. The two-part folding roof in aluminum provides excellent protection. Although when folded down it leaves only 6.4 cu.ft (180 liters) of storage space, this increases by 4.6 cu.ft (130 liters) when the hard top is in place.

Three engine variants were available when the Z4 sDrive was launched in May 2009—all of them classic straight 6-cylinders, with the 3-liter engine of the 35i providing additional power courtesy of its twin turbo and direct injection (high precision injection). The optional "seven-speed sport automatic double-clutch transmission" catapults this Z4 to 62 mph (100 kph) in only 5.1 seconds. The bandwidth of the maximum torque of 250 lb-ft (400 Nm) ranges from 1300 to 5000 rpm. Unfortunately, here too the driving fun suffers an electronic cut-off at 155 mph (250 kph). However, thanks to the excellent three-stage driving dynamic of this roadster-coupé combination, winding roads do still offer the ultimate driving experience. This is accompanied by an experience in sound—especially when shifting down through the gears using the double clutch.

The tasteful interior with plenty of useful storage niches mean that there is even room behind the seats for a briefcase or document holder. No less practical is the between-rows opening that will accommodate two pairs of skis in winter. Golf-lovers can stow two full bags with normal dimensions. After all, this sporty two-seater isn't a family vehicle that has to find room for everything except the kitchen sink!

With its extremely successful all-round concept, the Z4 does not have to fight for customers' favors, and one long-standing member of the BMW M team says "We're going to make sure it's a bestseller." Bad times, good times?

Abschied vom klassischen Roadster-Stoffverdeck, Retuschierung der Bangle-Design-Sicken, die der bisherigen Z4-Flanke ein Zorro-Z aufgedrückt hatten, Streckung des „Entenbürzels" in eine harmonische Abrisskante auf dem Kofferraum, in dem sich jetzt ein zweiteiliges Hardtop in 20 Sekunden versenkt, und eine aggressive, flache BMW-Niere, die V-förmig zusammenläuft: Der neue Z4 ist ein sportlicher Beau aus Bayern. Im Gegensatz zu seinen Vorgängern wird er nicht in Spartanburg, USA, sondern in Regensburg gebaut. „Ein feste Burg" ist auch das zweiteilige Faltdach aus Aluminium: Es lässt in versenktem Zustand zwar nur 180 Liter Stauraum übrig, doch mit geschlossenem Hardtop erhöht sich die Ladekapazität um 130 Liter.

Drei Motorvarianten begleiten die Markteinführung des Z4 sDrive im Mai 2009 – allesamt klassische 6-Zylinder in Reihe, wobei das 3-Liter-Triebwerk des 35i zusätzlichen Schub durch seinen Twin-Turbo und die Direkteinspritzung (High Precision Injection) erfährt. Mit dem optionalen „7-Gang Sport-Automatic Getriebe mit Doppelkupplung" lässt sich dieser Z4 in 5,1 Sekunden auf 100 km/h katapultieren. Die Bandbreite

BMW Z4 E89 | 2009

des maximalen Drehmoments von 400 Nm reicht von 1300 bis 5000 Touren. Leider resultiert auch hier der Fahrspaß bei 250 Sachen in einem Interruptus elektronischer Art. Dank der hervorragenden dreistufigen Fahrdynamik dieses Roadster-Coupé-Unisonos bescheren kurvenreiche Strecken dann doch noch den ersehnten „Driving-Orgasmus". Dazu gesellt sich ein akustisches Erlebnis, besonders beim Runterschalten mit Zwischengas.

Das geschmackvoll zusammengestellte Interieur mit vielen praktischen Ablagenischen lässt sogar hinter den Sitzen Platz für eine Aktentasche oder Dokumentenmappe. Nicht minder praktisch: die Durchreiche für zwei Paar Ski im Winter. Golfer können zwei gefüllte Bags mit normalen Dimensionen unterbringen. Schließlich ist dieser sportliche Zweisitzer keine Familienkutsche, in der Sack und Pack verstaut werden müssen!

Mit seiner rundum gelungenen Gesamtkonzeption muss der Z4 nicht um die Gunst der Kunden buhlen, und „wir machen eine gut gehende Granate daraus", so einer der langjährig gedienten BMW-M-Mannen. Schlechte Zeiten, gute Zeiten?

Abandon de la capote en toile classique sur les roadsters, réinterprétation du design imaginé par Bangle qui gravait un Z à la Zorro sur les flancs des Z4 précédentes, allongement de la « queue de canard » en une saillie harmonieuse sur le coffre dans lequel se glisse désormais en 20 secondes un toit rigide en deux parties, et enfin une retouche plus agressive des naseaux BMW désormais plats et en forme de V : la nouvelle Z4 est une vraie beauté sportive à la bavaroise. Contrairement à ses prédécesseurs, elle n'est d'ailleurs pas construite à Spartanburg aux États-Unis mais à Ratisbonne en Allemagne. Le toit escamotable en aluminium composé de deux parties est bien solide : s'il ne laisse que 180 litres de volume de stockage lorsqu'il est ouvert, la capacité de chargement augmente de 130 litres lorsqu'il est fermé.

Trois moteurs différents sont proposés lors du lancement sur le marché de la Z4 sDrive en mai 2009 – tous des six-cylindres en ligne classiques, le moteur 3 litres de la 35i offrant une poussée supplémentaire grâce à son double turbo et à la technologie d'injection directe (high precision injection). La « boîte de vitesses automatique Sport 7 rapports à double embrayage DKG » proposée en option catapulte cette

Z4 de 0 à 100 km/h en 5,1 secondes. Le couple maximal est de 400 Nm pour des régimes allant de 1300 à 5000 tours. Malheureusement, le plaisir de conduite s'arrête ici aussi à 250 km/h par un système électronique de limitation de la vitesse. Grâce à l'exceptionnelle régulation de comportement dynamique à trois modes de ce coupé-roadster, les itinéraires les plus sinueux procurent néanmoins toujours une véritable extase au volant à laquelle se greffe une expérience acoustique inoubliable, en particulier lors du double débrayage au rétrogradage.

L'intérieur raffiné aux nombreux vide-poches très pratiques réserve même de la place pour une sacoche ou un porte-documents à l'arrière des sièges. Tout aussi pratique : la trappe à skis prévue pour deux paires de skis en hiver. Les golfeurs peuvent emporter quant à eux deux sacs de taille standard bien remplis. Mais après tout, cette deux places sportive n'est pas une voiture familiale où entasser quantité de bagages !

Avec un concept d'ensemble très réussi, la Z4 n'a pas besoin d'implorer pour obtenir les faveurs des clients et « elle va faire l'effet d'une bombe », comme l'a déclaré un des capitaines de BMW M. Une éclaircie en temps de crise ?

Power under the hood: twin turbo on the Z4 sDrive 35i—and the corresponding looks. The Z4 generation E89 with aluminum folding roof replaces the roadster and the coupé.

Stark unter der Haube – Biturbo-Power beim Z4 sDrive 35i – und ansprechende Optik: Die Z4-Generation E89 mit Aluminium-Faltdach ersetzt Roadster und Coupé gleichermaßen.

De la puissance sous le capot, avec le Biturbo-Power sur la Z4 sDrive 35i, et une allure en adéquation : la génération E89 de la Z4 avec son toit escamotable remplace le roadster et le coupé.

BMW X1 E84 | 2009

BMW's SUVs come in a wide range of guises. A development that only shows the due respect to the 7 series as the flagship. The fact that the little 1 series is elevated to this pepped-up category with the "intelligent" all-wheel xDrive system is in line with the company's strategy of occupying as many niches as possible, especially in the lower and mid-segments. The little "X" had its debut at the Frankfurt IAA 2009 under BMW's motto of "efficient dynamics"—lots of driving fun despite a further reduction in fuel consumption and lower CO_2 emissions—and delighted with its tremendous performance and features: from the 143 bhp of the 18d to the 258 bhp of the xDrive 28i. Thanks to the ample exterior dimensions of 14 ft 7 in × 5 ft 11 in × 5 ft 1 in (4454 × 1798 × 1545 mm), the X1 has a commodious capacity of 17 cu.ft (480 liters) with the rear seat back in the "cargo position." Anyone who wants to—or has to—sit in the back with the backrest in this position has to adopt an extremely upright position. Of course, the back seats can also be folded down individually in order to transport a certain amount of "cargo." The capacity is then increased to just over 47 cu.ft (1350 liters). Pretty impressive for a compact SUV!

All kinds of storage areas, bottle and cup holders—slot-in or integrated in the back armrest—glasses compartment above the windscreen, net in rear storage area, or the between-rows openings for a ski and snowboard bag, testify to a functional, practical interior. Countless goodies that are available for a surcharge enhance this organization system.

The technology also has a number of treats for the "driver of this thoroughbred." It goes without saying that all X1s meet all EU5 standards, although it must also be said that the brake energy regeneration and flat tire monitor are standard features on the X1. The sDrive 18d is particularly efficient; with rear wheel drive the average mileage is 38 mpg (6.2 liters per 100 km in the EU test cycle) with a CO_2 emission of just 219 grams per mile (136 g/km).

Of course, every X1 also has a balanced chassis with double-joint spring strut front axle and multi-joint rear axle, dynamic stability control, a control system for the brake torque in fast corners, and the standard SUV hill descent control (HDC). The variable distribution of the drive torque between the front and rear wheels (xDrive versions only) is quite advantageous in rural areas with lots of dirt tracks.

With door reinforcements for maximum passenger safety and chassis deformation elements front and rear that absorb impacts at up to 10 mph (15 kph), as well as six well-positioned airbags, the passenger cell—which is already pretty stable—can truly be called a safety package. An optional safety element that is highly recommended is the special BMW telematics which, in the event of an accident, automatically transmits an emergency call with details of the vehicle's location and other information. All in all, the X1 most certainly does not have to hide from its big brothers. Thanks to its optimum axle load distribution and relatively low center of gravity, excellent traction, and direction stability, it is well-balanced all round. Which makes for the ultimate driving pleasure!

X-beliebig präsentieren sich die SUVs von BMW. Eine Entwicklung, die nur dem 7er als Flaggschiff den nötigen Respekt zollt. Dass auch der kleine 1er in diese aufgebockte Kategorie mit dem „intelligenten" Allradsystem xDrive erhoben wird, gehört zur Firmenstrategie, möglichst viele Nischen gerade im unteren und mittleren Fahrzeug-Segment zu besetzen. Auf der Frankfurter IAA 2009, die BMW ganz unter das Motto „Efficient Dynamics" stellt – viel Fahrspaß trotz erneut reduzierten Energieverbrauchs und weniger CO_2-Emission – debütiert der kleine „X" mit einem großen Leistungsspektrum: von 143 PS des 18d bis 258 PS, die der xDrive 28i auf die Räder verteilt. Durchaus stattliche Außenmaße (4454 × 1798 × 1545 mm) ermöglichen dem X1 in der „Cargostellung" der hinteren Rücklehne ein Laderaum-Volumen von 480 Litern. Wer bei dieser Lehnen-Position im Fond Platz nehmen will oder muss, wird zu einer äußerst aufrechten Haltung genötigt. Natürlich lassen sich die Rücksitze auch einzeln umlegen, um wirklich etwas „Cargo" transportieren zu können. Hierfür steht dann ein Raum von 1350 Litern zur Verfügung. Für einen SUV der Kompaktklasse recht ordentlich!

Ablagefächer aller Art, Flaschen- und Getränkehalter, aufsteckbar oder in die hintere Armauflage integriert, Brillenfach im Dachhimmel, Gepäckraum-Trenn-Netz oder die Durchreiche für eine Ski- und Snowboard-Tasche künden von einer funktionalen, praxisorientierten Inneneinrichtung. Ungezählte Goodies bereichern – gegen Aufpreis – dieses Ordnungssystem.

Auch die Technik hält – weitgehend serienmäßig – etliche Leckerbissen für den „Lenker auf hohem Ross" parat.

Dass die EU5-Normen bei allen X1 erfüllt werden, bedarf keiner Erklärung, doch dass auch die Bremsenergie-Rückgewinnung oder die Reifenpannen-Anzeige zum Standard des X1 gehören, ist eine Randnotiz wert. Besonders effizient schneidet der sDrive 18d ab, der mit Hinterradantrieb einen Verbrauchsschnitt von 5,2 Litern (EU-Testzyklus) erzielt und nur 136 g/km CO_2 ausstößt.

Natürlich verfügt jeder X1 über ein ausgewogenes Fahrwerk mit Doppelgelenk-Federbein-Vorderachse und Mehrlenker-Hinterachse, dynamische Stabilitätskontrolle, ein Kontrollsystem für Bremsmomente in schnell gefahrenen Kurven und die SUV-übliche Berg-Abfahrtskontrolle. Die variable Verteilung des Antriebsmoments zwischen Vorder- und Hinterrädern (nur bei den xDrive-Ausführungen) erweist sich in ländlichen Gegenden mit vielen Feldwegen als sehr vorteilhaft.

Ausgestattet mit Türverstärkungen für höchstmöglichen Insassenschutz und Karosserie-Deformationselemente vorn und hinten, die Aufprallkräfte bis 15 Stundenkilometer absorbieren, sowie mit sechs gut platzierten Airbags kann die ohnehin sehr stabile Fahrgastzelle als Sicherheits-Paket bezeichnet werden. Optional empfiehlt sich als zusätzliches Sicherheitselement eine spezielle BMW-Telematik, die bei einem Unfall automatisch einen Notruf mit Positionsbestimmung und detaillierten Angaben absetzt. Insgesamt gesehen braucht sich der X1 vor seinen großen Brüdern nicht zu verstecken. Dank seiner optimalen Achslastverteilung und einem relativ niedrigen Schwerpunkt, hervorragender Traktion und Spurtreue ist er rundum ausgewogen. Da kommt Freude am Fahren auf!

Les SUV de BMW se déclinent sous tous les numéros. Évolution qui n'épargne que la Série 7 compte tenu du respect qui lui est dû en tant que vaisseau amiral de la marque. Le fait que même la petite Série 1 soit élevée dans cette catégorie avec le système de transmission intégrale « intelligent » xDrive fait partie intégrante de la stratégie de l'entreprise visant à occuper le plus de niches possibles précisément dans le segment des véhicules d'entrée de gamme et moyenne gamme. C'est à l'IAA, le Salon de l'automobile de Francfort, de 2009, placé sous le signe de l'« Efficient Dynamics » par BMW, slogan désignant un ensemble de technologies destinées à réduire la consommation et les émissions sans nuire au plaisir de conduire, que la petite « X » a fait ses débuts avec une vaste gamme de motorisation : du moteur 143 ch de la 18d aux 258 ch de la xDrive 28i. Des dimensions extérieures plutôt généreuses (4454 × 1798 × 1545 mm) octroient à la X1 un volume de chargement de 480 litres lorsque les dossiers des places arrière sont en configuration « cargo ». Si des passagers veulent, ou doivent, prendre place à l'arrière, ils doivent alors s'asseoir le dos bien droit. Naturellement, les sièges arrière peuvent également être rabattus individuellement pour pouvoir transporter une véritable « cargaison ». On obtient ainsi un volume de 1350 litres. Très convenable pour un SUV de la classe compacte.

Des rangements de toutes sortes, des bacs pouvant accueillir une grande bouteille dans les portes, des porte-gobelets intégrés dans la console centrale, un compartiment à lunettes dans le plafonnier, un filet de séparation pour le coffre ou encore une trappe pour les sacs à skis ou à snowboard, témoignent d'un aménagement intérieur fonctionnel et pratique. D'innombrables « gadgets » en option payante complètent ce système de rangement.

La X1 réserve également de très agréables surprises, pour la plupart en série, sur le plan technique. Inutile de préciser que toutes les X1 répondent aux exigences de la norme Euro 5 ; en revanche, il convient d'ajouter que la récupération de l'énergie de freinage ou l'indicateur de crevaison font aussi partie de l'équipement standard de la X1. La sDrive 18d, avec une consommation moyenne de 5,2 litres (cycle essai de l'UE) pour une émission de CO_2 de seulement 136 g/km, s'avère très convaincante.

Toutes les X1 disposent naturellement d'un châssis équilibré avec train avant à double articulation des pivots de fusée et essieu arrière à cinq bras, du contrôle dynamique de la stabilité, un système de compensation du couple dans les virages négociés rapidement, ainsi que de la gestion de la motricité en descente usuelle sur les SUV. La répartition variable du couple entre les trains avant et arrière (seulement sur les versions xDrive) s'avère très avantageuse en environnement rural sur les chemins de terre.

Équipé de portières renforcées offrant une protection optimale des passagers, d'éléments sur les pare-chocs avant et arrière résistant sans déformation à une collision ayant lieu à une vitesse allant jusqu'à 15 km/h, ainsi que de six airbags judicieusement positionnés, l'habitacle déjà très stable de la X1 peut être qualifié de véritable pack de sécurité. En option, le constructeur conseille un élément de sécurité supplémentaire, le système télématique spécifique BMW, qui en cas d'accident émet automatiquement un appel d'urgence et transmet les données de positionnement et des indications précises sur la gravité de la situation. Avec une répartition optimale des charges sur les essieux, un centre de gravité relativement bas, une traction exceptionnelle et une grande stabilité directionnelle, elle est parfaitement équilibrée.

Compact, dynamic, agile, and elegant: the X1—seen here with the 4-cylinder turbodiesel engine—is equally appealing on the inside.

Kompakt, dynamisch, agil und elegant: Der X1 – hier mit dem 4-Zylinder-Turbo-Dieselmotor – überzeugt auch im Interieur.

Compact, dynamique, agile et élégant: la X1 – ici avec un moteur turbodiesel à 4 cylindres – est aussi convaincante à l'extérieur qu'à l'intérieur.

BMW 5 F07 F10 F11 | 2009

The aesthetic appearance of the sixth 5 series, with its powerful radiator grille, four inch longer wheelbase and more attractive tail than its predecessor, is matched by the engine, which peaks at 560 bhp in the M5. But the real fireworks under the hood come from the compression-ignition engine. The three-liter base engine of the 530d and 535d is triple-turbo-boosted to 381 bhp in the M550d xDrive, and the maximum torque of 546 lb-ft puts even the gasoline-driven M to shame. The three-stage turbo charge begins by over-revving the idling speed; at 1500 rpm, low pressure is used to generate compression; then at 2500 rpm, the real boost kicks in. The variable turbine geometry leaves no chance of a power gap. The two-ton vehicle accelerates smoothly from 0 to 60 mph in just under five seconds. With an average mileage of some 33.5 mpg and CO_2 emissions of 272 grams per mile, this dynamic power package scores highly on efficiency, and also complies with the Euro 6 emission standard.

Of course, the "M" in the M550d xDrive means "maximum"—the benchmark against which everything else is measured. It stands for a tight chassis with adapted absorbers and shorter springs, lowered by a fingerbreadth and developed by BMW M GmbH. 245 tires on 19-inch double-spoke aluminum alloy wheels emphasize the M550d xDrive's sporty character, and the way it corners is in keeping with the same theme. In order to differentiate it from the aggressive look

of the "true M", the M aerodynamics package offers a more modest aesthetic, with less extravagant front and rear aprons and understated sills.

Black window frames, B-pillars and wing mirror mountings—BMW's "high-gloss shadow line"—are also standard M equipment, just like the sport seats, leather steering wheel with high-grip rim and the anthracite ceiling on the interior.

While two of the six gasoline-powered models (528i and 535i) are also available with xDrive, the diesel fleet offers all-wheel drive to the 525d, 530d, and 535d; in the M550d it is standard. The same applies to sedans (F10) and station wagons (F11). The combination of xDrive and dynamic stability control offers directional stability and reliable road holding.

The GT (F07), this 5 series combination of grand tourer, sedan and fastback station wagon with a panoramic glass roof and integrated wind deflector certainly lives up to the BMW slogan "The first of its kind." With a width of 6 ft 3 in (190 cm) and at over 16 feet (just under 5 meters) in length, the impressive vehicle has the wheelbase of a 7 series.

The "Open Sesame" of the rear section and relatively small window contains a mechanism that is illuminating. The handle for the mini tailgate is just under the "M" of the BMW logo, while the "W"—for "widely open" —opens a big door to the boot. Behind it lies 60 cu.ft (1700 liters) of storage capacity with the seats folded down.

Zu dem ästhetischen Erscheinungsbild des sechsten 5ers, mit seiner kraftvollen Frontpartie, dem zehn Zentimeter längeren Radstand und dem optisch besser gelungenen Heck als beim Vorgänger passt die Motorisierung, die im M5 in 560 PS gipfelt. Doch die wirkliche Show unter der Haube bietet ein Selbstzünder. Das Drei-liter-Basistriebwerk von 530d und 535d erfährt im M550d xDrive eine dreifache Turboaufladung auf 381 PS, und das maximale Drehmoment von 740 Newtonmetern stellt sogar den M-Benziner in den Schatten. Die dreistufige Turboaufladung beginnt mit dem Überschreiten der Leerlaufdrehzahl, im Bereich von 1500 Touren wird mit Niederdruck komprimiert und bei 2500 Umdrehungen setzt der richtige Boost ein. Die variable Turbinengeometrie lässt kein Power-Loch zu. Nahtlos beschleunigt der Zweitonner in knapp fünf Sekunden auf 100 km/h. Mit einem Durchschnittsverbrauch unter sieben Litern und einer CO_2-Emission von 169 g/km erzielt dieses dynamische Kraftpaket eine ordentliche Note hinsichtlich seiner Effizienz und genügt auch der Abgasnorm EU6.

„M" bezeichnet beim M550d xDrive natürlich das Maß der Dinge. Es steht für ein von der BMW M GmbH entwickeltes, straff ausgelegtes, um einen Zentimeter abgesenktes Fahrwerk mit angepassten Dämpfern und kürzeren Federn. 245er-Walzen auf 19-Zoll-Doppelspeichen-Leichtmetall-rädern unterstreichen die sportliche Note. Entsprechend gebärdet sich der M550d xDrive auf kurvenreichem Terrain. Um nicht mit der aggressiven Optik des „echten M" zu

konkurrieren, gibt sich das M-Aerodynamik-Paket mit nur leicht aufgemotzter Front- und Heckschürze und dezenten Schwellern bescheidener.

Schwarze Fensterrahmen, B-Säulen und Außenspiegel- halterungen, von BMW als „Hochglanz Shadow Line" angepriesen, gehören ebenso zur M-Ausstattung wie die Sportsitze, das Lederlenkrad mit besonders griffigem Kranz und der anthrazitfarbene Dachhimmel im Interieur.

Während von den sechs Benzinern zwei (528i und 535i) auch als xDrive angeboten werden, wartet die Diesel- Fraktion gleich mit vier Allradlern auf: 525d, 530d, 535d und serienmäßig der M550d. Dieses Schema gilt für Limousine (F10) und Touring (F11) gleichermaßen. Die Kombination von xDrive und dynamischer Stabilitätskontrolle resultiert in Spurtreue und verlässlicher Bodenhaftung.

Der GT (F07), diese 5er-Mischung aus Gran Turismo, Limousine und Fastback-Kombi mit Panorama-Glasdach samt integriertem Windabweiser erfüllt zumindest den BMW-Slogan „Erster seiner Art". Das mit 190 Zentimetern Breite und knapp fünf Metern Länge gewaltige Fahrzeug war- tet immerhin mit dem Radstand eines 7er auf.

Das „Sesam öffne Dich" der Heckpartie mit relativ klein geratenem Fenster beherbergt einen Mechanismus, der ein- leuchtet. Just unter dem „M" des BMW-Logos liegt der Griff für die Mini-Heckklappe, während sich unter dem „W" – wie „wide open" – die große Heckklappe emporheben lässt. Hin- ter ihr verbirgt sich bei umgelegten Fondsitzen der Stauraum von satten 1700 Litern.

La ligne de la sixième série 5, avec sa partie avant puis- sante, un empattement plus long de dix centimètres et une partie arrière revue et améliorée par rapport au modèle précédent, est assortie à la motorisation, qui culmine à 560 ch pour la M5. Mais sous le capot, la vraie vedette du spectacle est un moteur diesel. Le moteur trois litres de base de la 530d et de la 535d est triplement turbocompressé à 381 ch dans la M550d xDrive, et le couple maximum de 740 Nm éclipse même la M à essence. La suralimentation turbo à trois étages se met en route juste au-dessus du régime de ralenti, aux alentours de 1500 tours la compression basse pression entre en scène, et à partir de 2500 tours on passe aux choses sérieuses. La géométrie variable de la tur- bine interdit toute défaillance de puissance. Cette voiture de deux tonnes accélère de 0 à 100 km/h d'une traite en moins de cinq secondes. Avec une consommation moyenne de moins de sept litres et des émissions de CO_2 de 169 g/km, ce concentré de puissance récolte une note respectable en efficience, et respecte la norme d'émissions Euro 6.

Le « M » de M550d xDrive signifie « maximum », bien entendu, la référence absolue. Il indique que le châssis rigide rabaissé d'un centimètre, doté d'amortisseurs adaptés et de ressorts raccourcis, a été développé par BMW M GmbH. Les pneus de 245 sur des jantes en alliage léger 19 pouces à rayons doubles accentuent le caractère sportif de la M550d xDrive, et son comportement dans les courbes est à l'avenant. Pour se différencier de la ligne agressive de la « vraie M », le

pack aérodynamique M offre une jupe avant et arrière moins extravagante et un bas de caisse plus modeste.

Encadrements de fenêtres, montants B et montures de rétroviseurs extérieurs en noir – la finition « Shadow Line » haute brillance de BMW – font également partie de l'équipe- ment M, tout comme les sièges sport, le volant cuir antidéra- pant et l'habillage de plafond gris anthracite.

Deux des six modèles essence (528i et 535i) sont égale- ment disponibles en version xDrive, mais la flotte diesel offre quatre variantes avec transmission intégrale : 525d, 530d, 535d et, de série, M550d. Le même schéma s'applique aux berlines (F10) et aux breaks (F11). La combinaison de xDrive et de contrôle dynamique de la stabilité offre stabilité direc- tionnelle et adhérence.

La GT (F07) de cette Série 5 mêlant grand tourisme, ber- line et break fastback au toit vitré panoramique avec déflec- teur intégré répond du moins au slogan choisi par BMW : « La première de son espèce ». Cette voiture imposante d'une largeur de 190 cm pour une longueur de tout juste 5 mètres, possède tout de même l'empattement d'une Série 7.

Le « sésame » de l'arrière doté d'une vitre relativement petite abrite un mécanisme très pratique. Juste en des- sous du « M » du logo BMW se trouve la poignée du mini- hayon tandis que sous le « W », comme *widely open*, se situe le levier du grand hayon. Il dissimule un vaste espace de rangement de 1700 litres lorsque les sièges arrière sont rabattus.

245 diesel bhp await inside this 530d GT. Clearly structured: the cockpit of this top-class vehicle.

In diesem 530d GT schlummern 245 Diesel-PS. Klar gegliedert: das Cockpit dieses Oberklasse-Wagens.

Sous le capot de la 530d GT, 245 ch attendent de se mettre en action. Le cockpit de cette voiture de grande classe est clairement structuré.

As BMW's longest-serving series, the 5 series combines elegance and sportiness. The "M Performance TwinPower Turbo" six-cylinder diesel engine turns out 381 bhp.

Erfolgreich und als Fahrzeug mit der längsten Ahnenreihe bei BMW, vereint der 5er Eleganz und Sportlichkeit. 381 PS aktiviert der „M Performance TwinPower Turbo" Sechszylinder-Diesel.

La série 5 est celle qui a le plus d'ancienneté chez BMW. Elle combine élégance et sportivité. Le moteur diesel six cylindres « M Performance TwinPower Turbo » libère 381 ch.

The 5 series's interior and exterior harmony is underlined by its sweeping lines at the rear, on the side grooves, the sill and the dashboard.

Harmonie zwischen Exterieur und Interieur betont der 5er durch den Schwung seiner Linienführung: ganz gleich ob am Heck, bei der seitlichen Sicke, dem Schweller oder auf dem Armaturenbrett.

L'harmonie entre extérieur et intérieur de la série 5 est soulignée par l'élan de sa ligne, qu'il s'agisse de l'arrière, des rainures latérales, des bas de caisse ou du tableau de bord.

Mini Countryman, Paceman | 2010

As a small car with a large load capacity, the Countryman has proven a valuable addition to the Mini product range since its debut at the Geneva International Motor Show in 2010. Since production in its home town of Oxford is already at full capacity, it is built by Magna Steyr in Austria. Taller, wider and a good 15 inches longer than the normal Mini, this rangy "Mini Maximus" appeals to us with three models. The Mini One Countryman, available as a gasoline variant with 98 bhp for 107 mph or a 106 mph, 90 bhp diesel variant, forms the basis of the more powerful Mini Cooper Countryman, whose compression-ignition variant with 112 bhp is also available as an "All4" with a variable all-wheel-drive system. In extreme cases, its drive power can even be assigned completely to the rear axle. "All4" is also on offer for the high-end Countrymen, the Cooper S with 184 bhp, the Cooper SD and—as standard—the John Cooper Works Countryman with 218 bhp.

Thanks to its extremely efficient two-liter engine, the power (143 bhp) and elasticity of which can also be seen in the BMW 118d, the Cooper SD has an outstanding mileage of 51 miles per gallon of diesel using the optional automatic Steptronic system. With the manual six-speed transmission, the engine goes ten extra miles.

Countryman drivers belong to the species of individualists who do not concern themselves with whether the rear of the vehicle seems a little unconventional. Instead, their design ideals tend more toward the choice of a white or black roof with matching stripes on the hood, perhaps a roof spoiler, a sunroof or the flat-lying roof rack for transporting luggage. Buyers can choose the right alloy wheel design from a range of five variants, including "silver" and "matt anthracite". The well-illustrated list of options for the Countryman interior is long, and should cater to any taste. For those who wish to avoid the technicalities of operating a navigation system, a rearview mirror with built-in compass is recommended—even if its display only uses eight directions.

Those with a more technical leaning, on the other hand, will be interested to know that the Countryman, too, can convert its braking energy into power. All the gasoline engines come with fully variable valve stroke control, and the small diesel engines make full use of the benefits of the common-rail technology.

The Paceman (R61) is effectively a two-door Countryman coupé. Comparison of the John Cooper Works version reveals that the 11 pound lighter and an inch lower Paceman is half a mile faster, and gains one-tenth of a second over 0 to 60 mph. That's all!

Als kleines Auto mit großer Ladekapazität bereichert der Countryman seit 2010, Premiere beim Genfer Salon, die Mini-Produktpalette. Da die Produktionskapazitäten in seiner Heimat Oxford völlig ausgelastet sind, baut ihn Magna Steyr in Österreich. Höher, breiter und gut 40 Zentimeter länger als der normale Mini, wirbt dieser hochbeinige Mini-Maximus mit drei Modellen um unsere Gunst. Der Mini One Countryman, als Benziner mit 98 PS gut für 173 km/h und 170 km/h mit dem 90-PS-Dieselmotörchen, bildet die Basis für den stärkeren Mini Cooper Countryman, dessen Selbstzünder-Variante mit 112 PS auch als „All4" mit einem variablen Allradsystem aufwartet. Im Extremfall kann die Antriebskraft sogar zu 100 Prozent auf die Hinterachse verteilt werden. „All4" haben auch die stärksten Countrymen zu bieten, der Cooper S mit 184 PS, der Cooper SD, und – serienmäßig – der John Cooper Works Countryman mit 218 PS. Dank des äußerst effizienten Zweilitermotors, der auch im BMW 118d seine Kraft elastisch und durchaus kraftvoll (143 PS) entfaltet, glänzt der Cooper SD mit einem kombinierten Verbrauchswert von 4,6 Litern Diesel mit dem serienmäßigen Sechsgang-Schaltgetriebe. Mit der Steptronic-Automatik schluckt das Triebwerk über eine 100-Kilometer-Distanz einen guten Liter mehr.

Wer einen Countryman fährt, dürfte zur Spezies der Individualisten gehören, die sich keine Gedanken darüber macht, ob das Wagenheck etwas eigenwillig geraten

ist. Stattdessen bezieht sie in ihre Gestaltungsüberlegungen die Option eines weißen oder schwarzen Daches mit entsprechenden Streifen über die Motorhaube ein, bestellt vielleicht einen Dach-Heckspoiler, ein Glas-Schiebe-Hebedach oder entscheidet sich für die flach anliegende Reling für den Lastentransport auf höchster Ebene. Unter fünf Leichtmetallräder-Designs in verschiedenen Varianten von „Silber" bis „Anthrazit matt" kann das Passende ausgewählt werden. Die gut bebilderte Auflistung werksseitiger Bereicherungen für das Countryman-Interieur ist lang und bedient wohl alle Geschmäcker. Und wem die Bedienung eines Navigationsgeräts technisch zu anspruchsvoll ist, dem sei ein Mini-Innenspiegel mit integriertem digitalen Kompass empfohlen. Dessen Display kennt freilich nur acht Himmelsrichtungen.

Technisch Versierte wird hingegen interessieren, dass auch der Countryman seine Bremsenergie in Strom umwandeln kann. Alle Benzinmotoren verfügen über eine vollvariable Steuerung des Ventilhubs, und die kleinen Dieseltriebwerke schöpfen alle Vorteile der Common-Rail-Technologie aus.

Quasi als zweitüriges Coupé des Countryman tritt der Paceman (R61) auf. Vergleicht man die John Cooper Works-Versionen miteinander, so ist der fünf Kilo leichtere und drei Zentimeter niedrigere Paceman einen Kilometer schneller und gewinnt beim Sprint auf Tempo 100 eine Zehntelsekunde. That's all!

En tant que petite voiture qui offre une grande capacité de chargement, la Countryman occupe une place bien à elle dans la gamme Mini depuis ses débuts au Salon de Genève en 2010. La production fonctionnant déjà à pleine capacité dans sa ville d'origine, Oxford, elle est construite par Magna Steyr en Autriche. Plus haute, plus large et plus longue de 40 bons centimètres par rapport à la Mini normale, cette «maxi Mini» haute sur jambes s'adapte aux goûts de chacun avec ses trois modèles. La Mini One Countryman, version essence avec 98 ch pour 173 km/h ou version diesel avec 90 ch pour 170 km/h, constitue la base de la Mini Cooper Countryman plus puissante, dont la variante diesel 112 ch est aussi disponible avec un système de transmission intégrale variable «All4». Dans les cas extrêmes, sa force motrice peut même être affectée à 100 pour cent à l'essieu arrière. Le système «All4» est aussi proposé sur les modèles Countryman haut de gamme, comme la Cooper S avec 184 ch, la Cooper SD et – en série – la John Cooper Works Countryman avec ses 218 ch. Grâce à son moteur deux litres extrêmement efficace, qui déploie aussi sa puissance élastique (143 ch) dans la BMW 118d, la Cooper SD affiche une excellente consommation de 4,6 litres de diesel avec sa boîte six vitesses de série. Avec le système automatique Steptronic, le moteur avale un bon litre tous les 100 kilomètres.

Le conducteur de la Countryman appartient en général à l'espèce des individualistes qui ne se préoccupent pas de savoir si l'arrière de la voiture semble un peu bizarre. Leurs préférences en matière de design tendent plutôt vers un toit noir ou blanc avec les rayures assorties sur le capot, peut-être un aileron de toit à l'arrière, un toit ouvrant en verre ou des barres de toit pour transporter les bagages. Ils pourront choisir parmi cinq modèles de jantes en alliage léger en couleur argent ou anthracite mat. La liste des options d'usine pour l'intérieur de la Countryman est longue et s'attache à satisfaire tous les goûts. Et pour ceux qui trouvent qu'un système de navigation est un gadget trop technique, le rétroviseur intérieur avec boussole numérique intégrée est recommandé, même si l'affichage est limité à huit directions.

Mais les amateurs de technique seront eux intéressés de savoir que la Countryman peut aussi convertir l'énergie de freinage en courant électrique. Tous les moteurs essence sont équipés d'un système de commande de course de soupape entièrement réglable, et les petits moteurs diesel tirent pleinement profit des avantages de la technologie de rampe commune.

La Paceman (R61) se présente presque comme un coupé deux portes de la Countryman. Si on compare les versions John Cooper Works entre elles, la Paceman, plus légère de cinq kilos et plus basse de trois centimètres, est plus rapide d'un km/h et passe de 0 à 100 km/h en un dixième de seconde de moins. C'est tout!

The dual exhaust differentiates the rear of the
Cooper SD from those of its less powerful fellow
Countrymen. Interior: a look around the cockpit.

Das Cooper-SD-Heck unterscheidet sich von dem
seiner schwächeren Countryman-Artgenossen durch
zwei Auspuffrohre. Interieur: alles rund im Cockpit.

La double sortie d'échappement différentie l'arrière de
la Cooper SD de celui des autres Countryman moins
puissantes. Intérieur: dans l'habitacle, tout est rond.

The front of the Countryman SD All4 is marked by its "hexagon" grille and additional air vents. Its two-liter diesel engine, transversally installed, delivers 143 bhp.

Frontal fällt der Allradler Countryman SD durch seinen Kühlergrill im sogenannten Hexagon-Look und zusätzliche Luftschlitze auf. Sein Zweiliter-Dieselmotor, quer eingebaut, leistet 143 PS.

L'avant de la Countryman SD à transmission intégrale est marqué par sa calandre «hexagone» et ses grilles d'aération supplémentaires. Son moteur diesel deux litres, monté transversalement, développe 143 ch.

The sloping roof contour, lower sports chassis, dynamic traction control, and powerful four-cylinder engine with twin-scroll turbocharger, direct fuel injection and variable valve control under the hood: the Mini John Cooper Works Paceman combines sporty attributes with space for four adults. Effectively the coupé version of the all-wheel-drive Countryman, the Paceman offers two quite comfortable individual seats.

Flach abfallende Dachkontur, tiefergelegtes Sportfahrwerk, dynamische Traktionskontrolle und ein kraftvoller Vierzylinder mit Twin-Scroll-Turbolader, Direkteinspritzung und variabler Ventilsteuerung unter der Haube: Der Mini John Cooper Works Paceman vereint sportliche Attribute mit einem Platzangebot für vier Erwachsene. Quasi als zweitürige Coupé-Variante des allradgetriebenen Countryman bietet der Paceman-Fond zwei durchaus komfortable Einzelsitze.

Ligne de toit en pente, châssis sport surbaissé, système antipatinage dynamique et puissant quatre-cylindres avec turbocompresseur twin-scroll, injection directe et commande variable de soupapes sous le capot: la Mini John Cooper Works Paceman réunit attributs sportifs et espace pour quatre adultes. C'est presque une variante coupé 2-portes de la Countryman à transmission intégrale, et sa banquette arrière offre deux places tout à fait confortables.

In contrast to the first X3 generation (E83), built to a run of 600,000 units by Magna Steyr, its successor—now manufactured in Spartanburg, South Carolina—really grabs the attention with its technical innovations and elegant lines. Its larger BMW kidney gives a more dynamic feel, boldly flanked by the headlamps with daytime driving light rings. Of course, xenon lighting adds to the price. The side grooves have also been made more dynamic; they now continue through to the tail light, and even the typical BMW Hofmeister kink found its way into the D-pillar. The car is perfectly proportioned from head to toe: a masterpiece by Erik Goplen, exterior designer at BMW's Californian design studio. A clear view of the sky: the generous dimensions of the optional tilt & slide panorama sunroof come highly recommended.

The X3 is driven by one of three petrol engines with variable camshaft and valve control, and direct injection from 184 to 306 bhp, or four common-rail diesel engines between 143 and 313 bhp, all boosted. The X3 sDrive 18d with its 143 bhp, four-cylinder diesel engine stands out: 265 lb-ft of torque, 0 to 62 mph in 9.9 seconds and a top speed of 121 mph. This performance is impressive, especially considering the factory specification of an average mileage of 46 mpg. In practice, of course, this will be a little lower, but a full 15-gallon tank will still contain easily enough fuel for more than 600 miles, not least thanks to the usual EfficientDynamics goodies, such as the auto start-stop function, electromechanical servo-assisted steering, regenerative braking and the "Eco Pro

mode" which reminds the driver to drive sensibly and allows the automatic transmission to shift more calmly.

The 306 bhp in the top xDrive 35i model is slightly lower than the 313 bhp in the 35d—however, the 100 pounds of extra weight from the diesel engine cost a mile per hour off the maximum speed (152 mph) and an extra tenth of a second on the acceleration (under six seconds). Nevertheless, the 35d does have outstanding emission and consumption figures: 261 grams of CO_2 per mile and 38.5 mpg of diesel. These place it well above the premium guzzler—referred to the fuel type, as the average consumption of the six-cylinder engine with twin-scroll turbocharger, variable camshaft and valve control, and direct injection is still quite respectable, at 26.5 mpg.

The X4 is slimmer and more elegant than its big brother, the X6. The coupé-roofed four-wheel drive, available since July 2014, quickly moved into the spotlight. It was an absolute eye-catcher, and by the end of the first year of production in Spartanburg, 21,688 had been manufactured. This exciting machine—BMW's fifth X-model—is abbreviated to "SAC" (Sports Activity Coupé), although it also provides all-terrain qualities. Based on the X3 platform, the X4 implies sportiness, especially in its driving behavior and its direct steering. This compensates for the turning circle, which at 39 feet can by no means be called small, and for the virtually zero visibility through the somewhat too small rear window when reverse parking.

Gegenüber der ersten, bei Magna Steyr in einer Auflage von 600 000 gebauten X3-Generation (E83) besticht der nunmehr im Werk Spartanburg, South Carolina, gefertigte Nachfolger durch technische Innovationen und eine elegantere Linienführung rundum. Seine größeren BMW-Nieren wirken dynamischer, schwungvoll flankiert von den Scheinwerfern mit Tagfahrlichtringen. Xenon-Beleuchtung verlangt natürlich nach einem Aufpreis. Schwung ist auch in die seitliche Sicke gekommen, die sich jetzt bis ins Rücklicht zieht, und sogar der BMW-typische Hofmeister-Knick findet sich nun in der D-Säule. Vom Scheitel bis zur Sohle stimmen die Proportionen bis ins kleinste Detail: eine Meisterleistung von Erik Goplen, Exterieurdesigner im kalifornischen BMW-Designstudio. Freier Blick nach oben: Das optionale Panorama-Glasdach mit Schiebe- und Hebefunktion empfiehlt sich durch seinen großzügig bemessenen Öffnungsbereich.

Drei Benziner mit variabler Nockenwellen- und Ventilsteuerung und Direkteinspritzung von 184 bis 306 PS und vier Common-Rail-Selbstzünder zwischen 143 und 313 PS dienen, allesamt zwangsbeatmet, der X3-Motorisierung. Besonders der X3 sDrive 18d mit dem 143-PS-Vierzylinder-Diesel entpuppt sich als Klassenprimus: 360 Newtonmeter Drehmoment, Beschleunigung auf 100 Stundenkilometer in 9,9 Sekunden, Spitze 195 km/h. Diese Performance beeindruckt angesichts eines vom Werk angegebenen kombinierten Kraftstoffverbrauchs von 5,1 Litern. In der Fahrpraxis werden es naturgemäß etwas mehr sein, eine 67-Liter-Tankfüllung reicht dennoch locker für 1000 Kilometer, was nicht zuletzt den üblichen EfficientDynamics-Goodies wie Auto-Start-Stopp-Funktion, elektromechani-

BMW X3, X4 F25, F26 | 2010

sche Servolenkung, Bremsenergie-Rückgewinnung bis zum sogenannten „Eco Pro Modus", der zu vernünftiger Fahrweise mahnt und die Automatik besonnener schalten lässt, zu verdanken ist.

Den 306 PS im Topmodell xDrive 35i stehen 313 PS im 35d gegenüber – die 45 Kilo Mehrgewicht des Dieselaggregats kosten allerdings einen Stundenkilometer bei der Höchstgeschwindigkeit (jeweils um 245 km/h) und eine Zehntelsekunde beim Beschleunigungswert (jeweils unter sechs Sekunden). Dafür glänzt der 35d mit seinen Emissions- und Verbrauchswerten, denn er liegt mit 162 g/km und 6,1 Litern naturgemäß deutlich vor dem Supersäufer – auf die Treibstoffsorte bezogen, denn der Normverbrauch des Sechszylinders mit Twin-Scroll-Turbolader, variabler Nockenwellen- und Ventilsteuerung und Direkteinspritzung bleibt mit 8,8 Litern im gemischten Betrieb schon noch im vertretbaren Bereich.

Schlanker und eleganter als sein großer Bruder X6 präsentiert sich der X4. Der seit Juli 2014 erhältliche Allradler mit Coupé-Dach rückte schnell ins Rampenlicht – ein Blickfang, von dem bis zum Ende des ersten Produktionsjahres in Spartanburg bereits 21688 Exemplare vom Band liefen. Dieses aufregende Gerät – BMWs fünftes X-Modell – läuft unter dem Kürzel „SAC" (Sports Activity Coupé), wobei man ihm attestieren muss, dass es auch mit Offroad-Qualitäten aufwarten kann. Auf der X3-Plattform aufgebaut, impliziert der X4 Sportlichkeit, besonders beim Fahrverhalten und hinsichtlich seiner direkten Lenkung. Diese tröstet darüber hinweg, dass der Wendekreis mit zwölf Metern nicht gerade knapp bemessen und die Sicht durch das etwas zu klein geratene Heckfenster beim rückwärts Einparken gleich Null ist.

Contrairement à la première génération de X3 (E83) construite à 600000 exemplaires par Magna Steyr, sa remplaçante, désormais fabriquée à Spartanburg, en Caroline du Sud, éblouit par ses innovations techniques et l'élégance de sa ligne. Sa calandre BMW plus grande lui donne un air plus dynamique, encadrée par les phares avec feux de circulation diurne. L'éclairage au xénon se traduit bien évidemment par un prix plus élevé. Les rainures latérales sont elles aussi plus dynamiques, et se prolongent maintenant jusqu'aux phares arrière, et même le fameux pli Hofmeister de BMW recule pour mordre sur le montant D. Du toit jusqu'aux roues, les proportions sont étudiées dans le moindre détail : un chef-d'œuvre d'Erik Goplen, designer extérieur pour le studio de design californien de BMW. Une vue dégagée sur le ciel : les dimensions généreuses du toit panoramique basculant et coulissant en font une option très recommandable.

La motorisation de la X3 se compose de trois moteurs essence à injection directe avec commande variable d'arbres à cames et de soupapes de 184 à 306 ch et de quatre moteurs diesel à rampe commune d'entre 143 et 313 ch, tous boostés. La X3 sDrive 18d, avec son moteur diesel quatre cylindres de 143 ch, s'avère être première de la classe : un couple de 360 Nm, une accélération à 100 km/h en 9,9 secondes, une vitesse de pointe de 195 km/h. Ces performances sont impressionnantes, si l'on considère les spécifications d'usine qui indiquent une consommation combinée de 5,1 litres. En pratique, bien sûr, ce chiffre sera légèrement plus élevé, mais son réservoir de 67 litres rempli devrait néanmoins suffire amplement pour parcourir 1000 kilomètres,

notamment grâce aux équipements EfficientDynamics habituels tels que la fonction start & stop, la direction à assistance électromécanique, la récupération de l'énergie au freinage et le mode «Eco Pro» qui favorise une conduite plus économique.

Les 306 ch du modèle supérieur xDrive 35i sont légèrement en dessous des 313 ch du modèle 35d – les 45 kilos supplémentaires du moteur diesel coûtent un km/h sur la vitesse de pointe (245 km/h) et un dixième de seconde sur l'accélération (en dessous de six secondes). Le 35d brille en revanche par ses performances en matière d'émissions et de consommation, car avec 162 g/km et 6,1 litres, il bat le soiffard d'essence haut la main – même si la consommation mixte du moteur six cylindres à injection directe avec turbocompresseur à deux volutes et commande variable d'arbres à cames et soupapes reste, avec 8,8 litres, assez respectable.

La X4 affiche une ligne plus svelte et plus élégante que sa grande sœur la X6. Superbe crossover à transmission intégrale avec toit coupé disponible depuis juillet 2014, il s'est vite imposé, et 21688 exemplaires en ont été fabriqués à Spartanburg dès la première année de production. Cette machine sensationnelle, le cinquième modèle X de BMW, porte l'abréviation «SAC» (Sports Activity Coupé), ce qui signifie que l'on peut également en attendre des performances de tout-terrain. Construite sur la plateforme de la X3, la X4 est une sportive, particulièrement en ce qui concerne son comportement sur la route et sa direction directe. C'est une consolation nécessaire pour un diamètre de braquage de douze mètres, et une vision quasiment nulle à travers la petite lunette arrière pour se garer en marche arrière.

The second generation of the X3—pictured here with the standard 17-inch, V-spoke wheels—is more curvaceous and aesthetically pleasing than its predecessor, as befits its Californian birthplace.

Die zweite Generation des X3 – hier mit den serienmäßigen 17-Zoll-V-Speichenrädern bestückt – wirkt nicht so eckig wie sein Vorgänger und demonstriert Ästhetik, kreiert im sonnigen Kalifornien.

La deuxième génération de la X3 (ici avec ses jantes de série 17 pouces à rayons en V) est moins anguleuse que la première, et affiche une esthétique plus plaisante, créée sous le soleil californien.

In detail: curved nose, BMW emblem protected under the tailgate sill, the four-cylinder turbo diesel of the 20d and a tidy cockpit.

En detail: gewölbter Bug, unter der Heckklappen-Sicke geschützt platziertes BMW-Emblem, der Vierzylinder-Turbodiesel des 20d und ein aufgeräumtes Cockpit.

En détail : nez bombé, logo BMW protégé sous la rainure du hayon, le moteur turbodiesel quatre cylindres du modèle 20d et un habitacle bien organisé.

It's better not even to try parking the X4 without using the parking assistant that is a standard feature.

Den Versuch, in eine Parklücke zu gelangen, ohne die serienmäßige Einpark-Distanz-Kontrolle einzuschalten, sollte man im X4 lieber unterlassen.

Il vaut mieux s'abstenir d'essayer de garer la X4 sans son système d'aide au stationnement de série.

Fans of the X4 don't mind that it holds 1¾ cu.ft less than the X3. This all-wheel-drive BMW with the electric tailgate still provides sufficient storage with the split rear seat backrests down and secured to tracks and loops, hooks and straps. The 313 bhp power pack in X4 xDrive 35d has this 2-ton beast at 62 mph in just 5.1 seconds.

Dass der Laderaum 50 Liter weniger als der des X3 fasst, stört die X4-Fangemeinde nicht. Dieser BMW-Allradler, dessen Heckklappe elektrisch betätigt wird, bietet nach Umlegen seiner geteilten Rückenlehne genügend Stauraum, der an Schienen und Ösen, Haken und Haltebändern sicher verzurrt beladen werden kann. Das 313-PS-Kraftpaket im X4 xDrive 35d schiebt den Zweitonner in 5,1 Sekunden auf 100 km/h.

Le fait que son volume de chargement soit inférieur de 50 litres à celui de la X3 ne dérange aucunement les fans de la X4. Une fois les dossiers individuels de la banquette arrière rabattus, cette transmission intégrale BMW à hayon électrique offre suffisamment de place, et les rails, anneaux, crochets et sangles permettent d'attacher la charge en toute sécurité. Le puissant moteur 313 ch de la X4 xDrive 35d propulse ses deux tonnes à 100 km/h en 5,1 secondes.

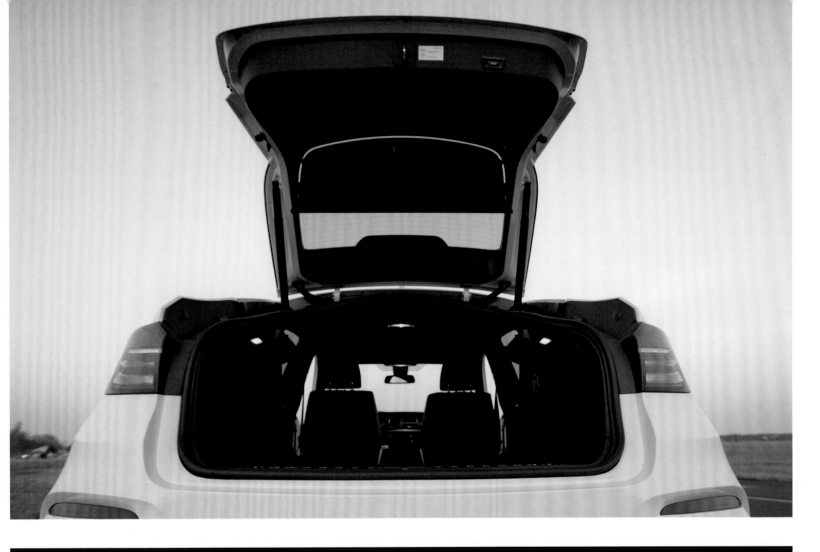

BMW 6 F06, F12, F13 | 2010

Following a complete design overhaul, especially on the rear section BMW presented the third 6 series generation at the end of 2010. Despite their length of 16 ft 1 in, the coupé (F12 series) and convertible (F13) are still two-seaters, with child seats in the back. Using the 4½ in-longer, non-shortened platform of the 5 series and with a total length of almost 16½ feet, BMW first revealed the 6 series as a four-door Gran Coupé (F06) in December 2011, and started shipping it in early summer 2012. As a direct competitor to the Mercedes CLS and Audi A7—and in a price range near the Porsche Panamera—the Gran Coupé is not short of rivals.

An elongated silhouette, flat, forward-curving kidney grille and broad cheeks over the wheels: the shape of the 6 series is an astoundingly beautiful combination of sportiness and elegance. Available as a 640i, 640d, 650i or M6 with the 560 bhp biturbo, the series has no shortage of power packages. The 640i's inline six-cylinder engine with twin-scroll turbocharger, Valvetronic and direct injection provides 320 bhp. The 640d pulls just seven bhp less out of its six-cylinder engine with common-rail direct injection and two-stage turbocharger, combined with variable turbine geometry. The V8 in the 650i with two turbochargers puts out 450 bhp, which accelerate the almost two-ton heavy Gran Coupé xDrive up to 62 mph in only 4.4 seconds. At maximum torque of 479 lb-ft,

2000 to 4500 revs generate enough power reserve to allow a little play in the muscles during driving. In "Sport+" mode of the dynamic absorber control, that is with tight suspension, great driving pleasure is assured. The 2500-dollar investment in adaptive absorbers definitely pays off here, as they work together with the "Dynamic Drive" to almost completely eliminate rolling motion. The automatic eight-speed sports transmission is combined with a start/stop function; the M6 uses the seven-speed dual-clutch transmission.

The extremely tasteful interior emits an air of exclusiveness. Whether your custom design includes the Nappa leather/Alcantara combo in anthracite with blue contrast seams in the sport seats of the M-package or the platinum/black full merino leather trim, the feel of this car just oozes luxury. Interior paneling in dark red sycamore, highly-polished aluminum or with black piano finish add an extra touch of elegance. Exterior coatings such as "Moonstone Metallic" and "Frozen Bronze Metallic" add a further custom feel to this high-end vehicle from the first glance.

Eye-catching, or even attention-grabbing: adaptive LED headlights or adaptive cornering light. In order to save weight and lower the center of gravity, the M6 Coupé and the M6 Gran Coupé are equipped with carbon fiber composite roofs instead of the tilting glass panel roofs.

Mit völlig überarbeitetem Design, besonders bei der Heckpartie, stellt BMW Ende 2010 die dritte 6er-Generation vor. Coupé (Baureihe F12) und Cabrio (F13) sind trotz ihrer Länge von 4,90 Metern nach wie vor Zweisitzer mit Kindersitzen im Fond. Auf der 113 Millimeter längeren, weil ungekürzten Plattform des 5ers und mit einer Gesamtlänge, die fünf Meter überschreitet, zeigt BMW den 6er im Dezember 2011 erstmals als viertüriges Gran Coupé (F06), das ab Frühsommer 2012 ausgeliefert wird. Als direktem Gegenspieler zu Mercedes CLS und Audi A7 – und preislich in Reichweite eines Porsche Panamera – mangelt es dem Gran Coupé nicht an Konkurrenz.

Gestreckte Silhouette, flache, nach vorn gewölbte Nieren und breite Backen über den Reifen: Die 6er vereinen Sportlichkeit und Eleganz in schönster Form. Als 640i, 640d, 650i und als M6 mit dem 560-PS-Biturbo verfügt die Reihe über adäquate Kraftpakete. 320 PS stellt der Reihensechszylinder mit Twin-Scroll-Turbolader, Valvetronic und Direkteinspritzung des 640i zur Verfügung. Nur sieben PS weniger entlockt der 640d seinem Sechszylinder mit CommonRail-Direkteinspritzung und zweistufiger Turboaufladung, kombiniert mit variabler Turbinengeometrie. Der V8 des 650i mit zwei Turboladern mobilisiert 450 PS, die etwa das fast zwei Tonnen schwere Gran Coupé xDrive in nur 4,4 Sekunden auf Tempo 100 beschleunigen. Im maximalen Drehmoment von 650 Newtonmetern schlummern zwischen 2000 und 4500 Touren genügend Kraftreserven,

um die Muskeln im Fahrbetrieb ein wenig spielen zu lassen. Im Modus „Sport+" der dynamischen Dämpferkontrolle, also mit gestrafftem Fahrwerk, ist viel Freude am Fahren vorprogrammiert. Hier lohnt sich noch die 2670 Euro teure Anschaffung adaptiver Dämpfer, die zusammen mit „Dynamic Drive" Wankbewegungen nahezu eliminieren. Das automatische Achtgang-Sportgetriebe ist mit einer Start-Stopp-Funktion kombiniert, im M6 arbeitet das Siebengang-Doppelkupplungsgetriebe.

Ein Hauch von Exklusivität schwebt durch den äußerst geschmackvoll eingerichteten Innenraum. Ob Nappaleder-Alcantara-Wechselspiel in Anthrazit mit blauen Kontrastnähten bei den Sportsitzen des M-Pakets oder Vollleder „Merino Feinnarbe Platin", mit schwarzem Kontrastkeder gesteppt, bei der Individual-Ausstattung: Das Ambiente dieses Wagens inspiriert zum Verweilen. Interieurleisten aus rotbrauner Platane, fein geschliffenem Aluminium oder mit schwarzem Pianolack betonen das elegante Environ. Außenlackierungen wie „Mondstein metallic" oder „Frozen Bronze metallic" ergänzen die individuelle Note dieses Oberklassenfahrzeugs auf den ersten Blick.

Augenscheinlich, ja auffällig: adaptive LED-Scheinwerfer oder adaptives Kurvenlicht. Solche Extras machen sich pekuniär ebenso bemerkbar wie ein elektrisches Glasdach. Um Gewicht zu sparen und den Schwerpunkt zu senken, bestehen die Dächer von M6 Coupé und M6 Gran Coupé aus kohlefaserverstärktem Kunststoff.

BMW a présenté en 2010 la troisième génération de la série 6 avec un design complètement revu, particulièrement à l'arrière. Malgré une longueur de 4,90 mètres, le coupé (F12) et le cabriolet (F13) restent des deux places, avec sièges enfants à l'arrière. En décembre 2011, BMW a présenté pour la première fois le Gran Coupé quatre portes (F06), commercialisé à partir du début de l'été 2012. Sa plateforme est plus longue de 113 millimètres, car c'est celle de la série 5, et sa longueur totale dépasse les cinq mètres. Rival direct de la Mercedes CLS et de l'Audi A7 – et dans la fourchette de prix de la Porsche Panamera – le Gran Coupé ne manque pas de concurrence.

Silhouette fuselée, calandre bombée vers l'avant et larges joues sur les pneus : la série 6 allie sportivité et élégance avec une ligne de toute beauté. Disponible en versions 640i, 640d, 650i et M6 avec turbo TwinPower 560 ch, on peut dire que cette série a du souffle. Le moteur six cylindres en ligne de la 640i avec turbocompresseur twin-scroll, Valvetronic et injection directe libère 320 ch. La 640d tire seulement sept chevaux de moins de son six cylindres à injection directe, rampe commune et turbocompression à deux étages, combiné avec une turbine à géométrie variable. Le V8 de la 650i avec deux turbocompresseurs mobilise 450 ch, qui font accélérer les presque deux tonnes du Gran Coupé xDrive de 0 à 100 km/h en seulement 4,4 secondes. Avec un couple maximal de 650 Nm entre 2000 et 4500 tours, il y a assez de réserves de puissance pour rouler un peu des mécaniques. En mode « Sport+ » du contrôle dynamique des amortisseurs, soit à suspension rigide, ça fait la part belle au plaisir de conduire. Ici, l'investissement de 4000 euros pour des amortisseurs adaptatifs vaut la peine, car ils forment avec le système antiroulis « Dynamic Drive » un tandem extrêmement efficace. La boîte de vitesses automatique sport à huit rapports se combine avec une fonction stop & start, et la M6 utilise une boîte de vitesses sept rapports à double embrayage.

L'intérieur extrêmement raffiné donne à la voiture une aura d'exclusivité. Que votre intérieur personnalisé comprenne les sièges sport en cuir nappa et alcantara anthracite avec surpiqûres bleues du pack M ou bien le cuir de mérinos « Platine » avec passepoil noir, cette voiture crée une atmosphère qui donne envie de s'y attarder. Les finitions intérieures en platane foncé, aluminium finement brossé ou « piano laqué noir » apportent une touche d'élégance supplémentaire. Les couleurs extérieures telles que « Mondstein métallisé » ou « Frozen Bronze mat métallisé » donnent à ce véhicule haut de gamme une personnalité encore plus singulière dès le premier coup d'œil.

Les phares LED adaptatifs ou feux de virage adaptatifs ne passent pas inaperçus. Ce genre d'extra a autant d'impact sur le budget qu'un toit panoramique entrebaillable électriquement. Pour économiser sur le poids et abaisser le centre de gravité, les toits du M6 Coupé et du M6 Gran Coupé sont faits de plastique renforcé de fibre de carbone.

Brawny, elegant and powerful—the 650i xDrive. The four-door Gran Coupé has set new BMW standards for the high-end luxury segment, and matches its competitors blow for blow.

Wuchtig, elegant und kraftvoll präsentiert sich dieser 650i xDrive. Das viertürige Gran Coupé setzt bei BMW neue Maßstäbe in der Oberklasse und bietet seinen Konkurrenten erfolgreich Paroli.

Présence, élégance et puissance: la 650i xDrive. Ce Gran Coupé quatre portes est une nouvelle référence BMW dans le segment H, et donne du fil à retordre à ses concurrents.

A wide transmission tunnel divides the space.
The eight-cylinder engine produces 450 bhp.

Ein breiter Kardantunnel gliedert den Raum.
Das achtzylindrige Kraftwerk produziert 450 PS.

Le large tunnel de transmission divise l'espace.
Le moteur huit cylindres produit 450 ch.

Three or five doors, gasoline or diesel: with its station wagon-style rear, the second-generation 1 series certainly isn't lacking in originality, and the M135i could even be seen as extroverted. The spectrum of engines ranges from the 1.6-liter, four-cylinder diesel with 95 bhp to the three-liter, inline six-cylinder with 320 bhp. Only the load (1168 lbs), roof load (165 lbs) and length (14 ft 2 in) remain the same throughout.

Three equipment packages add individual pep to everyday life with the 1 series. The "Urban Line" is designed for the extra comfort required by city-dwellers, while the details of the "Sport Line"—from the bucket seats to the design of the alloy wheels and the "Sport" mode—give the driver an extra boost. The M-Sport package offers a taster of the real M, the series heavyweight available in the form of the M135i.

Its new straight six engine combines the performance advantages of a twin-scroll turbocharger with variable valve control ("Valvetronic"), variable control of both camshafts ("double-Vanos") and direct gasoline injection, so you can feel the spontaneous engine response even at low speeds. 332 lb-ft of torque, 320 bhp, a sprint of 0 to 60 mph in under

five seconds and an electronic top speed cut-off of 155 mph bring this small BMW in line with the big boys.

The 118i with five doors, shown here, sits comfortably in the mid-performance range. If required, its compact four-cylinder engine can unleash 170 bhp. Like its cousin, this turbo machine is a high-tech piece of equipment whose manual six-speed transmission and regenerative braking make it extremely efficient, resulting in an average of 50 mpg. And at 140 mph, this 1 series is certainly no slow coach. The real "cost cutter" is the 116d "EfficientDynamics Edition," whose little thirst makes it run 62 miles on a gallon of diesel.

To match the 13 exterior colors—three solid, ten metallic—BMW offers several combination options for upholstery and interior paneling. Those who wish to shell out a little more can go the whole hog and splash out in the special equipment shop. Infotainment, hands-free kit with USB interface, function buttons on the leather steering wheel and all kinds of assistance systems—from "Real Time Traffic Information" in the satnav to the parking assistant, camera for lane departure and collision warning or speed limit display—await customers, together with a range of visual accessories that includes 13 aluminum alloy wheel designs from 16 to 18 inches.

Ob Drei- oder Fünftürer, ob Benziner oder Diesel: Die 1er-Reihe der zweiten Generation mit dem kombiähnlichen Heck entbehrt nicht einer gewissen Originalität und gibt sich als M135i sogar extrovertiert. Das Motorenspektrum reicht vom 1,6-Liter-Vierzylinder-Diesel mit 95 PS bis zum Dreiliter-Reihensechszylinder mit 320 PS. Gleichheit herrscht nur bei Zuladung (530 Kilo), Dachlast (75 Kilo) und Länge (4,32 Meter).

Individuellen Pepp in den 1er-Alltag bringen drei Ausstattungspakete. Die „Urban Line" soll wohl den gehobenen Komfortansprüchen eines Städters gerecht werden, während sich die „Sport Line" durch einige Details von den Sitzschalen über das Design der Leichtmetallräder bis zum Schaltmodus „Sport" abhebt. Das M-Sportpaket bildet sozusagen das Entrée zum eigentlichen M, der als M135i zum Kräftemessen einlädt.

Sein neuer Reihensechszylinder vereint die Leistungsvorzüge eines Twin-Scroll-Turboladers mit variabler Ventilsteuerung („Valvetronic"), variabler Steuerung beider Nockenwellen („Doppel-Vanos") und direkter Benzineinspritzung. So ist selbst im Drehzahlkeller ein spontanes Ansprechverhalten des Triebwerks spürbar. 450 Newtonmeter Drehmoment, 320 PS, ein Sprintwert von unter fünf Sekunden auf 100 km/h und die elektronisch bei 250 km/h abgeregelte

BMW 1, 2 F20, F21, F22, F23 | 2011

Höchstgeschwindigkeit reihen den kleinen BMW bei den Großen ein.

Leistungsmäßig im Mittelfeld angesiedelt ist der hier vorgestellte 118i mit fünf Türen. Sein kompakter Vierzylinder setzt bei Bedarf 170 PS frei. Auch dieser moderne Turbomotor ist ein High-Tech-Gerät, das in Verbindung mit einem handgeschalteten Sechsganggetriebe und Bremsenergie-Rückgewinnung äußerst effizient agiert. Daraus resultiert ein durchschnittlicher Spritverbrauch von knapp unter sechs Litern Super. Und mit 225 km/h gehört dieser 1er gewiss nicht zu den Hinterherfahrern. Als absolutes „Sparbrötchen" darf der 116d „EfficientDynamics Edition" bezeichnet werden. Seinem Durst genügen durchschnittlich nur 3,8 Liter Diesel.

Zu den 13 Außenfarben – davon zehn metallic – bietet BMW etliche Kombinationsmöglichkeiten mit den Polsterfarben und Interieurleisten an. Wer es sich leisten will, kann hier und auch im Sonderausstattungs-Shop kräftig zulangen. Infotainment, Freisprechanlage mit USB-Schnittstelle, Funktionsknöpfe am Lederlenkrad, allerlei Assistenzsysteme – von der „Real Time Traffic Information" im Navi über den Parkassistenten bis zur Kamera zur Spurverlassens- und Auffahrwarnung oder Verkehrszeichenerkennung – warten ebenso auf Käufer wie die optischen Accessoires, zu denen 13 Leichtmetallräder-Designs von 16 bis 18 Zoll gehören.

Trois ou cinq portes, essence ou diesel : avec son hayon de break, la série 1 deuxième génération ne manque certainement pas d'originalité, et l'on pourrait même considérer le modèle M135i comme extraverti. L'éventail de moteurs disponibles va du diesel quatre cylindres, 1,6 litre et 95 ch jusqu'au six cylindres en ligne, 3 litres et 320 ch. Seules la charge utile (530 kilos), la charge de toit (75 kilos) et la longueur (4,32 mètres) restent les mêmes.

Trois finitions individualisées donnent du pep au quotidien de la série 1. La finition «Urban Line» est conçue pour apporter aux citadins un surcroît de confort, tandis que la finition «Sport Line» se démarque par quelques détails tels que les sièges baquets, le design des jantes en alliage léger ou encore le mode « Sport ». Le pack M Sport offre un avant-goût de la réelle M, le poids lourd de la série, sous le numéro de modèle M135i.

Son nouveau moteur à six cylindres en ligne réunit les performances d'un turbocompresseur Twin-Scroll avec la commande variable des soupapes («Valvetronic»), le calage variable des arbres à cames («double Vanos») et l'injection d'essence directe. Même en bas régime, le conducteur sent parfaitement la réactivité du moteur. 450 Nm de couple, 320 ch, une accélération de 0 à 100 km/h en moins de cinq secondes et une vitesse maximale réglée électroniquement à 250 km/h placent cette petite BMW dans la cour des grands.

La 118i cinq portes montrée ici se situe quant à elle dans le milieu de gamme en termes de performances. Son moteur quatre cylindres compact peut libérer 170 ch. Ce moteur turbo moderne est lui aussi une machine high-tech, qui, utilisée avec une boîte de vitesses manuelle à six rapports et un système de récupération de l'énergie au freinage, se révèle extrêmement efficace, ce qui se traduit par une consommation moyenne de moins de six litres d'essence. Et avec une vitesse de pointe de 225 km/h, cette série 1 n'est certainement pas à la traîne. Le modèle 116d «EfficientDynamics Edition» est le grand champion des économies, et n'a besoin que de 3,8 litres de gazole pour étancher sa soif.

BMW propose 13 couleurs extérieures (dont dix métallisées) et une multitude de combinaisons possibles avec la sellerie et les inserts décoratifs. Ceux qui sont prêts à dépenser plus pourront se faire plaisir avec les équipements spéciaux. Système d'info-divertissement, kit mains libres avec port USB, boutons de fonction sur le volant cuir et toutes sortes de systèmes d'assistance – depuis l'information sur la circulation en temps réel du système de navigation jusqu'au système d'aide au stationnement en passant par la caméra, les systèmes d'avertissement de dérive de trajectoire et de collision ou encore la reconnaissance des panneaux de signalisation – attendent l'acheteur, et il faut ajouter à tout cela les accessoires esthétiques, dont treize jantes en alliage léger de 16 à 18 pouces.

The second generation of the 1 series is more than just a facelift. The differences can be seen both in the new rear section design and throughout the interior.

Mit mehr als nur Facelifts präsentiert sich die zweite Generation der 1er-Reihe. Die Unterschiede machen sich sowohl bei der neu gestalteten Heckpartie als auch im gesamten Interieur bemerkbar.

La deuxième génération de la série 1 a bénéficié de bien plus qu'un ravalement de façade. On peut observer les différences dans la nouvelle ligne de l'arrière, ainsi que dans tout l'intérieur.

The five-door offers easy-access luggage space of 12¾ to 42½ cu.ft in volume. The 1 series has a completely new front with headlights that taper dynamically to the kidney grille. The 118i's four-cylinder engine generates 180 bhp.

Gut zugänglichen Gepäckraum von 360 bis 1200 Litern Volumen bietet der Fünftürer. Völlig neu: die Front des 1ers mit dynamisch auf die Niere zulaufenden Scheinwerfern. 180 PS entwickelt der Vierzylinder des 118i.

Le modèle cinq portes offre un espace de chargement facile d'accès de 360 à 1200 litres. La série 1 est dotée d'un nouvel avant avec des phares dont la ligne dynamique flatte la calandre. Le moteur quatre cylindres de la 118i développe 180 ch.

This Series 2 appeals not only with the aggressive front and pleasing rear, but also as the M235i with a 3-liter, six-cylinder engine that reaches 62mph in 5 seconds. It's undeniably a two-seater, since there is hardly any room for adults in the rear.

Dieser 2er besticht nicht nur durch seine Optik mit aggressiver Front und gefälligem Heck, sondern als M235i mit einem Dreiliter-Sechszylinder bestückt, beschleunigt er in fünf Sekunden auf Tempo 100. Ein echter Zweier, denn auf den Rücksitzen haben Erwachsene kaum Platz.

Cette série 2 éblouit non seulement par sa ligne, avec un nez agressif et un arrière gracieux, mais aussi, dans sa variante M235i, par son six-cylindres de trois litres, qui l'emmène à 100 km/h en cinq secondes. C'est une vraie 2-places, car les adultes seront bien à l'étroit sur les sièges arrière.

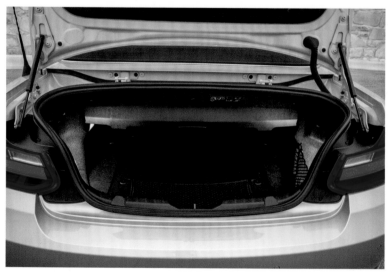

With two travelling in the Series 2 convertible, the wind deflector is raised behind the front seats to prevent any wind from leaving you with a hair out of place. The trunk with through-loading opening can easily hold two sets of golf equipment.

Zu zweit im 2er-Cabrio unterwegs, fährt man hinter den Vordersitzen das Windschott hoch und genießt die Fahrt ohne die Frisur bedrohende Turbulenzen. Der Kofferraum mit Durchladeluke ist groß genug für zwei Golfausrüstungen.

À deux dans ce cabriolet Série 2, il suffit de relever le pare-vent derrière les sièges avant pour profiter de la promenade sans se décoiffer. Le coffre avec trappe à skis peut accueillir deux sacs de golf.

The electric mechanism ensures that the fabric top glides down smoothly in less than 20 seconds even at speeds up to 30 mph.

Der elektrische Verdeckmechanismus sorgt sogar bei Geschwindigkeiten bis 50 Stundenkilometer für ein reibungsloses Versenken des Stoffdachs innerhalb von 20 Sekunden.

Le mécanisme électrique de la capote permet de la replier en 20 secondes et en tout confort jusqu'à une vitesse de 50 km/h.

BMW 3 F30/F80, F31, F34 | 2011

"The BMW tradition of expressing sporty elegance," says Head Designer Adrian van Hooydonk, "is reflected once again in the sixth-generation 3 series." The range of models is clear for all to see, with 27 possible engine/body combinations, from a gentle 316d's 116 bhp to the 340 bhp of the peak athlete ActiveHybrid 3; from the sedan (code name F30) and the station wagon (F31) to the GranTurismo (F34). According to BMW, the "power and poise" of this 3 series make it "the synonym for driving pleasure." This can be pre-programmed using "Driving Experience Control". Animated by the appearance of the now wider, longer car with more aggressive xenon headlamps with LED light rings that flank the kidney, the new 3 series oozes driving pleasure. This is particularly evident during load alteration, when the electronically controlled absorbers have to do heavy labor. Even for the extra price, the variable sport steering is highly recommended. This responds independently of the steering wheel angle, and makes fast cornering and maneuvering in tight parking spaces much easier. BMW also offers the speed-dependent Servotronic and the intelligent xDrive all-wheel drive system, as well as a sporty eight-speed automatic transmission.

The designation "Eco Pro" refers to a fuel-saving mode that increases the vehicle's range by driving more efficiently. Hardcore 3 series fans place greater importance on the Bavarians' sporting quality – and this is undisputed. And the diesels keep up well with the gasoline models. The common-rail diesel engine of the 320d, for example, with turbocharger and intercooler, produces 184 bhp and reaches a torque of 280 lb-ft. Its average mileage of more than 52 miles per gallon allows a range of a good 800 miles with a tank full of diesel. It also has a commendable greenhouse gas emissions value of 190 grams per mile—which the "EfficientDynamics Edition" even beats by some twelve grams.

The all-round pleasing exterior, free of annoying corners and sharp angles, is the perfect match for the tasteful interior, with more legroom for backseat passengers. The back seat division ratio is 40:20:40, thus allowing transport of longer items of luggage such as a golf bag.

The dashboard leans slightly toward the driver, harking back to an old BMW tradition that had fallen by the wayside for a time. "All the controls the driver needs are arranged ergonomically around the driver's seat for intuitive operation," says van Hooydonk, confirming expectations. He also notes that there are sufficient custom options available for customers who want something more than the ample standard equipment.

Die BMW-Tradition, sportliche Eleganz auszudrücken", so Chefdesigner Adrian van Hooydonk, „spiegelt sich auch in der sechsten 3er-Generation wider." Die Modellpalette mit 27 möglichen Karosserie-Motor-Kombinationen von zarten 116 PS (316d) bis zum Vorzeigeathleten mit 340 PS (ActiveHybrid 3), von der Limousine (Baureihe F30) über den Touring (F31) bis zum GranTurismo (F34) kann sich sehen lassen. Laut BMW ist dieser 3er „mit seiner Stärke und Souveränität das Synonym für Fahrfreude". Diese lässt sich per „Fahrerlebnisschalter" vorprogrammieren. Animiert durch die ansprechende Optik des in Länge und Breite gewachsenen Wagens mit aggressiveren Xenon-Scheinwerfern mit LED-Leuchtringen, die die Niere flankieren, lädt der neue 3er zum Fahrvergnügen ein. Dieses stellt sich besonders bei Lastwechseln, bei denen die elektronisch gesteuerten Dämpfer ganze Arbeit leisten müssen, ein. Wenn auch gegen Aufpreis, empfiehlt sich die Wahl der variablen Sportlenkung, die abhängig vom Lenkradeinschlag reagiert und schnelle Kurvenfahrten ebenso erleichtert wie das Rangieren in enge Parklücken. Daneben bietet BMW auch die geschwindigkeitsabhängige „Servotronic" an, wie auch das „intelligente" Allradsystem xDrive oder ein sportliches Achtgang-Automatikgetriebe.

Hinter der Bezeichnung „Eco Pro" verbirgt sich ein kraftstoffsparender Modus, der mehr Reichweite durch

effizienteres Fahren verheißt. Eingefleischte 3er-Freaks legen mehr Wert auf die sportlichen Qualitäten des Bajuwaren. Und diese sind unstrittig. Auch die Selbstzünder halten mit den Benzinern gut mit. Der Common-Rail-Dieselmotor des 320d etwa, mit Abgasturbo und Ladeluftkühler, produziert 184 PS und bringt es auf ein Drehmoment von 380 Newtonmetern. Sein durchschnittlicher Verbrauch von weniger als fünf Litern Diesel ermöglicht eine Reichweite von gut 1200 Kilometern pro Tankfüllung. Vorbildlich der CO_2-Emissionswert von 117g/km, den die „EfficientDynamics Edition" um weitere acht Gramm unterbietet.

Zu dem rundum gefälligen Äußeren ohne störende Ecken und Verwinkelungen passt die geschmackvolle Inneneinrichtung mit mehr Beinraum für die Fondpassagiere. Deren Rücksitzbank lässt sich im Verhältnis 40:20:40 teilen, damit auch Gepäckstücke wie ein Golfbag längs untergebracht werden können.

Das Armaturenbrett, Rückgriff auf zwischenzeitlich vernachlässigte BMW-Tradition, neigt sich dem Fahrer nun wieder etwas entgegen. „Alle fahrrelevanten Bedienelemente sind ergonomisch um den Fahrer herum angeordnet und intuitiv bedienbar", doziert van Hooydonk über Erwartetes, und weist darauf hin, dass dem Kunden neben der reichhaltigen Basisausstattung genügend Individualisierungsmöglichkeiten geboten werden.

D'après le designer en chef Adrian van Hooydonk, «la sixième génération de la série 3 reflète encore et toujours l'élégance sportive traditionnelle de BMW». La gamme de modèles est convaincante, avec 27 combinaisons de carrosserie et moteur possibles, de la tranquillité de 116 ch (316d) jusqu'à l'athlétisme de haut niveau avec 340 ch (ActiveHybrid 3), de la berline (F30) au Touring (F31) et au GranTurismo (F34). D'après BMW, «la puissance et la majesté» de cette série 3 en font «l'essence même du plaisir de conduire». Ces modèles peuvent être préprogrammés à l'aide du bouton de régulation du comportement dynamique. La série invite à découvrir le plaisir de la conduite avec une voiture plus longue et plus large dotée d'une belle ligne et dont la calandre est flanquée de phares au xénon plus agressifs avec des anneaux de LED. Cela se produit particulièrement lors des changements de charge, lorsque les amortisseurs à commande électronique doivent faire du bon travail. Même avec le supplément de prix, la direction sport variable est très recommandable. Elle répond en fonction de l'angle de braquage du volant et facilite la prise de courbe rapide ainsi que les manœuvres de stationnement dans les espaces réduits. BMW propose également la direction assistée «Servotronic» asservie à la vitesse, ainsi que le système de transmission intégrale «intelligente» xDrive ou une boîte de vitesses automatique sport à huit rapports.

La dénomination «Eco Pro» désigne un mode économique qui augmente l'autonomie du véhicule grâce à une conduite plus éco-efficiente. Les vrais amateurs de la série 3 accordent plus d'importance aux qualités sportives de la Bavaroise, et elles sont incontestables. Les moteurs diesel n'ont rien à envier aux essence. Le moteur diesel à rampe commune de la 320d, par exemple, avec turbo et intercooler, développe 184 ch et atteint un couple de 380 Nm. Sa consommation moyenne inférieure à cinq litres de diesel lui donne une autonomie d'au moins 1200 kilomètres par plein. Elle a également des performances exemplaires en matière d'émissions de CO_2, avec 117 g/km, seulement 8 grammes de plus que l'«EfficientDynamics Edition».

La ligne extérieure séduisante sans angles aigus est assortie d'un intérieur élégant avec plus de place pour les jambes à l'arrière. Les sièges arrière se divisent selon un rapport de 40:20:40 afin de pouvoir transporter confortablement un sac de golf, par exemple.

Le tableau de bord est incliné vers le conducteur, retour à une vieille tradition de BMW qui avait été quelque peu oubliée. «Toutes les commandes utiles sont disposées ergonomiquement autour du conducteur pour une utilisation intuitive», indique van Hooydonk. Il remarque également que les clients qui désirent davantage que l'ample équipement standard ont à leur disposition de nombreuses options de personnalisation.

The sixth-generation 3 series is markedly different from its predecessor, with a curved hood, an almost vertical kidney grille and headlight slits.

Die sechste 3er-Generation fällt gegenüber ihrer Vorgängerin sofort durch die gewölbte Haube, die fast senkrechte Niere und die Scheinwerferschlitze auf.

La série 3 sixième génération se distingue des générations précédentes par un capot bombé, une calandre pratiquement verticale et la fente des phares.

Even with the two-liter engine with twin-scroll turbo and 184 bhp, the 3 series loves to show off its well-shaped rear to its competitors.

Selbst mit dem Zweilitertriebwerk mit Twin-Scroll-Turbo und 184 PS zeigt der 3er Mitbewerbern gern seine formschöne Heckpartie.

Même avec le moteur deux litres avec turbocompresseur à deux volutes et 184 ch, la série 3 aime montrer à ses concurrentes son arrière-train à l'esthétique fort aboutie.

The functional design
of the tidy interior
of the 3 series is in
keeping with the BMW
tradition of radiating
sporty elegance.

Die funktionelle,
sauber verarbeitete
Inneneinrichtung
des 3ers folgt in
der Gestaltung
der BMW-Tradition,
sportliche Eleganz
auszustrahlen.

Le design fonctionnel
de l'intérieur épuré de la
série 3 suit la tradition
de BMW et respire
l'élégance sportive.

The rear section of the Series 3 GT is as massive as that of the Series 5 GT, but also a little more delicate in appearance and slightly elongated.

Gewaltig wie beim 5er GT, aber doch etwas filigraner und gestreckter wirkend, ragt das Heck des 3er GT empor.

Imposant comme pour la Série 5 GT, et pourtant avec une ligne plus fine et plus allongée, l'arrière de la Série 3 GT s'étire vers le haut.

There is more space behind the large tailgate of the Series 3 GT than of the Series 3 Touring. The rear seat backrests fold down in three sections which, combined with the option of storing the split luggage compartment cover inside the floor of the trunk, means the car can be loaded as required. The elegant lines of the sides hide a storage miracle.

Hinter der großen Klappe des 3er GT verbirgt sich mehr Ladekapazität als beim 3er Touring. Durch dreifach teilbares Umlegen der Rückenlehnen im Fond und die Möglichkeit, die ebenfalls teilbare Gepäckraumabdeckung im Kofferraumboden zu verstauen, kann nach Belieben beladen werden. Hinter der eleganten seitlichen Karosserieführung verbirgt sich ein kleines Raumwunder.

Le grand hayon de la Série 3 GT s'ouvre sur une capacité de chargement supérieure à celle de la Série 3 Touring. Grâce à ses dossiers arrière rabattables en trois parties et à la possibilité de ranger le cache-bagages également divisible dans le plancher du coffre, on peut charger à volonté. Derrière les lignes élégantes de la carrosserie se cache une petite merveille d'espace.

BMW X5, X6 F15/F85, F16/F86 | 2013

BMW's highlights in the SUV and SAC segment, the X5 and its coupé version X6, were presented in their top-of-the-range versions X5M and X6M at the November 2014 Los Angeles Auto Show to tremendous acclaim. After all, they were being presented to a target audience that is particularly widespread in North America. In order to enhance the coupé, which was not quite so well known in the USA, it was painted in the new color of "Long Beach Blue Metallic". With the double-strut kidney grille and aggressive-looking, massive honeycomb air intakes, these M-models soon roared into the hearts of people who love beefy "strongmen" like this one. The muscular looks are further enhanced by the flared fenders, which can also take 21-inch wheels (for a surcharge). Like the standard 20-inch option, they have wide tires—285/40 R20 at the front and 325/35 R20 at the back. The honeycomb is also repeated at the rear between the two muffler tail pipe pairs! With all this power on show, enhanced by the discreet M-emblems, let's not forget the potential under the hood: the most powerful BMW series engine, a 4.4-liter V8 turbo of 575 bhp and providing 553 lb-ft at between 2200 and 5000 revs. With a range of just under 20 mpg with normal driving, this power plant is actually quite easy to please. Despite the not insignificant weight (with driver, passenger, and a small amount of luggage we're talking about 2½ tons), the X5M/

X6M duo reaches the 62 mph mark in just 4.2 seconds. The actual top speed is limited electronically to 155 mph, but the "M Drivers' Package" for experienced drivers increases the limit to 174 mph. The fact that these four-wheel giants can hold their own against sportier numbers on the legendary Nordschleife of the Nürburgring also speaks for the suspension with electronically adjusting shock absorbers, reinforced springs and active roll stabilization.

Up to one hundred percent of the power transmission can be transferred to the front or rear wheels. The "Dynamic Performance Control" ensures the optimum distribution at the rear. BMW has also given its M-giant a more powerful braking system. For these large vehicles, 8.20 minutes through the "Green Hell" are truly and literally spectacular. Asphalt performance: even controlled drifts are possible in "M-Dynamic Mode". The 8-speed Steptronic with aluminum paddles on the leather steering wheel provides a sporty drive. Thanks to the Servotronic steering with three settings, these X models can be controlled with precision and relative ease. The tasteful, lavishly designed interior with a large display over the center console reveals that these four-wheel drives are not really intended for all-terrain driving, but for cruising down boulevards or showing off their power on the interstate.

BMWs Highlights im SUV- und SAC-Segment, der X5 und seine Coupé-Variante X6, paradierten in ihren höchsten Eskalationsstufen X5M und X6M auf der Los Angeles Auto Show im November 2014 brüderlich nebeneinander und fanden viel Anklang. Schließlich präsentieren sie sich einer Zielgruppe, die gerade in Nordamerika sehr verbreitet ist. Um das in den USA noch nicht so bekannte Coupé ein wenig hervorzuheben, stellte sich dieses in der neuen Außenfarbe „Long Beach Blue Metallic" vor. Mit Doppelstreben-Nieren und aggressiv wirkenden, gewaltigen Wabengitter-Lufteinlässen saugen sich diese M-Typen in die Herzen von Menschen, die bullige Kraftsportler mögen. Die Muscle-Optik unterstreichen auch die verbreiterten Kotflügel, die gegen Aufpreis auch 21-Zoll-Räder aufnehmen können. Diese – wie auch die serienmäßigen 20-Zöller – sind mit breiten Walzen (285/40 R20 vorn und 325/35 R20 hinten) bereift. Wabengitter auch am Heck zwischen den zwei Auspuff-Endrohrpaaren! Bei soviel Kraftausdruck, unterstrichen durch dezent verteilte M-Embleme, darf natürlich das entsprechende Potenzial unter der Haube nicht fehlen: der stärkste BMW-Serien-Motor, ein 4,4-Liter-V8-Turbo mit 575 PS und einem Drehmoment von 750 Newtonmetern zwischen 2200 und 5000 Touren. Bei normaler Gangart gibt sich dieses Kraftwerk mit einem Verbrauch von knapp 12 Litern relativ bescheiden. Trotz einer nicht unerheblichen Massenbewegung, die einschließlich Fahrer und Beifahrer mit etwas Gepäck im Bereich von zweieinhalb Tonnen liegt,

erreicht das X5M/X6M-Duo bereits in 4,2 Sekunden die 100-km/h-Marke. Die eigentliche Spitzengeschwindigkeit wird bei Tempo 250 elektronisch in die Schranken gewiesen, doch hebt ein „M Drivers Package" für versierte Fahrer das Limit auf 280 km/h an. Dass diese Allradriesen auf der Nordschleife des Nürburgrings im Vergleich mit sportlicher anmutenden Geräten munter mithalten können, spricht auch für deren Fahrwerk mit elektronisch verstellbaren Stoßdämpfern und härteren Federn sowie der aktiven Wankstabilisierung. Die Kraftübertragung kann bis zu einhundert Prozent auf die Hinter- oder Vorderräder übertragen werden. Zwischen den Hinterrädern sorgt eine „Dynamic Performance Control" für die optimale Verteilung. Außerdem spendierte BMW seinen M-Kolossen eine leistungsfähigere Bremsanlage. Zeiten um 8:20 Minuten durch die „Grüne Hölle" sind für diese voluminösen Gefährte also im wahrsten Sinne des Wortes kolossal. Asphalt-Performance: Im „M-Dynamic-Mode" lassen sich sogar kontrollierte Drifts hinlegen. Sportliches Schalten ermöglicht eine 8-Gang-Steptronic mit Alu-Paddeln am Lederlenkrad. Dank der Servotronic-Lenkung – in drei Stufen einstellbar – lässt sich diese X-Materie präzise und relativ leicht beherrschen. Auch das geschmackvoll und aufwendig gestaltete Interieur mit einem großen Display über der Mittelkonsole verrät, dass diese Allradler nicht zum Bewegen im Gelände gedacht sind, sondern sich eher zum Flanieren auf Boulevards oder zur Power-Demonstration auf der Autobahn eignen.

Vedettes de BMW sur le segment SUV et SAC, la X5 et sa version coupé la X6 ont paradé côte à côte dans leurs variantes les plus sélect X5M et X6M sur le Los Angeles Auto Show en novembre 2014 et ont fait sensation. Elles sont enfin présentées à un public cible très large en Amérique du Nord. Pour mettre en valeur le coupé, encore peu connu aux États-Unis, il a été revêtu de la nouvelle couleur «Long Beach Blue Metallic». Avec des naseaux à double traverse et d'énormes prises d'air nid d'abeille à l'air agressif, ces modèles M visent le cœur de ceux qui aiment les sportives musclées. Cette esthétique nerveuse est aussi soulignée par les ailes élargies, qui peuvent accueillir des roues de 21 pouces, à un coût supplémentaire. Elles sont chaussées de pneus larges (285/40 R20 à l'avant et 325/35 R20 à l'arrière) – tout comme la version 20 pouces standard. Le nid d'abeille est également présent à l'arrière entre les deux paires d'échappement ! Avec tous ces déploiements de force, accentués par le sigle M très exclusif, le potentiel correspondant ne doit bien sûr pas faire défaut sous le capot : le moteur BMW de série le plus puissant, un V8 turbo de 4,4 litres qui développe 575 ch, et un couple de 750 Nm entre 2200 et 5000 tours. Pour une conduite normale, cette petite centrale se montre relativement peu gourmande, avec à peine 12 litres. Malgré un poids non négligeable, qui se situe aux alentours de deux tonnes et demie avec le conducteur, un passager et quelques bagages, le duo X5M/X6M

atteint les 100 km/h en seulement 4,2 secondes. La vitesse maximale réelle est réduite électroniquement à 250 km/h, mais le «M Drivers Package» relève cette limite à 280 km/h pour les conducteurs expérimentés. Le fait que ces géantes de la transmission intégrale puissent faire jeu égal avec des machines qui semblent plus sportives sur la boucle nord du Nürburgring est aussi le résultat d'un châssis équipé d'amortisseurs électroniques et de ressorts renforcés, ainsi que de la stabilisation active du roulis. La transmission de l'effort peut être transférée jusqu'à cent pour cent sur les roues arrière ou sur les roues avant. Entre les roues arrière, le «Dynamic Performance Control» assure une distribution optimale. En outre, BMW a doté ses colosses M d'un système de freinage plus puissant. Pour ces engins volumineux, un temps de 8,20 minutes sur «l'enfer vert» est effectivement colossal, dans le vrai sens du terme. Performance sur l'asphalte : le mode «M-Dynamic» permet même de dominer le drift contrôlé. La boîte Steptronic à huit rapports avec touches en alu sur le volant cuir assure un passage sportif des vitesses. Grâce à la direction Servotronic à trois réglages, ces modèles X se laissent conduire avec précision et une certaine facilité. Leur intérieur élégant et somptueux, avec un grand écran sur la console centrale, révèle que ces engins à quatre roues motrices ne sont pas pensés pour le tout-terrain, mais plutôt pour se promener sur les boulevards ou se livrer à des démonstrations de puissance sur l'autoroute.

The combination of an SUV with the habitus of a sports car is further underscored by the eye-catching front with double-braced kidneys and the broad front apron with the extremely aggressive-looking air intakes. The side contours also reflect the sporty character. Colossal: the rear section of this powerhouse on wheels.

Die Kombination eines SUV mit dem Habitus eines Sportwagens wird auch optisch untermalt durch eine markante Front mit Doppelstreben-Nieren und einer breiten Frontschürze mit äußerst aggressiv wirkenden Lufteinlässen. Auch die seitlichen Konturen lassen den sportlichen Charakter nicht vermissen. Kolossal: das Heck dieses Kraftwerks auf Rädern.

La combinaison du SUV avec l'esprit d'une voiture de sport est aussi soulignée esthétiquement à l'avant par des naseaux marquants à traverses doubles et une jupe large avec des prises d'air très agressives. La ligne des côtés ne laisse aucun doute sur le caractère sportif de cette machine, et l'arrière est tout simplement colossal.

The interior with the multi-function seats and elegant features is spacious and comfortable. Exclusive touch on the interior and exterior: the M emblems that are even to be found on the door sill panels. The 575 bhp of the twin-turbo V8 accelerate this 2.3-ton vehicle to 62 mph in just 4.2 seconds.

Geräumig präsentiert sich das Interieur mit Multifunktionssitzen und nobler Ausstattung. Innen und außen nach Würdigung heischend: die M-Embleme, selbst auf den Einstiegsleisten. Die 575 PS des V8-Twin-Turbos beschleunigen das 2,3 Tonnen schwere Gefährt in 4,2 Sekunden auf Tempo 100.

L'intérieur équipé de sièges multifonctions et revêtu de matières nobles est spacieux. Le sigle M, présent même sur les barres de seuil, rappelle qu'il s'agit d'une voiture d'exception. Les 575 ch du V8 Twin-Turbo font accélérer ses 2,3 tonnes à 100 km/h en 4,2 secondes.

Highlight in BMW's SAC segment: the X6M, effectively the coupé version of the X5M, whose built-in speed limit can be raised to 175 mph as an option.

Highlight im SAC-Segment von BMW: der X6M, quasi das Coupé des X5M, dessen Massenbewegung auf Wunsch auf ein Limit von 280 km/h angehoben werden kann.

La X6M, version coupé de la X5M, est la vedette du segment SAC de BMW. Il est possible de relever la limitation de sa vitesse maximale à 280 km/h.

Functional and framed in fine wood and interior trims: the cockpit of the X6M with its clear gauges and leather steering wheel with shifting paddles. Two pairs of chrome-plated double mufflers flank the diffusor on the rear. All M design: blue-painted brake saddles and double-spoke alloy wheels.

Funktionell und eingerahmt von Edelholz und Interieur-Leisten: das Cockpit des X6M mit übersichtlichen Armaturen und einem Lederlenkrad mit Schaltwippen. Zwei verchromte Doppelauspuff-Paare flankieren den Diffusor am Heck. Ganz im M-Design: lackierte Bremssättel und Doppelspeichen-Leichtmetallräder.

Fonctionnel, habillé de bois noble et d'inserts de décoration, l'habitacle de la X6M offre des commandes claires et des palettes au volant cuir. Deux paires d'échappements chromés flanquent le diffuseur à l'arrière. Dans le plus pur style M: étriers de freins laqués et jantes en alliage léger à rayons doubles.

BMW i3 |01|2014

The idea of taking this little electric car, known as the i3, out on country roads and then stopping with barely a charging outlet in sight may not be exactly electrifying, but that isn't actually what it was designed for.

In 2008, project manager Ulrich Kranz and his team looked at exploring new options in urban mobility, and analyzed the volume and flow of traffic and the resulting environmental pollution in the major urban centers of the world. The result of this research and a wide range of tests was a compact electric urban car. On the road (depending on driving style), this emission-free car has a range of around 95 miles.

The compromise is suggested for longer distances: the i3 with "Range Extender". The 170 bhp electric motor is connected to a two-cylinder that develops 34 bhp from an engine capacity of 647 cc. This almost doubles the full range, although the extra 265 pounds slows acceleration to 62 mph from 7.2 to 7.9 seconds. By the same token, though, the i3 is not meant to be impressive at accelerating or for racing along the highway. Its top speed of 93 mph is more than reasonable.

As attractive as the DC express charging time of 30 minutes is, plugged into the domestic AC supply it will take between six and eight hours to charge. The BMW Wallbox shortens this process by two hours.

For its move into electrics, BMW is on the right track with the i3. In 2014, an impressive 16,052 units left the plant in Leipzig, and in fact demand was at times so high that the daily output had to be increased to 100 units.

The i3 architecture consists of two modules. The lower section has all the chassis and drive components plus the lithium-ion high-voltage battery that lasts up to eight years, while the upper section houses the passenger compartment. Made entirely of carbon, it is bonded to the aluminum chassis. Lightweight above, battery weight right at the bottom: it's not possible to get the center of gravity any lower on this 62-inch-tall four-seater. There's no dodging a B-pillar when getting in because there isn't one.

Having seen the elevated seating in a combination of climate-active wool and cowhide leather from South Germany tanned in an olive leaf extract, it is time to contemplate the origin of the wood paneling. In the "Lodge" and "Suite" versions it consists of open-pored eucalyptus wood, in other words a renewable resource. And naturally, the plastic and fabric elements are all made from recycled materials. Functionally, the i3 is oriented towards the future, but when it comes to the design—and especially to the profile—opinions are vastly divided.

Nicht gerade elektrisierend ist die Vorstellung, mit dem kleinen Stromer, genannt i3, auf einem Landausflug – keine Ladesäule weit und breit – stehen zu bleiben, doch ein derartiger Exkurs ist eigentlich auch nicht vorgesehen.

Neue Wege urbaner Mobilität zu beschreiten, stand 2008 auf der Agenda von Projektleiter Ulrich Kranz und seinem Team, das sorgfältig Verkehrsaufkommen und -fluss sowie die daraus resultierende Umweltbelastung in den großen Ballungszentren dieser Erde analysiert hatte. Resultat der Forschung und eines umfangreichen Testprogramms: ein kompakter, elektrisch angetriebener Stadtwagen. Dieser emissionslose Wagen schafft in der Praxis – je nach Fahrweise – etwa 150 Kilometer.

Für längere Distanzen am Stück empfiehlt sich der Kompromiss: i3 mit „Range Extender". Hierbei wird das 170-PS-Elektromobil mit einem Zweizylinder gekoppelt, der aus 647 cm³ Hubraum 34 PS schöpft. Die Gesamtreichweite kann dadurch nahezu verdoppelt werden, wenngleich das Mehrgewicht von 120 Kilo die Beschleunigung auf Tempo 100 von 7,2 auf 7,9 Sekunden verlangsamt. Andererseits ist der i3 weder als Ampelsprinter noch als Autobahn-Renner gedacht. Ergo liegt seine Spitze von 150 km/h durchaus im vernünftigen Bereich.

So verlockend die Gleichstrom-Schnellladezeit von 30 Minuten sein mag, an der Wechselstrom-Haushaltssteckdose muss der Elektrowagen sechs bis acht Stunden

hängen. Die sogenannte Wallbox von BMW verkürzt diese Prozedur um zwei Stunden.

BMW – elektrisch in Bewegung geraten – sieht sich mit dem i3 auf dem richtigen Weg. 2014 verließen immerhin 16 052 Einheiten das Werk in Leipzig, das teilweise derart unter Strom stand, dass die tägliche Stückzahl bis auf 100 Einheiten angehoben werden musste.

Die Architektur des i3 besteht aus zwei Modulen: Das untere mit allen Fahrwerks- und Antriebskomponenten sowie dem Lithium-Ionen-Hochvolt-Batterie-Segment, dem eine Lebensdauer von acht Jahren zugestanden wird, und darüber das obere Modul, die Fahrgastzelle. Diese, ganz aus Carbon gebacken, wird mit dem Alu-Chassis verklebt. Leichtbau oben, Batteriegewicht ganz unten: Niedriger lässt sich der Schwerpunkt bei dem knapp 158 Zentimeter hohen Viersitzer nicht setzen. Beim Einsteigen muss man sich nicht an einer B-Säule vorbei jonglieren – sie gibt es nicht.

Ist die erhöhte Sitzposition im Ensemble aus klimaaktiver Wolle und mit Olivenblattextrakt gegerbtem Leder süddeutscher Rinder eingenommen, darf über die Herkunft der Holztäfelung sinniert werden. Bei den Interieur-Variationen „Lodge" und „Suite" besteht sie aus offenporigem Eukalyptus-Holz, also einem nachwachsenden Rohstoff. Selbstverständlich sind Kunststoffteile und Stoffverkleidungen aus recyceltem Material. Die Funktion des i3 orientiert sich an der Zukunft, beim Design – besonders der seitlichen Linienführung – gehen die Meinungen jedoch weit auseinander.

Prendre cette petite électrique, baptisée i3, pour une balade à la campagne sans borne de chargement en vue, n'a rien d'une idée précisément électrisante. Mais elle n'a pas été prévue pour ça.

L'exploration de nouveaux modes de mobilité urbaine était au programme du chef de projet Ulrich Kranz et de son équipe en 2008. Ils réalisèrent une analyse détaillée des volumes et flux de trafic ainsi que de la pollution environnementale résultante dans les grands centres urbains du monde. Le résultat de ces recherches et d'un vaste programme d'essais : une citadine électrique compacte. Ce véhicule sans émissions atteint une autonomie de quelques 150 kilomètres – selon la conduite.

Pour les distances plus longues, le compromis est conseillé : l'i3 peut s'accompagner d'un «range extender» qui augmente son autonomie. Le moteur électrique de 170 ch est dans ce cas couplé à un bicylindre qui développe 34 ch avec une cylindrée de 647 cm³. Cela permet de pratiquement doubler l'autonomie, mais le poids supplémentaire de 120 kilos ralentit l'accélération à 100 km/h de 7,2 à 7,9 secondes. Cela étant, l'i3 n'a été conçue ni pour sprinter, ni pour faire la course sur l'autoroute. C'est pourquoi sa vitesse de pointe de 150 km/h est tout à fait raisonnable.

Aussi séduisant que puisse être son temps de charge rapide sur courant continu, de 30 minutes, pour un chargement sur prise domestique de courant alternatif il faut compter

six à huit heures. La Wallbox de BMW raccourcit cette procédure de deux heures.

Avec l'i3, BMW est sur la bonne voie pour faire bouger l'électrique. Quelque 16 052 unités sont sorties de l'usine de Leipzig en 2014, et la tension a monté de sorte qu'il a fallu faire passer le nombre d'unités à 100 par jour.

L'architecture de l'i3 se compose de deux modules : Un module inférieur avec tous les composants du châssis et de la transmission, ainsi que la batterie lithium-ion haute tension, dont la durée de vie atteint huit ans, sur lequel est posé le module supérieur, l'habitacle. Il est entièrement renforcé au carbone, et collé sur le châssis en alu. Légèreté en haut, poids de la batterie en bas : Impossible de situer le centre de gravité plus bas sur cette quatre places qui atteint à peine 158 centimètres de haut. Pour monter à bord, pas la peine d'esquiver le montant central – elle n'en a pas.

Après avoir apprécié les sièges surélevés revêtus de laine climactive et de cuir de vache d'Allemagne du Sud tanné à l'extrait de feuille d'olivier, il faut encore méditer sur l'origine des boiseries. Pour les finitions «Lodge» et «Suite» elles se composent d'eucalyptus à pores ouverts, encore une matière renouvelable. Bien évidemment, les éléments en plastique et en tissu sont fabriqués en matériaux recyclés. La fonction de l'i3 s'oriente vers l'avenir, mais son design – surtout lorsqu'elle est vue de profil – divise les opinions.

Even if the contours of the i3—seen here in "Solar Orange" with accents in "Frozen Grey"—take a little getting used to, this zero-emission car is electrifying. The 20-inch double-spoke wheels with mixed tires add a touch of sportiness. A standard cable connects the charging socket to a standard wall socket or, alternatively, a "Wallbox" that accelerates the charging process.

Auch wenn die Konturen des i3 – hier in der Farbe „Solarorange" mit Akzenten in „Frozen Grey" – etwas gewöhnungsbedürftig sind, elektrisiert dieses abgasfreie Mobil. Einen Touch Sportlichkeit vermitteln die 20-Zoll-Doppelspeichenräder mit Mischbereifung. Ein Standardkabel verbindet die Elektro-Ladebuchse mit einer normalen Steckdose oder einer „Wallbox", die den Ladevorgang beschleunigt.

Même si la ligne de l'i3 – ici en couleur « Solar Orange » avec des accents « Frozen Grey » – est un peu surprenante, cette voiture sans émissions est électrisante. Les jantes 20 pouces à branches doubles et les pneus mixtes lui donnent une touche de sportivité. C'est un câble standard qui relie la prise de chargement électrique à une prise normale ou à une « Wallbox » qui accélère le chargement.

Entry into BMW's carbon age is easy thanks to the rear coach doors and the lack of a B-pillar; moreover, there is no irritating center console, the steering column is free, and the position of the olive leaf tanned leather seating is elevated.

Dank gegenläufiger Türen ohne B-Säule fällt der Einstieg in das Carbonzeitalter von BMW leicht, zumal keine Mittelkonsole stört, das Lenkrad frei steht, und die Sitzposition der Fauteuils aus mit Olivenblattextrakt gegerbtem Leder erhöht ist.

Ses portes qui s'ouvrent en sens contraire et l'absence de montant central facilitent la montée dans cette BMW de l'âge du carbone, surtout qu'aucune console centrale ne gêne les mouvements, le volant est dégagé, et la position du siège en cuir tanné à l'extrait de feuilles d'olivier est surélevée.

The optional glass roof that either opens or tilts increases the feeling of spaciousness. D, N, R: the least in being spoilt for choice as there is none, a gear shift is needless. The entertainment and navigation screen is embedded in open-pore eucalyptus wood, and includes a range map. The speedometer with battery display is also digital.

Mehr Raumgefühl verleiht das optionale Glasdach zum Öffnen oder Kippen. D, N, R: Wer die Wahl hat, hat hier keine Qual, denn für die Fortbewegung ist eine Gangschaltung überflüssig. Das in offenporiges Eukalyptusholz eingebettete Entertainment- und Navi-Display beinhaltet auch eine Reichweitenkarte. Ebenfalls digital informiert der Tacho mit Ladestatus.

Le toit ouvrant coulissant et entrebaillable en option augmente l'impression d'espace. D, N, R: le choix sans l'embarras, car pour la marche avant, tout changement de vitesse est superflu. L'écran de navigation et de divertissement monté dans le bois d'eucalyptus à pores ouverts comprend également un indicateur d'autonomie avec carte. Le compteur numérique indique quant à lui le niveau de chargement.

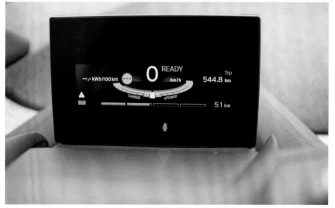

The 4-series BMWs—and there are now five of them—are distancing themselves from their predecessor, the 3-series coupé: by a few inches in the dimensions, by a carefully redesigned chassis, and by a sporty esthetic that is beyond compare. With the exception of the 430d, the coupé (F32) and convertible (F33) are also available with all-wheel drive, whereas the Gran Coupé (F36), the weakest link in terms of the engine, the 418d with 143bhp, has had to go without the "xDrive".

Like the M3 sedan (F80), the M4 coupé (F82) and convertible (F83) are in the same M-TwinPower league with 431bhp. The rear drive invites a slight drift, although the driving behavior of the slightly front-heavy vehicle is decidedly neutral. The return from a V8 to the classic straight six, twin-turbocharged of course, not only provides an additional 11bhp and higher torque, but also pays off with an improvement in fuel economy. The powerful sound through flap systems provides acoustic support for the M-instrument, which comes with a 6-gear transmission with conventional manual shift as standard. Of course, a 7-gear M dual-clutch version with "Drivelogic" is available as an option for just about 5000 dollars. The M-generation provides pure driving fun that is best experienced in the corners of the Nürburgring Nordschleife. Along with the carbon, aluminum, and magnesium used in the M4's lightweight construction, BMW has also added a healthy dash of adrenalin.

Nor does the performance of the Coupé without the "M" in its name give any cause for complaint. Both the 435i (306bhp) and the turbodiesel 435d (313bhp) are powerful enough to reach 62mph in 5.5 seconds, and to bring in the electronic speed limiter at 155mph. Thanks to the M-sports package, which includes aerodynamic accessories from the front to the rear apron, the 18- or 19-inch double-spoke alloy wheels or a sporty chassis, along with M-styling on the inside, it can pretty much hold its own against the "M." Three other versions, the "Sport Line," "Luxury Line," and "Modern Line," offer a multitude of customization options that are also included in the GranCoupé's repertoire. This four-door, about half an inch higher than the coupé but otherwise with the same dimensions, weighs an average of 110 to 130 pounds more, although this translates to just a split second more on the way to 62mph.

For all its elegance, this "beau on wheels" also offers plenty of practical advantages. With a trunk capacity of 17cu.ft—which increases to 46 with the back seats down—that is easily accessed via the large power lift gate, luggage space, or a lack thereof, will not give cause for complaint. And practicality will probably not top the list of any Series 4 customer's list of priorities, since the idea is to stand out from the Series 3, and that is achieved with the harmony of its proportions and its flowing silhouette that ends in the elegant rear section.

Die 4er-BMW – und das sind immerhin deren fünf – gehen zu ihrem Vorläufer, dem 3er-Coupé, auf Distanz: um einige Millimetersprünge bei den Dimensionen, durch ein sorgfältig überarbeitetes Fahrwerk und rein optisch durch sportliche Ästhetik par excellence. Abgesehen vom motorisch schwächsten Glied, dem 418d mit 143 PS, sind Coupé (F32), Cabrio (F33) und GranCoupé (F36) auch mit Allradantrieb erhältlich.

Wie auch die M3-Limousine (F80) spielen M4 Coupé (F82) und Cabrio (F83) in der M-TwinPower-Liga, die sich mit 431 PS bemerkbar macht. Der Heckantrieb lädt auch zu einem leichten Drift ein, wenngleich das Fahrverhalten der leicht frontlastigen PS-Protze durchaus sehr neutral ausfällt. Die Rückkehr vom V8-Sauger zum klassischen Reihensechszylinder, freilich mit doppeltem Turbolader, beschert nicht nur zusätzliche elf PS und ein höheres Drehmoment, sondern macht sich auch durch bessere Verbrauchswerte bezahlt.

Kraftvoller Klang durch Klappensysteme unterstützt akustisch das M-Instrument, dessen serienmäßiges 6-Gang-Getriebe konventionell von Hand geschaltet wird. Natürlich ist auch eine siebengängige M-Doppelkupplungs-Variante mit „Drivelogic"-System für knapp 4000 Euro optional. Diese M-Generation bringt Fahrspaß pur, der sich besonders im Kurvengeschlängel einer Nürburgring-Nordschleife einstellt. Der M4-Leichtbauweise mit einigen Carbon-, Aluminium- und Magnesium-Zutaten fügt BMW noch einen gehörigen Schuss Adrenalin hinzu.

BMW 4 F32/F82 F33/F83 F36|2014

Über mangelnde Leistung braucht man sich aber auch beim Coupé ohne „M" im Vorspann nicht beklagen. Mit dem 435i (306 PS) und dem Turbodiesel 435d (313 PS) ist genügend Vortrieb vorhanden, um in 5,5 Sekunden auf Tempo 100 zu beschleunigen und bei 250 km/h die elektronische Abregelung auf den Plan zu rufen. Dank M-Sportpaket, zu dem auch aerodynamische Accessoires von der Front- bis zur Heckschürze, Leichtmetall-Doppelspeichenräder in 18 oder 19 Zoll oder ein Sportfahrwerk sowie M-Lastiges im Interieur gehören, kann mit „M" im Nachspann Staat gemacht werden. Drei weitere Ausstattungsvarianten – „Sport Line", „Luxury Line" und „Modern Line" – warten mit einer Fülle von Individualisierungsmöglichkeiten auf, die auch zum Repertoire des Gran Coupés gehören. Dieser Viertürer, zwölf Millimeter höher als das Coupé, ansonsten mit gleichen Abmessungen, bringt durchschnittlich 50 bis 60 Kilo mehr auf die Waage, was der Beschleunigung auf 100 km/h lediglich eine Zehntelsekunde kostet.

Bei aller Eleganz offenbart dieser Beau auf Rädern auch viele praktische Aspekte: Mit 480 Litern Gepäckraumvolumen – bei umgeklappten Rücksitzlehnen sogar 1300 – bequem erreichbar über eine große, elektrisch betätigte Heckklappe, mangelt es an Stauraum nicht. Alltagstauglichkeit dürfte bei einem 4er-Kunden sicherlich nicht ganz oben auf der Prioritätenliste stehen, denn man will sich ja vom 3er abheben, und das gelingt durch die Harmonie seiner Proportionen und seine fließende Silhouette, die in einer anmutigen Heckpartie mündet.

Les BMW Série 4 prennent leurs distances d'avec leur prédécesseur le Série 3 Coupé : à pas comptés de quelques millimètres dans les dimensions, avec un châssis soigneusement retravaillé, et avec une ligne sportive par excellence. À part le 418d, maillon faible sur le plan de la motorisation avec 143 ch, le Coupé (F32), le Cabriolet (F33) et le GranCoupé (F36) sont aussi disponibles avec transmission intégrale.

Tout comme la M3 Berline (F80), le M4 Coupé (F82) et le Cabriolet (F83) jouent dans la ligue M TwinPower, qui se distingue avec 431 ch. La transmission arrière invite également à un léger drift, même si le comportement de cet engin puissant un peu chargé à l'avant reste plutôt neutre. L'abandon du V8 en faveur d'un six cylindres en ligne classique, bien qu'avec double turbocompresseur, apporte non seulement onze chevaux supplémentaires et plus de couple, mais se révèle aussi payant en améliorant les économies de carburant.

Le son puissant des systèmes à clapets souligne acoustiquement cet engin blasonné M, dont les 6 vitesses de série se passent manuellement. Bien entendu, une version sept vitesses à double embrayage M avec système «Drivelogic» est également disponible en option pour près de 4000 euros. Cette génération M sait apporter un pur plaisir de conduire, et trouve sa meilleure expression dans les courbes telles que celles de la boucle nord du Nürburgring. Avec des ingrédients tels que le carbone, l'aluminium et le magnésium, BMW injecte une dose considérable d'adrénaline supplémentaire à la M4 légère.

Mais le Coupé qui ne porte pas de «M» n'attirera pas non plus de critiques sur un éventuel manque de performance. Le 435i (306 ch) et le turbodiesel 435d (313 ch) sont assez puissants pour atteindre les 100 km/h en 5,5 secondes, et pour déclencher la limitation électronique à partir de 250 km/h. Grâce au pack M-Sport, qui comprend également des accessoires aérodynamiques du nez au pare-chocs arrière, des jantes à branches doubles en alliage léger de 18 ou 19 pouces ou un châssis sport et un intérieur de style M, il est possible de se rapprocher considérablement du «M».

Trois autres finitions sont disponibles avec une multitude de possibilités de personnalisation, qui appartiennent aussi au répertoire du Gran Coupé. Cette quatre-portes, plus haute que le Coupé de douze millimètres, mais avec les mêmes dimensions, pèse en moyenne 50 à 60 kilos de plus, ce qui ne se traduit que par un dixième de seconde supplémentaire pour atteindre les 100 km/h.

L'élégance et la beauté ne sont pas ses seuls atouts, elle offre aussi de nombreux avantages pratiques : avec une capacité de 480 litres – et même 1300 avec les sièges arrière rabattus – faciles d'accès grâce au grand hayon électrique, elle ne manque pas de place pour les bagages. L'aspect pratique n'est sans doute pas la première priorité des clients de la Série 4, car il faut se démarquer de la Série 3, et c'est précisément le résultat de l'harmonie de ses proportions et de sa silhouette fluide, résolue dans une partie arrière toute de grâce.

Impressive looks: the Gran Coupé of the Series 4 is over 15 feet long. As the 430d with the M Performance package, this two-ton vehicle has all the power and the glory of the premium range. Eight-speed automatic, four-wheel drive, beautifully matched components—be still, my beating heart…

Eine imposante Erscheinung: das Gran Coupé des 4er von über 4,60 Metern Länge. Als 430d mit dem M-Performance-Paket verfügt der Zweitonner über die Kraft und die Herrlichkeit des Premiumbereichs. 8-Stufen-Automatik, Allradantrieb, hervorragend abgestimmte Fahrwerkskomponenten: Herz, was willst Du mehr?

Avec plus que 4,60 mètres de longueur, le Gran Coupé Série 4 est imposant. Dans sa version 430d avec le pack M Performance, cet engin de deux tonnes déploie puissance et majesté. Boîte automatique à huit rapports, transmission intégrale et excellent ensemble de composants de châssis : que demander de plus ?

Sporty cockpit with
M features, and under
the hood a 3-liter
turbo with 381bhp and
torque of 413lb-ft at just
1500 revs.

Sportliches Cockpit mit
M-Attributen und unter
der Haube ein 3-Liter-
Turbo mit 381 PS und
einem Drehmoment
von 560 Newtonmetern
schon bei 1500 Touren.

Cockpit sportif avec des
attributs «M», et sous
le capot un trois-litres
turbo de 381 ch et un
couple de 560 Nm dès
1500 tours.

BMW 2 Active

BMW is entering uncharted territory with the Series 2 Active Tourer. Like its minivan competitors, which include the Mercedes B-Class, this first front-wheel drive by the Bavarian brand requires a transverse engine. And here, BMW offers two powerful petrol and diesel turbo engines with four cylinders, and two three-cylinders in the 218i and 216d, also with TwinPower turbo. Whereas the four-cylinders reach between 150 (218d) and 231 bhp (225i), the three-cylinders achieve 136 (218i) and 116 bhp (216d). With emission levels between 104 and 99 grams, the latter is the top of the class in the Series 2 league.

The new 2-liter engine of the 218d, a high-performance turbo with common-rail direct injection of the latest generation, deserves special attention. An eight-speed automatic transmission (available for a surcharge) provides the best possible efficiency. In addition to this convenience, all Active Tourers also offer excellent driving behavior, especially on winding roads. Thanks to the sporty steering, relatively little effort is required on the wheel since the Servotronic provides optimum handling around all kinds of corners and is extremely helpful when parking. The "Performance Control" that monitors the distribution of the driving and braking forces and comes as standard also improves driving dynamics.

As is usual at BMW, three other versions compete for the customer's favor as well as the basic version. The benefits of the "Advantage" lie in the dual-zone climate control, the multifunctional leather steering wheel, cruise control with braking function, the parking distance control and integrated fog lights in the bumper. "Luxury Line" earns its name with 14 additional treats on the inside and eight external features, some in chrome. "Sport Line" goes even further (in price as well), and offers 16- and 17-inch light alloy wheels.

The "M Sport" leaves nothing to be desired. In combination with the 225i engine, it turns the Active Tourer into an adventure machine that offers lots of practical details and various storage options along with its sporty touch. The rear seat backrests divide into three for folding, as does the passenger backrest (optionally) for ultimate loading flexibility.

Mit dem 2er Active Tourer beschreitet BMW Neuland. Dieser erste Fronttriebler der weiß-blauen Marke verlangt wie bei seinen Minivan-Mitbewerbern, zu denen auch die B-Klasse von Mercedes gehört, nach einem quer eingebautem Triebwerk. Und hier offeriert BMW je zwei starke Benziner- und Diesel-Turbomotoren als Vierzylinder und mit dem 218i und dem 216d zwei Dreizylinder, ebenfalls mit „TwinPower"-Turbo. Während das Kraftspektrum der Vierzylinder von 150 (218d) bis 231 PS (225i) reicht, entfalten die Dreizylinder 136 (218i) und 116 PS (216d). Letzterer ist mit einem Emissionswert zwischen 104 und 99 Gramm Klassenprimus in dieser 2er-Riege.

Besonderes Augenmerk verdient das neue 2-Liter-Aggregat des 218d, ein Hochleistungs-Turbomotor mit einer Common-Rail-Direkteinspritzung der jüngsten Generation. Für bestmögliche Effizienz sorgt ein gegen Aufpreis erhältliches Acht-Stufen-Automatikgetriebe. Zu diesem Schaltkomfort gesellt sich bei allen Active Tourern ein hervorragendes Fahrverhalten, besonders auf kurvenreichen Strecken. Hierbei ist dank der sportlichen Lenkung ein relativ geringer Aufwand am Volant erforderlich, da die Servotronic für optimales Handling in Kurvenpassagen aller Art sorgt und auch beim

Einparken äußerst hilfreich ist. Der Fahrdynamik förderlich erweist sich auch die serienmäßige „Performance Control", die sich um die Verteilung der Antriebs- und Bremskräfte kümmert.

Wie bei BMW üblich, wetteifern neben der Basisversion drei weitere Varianten um die Gunst der Kunden. Beim Modell „Advantage" liegt der Zugewinn in einer Zweizonen-Klimaautomatik, einem Multifunktionslederlenkrad, Tempomat mit Bremsfunktion, dem Einpark-Warnsystem und integrierten Nebelscheinwerfern im Stoßfänger. „Luxury Line" macht dem Namen mit 14 zusätzlichen Goodies im Interieur und acht äußerlichen Merkmalen, teilweise in Chrom, alle Ehre. „Sport Line" setzt, auch preislich, noch eins drauf und bietet Leichtmetallräder in 16 und 17 Zoll an.

Keine Wünsche offen lässt das Modell „M Sport". Dieses im Verbund mit dem 225i macht den Active Tourer zu einer kleinen Erlebnismaschine, die neben ihrem sportlichen Touch mit vielen praktischen Details und diversen Ablagemöglichkeiten aufwartet. Die dreifach geteilten Fondsitzlehnen lassen sich ebenso umlegen wie optional die Beifahrer-Sitzlehne, so dass bei der Beladung variiert werden kann.

Avec la Série 2 Active Tourer, BMW emprunte une nouvelle voie. Cette première traction avant de la marque bleue et blanche exige, comme les monospaces qui lui font concurrence, dont fait partie la Classe B de Mercedes, un moteur installé transversalement. Et ici, BMW propose deux puissants moteurs turbo essence et diesel quatre cylindres, et avec la 218i et la 216d trois cylindres, également avec turbo «TwinPower». Les quatre-cylindres atteignent 150 (218d) à 231 ch (225i), tandis que les trois-cylindres développent 136 (218i) et 116 ch (216d). Avec des émissions d'entre 104 et 99 g/km, ce dernier est premier de la classe de la Série 2.

Le nouveau moteur 2 litres de la 218d mérite une attention particulière. C'est un turbo haute performance à injection directe à rampe commune de dernière génération. Pour un rendement maximal, la transmission automatique à huit rapports est disponible en option. Outre ce confort dans le passage des vitesses, tous les Active Tourer ont un excellent comportement, particulièrement sur les routes sinueuses. La direction sportive réduit les efforts au volant, car le Servotronic assure une maniabilité optimale dans toutes les courbes, et se révèle très utile pour se garer. Le «Performance Control» améliore également la dynamique de conduite en se chargeant de la répartition des forces motrice et de freinage.

Comme c'est l'habitude chez BMW, la version de base doit rivaliser avec trois autres variantes pour plaire aux clients. Le modèle «Advantage» se distingue par une climatisation à deux zones, un volant cuir multifonctions, un régulateur de vitesse avec fonction de freinage, le système d'aide au stationnement et des phares antibrouillards intégrés au pare-chocs. «Luxury Line» mérite bien son nom, avec 14 équipements supplémentaires à l'intérieur et huit éléments extérieurs dont certains en chrome. Quant au «Sport Line», il se situe encore un cran au-dessus et propose des jantes en alliage léger de 16 et 17 pouces.

Le modèle «M Sport» ne laisse rien à désirer. En combinaison avec le 225i, l'Active Tourer devient une machine à aventure, dont la touche sportive est complétée par de nombreux détails pratiques et diverses possibilités de rangement. La banquette arrière en trois parties est rabattable, ainsi que (en option) le siège passager, pour un chargement pratique.

The Series 2 Active Tourer is BMW's first van, and faces strong competition. BMW is also venturing into terrain—front-wheel drive!—that has been chartered by other manufacturers a long time ago. This family car has an attractive lightweight body featuring elegantly swung lines and the traditional Hofmeister kink in the D-pillar.

Als erster Van von BMW tritt der 2er Active Tourer gleich gegen starke Konkurrenz an, und auch beim Antrieb – auf die Vorderräder! – beschreitet BMW Neuland, das andere Hersteller längst erschlossen haben. Über diese Familienkutsche stülpt sich eine ansehnliche Karosserie in intelligenter Leichtbauweise, elegant geschwungen und nach Art des Hauses mit Hofmeister-Knick in der D-Säule.

Premier monospace de BMW, la Série 2 Active Tourer a dû faire face à une forte concurrence, et même sa traction – sur les roues avant ! – est une nouveauté chez BMW, que d'autres constructeurs exploitent depuis longtemps. Cette familiale est habillée d'une carrosserie très honorable, à la construction légère intelligente, élégamment galbée, et pourvue du pli Hofmeister typique de la maison sur le montant D.

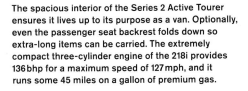

The spacious interior of the Series 2 Active Tourer ensures it lives up to its purpose as a van. Optionally, even the passenger seat backrest folds down so extra-long items can be carried. The extremely compact three-cylinder engine of the 218i provides 136 bhp for a maximum speed of 127 mph, and it runs some 45 miles on a gallon of premium gas.

Mit einem großzügigen Raumangebot wird der 2er Active Tourer seiner Bestimmung als Van gerecht. Um auch überlanges Gepäck verstauen zu können, lässt sich auf Wunsch sogar die Beifahrersitz-Rückenlehne umklappen. Der äußerst kompakte Dreizylinder des 218i aktiviert 136 PS, sorgt für eine Höchstgeschwindigkeit von 205 km/h und verbraucht nur fünf Liter Super auf 100 Kilometer.

La Série 2 Active Tourer est généreuse en espace, comme l'exige sa vocation de monospace. Même le dossier du siège passager est (en option) rabattable, afin d'accommoder aussi les chargements très longs. Le trois-cylindres extrêmement compact de la 218i développe 136 ch, atteint une vitesse de pointe de 205 km/h et ne consomme que cinq litres de super sur 100 kilomètres.

BMW i8 |12|2014

Dynamic and unmistakable: this vision of an eco-friendly sports car that was presented at the 2009 Frankfurt Motor Show and celebrated its premiere as the i8 at the same event four years later is a breathtakingly beautiful success. In the first six months of 2015, 1741 units of this hybrid car, which is only 4¼ feet high, left the plants in Leipzig. And the trend is rising!

Despite the weight of the massive lithium-ion battery on the bottom—effectively the connection between the electric engine at the front and the three-cylinder turbo at the back—the i8 is a lightweight at only 3273 pounds. The carbon fibers that are produced in the USA and made into mats at the BMW plant in Wackersdorf, are then pressed into passenger cell components in Landshut and Leipzig before going to the final assembly in the Saxon trade fair metropolis. These passenger cell components are almost 30 percent lighter than the same structures made of aluminum.

The "eco wonder" with a drag coefficient of 0.26 has a synchronous electric motor that provides 131bhp and a 1.5-litre gasoline engine with 231bhp. This power combination accelerates the intelligent all-wheel drive to 62mph in 4.4 seconds and to a limited top speed of 155mph. In pure electric mode, the i8 needs a little over 11 seconds to get to 62mph, and after 22 miles at the most, the silent, emission-free stage of this magic carpet ride is over. The

batteries are flat! Racing the highway as a sports car, the i8 goes 21 miles per gallon of premium petrol, but with more moderate driving, this can be extended to between 33 and 47 miles. Its tank capacity of 8 gallons gives it a total range of about 336 miles.

The scissor doors invite you into the futuristic cockpit. A digital, three-dimensional control display provides the driver with all the relevant information. Whether the chassis, six-speed automatic transmission that can also be changed manually using switches on the steering wheel, the steering, or the seat position, the i8 is sportier than its narrow tires would suggest: 195s are fitted to the front and 215s to the back as standard! Although there is fortunately the option of mixed tires, with 215s at the front and 245s at the back providing a little more rolling resistance, the look is more that of a sports car.

Thanks to every conceivable modern driving aid and the good traction achieved by independently driven axles, the i8 is almost as stiff as a board in sport mode. Fast cornering, with a slight understeer but no swaying, it provides a driving experience that could be improved with wider tires. However, a little provocation is required before the rear responds. By contrast, the sound generator in the little engine produces an excellent melody in perfect harmony, composed by the sound engineers at BMW.

Dynamisch und unverwechselbar: Die auf der Frankfurter IAA 2009 präsentierte Vision eines nachhaltigen Sportwagens, der vier Jahre danach auf der gleichen Automobilausstellung als i8 Premiere feiert, ist atemberaubend schön gelungen. 1741 dieser nur 1,29 Meter hohen Hybrid-Renner verließen innerhalb des ersten Produktionshalbjahres 2014 die Leipziger Hallen. Tendenz steigend!

Trotz des Gewichts der gewaltigen Lithium-Ionen-Hochvolt-Batterie in der Bodengruppe – quasi Bindeglied zwischen dem Elektromotor vorn und dem Turbo-Dreizylinder über der Hinterachse – bringt der i8 nur 1485 Kilo auf die Waage. Die in den USA hergestellten Kohlefasern, im BMW-Werk Wackersdorf zu Matten verarbeitet, werden in Landshut und Leipzig zu Fahrgastzellen-Komponenten gepresst und gehen in der sächsischen Messemetropole in die Endmontage. Diese Fahrgastzellen wiegen fast 30 Prozent weniger als vergleichbare Aufbauten aus Aluminium.

Die „Öko-Wunder-Flunder", die mit einem Luftwiderstandsbeiwert von 0,26 glänzt, bringt 131 PS vom Elektro-Synchron-Motor und dazu 231 PS des 1,5-Liter-Ottomotors auf die Räder. Diese Kraftquellenkombination beschleunigt den intelligenten Allradler in 4,4 Sekunden auf 100 km/h und auf eine abgeregelte Spitze von 250 km/h. Rein elektrisch betrieben, braucht der i8 etwas mehr als 11 Sekunden auf Tempo 100, und nach höchstens 35 Kilometern ist die ton- und emissionslose Phase des leisen Dahinschwebens schon vorbei. Akkus leer! Als Sportwagen über die Autobahn

gescheucht, schluckt der i8 gut elf Liter Super, doch bei gemäßigter Fahrweise lässt sich der Durst auf fünf bis sieben Liter reduzieren. Mit einem nutzbaren Tankvolumen von 30 Litern ist eine Gesamtreichweite von etwa 540 Kilometern also möglich.

Ausladende Schmetterlingstüren bitten zum Einstieg in das futuristische Cockpit. Ein digitales, dreidimensionales Kontrolldisplay übermittelt alle für das Fahrerlebnis relevanten Informationen. Ob Fahrwerk, Sechsgang-Automatik, manuell auch über Lenkradwippen zu bedienen, Lenkung oder Sitzposition: Der i8 ist sportlicher orientiert, als man angesichts der „Schmalspur"-Bereifung glauben könnte – serienmäßig nur 195er Pneus vorn und 215er hinten! Gegen Aufpreis gibt es zum Glück eine Mischbereifung, die mit den Dimensionen 215 vorn und 245 hinten zwar etwas mehr Rollwiderstand leistet, aber optisch eher zu einem Sportwagen passt.

Dank aller erdenklichen modernen Fahrhilfen und der insgesamt guten Traktion, erzeugt durch unabhängig voneinander angetriebene Achsen, liegt der i8 im Sportmodus fast wie ein Brett. Schnelles Kurvenfahren, leicht untersteuernd aber ohne Wankbewegungen, bereitet ein Fahrvergnügen, das mit breiteren „Sohlen" eine Steigerung erfahren könnte. Das Heck ein wenig kommen zu lassen, muss allerdings provoziert werden. Stimmig dagegen der Soundgenerator des kleinen Motors: hervorragend komponiert von den BMW-Klang-Ingenieuren.

Dynamique et unique : cette vision d'une voiture de sport respectueuse de l'environnement présentée à l'IAA de Francfort en 2009, et célébrée quatre ans plus tard au même endroit en tant qu'i8, est une réussite époustouflante. Les six premiers mois de production de ce bolide hybride de seulement 1,29 mètre de haut ont vu 1741 exemplaires quitter les ateliers de Leipzig. La tendance est à la hausse !

Malgré le poids de l'énorme batterie lithium-ion haute tension dans l'ensemble de plancher, qui relie pratiquement le moteur électrique à l'avant et le trois-cylindres turbo sur l'axe arrière, l'i8 n'affiche que 1485 kilos sur la balance. La fibre de carbone fabriquée aux États-Unis est assemblée en mats stratifiés à l'usine BMW de Wackersdorf, puis pressée en forme de composants d'habitacle à Landshut et Leipzig, qui partent pour la métropole saxonne des salons afin d'être montés. Ces habitacles pèsent presque 30 pour cent de moins que les structures analogues en aluminium.

Cette « éco-limande prodigieuse » qui brille par son coefficient de traînée de 0,26 est dotée d'un moteur électrique à synchronisation de 131 ch et d'un moteur à combustion 1,5 litre de 231 ch. C'est grâce à cette combinaison que cette transmission intégrale intelligente accélère à 100 km/h en 4,4 secondes et atteint une vitesse de pointe limitée à 250 km/h. En mode purement électrique, il faut à l'i8 un peu plus de 11 secondes pour atteindre les 100 km/h, et après

35 kilomètres maximum la phase sans bruit et sans émissions sur ce tapis volant prend déjà fin. La batterie est vide ! En mode sportif sur autoroute, l'i8 avale onze litres de super, mais avec une conduite plus modérée elle étanche sa soif avec cinq à sept litres. Son réservoir de 30 litres lui donne une autonomie totale d'environ 540 kilomètres.

Ses grandes portes papillons invitent à entrer dans son cockpit futuriste. Un écran numérique tridimensionnel relaie toutes les informations utiles à la conduite. Qu'il s'agisse du châssis, de la transmission automatique à huit rapports, à commande manuelle ou au volant, de la direction ou de la position d'assise, l'i8 est plus sportive que ne le laissent penser ses pneus étroits : de série, seulement 195 à l'avant et 215 à l'arrière ! Heureusement, une option permet de la chausser de pneus mixtes, 215 à l'avant et 245 à l'arrière, qui lui confèrent une meilleure résistance au roulis, mais conviennent plutôt à l'esthétique d'une voiture de sport.

Grâce à tous les équipements d'aide à la conduite imaginables et à sa traction satisfaisante dans l'ensemble, avec des essieux moteur indépendants, en mode sportif l'i8 est pratiquement raide comme une planche. Rapide dans les courbes, avec un léger sous-virage mais sans roulis, elle procure un plaisir de conduite qui se trouverait renforcé par des « semelles » plus larges. Le générateur de son du petit moteur est quant à lui un vrai plaisir, et émet une composition excellente des ingénieurs du son de BMW.

Breathtaking shape: the i8, seen here with W-spoke rims for mixed tires, even looks dynamic when it's not moving. The lightweight coupé—aluminum chassis and carbon passenger cell—combines all the features of a hybrid sports car with the performance of the electric 131 bhp motor and the turbocharged 231 bhp 1.5-liter, three-cylinder engine.

Atemberaubende Formgebung: Der i8, hier mit W-Speichen-Felgen für Mischbereifung bestückt, wirkt selbst im Stand dynamisch. Das Leichtbau-Coupé – Aluminium-Fahrgestell und Fahrgastzelle aus Carbon – verbindet alle Anforderungen an einen Hybrid-Sportwagen, dessen Leistung sich aus 131 Elektro-PS und 231 PS des 1,5-Liter-Dreizylinder-Turbotriebwerks addiert.

Une ligne à couper le souffle : l'i8, ici équipée de jantes à branches en W sur pneus mixtes, semble être en mouvement même à l'arrêt. Ce coupé léger – châssis en aluminium et habitacle en carbone – satisfait à tous les critères pour une sportive hybride, avec 131 ch électriques et les 231 ch de son moteur turbo 1,5-litre à trois cylindres.

Lift up your heads, ye mighty gates…: the scissor doors, which consist of a CFRP structure clad in sheet aluminum, contribute to the curb weight of just 3455 lbs. When open, they rise up to just 6½ ft.

Macht hoch die Tür…: Zum Leergewicht von nur 1485 Kilo tragen auch die Flügeltüren aus einem CFK-Träger mit Aluminium-Außenhaut bei. In geöffnetem Zustand ragen sie knapp zwei Meter nach oben.

Portes, élevez vos linteaux…: les portes en élytre en plastique renforcé de fibres de carbone et revêtu d'aluminium contribuent aussi à un poids à vide de seulement 1485 kilos. Ouvertes, elles atteignent presque deux mètres de haut.

The interior of the i8, seen here in "Carpo Ivory", delights with the dark/light contrast of the leather seats and black leather of the dashboard with multifunctional display. The green speedometer backlighting indicates the electric comfort mode up to 40 mph, whereas red illumination augurs sportiness with maximum boost. Concealed at the rear: the turbocharged gasoline engine.

Das Interieur des i8, hier in „Carpo-Elfenbeinweiß", besticht durch seinen Hell-Dunkel-Kontrast der Ledersitze und der schwarzen Lederbespannung der Instrumententafel mit Multifunktionsdisplay. Die grüne Tacho-Beleuchtung signalisiert den Elektro-Komfort-Modus bis 65 km/h, wohingegen die rote Sportlichkeit mit maximalem Boost verheißt. Verborgen im Heck: der Turbo-Benzinmotor.

L'intérieur de l'i8, ici en «Carpo Ivory White», se distingue par un séduisant contraste entre les sièges en cuir clair et le cuir noir du tableau de bord avec écran multifonctions. L'éclairage vert du compteur indique le mode électrique Confort jusqu'à 65 km/h, tandis que l'éclairage rouge indique le mode Sport avec performances maximales. Dissimulé à l'arrière : le moteur turbo à essence.

Specifications · Technische Daten · Caractères techniques

Baureihe	Wartburg Motorwagen	Dixi 3/15 PS	Wartburg DA3
Baujahre	1898–1900	1927–1929	1930–1931
Modell	Wartburg Kutschierwagen	DA1	DA3 Sport-Zweisitzer
Motor	2 Zylinder, luftgekühlt	4 Zylinder in Reihe	4 Zylinder in Reihe
Hubraum	479 cm³	748,5 cm³	748,5 cm³
Bohrung × Hub	66 × 70 mm	56 × 76 mm	56 × 76 mm
Kraftstoffversorgung	Oberflächenvergaser	Flachstromvergaser Solex	Flachstromvergaser Solex
Leistung	3,5 PS bei 1100/min	15 PS bei 3000/min	18 PS bei 3500/min
Getriebe	2-Gang	3-Gang	3-Gang
Chassis Rahmen	Rohrrahmen	U-Profilrahmen	U-Profilrahmen
Aufhängung vorn	gekapselte Schraubenfedern, Querfeder	Starrachse, Querfeder	Starrachse, Querfeder
Aufhängung hinten	Starrachse, ungefedert	Starrachse, Ausleger-Viertelfedern	Starrachse, Ausleger-Viertelfedern
Maße Radstand	1600 mm	1905 mm	1905 mm
Länge × Breite × Höhe	2300 × 1250 × 1450 mm	2800 × 1170 × 1625 mm	3100 × 1150 × 1400 mm
Gewicht	315 kg	440 kg	410 kg
Höchstgeschwindigkeit	40–45 km/h	75 km/h	90 km/h

Baureihe	3/20 PS	303	315/1
Baujahre	1932–1934	1933–1934	1934–1936
Modell	AM4	303	315/1 Sport-Zweisitzer
Motor	4 Zylinder in Reihe	6 Zylinder in Reihe	6 Zylinder in Reihe
Hubraum	782 cm³	1173 cm³	1490 cm³
Bohrung × Hub	56 × 80 mm	56 × 80 mm	58 × 94 mm
Kraftstoffversorgung	Flachstromvergaser Solex	2 Vertikalvergaser Solex	3 Flachstromvergaser Solex
Leistung	20 PS bei 3500/min	30 PS bei 4000/min	40 PS bei 4300/min
Getriebe	4-Gang	4-Gang	4-Gang
Chassis Rahmen	Zentralkasten-Niederrahmen	Leiterrohrrahmen, Kastenquerträger	Leiterrohrrahmen, Kastenquerträger
Aufhängung vorn	achslos, Querfedern	Querlenker unten, Querfedern oben	Querlenker unten, Querfedern oben
Aufhängung hinten	Pendelachse, Querfedern	Starrachse, Halbfedern	Starrachse, Halbfedern
Maße Radstand	2150 mm	2400 mm	2400 mm
Länge × Breite × Höhe	3200 × 1420 × 1550 mm	3900 × 1440 × 1550 mm	3800 × 1440 × 1350 mm
Gewicht	650 kg	820 kg	780 kg
Höchstgeschwindigkeit	80 km/h	90 km/h	130 km/h

Baureihe	326	328	325
Baujahre	1936–1941	1936–1940	1937–1940
Modell	326 Cabriolet	328 Roadster	Leichter Einheits-Pkw
Motor	6 Zylinder in Reihe	6 Zylinder in Reihe	6 Zylinder in Reihe
Hubraum	1971 cm³	1971 cm³	1971 cm³
Bohrung × Hub	66 × 96 mm	66 × 96 mm	66 × 96 mm
Kraftstoffversorgung	2 Vertikalvergaser Solex	3 Fallstromvergaser Solex	2 Steigstromvergaser Solex 26 BFLV
Leistung	50 PS bei 3750/min	80 PS bei 5000/min	50 PS bei 3750/min
Getriebe	4-Gang	4-Gang	5-Gang
Chassis Rahmen	Tiefbett-Kastenrahmen	Rohrrahmen, Kastenquerträger	Kastenrahmen
Aufhängung vorn	Querfedern unten, Querlenker oben	Querlenker unten, Querfedern oben	Doppelquerlenker, doppelte Schraubenfedern
Aufhängung hinten	Starrachse, Halbfedern	Starrachse	Doppelquerlenker, doppelte Schraubenfedern
Maße Radstand	2750 mm	2400 mm	2400 mm
Länge × Breite × Höhe	4600 × 1600 × 1500 mm	3900 × 1550 × 1450 mm	3900 × 1690 × 1900 mm
Gewicht	1100 kg	830 kg	1775 kg
Höchstgeschwindigkeit	115 km/h	150 km/h	80 km/h

Baureihe	327	335	502
Baujahre	1937–1941	1939–1941	1954–1956
Modell	327 Cabriolet	335 Cabriolet (Graber)	502 Cabrio 2/2 (Baur)
Motor	6 Zylinder in Reihe	6 Zylinder in Reihe	V8, 90°
Hubraum	1971 cm³	3485 cm³	2580 cm³
Bohrung × Hub	66 × 96 mm	82 × 110 mm	74 × 75 mm
Kraftstoffversorgung	2 Vertikalvergaser Solex	2 Vertikal-Doppel-Registervergaser Solex	Doppel-Fallstromvergaser Zenith 32 NDIX
Leistung	55 PS bei 4500/min	90 PS bei 3500/min	100 PS bei 4800/min
Getriebe	4-Gang	4-Gang	4-Gang
Chassis Rahmen	Tiefbett-Kastenrahmen	Tiefbett-Kastenrahmen	Kastenrahmen, Rohrquerträger
Aufhängung vorn	Querfeder unten, Querlenker oben	Querlenker, Querfedern oben	Doppelquerlenker, Längslenker
Aufhängung hinten	Starrachse, Halbfedern	Starrachse, Längsfederstäbe	Banjo-Achse, Federhebel, Dreieckslenker
Maße Radstand	2750 mm	2984 mm	2835 mm
Länge × Breite × Höhe	4500 × 1600 × 1420 mm	4988 × 1700 × 1685 mm	4720 × 1780 × 1530 mm
Gewicht	1100 kg	1300 kg	1400 kg
Höchstgeschwindigkeit	125 km/h	145 km/h	170 km/h

Baureihe	Isetta	507	503
Baujahre	1955–1962	1956–1959	1956–1959
Modell	**Isetta 300**	**507**	**503**
Motor	1 Zylinder	V8 90°	V8 90°
Hubraum	298 cm³	3168 cm³	3168 cm³
Bohrung × Hub	72 × 73 mm	82 × 75 mm	82 × 75 mm
Kraftstoffversorgung	Schiebervergaser	2 Doppel-Fallstromvergaser Zenith 32 NDIX	2 Doppel-Fallstromvergaser Zenith
Leistung	13 PS bei 5200/min	150 PS bei 5000/min	140 PS bei 4800/min
Getriebe	4-Gang	4-Gang	4-Gang
Chassis Rahmen	Rohrrahmen	Kastenrahmen, Rohrquerträger	Kastenrahmen, Rohrquerträger
Aufhängung vorn	geschobene Längsschwingen, Schraubenfedern	Doppelquerlenker, Stabilisator, Längsfederstäbe	Doppelquerlenker, Längsfederstäbe
Aufhängung hinten	Starrachse, Ausleger-Viertelfedern	Starrachse	Starrachse, Dreieckslenker, Längsfederstäbe
Maße Radstand	1500 mm	2480 mm	2835 mm
Länge × Breite × Höhe	2285 × 1380 × 1340 mm	4380 × 1650 × 1300 mm	4750 × 1710 × 1440 mm
Gewicht	360 kg	1330 kg	1500 kg
Höchstgeschwindigkeit	85 km/h	200 km/h	190 km/h

Baureihe	700	1500	3200 CS
Baujahre	1959–1965	1962–1964	1962–1965
Modell	**700 LS Luxus**	**1500**	**3200 CS**
Motor	2 Zylinder Boxer	4 Zylinder in Reihe, 30° geneigt	V8 90°
Hubraum	697cm³	1499 cm³	3168 cm³
Bohrung × Hub	78 × 73 mm	82 × 71 mm	82 × 75 mm
Kraftstoffversorgung	Fallstromvergaser Solex 34 PCI	Fallstromvergaser Solex	2 Doppel-Fallstromvergaser Zenith
Leistung	30 PS bei 5000/min	80 PS bei 5700/min	160 PS bei 5600/min
Getriebe	4-Gang	4-Gang	4-Gang
Chassis Rahmen	selbsttragende Karosserie	selbsttragende Karosserie	Kastenrahmen, Rohrquerträger
Aufhängung vorn	geschobene Längsschwingen, Schraubenfedern	McPherson-Federbeine	Doppelquerlenker, Längsfederstäbe, Stabilisator
Aufhängung hinten	Schräglenker, Schraubenfedern, Gummihohlfedern	Schraubenfedern, Schräglenker	Starrachse
Maße Radstand	2280 mm	2550 mm	2835 mm
Länge × Breite × Höhe	3860 × 1480 × 1360 mm	4500 × 1710 × 1450 mm	4830 × 1720 × 1460 mm
Gewicht	680 kg	1060 kg	1500 kg
Höchstgeschwindigkeit	120 km/h	148 km/h	200 km/h

Baureihe	502	2000	02
Baujahre	1963	1965–1969	1966–1977
Modell	**3200 S Staatslimousine**	**2000CS**	**2002tii**
Motor	V8 90°	4 Zylinder in Reihe, 30° geneigt	4 Zylinder in Reihe, 30° geneigt
Hubraum	3168 cm³	1990 cm³	1990 cm³
Bohrung × Hub	82 × 75 mm	89 × 80 mm	89 × 80 mm
Kraftstoffversorgung	2 Doppel-Fallstromvergaser	2 Doppel-Flachstromvergaser Solex	Einspritzpumpe Kugelfischer
Leistung	160 PS bei 5600/min	120 PS bei 5500/min	130 PS bei 5800/min
Getriebe	4-Gang	4-Gang	4-Gang
Chassis Rahmen	Kastenrahmen, Rohrquerträger	selbsttragende Karosserie	selbsttragende Karosserie
Aufhängung vorn	Doppelquerlenker, Längsfederstäbe	McPherson-Federbeine, Stabilisator	McPherson-Federbeine, Drehstab-Stabilisator
Aufhängung hinten	Starrachse, Dreieckslenker, Längsfederstäbe	Schraubenfedern, Stabilisator, Schräglenker	Schraubenfedern, Drehstab-Stabilisator, Schräglenker
Maße Radstand	2835 mm	2550 mm	2500 mm
Länge × Breite × Höhe	4870 × 1780 × 1530 mm	4530 × 1675 × 1360 mm	4230 × 1590 × 1410 mm
Gewicht	1490 kg	1200 kg	1010 kg
Höchstgeschwindigkeit	190 km/h	185 km/h	190 km/h

Baureihe	2500 (E3)	3.0 CS (E9)	5er-Reihe (E12)
Baujahre	1968–1977	1971–1975	1972–1977
Modell	**2500**	**3.0 CSi**	**520**
Motor	6 Zylinder in Reihe, 30° geneigt	6 Zylinder in Reihe, 30° geneigt	4 Zylinder in Reihe, 30° geneigt
Hubraum	2494 cm³	2985 cm³	1990 cm³
Bohrung × Hub	86 × 71,6 mm	89 × 80 mm	89 × 80 mm
Kraftstoffversorgung	2 Fallstrom-Registervergaser	elektronische Einspritzung Bosch	1 Fallstromvergaser
Leistung	150 PS bei 6000/min	200 PS bei 5500/min	115 PS bei 5800/min
Getriebe	4-Gang	4-Gang	4-Gang
Chassis Rahmen	selbsttragende Karosserie	selbsttragende Karosserie	selbsttragende Karosserie
Aufhängung vorn	McPherson-Federbeine, Gummizusatzfedern, Drehstab-Stabilisator	McPherson-Federbeine, Drehstab-Stabilisator	McPherson-Federbeine, Drehstab-Stabilisator
Aufhängung hinten	Federbeine, Schraubenfedern, Gummizusatzfedern, Stabilisator, Boge-Nivomat	Federbeine, Schraubenfedern, Drehstab-Stabilisator, Schräglenker	Federbeine, Schraubenfedern, Drehstab-Stabilisator, Schräglenker
Maße Radstand	2692 mm	2625 mm	2636 mm
Länge × Breite × Höhe	4700 × 1750 × 1450 mm	4630 × 1730 × 1370 mm	4620 × 1690 × 1425 mm
Gewicht	1360 kg	1400 kg	1275 kg
Höchstgeschwindigkeit	190 km/h	220 km/h	175 km/h

Baureihe	02	3er-Reihe (E21)	6er-Reihe (E24)
Baujahre	1973	1975–1982	1976–1989
Modell	**2002 turbo**	**323i**	**M 635CSi**
Motor	4 Zylinder in Reihe, Turbolader	6 Zylinder in Reihe, 30° geneigt	6 Zylinder in Reihe, 30° geneigt
Hubraum	1990 cm³	2315 cm³	3453 cm³
Bohrung × Hub	89 × 80 mm	80 × 76,8 mm	93 × 84 mm
Kraftstoffversorgung	mechanische Einspritzung Kugelfischer	Saugrohreinspritzung Bosch	elektronische Einspritzung Bosch
Leistung	170 PS bei 5800/min	143 PS bei 6000/min	286 PS bei 6500/min
Getriebe	4-Gang	5-Gang	5-Gang
Chassis Rahmen	selbsttragende Karosserie	selbsttragende Karosserie	selbsttragende Karosserie
Aufhängung vorn	Federbeine, Querlenker, Stabilisator	McPherson-Federbeine, Gummizusatzfedern, Drehstab-Stabilisator	McPherson-Federbeine, Drehstab-Stabilisator
Aufhängung hinten	Schräglenker, Schraubenfedern, Gummizusatzfedern	Federbeine, Schräglenker, Schraubenfedern, Gummizusatzfedern, Drehstab-Stabilisator	Federbeine, Schraubenfedern, Drehstab-Stabilisator, Schräglenker
Maße Radstand	2500 mm	2563 mm	2626 mm
Länge × Breite × Höhe	4220 × 1620 × 1410 mm	4355 × 1610 × 1380 mm	4755 × 1725 × 1354 mm
Gewicht	1080 kg	1180 kg	1510 kg
Höchstgeschwindigkeit	210 km/h	192 km/h	255 km/h

Baureihe	7er-Reihe (E23)	M1 (E26)	3er-Reihe (E30)
Baujahre	1977–1986	1978–1981	1982–1994
Modell	**728i**	**M1**	**318i Cabrio** (E30/2C)
Motor	6 Zylinder in Reihe, 30° geneigt	6 Zylinder in Reihe	4 Zylinder in Reihe, 30° geneigt
Hubraum	2788 cm³	3453 cm³	1796 cm³
Bohrung × Hub	86 × 80 mm	93,4 × 84 mm	84 × 81 mm
Kraftstoffversorgung	elektronische Einspritzung Bosch	mechanische Einspritzung Kugelfischer	elektronische Einspritzung Bosch
Leistung	184 PS bei 5800/min	277 PS bei 6500/min	113 PS bei 5500/min
Getriebe	4-Gang	5-Gang	5-Gang
Chassis Rahmen	selbsttragende Karosserie	Gitterrohrrahmen, Kunststoffkarosserie	selbsttragende Karosserie
Aufhängung vorn	McPherson-Federbeine, Drehstab-Stabilisator	Doppelquerlenker, Schraubenfedern, Drehstab-Stabilisator, Gasdruckdämpfer	McPherson-Federbeine, Drehstab-Stabilisator
Aufhängung hinten	Federbeine, Schräglenker, Schraubenfedern	Doppelquerlenker, Schraubenfedern, Drehstab-Stabilisator, Gasdruckdämpfer	Schraubenfedern, Schräglenker, Drehstab-Stabilisator
Maße Radstand	2795 mm	2560 mm	2570 mm
Länge × Breite × Höhe	4860 × 1800 × 1430 mm	4360 × 1824 × 1140 mm	4325 × 1645 × 1380 mm
Gewicht	1530 kg	1440 kg	1230 kg
Höchstgeschwindigkeit	200 km/h	260 km/h	190 km/h

Baureihe	7er-Reihe (E32)	5er-Reihe (E34)	8er-Reihe (E31)
Baujahre	1987–1994	1988–1995	1989–1992
Modell	**750iL**	**M5**	**850i**
Motor	V12 60°	6 Zylinder in Reihe, 30° geneigt	V12 60°
Hubraum	4988 cm³	3535 cm³	4988 cm³
Bohrung × Hub	84 × 75 mm	93,4 × 86 mm	84 × 75 mm
Kraftstoffversorgung	elektronische Einspritzung Bosch	Bosch Motronic	elektronische Einspritzung Bosch
Leistung	300 PS bei 5200/min	315 PS bei 6900/min	300 PS bei 5200/min
Getriebe	4-Gang-Automatik	5-Gang	6-Gang
Chassis Rahmen	selbsttragende Karosserie	selbsttragende Karosserie	selbsttragende Karosserie
Aufhängung vorn	McPherson-Federbeine, Drehstab-Stabilisator	Doppelgelenk-Federbeine, Stabilisator, Querkraftausgleich, Bremsnickausgleich	Doppelgelenk-Federbeine, Stabilisator, Querkraftausgleich
Aufhängung hinten	Federbeine, Schräglenker, Drehstab-Stabilisator, Niveauregulierung	Schräglenkerachse, Anfahr- und Bremsnickausgleich, Stabilisator	Fünflenkerachse, Stabilisator
Maße Radstand	2947 mm	2761 mm	2684 mm
Länge × Breite × Höhe	5024 × 1845 × 1400 mm	4720 × 1751 × 1396 mm	4780 × 1855 × 1340 mm
Gewicht	1930 kg	1720 kg	1840 kg
Höchstgeschwindigkeit	250 km/h, elektronisch begrenzt	250 km/h, elektronisch begrenzt	250 km/h, elektronisch begrenzt

Baureihe	Z1	3er-Reihe (E30)	3er-Reihe (E36)
Baujahre	1988–1991	1990	1993–1999
Modell	**Z1**	**M3 Sport Evolution** (E30/2S)	**318i Cabrio** (E36/2C)
Motor	6 Zylinder in Reihe, 20° geneigt	4 Zylinder in Reihe, 30° geneigt	4 Zylinder in Reihe
Hubraum	2494 cm³	2467 cm³	1796 cm³
Bohrung × Hub	84 × 75 mm	95 × 87 mm	84 × 81 mm
Kraftstoffversorgung	Bosch Motronic	elektronische Einspritzung Bosch	elektronisches Motormanagement BMS 43
Leistung	170 PS bei 5800/min	238 PS bei 7000/min	115 PS bei 5500/min
Getriebe	5-Gang	5-Gang	5-Gang
Chassis Rahmen	Stahlblechgerüst mit Kunststoff- und Verbundstoffteilen	selbsttragende Karosserie	selbsttragende Karosserie
Aufhängung vorn	McPherson-Federbeine, Drehstab-Stabilisator	McPherson-Federbeine, Drehstab-Stabilisator	Eingelenk-Federbeine, Querkraftausgleich, Bremsnickausgleich
Aufhängung hinten	Zentrallenkerachse, Längslenker, Querlenker, Schraubenfedern, Drehstab-Stabilisator	Schräglenker, Schraubenfedern, Drehstab-Stabilisator	Zentrallenkerachse, Doppelquerlenker, Längslenker, Anfahr- und Bremsnickausgleich
Maße Radstand	2450 mm	2565 mm	2700 mm
Länge × Breite × Höhe	3925 × 1690 × 1248 mm	4345 × 1680 × 1370 mm	4433 × 1710 × 1348 mm
Gewicht	1290 kg	1200 kg	1370 kg
Höchstgeschwindigkeit	225 km/h	248 km/h	194 km/h

Baureihe	M3 (E36)	7er-Reihe (E38)	5er-Reihe (E39)
Baujahre	1992–1999	1994–2001	1995–2004
Modell	M3 Cabrio (E36/2CS)	740i	540i
Motor	6 Zylinder in Reihe, 24 Ventile	V8 90°, 32 Ventile	V8 90°, 32 Ventile
Hubraum	3201 cm³	4398 cm³	4398 cm³
Bohrung × Hub	86,4 × 91 mm	92 × 82,7 mm	92 × 82,7 mm
Kraftstoffversorgung	elektronisches Motormanagement MSS50	elektronisches Motormanagement M5.2	elektronisches Motormanagement M5.2
Leistung	321 PS bei 7400/min	286 PS bei 5700/min	286 PS bei 5700/min
Getriebe	6-Gang	6-Gang	6-Gang
Chassis Rahmen	selbsttragende Karosserie	selbsttragende Karosserie	selbsttragende Karosserie
Aufhängung vorn	Eingelenk-Federbeine, Querkraftausgleich, Bremsnickausgleich	Doppelgelenk-Federbeine, Querkraftausgleich, Bremsnickausgleich	Druckstreben-Doppelgelenk-Federbeine, Querkraftausgleich, Bremsnickausgleich
Aufhängung hinten	Zentrallenkerachse, Doppelquerlenker, Längslenker, Anfahr- und Bremsnickausgleich	Integralachse, Anfahr- und Bremsnickausgleich	Integralachse, Anfahr- und Bremsnickausgleich
Maße Radstand	2710 mm	2930 mm	2830 mm
Länge × Breite × Höhe	4433 × 1710 × 1355 mm	4984 × 1862 × 1435 mm	4775 × 1800 × 1435 mm
Gewicht	1460 kg	1800 kg	1585 kg
Höchstgeschwindigkeit	250 km/h, elektronisch begrenzt	250 km/h, elektronisch begrenzt	250 km/h, elektronisch begrenzt

Baureihe	Z3 (E36/7)	Z3 (E36/8)	3er-Reihe (E46)
Baujahre	1995–2002	1998–2002	1998–2007
Modell	M roadster (E36/7S)	Z3 coupé 2.8	328i (E46/4)
Motor	6 Zylinder in Reihe, 24 Ventile	6 Zylinder in Reihe, 24 Ventile	6 Zylinder in Reihe, 24 Ventile
Hubraum	3201 cm³	2793 cm³	2793 cm³
Bohrung × Hub	86,4 × 91 mm	84 × 84 mm	84 × 84 mm
Kraftstoffversorgung	elektronisches Motormanagement MSS50	elektronisches Motormanagement MS41.0	elektronisches Motormanagement
Leistung	321 PS bei 7400/min	192 PS bei 5300/min	193 PS bei 5500/min
Getriebe	5-Gang	5-Gang	5-Gang
Chassis Rahmen	selbsttragende Karosserie	selbsttragende Karosserie	selbsttragende Karosserie
Aufhängung vorn	Eingelenk-Federbeine, Querkraftausgleich, Bremsnickausgleich	Eingelenk-Federbeine, Querkraftausgleich, Bremsnickausgleich	Eingelenk-Federbeine, Bremsnickausgleich, Stabilisator
Aufhängung hinten	Schräglenker, Federn, Dämpfer, Anfahr- und Bremsnickausgleich	Schräglenker, Federn, Dämpfer, Anfahr- und Bremsnickausgleich	Zentrallenkerachse, Doppelquerlenker, Längslenker, Anfahr- und Bremsnickausgleich
Maße Radstand	2459 mm	2446 mm	2725 mm
Länge × Breite × Höhe	4025 × 1740 × 1266 mm	4025 × 1740 × 1293 mm	4471 × 1932 × 1415 mm
Gewicht	1350 kg	1280 kg	1470 kg
Höchstgeschwindigkeit	250 km/h, elektronisch begrenzt	231 km/h	240 km/h

Baureihe	X5 (E53)	Z8 (E52)	7er-Reihe (E65–E68)
Baujahre	1999–2006	2000–2003	2001–2008
Modell	X5 3.0i	Z8 Roadster	745i (E65)
Motor	6 Zylinder in Reihe, 24 Ventile	V8 90°, 32 Ventile	V8 90°, 32 Ventile
Hubraum	2979 cm³	4941 cm³	4398 cm³
Bohrung × Hub	84,0 × 89,6 mm	94,0 × 89,0 mm	92,0 × 82,7 mm
Kraftstoffversorgung	elektronisches Motormanagement MS43	elektronisches Motormanagement MSS52	elektronisches Motormanagement ME9
Leistung	231 PS bei 5900/min	400 PS bei 6600/min	333 PS bei 6100/min
Getriebe	6-Gang	6-Gang	6-Gang-Steptronic
Chassis Rahmen	selbsttragende Karosserie	Space Frame	selbsttragende Karosserie
Aufhängung vorn	McPherson-Federbeine	McPherson-Federbeine, Querlenker	McPherson-Federbeine, Querkraftausgleich, Bremsnickausgleich
Aufhängung hinten	Integralachse, Anfahr- und Bremsnickausgleich	Integral-Mehrlenkerachse, Schraubenfedern, Stabilisator	Integral-Mehrlenkerachse, Anfahr- und Bremsnickausgleich
Maße Radstand	2820 mm	2505 mm	2990 mm
Länge × Breite × Höhe	4667 × 1872 × 1715 mm	4400 × 1830 × 1317 mm	5029 × 1902 × 1492 mm
Gewicht	2070 kg	1690 kg	1945 kg
Höchstgeschwindigkeit	210 km/h	250 km/h, elektronisch begrenzt	250 km/h, elektronisch begrenzt

Baureihe	Mini (R50, R52, R53, R55–R59)	3er-Reihe (E46)	Z4 (E85, E86)
Baujahre	2001–2006	6/2003–12/2003	2002–2008
Modell	Mini Cooper S (R53)	M3 CSL	Z4 3.0i (E85)
Motor	4 Zylinder in Reihe, quer, 16 Ventile, Kompressor	6 Zylinder in Reihe, 24 Ventile	6 Zylinder in Reihe, 24 Ventile
Hubraum	1598 cm³	3246 cm³	2979 cm³
Bohrung × Hub	77,0 × 85,8 mm	87,0 × 91,0 mm	84,0 × 89,6 mm
Kraftstoffversorgung	elektronisches Motormanagement EMS 2000	elektronisches Motormanagement MSS54HP	elektronisches Motormanagement MS45
Leistung	163 PS bei 6000/min	360 PS bei 7900/min	231 PS bei 5900/min
Getriebe	6-Gang	6-Gang, sequenziell	6-Gang
Chassis Rahmen	selbsttragende Karosserie	selbsttragende Karosserie	selbsttragende Karosserie
Aufhängung vorn	McPherson-Federbeine	Eingelenk-Federbeine, Querlenker, Stabilisator, Bremsnickausgleich	Eingelenk-Federbeine, Querkraftausgleich, Bremsnickausgleich
Aufhängung hinten	Mehrlenkerachse	Zentrallenkerachse, Doppelquerlenker, Längslenker, Anfahr- und Bremsnickausgleich	Zentrallenkerachse, Querlenker, Dämpfer, Federn, Stabilisatoren, Anfahr- und Bremsnickausgleich
Maße Radstand	2467 mm	2729 mm	2495 mm
Länge × Breite × Höhe	3665 × 1688 × 1416 mm	4492 × 1780 × 1365 mm	4091 × 1781 × 1299 mm
Gewicht	1140 kg	1385 kg	1365 kg
Höchstgeschwindigkeit	218 km/h	250 km/h, elektronisch begrenzt	250 km/h, elektronisch begrenzt

Baureihe	5er-Reihe (E60, E61))	6er-Reihe (E63)	X3 (E83)
Baujahre	2003–2007	2003–2010	2003–2010
Modell	**530d** (E60)	**645Ci Coupé**	**X3 3.0i**
Motor	6 Zylinder in Reihe, 24 Ventile	V8 90°, 32 Ventile	6 Zylinder in Reihe, 24 Ventile
Hubraum	2993 cm³	4398 cm³	2979 cm³
Bohrung × Hub	90,0 × 84,0 mm	92,0 × 82,7 mm	84,0 × 89,6 mm
Kraftstoffversorgung	Common-Rail-Dieseleinspritzung Bosch DDE 5	elektronisches Motormanagement Bosch ME 9.2.1	elektronisches Motormanagement Siemens MS 45
Leistung	218 PS bei 4000 km/h	333 PS bei 6100/min	231 PS bei 5900/min
Getriebe	6-Gang	6-Gang	6-Gang
Chassis Rahmen	selbsttragende Karosserie	selbsttragende Karosserie	selbsttragende Karosserie
Aufhängung vorn	McPherson-Federbeine, Querkraftausgleich, Bremsnickausgleich	McPherson-Federbeine, Querlenker	McPherson-Federbeine, Querkraftausgleich, Bremsnickausgleich
Aufhängung hinten	Integral-Mehrlenkerachse, Anfahr- und Bremsnickausgleich	Integralachse	Zentrallenkerachse, Doppelquerlenker, Längslenker, Anfahr- und Bremsnickausgleich
Maße Radstand	2888 mm	2780 mm	2795 mm
Länge × Breite × Höhe	4841 × 1846 × 1468 mm	4820 × 1855 × 1373 mm	4565 × 1853 × 1674 mm
Gewicht	1670 kg	1690 kg	1835 kg
Höchstgeschwindigkeit	245 km/h	250 km/h, elektronisch begrenzt	224 km/h

Baureihe	1er-Reihe (E81, E82, E87, E88)	3er-Reihe (E90–E93)	3er-Reihe (E90–E93)
Baujahre	2004–2013	2005–2013	2005–2013
Modell	**120i** (E87)	**330d Coupé** (E92)	**M3 Cabriolet** (E93)
Motor	4 Zylinder in Reihe, 16 Ventile	6 Zylinder in Reihe, Turbo, 24 Ventile	V8, 90°, 32 Ventile
Hubraum	1995 cm³	2993 cm³	3999 cm³
Bohrung × Hub	90,0 × 84,0 mm	84 × 90 mm	92,0 × 75,2 mm
Kraftstoffversorgung	Saugrohreinspritzung	Common-Rail-Dieseleinspritzung	elektronisches Motormanagement MSS 60
Leistung	150 PS bei 6200/min	231 PS bei 4000/min	420 PS bei 8300/min
Getriebe	6-Gang	6-Gang	7-Gang, Doppelkupplung
Chassis Rahmen	selbsttragende Karosserie	selbsttragende Karosserie	selbsttragende Karosserie
Aufhängung vorn	McPherson-Federbeine	McPherson-Federbeine	McPherson-Federbeine
Aufhängung hinten	Fünflenkerachse	Fünflenkerachse	Fünflenkerachse, Anfahr- und Bremsnickausgleich
Maße Radstand	2660 mm	2760 mm	2761 mm
Länge × Breite × Höhe	4227 × 1751 × 1430 mm	4580 × 1782 × 1395 mm	4615 × 1804 × 1397 mm
Gewicht	1335 kg	1525 kg	1885 kg
Höchstgeschwindigkeit	217 km/h	250 km/h, elektronisch begrenzt	250 km/h, elektronisch begrenzt

Baureihe	X5 (E70)	X6 (E71)	7er-Reihe (F01–F04)
Baujahre	2006–2013	2008–2014	2008–2015
Modell	**X5 xDrive 40d**	**X6 xDrive 35d**	**740i** (F01)
Motor	6 Zylinder in Reihe, Turbo, 24 Ventile	6 Zylinder in Reihe, Turbo, 24 Ventile	6 Zylinder in Reihe, 24 Ventile
Hubraum	2993 cm³	2993 cm³	2979 cm³
Bohrung × Hub	84 × 90 mm	84 × 90 mm	89,6 × 84,0 mm
Kraftstoffversorgung	Common-Rail-Dieseleinspritzung	Common-Rail-Dieseleinspritzung	elektronisches Motormanagement MS D87
Leistung	306 PS bei 4400/min	286 PS bei 4400/min	326 PS bei 5800/min
Getriebe	6-Gang, Allradantrieb	6-Gang-Automatik	6-Gang-Automatik
Chassis Rahmen	selbsttragende Karosserie	selbsttragende Karosserie	selbsttragende Karosserie
Aufhängung vorn	Doppelquerlenkerachse	Doppelquerlenkerachse, Stabilisator	Doppelquerlenkerachse
Aufhängung hinten	Zentrallenkerachse	Integral-Mehrlenkerachse, Schraubenfedern, Stabilisator	Integral-Mehrlenkerachse, Anfahr- und Bremsnickausgleich
Maße Radstand	2933 mm	2933 mm	3070 mm
Länge × Breite × Höhe	4857 × 1933 × 1776 mm	4877 × 1983 × 1690 mm	5072 × 1902 × 1479
Gewicht	2185 kg	2185 kg	1860 kg
Höchstgeschwindigkeit	236 km/h	236 km/h	250 km/h, elektronisch begrenzt

Baureihe	Z4 (E89)	X1 (E84)	5er-Reihe (F07, F10, F11))
Baujahre	2009–	2009–	2009–
Modell	**Z4 sDrive 35i**	**X1 sDrive 20d**	**530d GT** (F07)
Motor	6 Zylinder in Reihe, 24 Ventile, Bi-Turbo	4 Zylinder in Reihe, Turbo	6 Zylinder in Reihe, Turbo
Hubraum	2979 cm³	1995 cm³	2993 cm³
Bohrung × Hub	84,0 × 89,6 mm	84,0 × 90,0 mm	84,0 × 90,0 mm
Kraftstoffversorgung	elektronisches Motormanagement MS D81, Direkteinspritzung	Common-Rail-Dieseleinspritzung	Common-Rail-Dieseleinspritzung
Leistung	306 PS bei 5800/min	177 PS bei 4000/min	245 PS bei 4000/min
Getriebe	6-Gang	6-Gang	8-Gang-Steptronic
Chassis Rahmen	selbsttragende Karosserie	selbsttragende Karosserie	selbsttragende Karosserie
Aufhängung vorn	McPherson-Federbeine	McPherson-Federbeine	Doppelquerlenkerachse
Aufhängung hinten	Zentrallenkerachse, Anfahr- und Bremsnickausgleich	Fünflenkerachse	Integral-Mehrlenkerachse, Luftfederung
Maße Radstand	2496 mm	2760 mm	3070 mm
Länge × Breite × Höhe	4239 × 1790 × 1291 mm	4454 × 1798 × 1545 mm	4998 × 1901 × 1559 mm
Gewicht	1580 kg	1565 kg	2035 kg
Höchstgeschwindigkeit	250 km/h, elektronisch begrenzt	218 km/h	240 km/h

Baureihe	5er-Reihe (F07, F10, F11)	Mini Countryman (R60)	X3 (F25)
Baujahre	2010–	2010–	2010–
Modell	**M550d xDrive** *(F10)*	**Mini Cooper SD Countryman All 4**	**X3 xDrive 20d**
Motor	6 Zylinder in Reihe, Tri-Turbo, 24 Ventile	4 Zylinder in Reihe, quer, Turbo, 16 Ventile	4 Zylinder in Reihe, Turbo, 16 Ventile
Hubraum	2993 cm³	1995 cm³	1995 cm³
Bohrung × Hub	84,0 × 90,0 mm	84,0× 90,0 mm	84,0 × 90,0 mm
Kraftstoffversorgung	Common-Rail-Dieseleinspritzung	Common-Rail-Dieseleinspritzung	Common-Rail-Dieseleinspritzung
Leistung	381 PS bei 4400/min	143 PS bei 4000/min	184 PS bei 4000/min
Getriebe	8-Stufen-Automatik, Allradantrieb	6-Gang, Allradantrieb	6-Gang, Allradantrieb
Chassis Rahmen	selbsttragende Karosserie	selbsttragende Karosserie	selbsttragende Karosserie
Aufhängung vorn	Doppelquerlenkerachse	McPherson-Federbeine	McPherson-Federbeine, Querkraftausgleich, Bremsnickausgleich
Aufhängung hinten	Mehrlenkerachse	Mehrlenkerachse	Zentrallenkerachse, Anfahr- und Bremsnickausgleich
Maße Radstand	2968 mm	2595 mm	2810 mm
Länge × Breite × Höhe	4910 × 1860 × 1462 mm	4110 × 1789 × 1561 mm	4648 × 1881 × 1661 mm
Gewicht	1955 kg	1395 kg	1790 kg
Höchstgeschwindigkeit	250 km/h, elektronisch begrenzt	198 km/h	210 km/h

Baureihe	6er-Reihe (F06, F12, F13)	1er-Reihe (F20, F21)	3er-Reihe (F30, F31, F34)
Baujahre	2011–	2011–	2012–
Modell	**650i xDrive** *(F06)*	**118i** *(F20)*	**320d** *(F30)*
Motor	V8, Bi-Turbo, 32 Ventile	4 Zylinder in Reihe, Turbo, 16 Ventile	4 Zylinder in Reihe, Turbo, 16 Ventile
Hubraum	4395 cm³	1598 cm³	1995 cm³
Bohrung × Hub	89,0 × 88,3 mm	77,0 × 85,8 mm	84,0 × 90,0 mm
Kraftstoffversorgung	Direkteinspritzung	Direkteinspritzung	Common-Rail-Dieseleinspritzung
Leistung	450 PS bei 5500/min	170 PS bei 4800/min	184 PS bei 4000/min
Getriebe	8-Stufen-Automatik, Allradantrieb	6-Gang	6-Gang
Chassis Rahmen	selbsttragende Karosserie	selbsttragende Karosserie	selbsttragende Karosserie
Aufhängung vorn	McPherson-Federbeine, Querlenker	McPherson-Federbeine	McPherson-Federbeine
Aufhängung hinten	Integralachse	Mehrlenkerachse	Mehrlenkerachse
Maße Radstand	2968 mm	2690 mm	2810 mm
Länge × Breite × Höhe	5007 × 1894 × 1392 mm	4324 × 1765 × 1421 mm	4624 × 1811 × 1429 mm
Gewicht	2015 kg	1370 kg	1495 kg
Höchstgeschwindigkeit	250 km/h, elektronisch begrenzt	225 km/h	235 km/h

Baureihe	Mini Roadster (R59)	3er-Reihe (F30, F31, F34)	X5 (F15/F85)
Baujahre	2012–	2012–	2013–
Modell	**Mini John Cooper Works Roadster**	**320d GT** *(F34)*	**X5 M** *(F85)*
Motor	4 Zylinder in Reihe, quer, Turbo, 16 Ventile	4 Zylinder in Reihe, Turbo, 16 Ventile	V8, Bi-Turbo, 32 Ventile
Hubraum	1598 cm³	1995 cm³	4395 cm³
Bohrung × Hub	77,0 × 85,8 mm	90,0 × 84,0 mm	89,0 × 88,3 mm
Kraftstoffversorgung	elektronisches Motormanagement	Common-Rail-Dieseleinspritzung	Direkteinspritzung
Leistung	211 PS bei 6000/min	184 PS bei 4000/min	575 PS bei 6000–6500/min
Getriebe	6-Gang	6-Gang	6-Gang, Allradantrieb
Chassis Rahmen	selbsttragende Karosserie	selbsttragende Karosserie	selbsttragende Karosserie
Aufhängung vorn	McPherson-Federbeine	McPherson-Federbeine	Doppelquerlenkerachse
Aufhängung hinten	Mehrlenkerachse	Mehrlenkerachse	Integral-Mehrlenkerachse, Luftfederung
Maße Radstand	2467 mm	2920 mm	2933 mm
Länge × Breite × Höhe	3734 × 1603 × 1390 mm	4824 × 1828 × 1508 mm	4880 × 1985 × 1754 mm
Gewicht	1185 kg	1640 kg	2350 kg
Höchstgeschwindigkeit	237 km/h	230 km/h	250 km/h, elektronisch begrenzt

Baureihe	4er-Reihe (F32, F33, F36)	Mini (F55, F56)	X4 (F26)
Baujahre	2013–	2014–	2014 –
Modell	**430d GranCoupé** *(F36)*	**Mini Cooper S 5-door** *(F55)*	**X4 xDrive 35d**
Motor	6 Zylinder in Reihe, Turbo, 24 Ventile	4 Zylinder in Reihe, quer, Turbo, 16 Ventile	6 Zylinder in Reihe, Bi-Turbo, 24 Ventile
Hubraum	2993 cm³	1998 cm³	2993 cm³
Bohrung × Hub	84,0 × 90,0 mm	82 × 94,6 mm	84,0 × 90,0 mm
Kraftstoffversorgung	Common-Rail-Dieseleinspritzung	Direkteinspritzung	Common-Rail-Dieseleinspritzung
Leistung	258 PS bei 4000/min	192 PS bei 6000/min	313 PS bei 4400/min
Getriebe	8-Stufen-Automatik	6-Gang	6-Gang, Allradantrieb
Chassis Rahmen	selbsttragende Karosserie	selbsttragende Karosserie	selbsttragende Karosserie
Aufhängung vorn	Doppelquerlenkerachse	McPherson-Federbeine	McPherson-Federbeine, Querkraftausgleich, Bremsnickausgleich
Aufhängung hinten	Mehrlenkerachse	Mehrlenkerachse	Zentrallenkerachse, Anfahr- und Bremsnickausgleich
Maße Radstand	2810 mm	2567 mm	2810 mm
Länge × Breite × Höhe	4638 × 1825 × 1389 mm	3982 × 1727 × 1425 mm	4671 × 1881 × 1624 mm
Gewicht	1680 kg	1220 kg	1935 kg
Höchstgeschwindigkeit	250 km/h, elektronisch begrenzt	237 km/h	247 km/h

Baureihe	X6 (F16/F86)	2er-Reihe Tourer (F45, F46)
Baujahre	2014–	2014-
Modell	X6 M *(F86)*	218i Active Tourer *(F45)*
Motor	V8, Bi-Turbo, 32 Ventile	3 Zylinder in Reihe, quer, Turbo, 12 Ventile
Hubraum	4395 cm³	1499 cm³
Bohrung × Hub	89,0 × 88,3 mm	82,0 × 94,6 mm
Kraftstoffversorgung	Direkteinspritzung	Direkteinspritzung
Leistung	575 PS bei 6000–6500/min	136 PS bei 4400/min
Getriebe	6-Gang, Allradantrieb	6-Gang, Frontantrieb
Chassis Rahmen	selbsttragende Karosserie	selbsttragende Karosserie
Aufhängung vorn	Doppelquerlenkerachse	McPherson-Federbeine
Aufhängung hinten	Mehrlenkerachse, Luftfederung	Mehrlenkerachse
Maße Radstand	2933 mm	2670 mm
Länge × Breite × Höhe	4909 × 1989 × 1689 mm	4342 × 1800 × 1586 mm
Gewicht	2340 kg	1395 kg
Höchstgeschwindigkeit	250 km/h, elektronisch begrenzt	205 km/h

Baureihe	i3 (I01)	I8 (I12)
Baujahre	2014 –	2014 –
Modell	i3	i8
Verbrennungsmotor		3 Zylinder in Reihe, quer, Turbo, 12 Ventile
Hubraum		1499 cm³
Bohrung × Hub		82,0 × 94,6 mm
Kraftstoffversorgung		Direkteinspritzung
Leistung		231 PS bei 5800/min
Elektromotor	Synchronmotor	Synchronmotor
Akku	Samsung Li-Ion 360V	Samsung Li-Ion 360V
Kapazität	18,8 kWh	5,2 kWh
Leistung	170 PS	131 PS
Systemleistung	170 PS	362 PS
Getriebe	1-Gang	6-Gang Automatik, Hinterradantrieb (Verbrennungsmotor)
		2-Gang Automatik, Frontantrieb (Elektromotor)
Chassis Rahmen	Aluminium-Profilrahmen, CFK-Kunststoff-Karosserie	Aluminium-Profilrahmen, CFK-Kunststoff-Karosserie
Aufhängung vorn	McPherson-Federbeine	McPherson-Federbeine
Aufhängung hinten	Mehrlenkerachse	Mehrlenkerachse
Maße Radstand	2570 mm	2800 mm
Länge × Breite × Höhe	3999 × 1775 × 1578 mm	4689 × 1942 × 1291 mm
Gewicht	1195 kg	1485 kg
Höchstgeschwindigkeit	150 km/h, elektronisch begrenzt	250 km/h, elektronisch begrenzt

Glossary · Glossaire

Baureihe	**Series**	**Gamme**
Baujahre	**Years of Production**	**Millésimes**
Modell	**Model**	**Modèle**
Motor	**Engine**	**Moteur**
Verbrennungsmotor	**Combustion engine**	**Moteur thermique**
Boxer	boxer	à plat
geneigt	inclined	incliné
in Reihe	straight	en ligne
Kompressor	supercharger	compresseur
luftgekühlt	air-cooled	refroidi par air
quer	transversal	transversal
Turbo	turbocharger	turbocompresseur
Ventile	valves	soupapes
Zylinder	cylinders	cylindres
Hubraum	**Displacement**	**Cylindrée**
Bohrung × Hub	**Bore × Stroke**	**Alésage × Course**
Kraftstoffversorgung	**Fuel supply**	**Alimentation en carburant**
Common-Rail-Dieseleinspritzung	common-rail diesel injection	injection directe diesel à rampe commune
Direkteinspritzung	direct injection	injection directe
Doppel-	double, twin	double
Einspritzpumpe	injection pump	pompe d'injection
Einspritzung	injection	injection
elektronische(s)	electronic	électronique
Fallstromvergaser	downdraft carburetor	carburateur inversé
Flachstromvergaser	sidedraft carburetor	carburateur horizontal
mechanische	mechanical	mécanique
Motormanagement	engine management	gestion moteur
Oberflächenvergaser	surface carburetor	carburateur à surface
Piezo-Injektoren	piezo injectors	injecteurs piezo
Registervergaser	two-stage carburetor	carburateur étagé
Saugrohreinspritzung	manifold injection	injection indirecte dans le collecteur d'admission
Schiebervergaser	slide carburetor	carburateur à vanne
Steigstromvergaser	updraft carburetor	carburateur vertical ascendant
Vertikalvergaser	vertical carburetor	carburateur vertical
Leistung	**Output**	**Puissance**
PS bei …/min	bhp at … rpm	ch à … tr/min
Elektromotor	**Electric motor**	**Machine électrique**
Synchronmotor	synchronous motor	machine synchrone
Akku	**Battery**	**Accumulateur**
Kapazität	**Capacity**	**Capacité**
Systemleistung	**System output**	**Puissance totale**
Getriebe	**Transmission**	**Boîte de vitesses**
…-Gang	…-speed	… vitesses
Allradantrieb	four-wheel drive	transmission intégrale
Automatik	automatic	automatique
Doppelkupplung	dual clutch	double embrayage
Frontantrieb	front-wheel drive	traction
Hinterradantrieb	rear-wheel drive	propulsion
sequenziell	sequential	séquentiel
Chassis	**Chassis**	**Châssis**
Rahmen	**Frame**	**Cadre**
Aluminium-Profilrahmen	aluminum profile frame	cadre en aluminium profilé
CFK-Kunststoff-Karosserie	CFRP and plastic body	coque en PRFC et plastique
Gitterrohrrahmen	tubular space frame	squelette tubulaire
Kastenquerträger	box-section cross beams	poutres transversales
Kastenrahmen	box-section frame	cadre-caisson
Kunststoffkarosserie	plastic body	carrosserie en plastique
Leiterrohrrahmen	tubular ladder frame	cadre-échelle
Rohrquerträger	tubular cross beams	poutres tubulaires transversales
Rohrrahmen	tubular frame	cadre tubulaire
selbsttragende Karosserie	integral body	carrosserie autoporteuse
Space Frame	space frame	*space frame*
Stahlblechgerüst mit Kunststoff- und Verbundteilen	sheet steel frame with plastic and composite parts	squelette d'acier avec pièces de plastique et de composites
Tiefbett-Kastenrahmen	drop base box frame	cadre-caisson surbaissé
U-Profilrahmen	U-section frame	cadre de profilés en U
Zentralkasten-Niederrahmen	central box-section low frame	cadre surbaissé à caisson central

Aufhängung vorn/hinten	**Suspension front/rear**	**Suspension avant/arrière**
achslos	shaftless	sans essieu
Anfahr- und Bremsnickausgleich	anti-squat and anti-dive mechanism	compensation du tangage au démarrage et au freinage
Ausleger-Viertelfedern	cantilever quarter spring	ressorts à lames à quart cantilever
Banjo-Achse	banjo axle	essieu banjo
Bremsnickausgleich	anti-dive mechanism	compensation du tangage au freinage
Dämpfer	absorber	amortisseur
Doppelgelenk-	double joint	à double articulation
Doppelquerlenkerachse	double wishbone axle	essieu à double bras transversaux
doppelte	double, twin	double
Drehstab	torsion bar	barre de torsion
Dreieckslenker	wishbones	bras triangulaires
Druckstreben	push rods	bras de pression
Eingelenk-	single joint	à une articulation
Federbeine	spring struts	jambes de suspension
Federhebel	spring lever	levier de ressort
Federn	springs	ressort
Fünflenkerachse	five-link suspension	suspension à cinq bras
Gasdruckdämpfer	gas filled shock absorber	amortisseurs à gaz
gekapselte Schraubenfedern	encapsulated coil springs	ressorts helicoïdaux encapsulés
geschobene Längsschwingen	leading swing arms	bras poussés
Gummihohlfedern	hollow rubber springs	ressorts creux en caoutchouc
Gummizusatzfedern	auxiliary rubber springs	ressorts supplémentaires en coutchouc
Halbfedern	semi-elliptic springs	ressorts semi-elliptiques
Integralachse	integral suspension	train intégral
Längsfederstäbe	longitudinal torsion bars	barres de torsion longitudinaux
Längslenker	longitudinal control arm	bras longitudinaux
Luftfederung	air suspension	suspension pneumatique
McPherson-Federbeine	MacPherson struts	jambes McPherson
Mehrlenkerachse	multi-link suspension	essieu multibras
Niveauregulierung	level control	régulation de niveau
oben	above	au-dessus
Pendelachse	swing axle	essieu pendulaire
Querfeder(n)	transverse spring(s)	ressorts transversaux
Querkraftausgleich	lateral force compensation	compensation des accélérations latérales
Querlenker	transverse arm	bras transversal
Schräglenker	diagonal control arm	bras diagonal
Schräglenkerachse	diagonal control arm axle	essieu à bras diagonaux
Schraubenfedern	coil springs	ressorts hélicoïdaux
Stabilisator	anti-roll bar	barre stabilisatrice
Starrachse	beam axle	essieu rigide
ungefedert	unsprung	non suspendu
unten	below	au-dessous
Zentrallenkerachse	centrally articulated multi-link suspension	essieu multibras en guidage central
Zugstreben	tie rods	tiroirs
Maße	**Dimensions**	**Dimensions**
Radstand	**Wheelbase**	**Empattement**
Länge × Breite × Höhe	**Length × width × height**	**Longueur × largeur × hauteur**
	100 mm = 3.937 in	
Gewicht	**Weight**	**Poids**
	1 kg = 2.205 lbs	
Höchstgeschwindigkeit	**Maximum speed**	**Vitesse de pointe**
elektronisch begrenzt	electronically limited	bridée électroniquement
	1 km/h (kph) = 0.622 mph	

Acknowledgments

I would like to express my thanks to everyone who made it possible for this book to happen by allowing their cars to be used:

Danksagung

Ich danke allen, die mir die Verwirklichung dieses Buches durch die Bereitstellung ihrer Fahrzeuge ermöglicht haben:

Remerciements

Je remercie tous ceux qui m'ont permis de réaliser ce livre en mettant leurs voitures à ma disposition:

Hans-Friedrich Andexer, Udo Beckmann, Jochen Burgdorf, Helmut & Thomas Feierabend, Baldur Glaas, Gunter Herz, Dr. August Kau, Dr. Jürgen & Brigitte Klöckner, Michael Knittel, Prof. Dr. Gerhard Knöchlein, Dr. Bernhard Knöchlein, Sepp Mayer, Yvonne Mittler, Jürgen Pollack, Karl Heinz Wedel.

I would also like to thank the members of the press department of BMW AG, BMW Mobile Tradition, BMW Motorsport Ltd., the BMW office in Frankfurt/Main, and BMW dealer Karl+Co in Mainz and Wiesbaden:

Ich bedanke mich ebenso bei den Mitarbeitern der Presseabteilung der BMW AG, der BMW Mobile Tradition, der BMW Motorsport Ltd., der BMW Niederlassung Frankfurt am Main und dem Autohaus Karl+Co Mainz/Wiesbaden:

Je remercie tout autant les collaborateurs de BMW AG, de BMW Mobile Tradition, de BMW Motorsport Ltd., de la succursale de BMW de Francfort/Main et du concessionnaire BMW Karl+Co Mayence/Wiesbaden:

Franz Joseph Bötsch, Thorsten Diemer, Christian W. Eich, Seçkin Emre, Jana Gaspar, Richard Gerstner, Thomas Giuliani, "Bepi" Grassl, Helmut Grünwald, Friedbert Holz, Franz Inzko, Fred Jakobs, Raimund Kupferschmid, Klaus Kutscher, Uwe Mahla, Joachim Pietzsch, Bruno Santic, Christian Stockmann, Ali Strasser, Dirk-Henning Strassl, Walter Zeichner, Axel Zimmermann.

My gratitude to all those in positions of responsibility at Egelsbach, Michelstadt, Lauf-Lillinghof and Siegerland airports for their kind support when I was photographing there. And finally, thanks are due to Hartmut Lehbrink and Jochen von Osterroth for their texts, as well as Christian Maiwurm, Monika Dauer, Sabine Gerber and the publishing team for the inspired way in which they handled the project.

Rainer W. Schlegelmilch

Für die freundliche Unterstützung bei meinen Aufnahmen danke ich den Verantwortlichen der Flugplätze Egelsbach, Michelstadt, Lauf-Lillinghof und des Flughafens Siegerland. Und zu guter Letzt gilt mein Dank Hartmut Lehbrink und Jochen von Osterroth für ihre Texte sowie Christian Maiwurm, Monika Dauer, Sabine Gerber und dem Verlagsteam für die geniale Realisation.

Rainer W. Schlegelmilch

Je tiens à remercier les responsables des aéroports d'Egelsbach, Michelstadt, Lauf-Lillinghof et de l'aéroport du Siegerland pour leur aide.
Enfin, je souhaite également remercier Hartmut Lehbrink et Jochen von Osterroth pour leurs textes, ainsi que Christian Maiwurm, Monika Dauer, Sabine Gerber et toute l'équipe éditoriale pour la qualité de leur travail.

Rainer W. Schlegelmilch

© h.f.ullmann publishing GmbH

Original title: *BMW*
ISBN 978-3-8331-1059-7

Photography: Rainer W. Schlegelmilch
Text: Hartmut Lehbrink, Jochen von Osterroth
Layout: Christian Maiwurm, Oliver Hessmann
Translations into English: Christian von Arnim, Stephen Hunt, Paul Motley, Russell Cennydd
Translation into French: Jean-Luc Lesouëf

Photos pp. 8–13, 300–301, 378–379, 400–403: BMW Group

www.ullmann-publishing.com
newsletter@ullmann-publishing.com
facebook.com/hfullmann
facebook.com/ullmann.social

© for this updated edition: h.f.ullmann publishing GmbH

Special edition

Project management for h.f.ullmann: Lars Pietzschmann

Translation into English: Mo Croasdale in association with First Edition Translations Ltd, Cambridge, UK; Edited by David Price in association with First Edition Translations Ltd, Cambridge, UK; except for pp. 296–299, 348–351, 366–367, 370–377, 380–385, 390–399, 404–409: by Ian Farell in association with Delivering iBooks & Design, Barcelona

Translation into French: Marion Villain in association with Intexte Édition, Toulouse; except for pp. 13, 296–301, 348–351, 366–367, 370–378, 380–388, 390–455: by Aurélie Daniel in association with Delivering iBooks & Design, Barcelona

Cover photo: Uwe Fischer, Munich

Slipcase Design: Oliver Hessmann
Slipcase photos: Rainer W. Schlegelmilch

Overall responsibility for production: h.f.ullmann publishing GmbH, Potsdam, Germany

Printed in China, 2015

ISBN 978-3-8480-0883-4
ISBN 978-3-8480-0885-8 (with slipcase/mit Schuber/avec coffret)

10 9 8 7 6 5 4 3 2 1
X IX VIII VII VI V IV